MW00803616

"This book set my heart and head aflame!! I cannot believe how many of these women I'd never heard of. What a tremendous gift Jennifer Ashley Tepper has bestowed upon us—a delicious coup d'œil into the kaleidoscope of badass women who, for decades, have been shaping American Musical Theatre as we know it."
—**Jenn Colella**, Tony Award-nominated actor of *Come From Away*

"Any new work from the incomparable Jennifer Ashley Tepper is cause for celebration. This book feels especially essential in the way it celebrates and amplifies female writers who history has embarrassingly ignored. It does more than shine a light on under-appreciated artists, it gives them a stage and puts their talents on full display. Tepper has the singular ability to make history feel alive, legacy feel active, and art feel like the lifeblood of the human race. The book provides the electric thrills of a live performance and I am so grateful to be in the audience for this particular show." —**Joe Iconis**, Tony Award-nominated writer of *Be More Chill*

"As a woman with a career in the rarified world of musical theatre, I really appreciate Jennifer Ashley Tepper's thrilling deep dive into the history and meaning of our work. This book is a rich and timely addition to our canon of musical theatre literature." —**Lynn Ahrens**, Tony Award-winning lyricist of *Ragtime*

"Where are all the female musical theatre writers? Turns out, they've always been there, but they've been hidden away behind a mist, like *Brigadoon*! However, an intrepid explorer named Jennifer Ashley Tepper has found them and is finally giving us their amazing herstories in this gem of a book!! Let's give these creative and groundbreaking women their long overdue bravas!" —**Seth Rudetsky**, Sirius XM host, author of *Seth's Broadway Diary* and *Musical Theatre for Dummies*

"How wonderful that Jennifer Ashley Tepper has written such a loving and informative book about this fabulous collection of female theatre songwriters. Whether from today or years ago, the beautifully detailed stories highlight the highs and lows of the mysterious craft of musical theatre, and the women who created it." —**Liz Callaway**, Emmy Award-winning actor and singer

"Reading Jennifer Ashley Tepper's remarkable book, I was gobsmacked at the breadth and depth of women composing and writing musicals in America and found myself wondering, why didn't I know about so many of them before? Well, thanks to her, now we do. It is galvanizing and humbling to learn that women have always found a way to create and get their work produced and forged incredible careers for themselves, even when there was no way. In concise, fascinating and illuminating histories, we learn about each woman's work and career and, in the aggregate, we get to see how many of us there are and how long we've been part of the landscape of the American musical. Thanks to Tepper, our stories are unsung no more." —**Amanda Green**, Tony Award-nominated writer of *Hands on a Hardbody*

"Nobody knows the history of Broadway—or the women who make it sing—like Jennifer Ashley Tepper. At once reverent, dishy, and passionately researched, this is an essential book for any fan of the Great White Way." —**Tim Federle**, Emmy-nominated creator of *High School Musical: the Musical: The Series*

WOMEN WRITING MUSICALS

WOMEN WRITING MUSICALS
The Legacy That the History Books Left Out

JENNIFER ASHLEY TEPPER

APPLAUSE
THEATRE & CINEMA BOOKS

APPLAUSE
THEATRE & CINEMA BOOKS

Bloomsbury Publishing Group, Inc.
ApplauseBooks.com

Distributed by NATIONAL BOOK NETWORK

Library of Congress Cataloging-in-Publication Data

Names: Tepper, Jennifer Ashley, author.
Title: Women writing musicals : the legacy that the history books left out / Jennifer Ashley Tepper.
Description: Essex, Connecticut : Applause Theatre & Cinema, an imprint of Globe Pequot, a trade division of The Rowman & LIttlefield Publishing Group, Inc., [2024] | Includes index. | The 18th and 19th Centuries : Beginnings—1900s : Revues, Large Teams, and Multi-Hyphenates—1910s : Operettas and Specialty Material—1920s : Vaudeville Origins, One-Show Wonders, and Pop Hits—1930s : Musicals of the Great Depression—1940s : Hit Tunesmiths with Broadway Flops, Writers with Major Careers in Other Fields, and the Longest Running Team in Broadway History—1950s : Comediennes, Radio Personalities, and Women at the Piano—1960s : Family Musicals, Musical Families, and Conceiver Credits—1970s : Protest Musicals, Female Teams, and Writers of Color—1980s : Jukebox Musicals and a Return to Revues—1990s : Disney, Blues Music, and Autobiographical Work—2000s : Tongue-In-Cheek Comedy, Jukebox Phenomenons, and New Media—2010s : Celebrities, Playwrights, and Crossover Artists. | Summary: "Women writing musicals: the legacy that the history books left out"—Provided by publisher.
Identifiers: LCCN 2024009445 (print) | LCCN 2024009446 (ebook) | ISBN 9781493080311 (cloth) | ISBN 9781493080328 (epub)
Subjects: LCSH: Women composers—United States. | Women lyricists—United States. | Women librettists—United States. | Musicals—New York (State)—New York—History and criticism.
Classification: LCC ML82 .T47 2024 (print) | LCC ML82 (ebook) | DDC 782.1082/7471—dc23/eng/20240307
LC record available at https://lccn.loc.gov/2024009445
LC ebook record available at https://lccn.loc.gov/2024009446

For my mom, Janis
The most incredible woman I know

Contents

Introduction

DURING THE SUMMER OF 2020, I WAS ISOLATED IN MY HOME LIKE SO MANY others, due to the COVID-19 pandemic. While looking out my window in midtown Manhattan, I began to think about other New Yorkers who worked in theatre, and lived through unprecedented historic events. What was it like to live through the 1918 influenza pandemic in my neighborhood? What was it like working on Broadway during World War II? What was it like to create a protest musical in the 1960s?

It was during this time that I had the idea for *Women Writing Musicals: The Legacy That the History Books Left Out.*

I began thinking specifically about female theatre makers who had overcome obstacles throughout the decades, and created notable works—and yet were not adequately represented in history books. How did their identities intersect with their career paths, their work, their legacies?

As a theatre historian, I've previously authored *The Untold Stories of Broadway* book series. For these books, I've conducted over three hundred interviews with Broadway professionals from various fields. Four volumes of *The Untold Stories of Broadway* have been published and there are two to come. One question that came up repeatedly while I was writing these books was:

Who is left out of the history books and why?

In my exploration of this question, I became fascinated specifically by women who wrote musicals. So many of them achieved amazing and fascinating accomplishments, and yet were not adequately remembered or celebrated. And in the summer of 2020, these women came to mind again, as I thought about New Yorkers who lived through extraordinary times and the challenges they overcame in order to create.

The women featured in this book are those who wrote stage musicals that were produced on Broadway and off-Broadway, starting in the eighteenth century and through to present day. After chapter 1, about the women in the 1700s and 1800s Manhattan who wrote early musicals as New York City became a melting pot, each chapter takes the reader through one decade of women writing musicals in the twentieth or twenty-first century. In the 1900s, we meet Clara Driscoll, who saved the Alamo, and also wrote a Broadway musical, as well as well as Clare Kummer, who was the first woman to be the sole writer of a Broadway production, two one acts. The 1910s presents women who created operettas and specialty material, women who wrote under male pseudonyms, and Elsie Janis, whose work made a significant impact on the war effort during World War I. In the 1920s, we meet women who came from vaudeville, women who were also historians and critics, and Kay Swift, who was the first woman to be the sole composer of a hit, full-length Broadway musical. The Great Depression in the 1930s found women pounding the pavement in Tin Pan Alley, women collaborating with their husbands, and the first woman to write a full-length Broadway score alone, Ann Ronell. The 1940s gave us Broadway women writing musicals inspired by their heritage, from Mexican (María Grever) to Jewish (Molly Picon), an Olympic Tennis Champion turned Broadway musical theatre writer, Marion Jones Farquhar, and Betty Comden who, with Adolph Green, became the longest-running writing team in Broadway history. Comedians, radio personalities, and women at the piano took the spotlight in the 1950s, the decade that gave us Mary Rodgers, legend and composer of *Once Upon a Mattress*; Dorothy Reynolds, co-librettist of the show *Salad Days*, which for a time was the longest running musical in history; and Carolyn Leigh, lyricist of the classic *Peter Pan*.

In the second half of the twentieth century, the 1960s featured women who wrote family musicals, environmental theatre, and rock musicals, among other projects; that decade also gave us the first Black woman to direct on Broadway, Vinnette Carroll, who was also a writer, and the groundbreaking all-female team of Gretchen Cryer and Nancy Ford. In the 1970s, we got musicals by women who crossed over to pop music, from Carole Bayer Sager to Toni Tennille to Carol Hall; New York's first long-running musical in Spanish, *El Grande de Coca-Cola*, by Diz White; and Micki Grant, the first Black woman to write book, music, and lyrics for a Broadway musical—which became a giant hit. Some of the women who wrote musicals in the 1980s also found significant success writing for television—how did Marta Kauffman's off-Broadway musical point to the TV show she would later cocreate: *Friends*? The 1980s also brought us one of the greatest theatrical lyricists of all time, Lynn Ahrens; a Broadway writer who was also a makeup line entrepreneur, Jane Iredale; and Winnie Holzman, who would give the world *Wicked*. The 1990s saw Broadway mega-hits like *The Lion King* contributed to by women (Tsidii Le Loka, Irene Mecchi, Julie Taymor, Linda Woolverton), as well as the landmark musical *The Secret Garden* (by Marsha Norman and Lucy Simon). In the 2000s, women wrote more tongue-in-cheek comedy, jukebox musicals, and boundary-breaking original musicals, from Kait Kerrigan and Bree Lowdermilk, who changed musical theatre with new technology, to Pulitzer Prize winner Quiara Alegría Hudes, who penned the book of *In the Heights*. More celebrity writers joined the game in the 2010s, with crossover artists like Cyndi Lauper, Sara Bareilles, and Tina Fey making Broadway musicals, alongside theatre-centric creators like Jeanine Tesori and Lisa Kron, who wrote *Fun Home*, the first Tony Award–winning Best Musical solely penned by women. That overview contains just a small fraction of highlights of the many writers featured in this book.

The women featured at the beginning of this book wrote musicals before the word "Broadway" was ever used to denote theatre. While trying to label productions in the index for the sake of a continuum, best efforts were made to determine whether a show from an era before the terms *Broadway* and *off-Broadway* were clearly defined might unofficially fall into one category or the other.

The stories of the writers featured in this book are reflective of the way the art form of musical theatre, the industry of Broadway, and arts and entertainment in general evolved, over the period of time examined in this work. From the types of revues contributed to by women of the 1910s, to the styles of comedy employed by women of the 1950s, to the genres of music utilized by women of the 1980s, the writers explored in these pages present a fascinating cross section of Broadway creators from each era. Important elements of theatre history, from how revues changed, to how the "theatre season" adjusted, are explored based on how they intersect with specific women's stories. That said, this book does not include an overall background on the history of Broadway. If you find that reading one would enhance reading this specialized work, I recommend seeking out your own choices of books about the history of Broadway.

By writing about who was "left out of the history books," I am referring to the literal books written about the art form of musical theatre and the industry of Broadway. But I also mean: Who was omitted from the cast recording releases, the licensing rosters, the think-pieces, the adaptation opportunities, the media round-ups, the class syllabi, and so on? Who was less often written about, and given opportunities for their work to live on, whether they were celebrated in their own time or not?

I focus here on women who had prominent credits, and not every woman who had a credit writing a musical was included. The book is nearly exhaustive, but not all writers could be included due to lack of space, lack of information, and other limitations. While this is somewhat paradoxical in a work about women who were left out of history books, I hope that in stating it explicitly I can be transparent. There are always some pages missing from history, and it is a collective responsibility to look out for those whenever we can. I also apologize to anyone I inadvertently left out.

Some women received less space even though they are important figures in history, because of the ratio of their careers that they spent writing musicals. I wanted to include relevant theatre directors who had the occasional conceiver credit (examples: Susan Stroman, Graciela Daniele), writers who specialized in another genre but spent a little time on musicals (examples: Dorothy Parker, Gertrude Stein), and so on, while giving the majority of space to those who focused on stage musicals. I also determined it to be valuable to include select writers of plays with music that are not explicitly categorized as musicals but that deserved to be part of the conversation, such as Ntozake Shange and Lucia Hwong.

There is an unfortunate dearth of writers of color among the women who had musicals produced. I sought to celebrate the extraordinary work of these women of color, while also chronicling the specific obstacles they faced within the industry.

This book includes women who not only wrote musicals but who had their musicals produced. There were women *writing* musicals during each of these decades who, for reasons of circumstance, sometimes intersecting with privilege and class, did not see productions of their work. The determinations about what was produced and what wasn't intersect with identity in a way that is explored throughout. The women writers who are missing from these pages because their work was not chosen to be produced affected how this book was written.

There are many worthwhile artists who have been egregiously forgotten in the history books; this distinction is not limited to female musical theatre writers. The topic of who is left out and why works or creators are not celebrated or remembered is complex. And, while it significantly intersects with who has been historically marginalized based on their identity, it also includes those omitted for other reasons.

Many women were given a place at the table because of a male relative. It is not intended to be derogatory to note that, in some instances, a woman received an opportunity because her father, brother, or spouse, was a fellow writer or in the industry otherwise. This does not mean that those women were not talented or did not deserve an opportunity, but their connection via a male relative is part of the story. This topic is certainly not unique to the theatre industry. "Joining the family business" has roots that are centuries old, in every industry. For generations, it was an accepted societal norm for men to pass a family business or a family trade down to their sons. This of course comes with positive connotations regarding legacy and familial tradition, as well as negative connotations regarding privilege. As women entered the workforce in increasing numbers, how did nepotism interact with their entry, specifically in theatre? And how did this evolve as societal attitudes toward nepotism evolved overall?

Also evolving throughout the decades is the question of *when* women were to be allowed to work in the theatre, based on their personal lives. In several instances in the early decades of the twentieth century, women of a certain class were expected to retire from writing once they were married. In other instances, societal demands on women, including childcare needs, affected whether it was possible for them to fulfill what was expected in order to get their shows produced. When a workplace element was established at a time before women were expected to participate professionally, how did its foundation continue to impact how women were included?

When I interviewed the legendary Broadway music coordinator Red Press for *The Untold Stories of Broadway*, he told me: "When I started doing theatre, there were very few women in the pit, except for the occasional harpist. When I hired some women to play *Lorelei*, a man who was one of my house musicians said to me, 'How dare you hire a woman! There is a man sitting at home trying to support a family who is unemployed!' I will never forget that. Things were different."[1]

This might seem like a sexist, out-of-date practice and mind-set, worthy of dismissing outright—but the unexamined cannot be properly fixed. We are not divorced from the past, and imagining we are is counterproductive. We are part of a continuum of history. The overall societal expectation in 1974, when this production occurred, was still overwhelmingly that men had to earn a living for their families, and women had to stay home and take care of those families. The structuring of the workforce and of American life in general was (and to a degree, still is) shaped around this. So, if a woman was hired over a man, the perception that the woman was working for fun and a man was suffering in a real way and not able to feed his family, was a straight line from that widespread societal expectation. This of course not only affected who was hired but also who was promoted, how those hired were paid, and so on. Then, it affected how subsequent generations of professionals functioned, based on hiring practices they'd observed. There was never a dividing day when these stereotypes and assumed structures suddenly changed. Rather, we are on a straight line from that time to now, with incremental changes having happened along the way, so the past cannot be ignored. Broadway is also not divorced from the outside world, from how women are treated within the larger job force, from how society expects gender roles to be fulfilled today, and how it affects a professional trajectory. The reasons why women have lacked certain opportunities are complex and deserve educated and complete consideration.

While acknowledging writers and creatives who were part of a given production, who are in some cases more well known than the featured writer, the intention is to impart information and context. It is my hope that others mentioned will not overshadow the women being celebrated. An unfortunate by-product of speaking about more famous collaborators and relatives is that their presence

---

1. Tepper, Jennifer Ashley. *The Untold Stories of Broadway*, vol. 1. New York: Dress Circle Publishing, 2013.

can overwhelm the story. One cannot tell the story of Kay Swift without George Gershwin, or the story of Mary Rodgers without Richard Rodgers, but the point is to be aware of the potential pitfalls of these narratives.

In this book that involves the intersection of identity and art, I included various aspects of identity where it felt appropriate to the conversation. I also strove to avoid reducing any writer's profile to be singularly focused on their identity. Women featured in this tome identified across the spectrum of sexuality, impacted by (among other things) the terms used by society during the era when each lived. They are also racially diverse, neurodiverse, differently abled, and diverse in other ways. While not always explicitly stated, sometimes due to a lack of existing, fully confirmed research, the writers featured represent an intersection of many different aspects of identity. By its very nature, this book lumps all women together in ways they shouldn't necessarily always be, and it's worth noting that within the label of "women writing musicals," all of the artists featured here are unique.

The language about aspects of identity, including gender and race, which was used by artists, reviewers, and others in media during each era, is laid bare. In an effort to honestly explore the past in order to illuminate the present and future, quotes from reviews and articles that may seem offensive or shocking are included. In chronicling, for example, the sexist ways that female writers were written about, the intention is not to perpetuate misogynist standards but rather to explore how media representation and societal standards have evolved and how they have impacted theatre. Even the word *feminist* has different meanings and intent throughout the decades, and among different people in the same decade, whether being used to self-identify, as a pejorative in a review, or in the way we look at a historic achievement in perspective as being feminist by today's terms. Sometimes the best way to examine a point of misogyny or racism was to let a given quote speak for itself. Mentions of women's appearances in reviews, articles, and books proliferated throughout different eras, and this is deliberately displayed in order to call it out. Review quotes do not represent the opinion of the author about a given work.

Which came first—media writing about women a certain way, or women in theatre being treated a certain way and this being reflected in the media? An article about the 1975 Broadway musical *The Lieutenant* wrote jokingly that a male writer had agreed to collaborate with a female writer since she "looked like a great source of home-cooked meals."[2] When this kind of societal expectation was the norm, can we hold yesterday's journalism, honestly depicting a bygone era, to today's standards? How do we examine the affect that these types of comments had?

---

2. "Tony-Award Nominee from Queens," *New York Times*, 6 April 1975, p. 94.

Women are written about in chronological order, based on when the first major show they wrote for premiered. The final chapter is about the 2010s, and thus I stopped with writers whose debuts were after 2019, but did include relevant projects that happened up to the present wherever possible. There are many extraordinary women who have debuted as musical theatre writers on or off-Broadway since 2019, and happily, more are emerging every year.

Effort was made to include quotes directly from the women themselves, speaking about their own work, careers, and lives. I consumed thousands of books, articles, reviews, cast recordings, and more in order to paint the fullest possible picture of the writers being discussed in the space allotted. I recommend perusing the source list for further reading. I am particularly grateful to *The Interval* and its creator Victoria Myers for the abundance of commendable, in-depth interviews with contemporary writers.

Stage musicals live on in a large variety of ways after their Broadway or off-Broadway premieres—through collective memory of course, and also through film and TV adaptations and live captures; tours; regional, stock, amateur, and school productions; and more. One significant way that musicals live on is via cast recordings. If a cast recording isn't made, it impacts greatly how much a show is produced and remembered. With no cast album, the creators' popularity isn't expanded, with new fans discovering them through their songs, so not only is that project impacted—their next project is impacted as well. A theatre doesn't become familiar with a writer's work through their cast album, so that writer is not on their radar. Who was making decisions about what show received a cast album throughout history? What factors affected how those cast albums were released? What determined whether a cast album made the leap from vinyl to CD or from CD to streaming service? Asking questions about the opportunities musicals were given to live on throughout other media was essential to the topic of this book.

The lack of parity in hiring for theatre has deep roots in societal elements that go back centuries. By exploring a timeline of women writing for theatre that goes from the eighteenth century to present day, I hoped to meaningfully show the extent to which something that happened in 1913 is related to something that happened last season on Broadway. The lines we can draw between past, present, and future will help us solve problems with greater tools of understanding.

At the same time, I wanted to shine a light on the accomplishments, triumphs, and great art made by women. I wanted to spend time exploring the careers and lives of extraordinary women theatre writers, without spending *every* line bemoaning their lack of opportunities or misogynist comments about their work. In this book, there is documentation of systemic sexism, but there is also an abundance of celebration about what women achieved. Several of the writers featured in this book lamented that in interviews, they were sick of being asked about their identity, and wanted to be asked more about the work. I sought to achieve a balance between a necessary exploration of how identities and society impacted individual writers' work, without reducing them to just their identities and personal lives. When asked by the *Guardian* about her opinion that she has to speak for her gender, class, and race in a way that white men are never required to do, Lynn Nottage said, "We feel this need to assert ourselves because we are absent in mainstream spaces, but at the same time feel the frustration that there is even a need to assert our voices. So that's the paradox."[3]

And what of the work? Were there musicals by women that were not produced, or not transformed into hits, or not remembered, because they were perceived as only written for one segment of the population, fellow women, and thus considered more disposable? Were women only produced when they wrote specific kinds of stories, or did they *choose* to write specific kinds of stories? Does a focus on identity cause writers to only be hired for certain jobs, or pigeonholed as only able to be produced successfully if they write about certain topics? Micki Grant expressed her opinion in a 1981 interview: "A woman or a Black person should be allowed to write about universal themes. It's as if we had no right as women and blacks to get involved in anything other than black and white issues. . . . If you get up in the morning and look in the mirror and you have a headache, you don't have a Black headache."[4]

There were several instances where a woman wrote about being a woman in a certain time frame, and this depiction was considered problematic by a later generation. The experience of being a woman changed, so "women's shows" of the 1960s were perceived as out-of-date in the 1980s. Being perceived as "dated" is a problem more often experienced by marginalized writers, whose collective experience changes more throughout the years. This perpetuates disparities surrounding whose work is revived and whose isn't.

Sometimes a writer was considered "the most beloved woman composer to ____," or some similar accolade that qualified the writer as a woman. Other times, I found it necessary to point out that a writer was the first woman to achieve a specific milestone. When is qualifying a woman helpful in pointing out an accomplishment or a discrepancy, and when is it perpetuating sexism?

Often when the media acknowledged women, it was done without appropriate credit being given to those who had come before. When in 1931 the press praised Charlotte Kent, the newspaper article stated that she had no path to follow, since only two women had ever written musicals before. A quick perusal

---

3. Crompton, Sarah. "Playwright Lynn Nottage: 'We are a country that has lost our narrative.'" *Guardian*, 2 December 2018, https://www.theguardian.com/stage/2018/dec/02/lynn-nottage -interview-play-sweat-america.

4. "Lyricist Micki Grant Is That and More." *Evening Sun*, 12 November 1981.

in the table of contents of this book of the dozens of women who had credits that came before hers, makes the point that this journalist, like many, had a lack of knowledge and research about women who had already made history. As Lisa Kron told the *Interval*, "It's always, 'Here's this person who has done amazing work and now things will be different,' and then it's not different. Part of the reason it's not different is that we forget those productions, we forget those women."[5]

All of this is being examined, with the understanding that all opinions about art itself are subjective. One person might think a musical is a masterpiece, and another might think it's terrible. One person might think a writer is immensely talented, and another might think that writer should never be hired. Different opinions are a healthy, positive aspect of humans reacting honestly to art. So there's no definitive judgment to be made on whether one person or another would be better for a particular job or opportunity. The point isn't that women need to be hired for specific shows or jobs in order to fill quotas, represent specific topics, or put band-aids on problems, but that by being more aware of all that has affected female musical theatre writers, educated decisions can be made in a multitude of ways. Whose forgotten catalog might be worthwhile to explore in an evening of song? Which critical perspective might we need to consider when examining why a show was a flop? What conversations are needed, regarding how identity intersects with show content? How can women be supported in order to be given full and fair consideration for opportunities, without being blindly hired just because of their identity?

Addressing complicated problems that go back generations is never going to be a quick fix. In fact, attempting a quick fix sometimes just exacerbates issues; not every wound is helped by a band-aid. Thoughtful, educated dialogue based on accurate information is key, and that's what this book seeks to provide. This is not a book about hiring practices, or statistics, or American workplace policies. It is a book about what women have accomplished in the field of musical theatre writing and about worthwhile work you may not have heard of that can provide context for valuable conversations.

In exploring the detailed stories of dozens of women throughout history who wrote musicals, I hope readers are inspired and excited. I hope they are galvanized to listen to cast recordings, discover productions, and otherwise champion the shows written about in these pages. I hope they want to independently seek out creators and works in their own time, who might not be receiving the attention they deserve otherwise.

---

5. Myers, Victoria. "An Interview with Lisa Kron." *Interval*, 13 May 2015, https://www.theinterval ny.com/interviews/2015/05/an-interview-with-lisa-kron/.

Take to heart the phenomenal legacy that the women explored in *Women Writing Musicals* left behind. It's time for them to be celebrated and to bring their collective accomplishments to the forefront.

1

The Eighteenth and Nineteenth Centuries

Beginnings

CHAPTER I

ANN JULIA HATTON
First Woman to Write a Libretto

In the late eighteenth century, only a decade after American independence became a reality, Ann Julia Hatton made a name for herself with her shows, particularly one political musical.

In 1793, Hatton collaborated with a writer credited only as Mrs. Pownall on a show titled *Needs Must; or, The Ballad Singers*, which was considered just an excuse for Pownall, who had broken her leg, to be stationary on stage and sing her favorite songs.[1] The show played at the John Street Theatre, considered the first permanent theater in New York City, which was in use from 1767 to 1798. Hatton wrote the lyrics and some of the music, with the rest of the piece by Pownall.

Hatton's next show was a more illustrious venture, and it was also the next production at the John Street Theatre. *Tammany; or, The Indian Chief* was billed as a "serious opera."[2] Hatton wrote the libretto to this show with a strong anti-Federalist stance. In 1794, anti-Federalists were in favor of the French Revolution. The Tammany Society, New York's powerful political organization, was also anti-Federalist, so Hatton based her libretto on their patron namesake.[3]

The show was about Native American Chief Tamanend, who is the namesake of Tammany Hall. The cast played Native American and Spanish characters. Lewis Hallam Jr., son of Sarah Hallam Douglass, cofounder of the Old American Company, who ran the John Street Theatre played Christopher Columbus. John Durang, known as the first American-born professional actor and ancestor of playwright Christopher Durang, was in the cast as well, playing a Native American dancer. John Hodgkinson, a leading actor at the time, was Chief Tamanend.

The story, concocted by Hatton, was about Tammany and his love interest, Manana. In the show, the two are tragically burned to death by the Spaniards. Hatton wrote original lyrics for the piece and also adapted some lyrics from old Native American songs, which she acknowledged as such.[4]

Tammany; or, The Indian Chief is widely considered the first libretto written by a woman. Hatton was also known for her poetry and novels.

1. Sonneck, Oscar George Theodore. *Early Opera in America.* New York: G. Schirmer, 1915.

2. Ibid.

3. Howard, John Tasker. *Our American Music; Three Hundred Years of It.* New York: Crowell, 1954.

4. Bordman, Gerald. *American Musical Theater: A Chronicle.* New York: Oxford University Press, 2001.

MRS. POWNALL
Singer, Actor, and Writer at the John Street Theatre

In the eighteenth century, women on the American stage were often billed without first names. Mrs. Pownall started as Miss Marshall in England, then became Mrs. Wrighten after her marriage, and starred on the British stage under that name. In America, she was an acclaimed actor under the name Mrs. Pownall, performing dramatic and musical roles after her arrival in the early 1790s.[5]

Pownall's writing credit came in 1793, when she sang the numbers she was most known for in *Needs Must; or, The Ballad Singers*, on which she collaborated with Ann Julia Hatton at the John Street Theatre.

LOUISA MEDINA
First Woman in America to Make Her Living Writing for the Stage?

Louisa Medina is known as the first woman in America to make her living solely as a dramatist. She is also known as the writer of a stage adaptation of *Last Days of Pompeii*, which had a long run of twenty-nine days at a time when most productions ran for only a few days.[6]

Medina died at the age of twenty-five, yet in her short life, she became acclaimed as a writer for the stage. All thirty-four of her works for the stage were written in the span of five years, starting in 1833.[7] Her work was credited with saving the Bowery Theatre, a center for American drama in nineteenth century New York. The Bowery burned down and was rebuilt five times, during an era when fires were frequent and devastating to live performance venues. Medina wrote the dedication for the Bowery's 1937 reopening after a fire, and also saved the theater from debt with her hit shows. Sadly, the scripts for many of Medina's shows were lost in fires at the Bowery Theatre, making them unknown to later generations.

Medina became involved with the Bowery Theatre through its manager, Thomas Hamblin. After emigrating from Spain, Medina was first the governess for Hamblin's daughter. She was an educated, independent woman, who pursued avenues not frequently open to women at the time. She spoke three languages;

---

5. Seilhamer, George O. *History of the American Theatre: New Foundations, Volume 3*. New York: Haskell House, 1968.

6. Kritzer, Amelia Howe. "Antebellum Plays by Women: Context and Themes." *The Oxford Handbook of American Drama*. Edited by Jeffrey H. Richards and Heather S. Nathans. New York: Oxford University Press, 2014.

7. Tobiason, Aaron M. "So as to Compass the Interest: Artisan Dramaturgy, Copyright Reform, and the Theatrical Insurgency of 1856." 2014, PhD diss., University of Maryland, https://drum.lib.umd.edu/bitstream/handle/1903/15240/Tobiason_umd_0117E_15036.pdf.

3

studied subjects considered too challenging for women,[8] including geometry and algebra, and pursued publication of her writing successfully in London. When given the opportunity to write for the Bowery Theatre, Medina quickly became its most popular dramatist. She had an ongoing affair with Hamblin, which resulted in scandal. After Hamblin left his wife for Medina, he carried on an affair with a young actor named Louisa Missouri Miller, who died under somewhat mysterious circumstances shortly before Medina did.

While the majority of Medina's works were melodramas, several contained musical elements. One of her most popular works was *Norman Leslie*, which in 1836, earned $6,000 in its first week, enough to save the Bowery Theatre from debt for the umpteenth time. *Norman Leslie*, which Medina adapted from a novel by Theodore S. Fay, continued to be produced after her death.[9]

Medina is often forgotten by historians of early American theatre, with credit for the Bowery Theatre's successes being attributed to Hamblin and others. In his 1889 memoir, *Memories of Fifty Years*, actor-manager Lester Wallack called Medina, "one of the most brilliant women I ever met. She was very plain, but a wonderful bright woman, charming in every way." The rare write-ups of Medina often mention her appearance in a derogatory way. Some historians speculate this may be the reason there is no known image of her.[10] One might also assume that these condescending remarks are simply because Medina went against what society expected and was put down as a result.

ANNA AND EMMA HYERS
Pioneers in Black Musical Comedy

The Hyers Sisters, Anna and Emma, started out as performers under the management of their enterprising father Samuel B. Hyers, in the 1860s. Making their debut on stage in Sacramento in 1867, the sisters followed this by touring many shows successfully across America, through the 1890s. They have been called "pioneers in Black musical comedy."[11]

Had Anna and Emma Hyers lived in a different era, or been of a different race and/or gender in their own era, they might have been rightfully credited with conceiver credits more explicitly. As it was, the Hyers Sisters performed in

---

8. Rodriguez, Miriam López. "Louisa Medina: Uncrowned Queen of Melodrama." PhD diss., Universitat de València, 2004, https://www.academia.edu/911059/Louisa_Medina_Uncrowned_Queen_of_Melodrama.

9. Ibid.

10. Wallack, Lester. *Memories of Fifty Years*. Lancaster, PA: Wentworth Press, 2016.

11. Hill, Errol. "The Hyers Sisters: Pioneers in Black Musical Comedy." In *The American Stage*. Edited by Ron Engle and Tice L. Miller. Cambridge, MA: Cambridge University Press, 1993.

many original works, musical and otherwise—some written by Pauline Elizabeth Hopkins—and often had notable input in their productions. The Hyers family produced their own shows.

One of the Hyers sisters' most popular productions was *In and Out of Bondage*, by Joseph Bradford. In 1876, this show about a Black family set before and after the Civil War was concluded by a concert featuring the sisters' regular repertoire. This was integral to the show, in which several characters in the plot became free men and women who were paid as vocalists and singers in post–Civil War America.[12] Anna and Emma Hyers kept *In and Out of Bondage* in their performance repertoire for fifteen years, and varied which songs they would perform.

Anna Hyers, appearing in the opera *Urlina the African Princess*, circa 1879. BY UNKNOWN PHOTOGRAPHER/ WIKIMEDIA COMMONS.

In much of their work, the Hyers sisters similarly lent creative contributions to the script, while simultaneously excelling as groundbreaking performers. They "pushed boundaries of acceptable and expected roles for Black and female performers by developing works that moved beyond stereotypical caricatures of African American life."[13]

PAULINE ELIZABETH HOPKINS
Multitalented Groundbreaking Black Female Writer

Pauline Elizabeth Hopkins was one of the most prolific and produced Black female writers in the late nineteenth and early twentieth centuries. She was a writer of many forms, penning stage musicals, novels, stories, speeches, and articles and was a pioneer of horror, science fiction, and fantasy writing.[14] She was a leader at several magazines and worked as a literary editor as well. She was an accomplished performer and orator.

Hopkins's first well-known work was a musical play called *Slaves' Escape; or, The Underground Railroad*. In her writing, she explored racism in different eras of American history. *Slaves' Escape*, later retitled *Peculiar Sam*, was produced in 1879, when Hopkins was only twenty years old. The piece was highly regarded

---

12. Ibid.

13. Buckner, Jocelyn L. "'Spectacular Opacities: The Hyers Sisters' Performances of Respectability and Resistance." *African American Review*, 45, no. 3 (Fall 2012).

14. Ouellette, Katherine. "The Literary Legacy of Pauline Hopkins." WBUR, February 12, 2021. https://www.wbur.org/news/2021/02/12/pauline-hopkins-of-one-blood-hagars-daughter.

Pauline Elizabeth Hopkins, circa 1901.
BY *COLORED AMERICAN MAGAZINE* / WIKIMEDIA COMMONS

by Hopkins's contemporaries. In it, she "provided American audiences with the first staged reenactments of slavery that were not offered through the lens of the white imagination."[15]

Raised in a prominent Black family in Boston, Hopkins was well educated and became a prominent intellectual force as a founding member of the Boston Literary and Historical Association.[16] Her most popular novel, *Contending Forces: A Romance Illustrative of Negro Life North and South*, gave voice to Black families living in America after the Civil War. In writing *Contending Forces*, Hopkins used her own family history; she was born to free parents whose ancestors had been enslaved. Through Hopkins's work with *The Colored American Magazine*, her founding of the Colored American League in Boston, and many other accomplishments, she fought for the advancement of Black Americans.

According to Dr. Cherene Sherrard-Johnson, president of the Pauline Elizabeth Hopkins Society, "Hopkins was very forthright in her activism against lynching and sexual violence against Black women. These subjects were not talked about, especially sexual abuse, and Hopkins talked about them as openly as she could in her novels. . . . [Hopkins] wanted to share race in a way that was authentic and humanizing, but she also wanted to entertain."[17]

One of Hopkins's lost works, the novel *Of One Blood; or, The Hidden Self*, was published in a new edition in 2020, with the subtitle "A Lost Heritage Rediscovered, from the First Great Female Horror Writer of Color."[18] *Of One Blood*'s 2020 edition has an introduction by writer Nisi Shawl. Shawl notes that Hopkins, less than forty years after the Civil War created a "proto-Wakanda" for her book, an advanced Black civilization with "all the arts and cunning inventions that make your modern glory," kept secret by its inhabitants.

15. Ibid.

16. Dworkin, Ira. "Biography of Pauline E. Hopkins." Pauline Hopkins Society. https://www.paulinehopkinssociety.org/biography/.

17. Ouellette, Katherine. "The Literary Legacy of Pauline Hopkins." WBUR, February 12, 2021. https://www.wbur.org/news/2021/02/12/pauline-hopkins-of-one-blood-hagars-daughter.

18. Hopkins, Pauline. *Of One Blood; or, The Hidden Self.* Scottsdale, AZ: Poisoned Pen Press, 2021.

Josie DeWitt
Actor, Writer, Violinist

By the Sad Sea Waves was an 1898 musical comedy at the Herald Square Theatre. Josie DeWitt appeared in the cast and also composed one song for the hit show, which ran for forty-seven performances. DeWitt was known as both a singer and a violinist; she was highly praised for playing her ribbon-covered violin in the production.[19]

By the Sad Sea Waves, while largely forgotten, made a small pop culture appearance in the 2012–2015 Australian television series *Miss Fisher's Murder Mysteries*. Its poster appears in several episodes.

---

19. "Miss Jessie Wood." *New York Evening Journal*, 27 June 1898, p. 8.

2

1900s

Revues, Large Teams, and Multihyphenates

NELLIE AND ROSE BEAUMONT
The Seltzer Sisters

Sisters Nellie and Rose Beaumont were perhaps the first women to write a song for Broadway in the twentieth century. The Beaumont sisters started out in vaudeville and eventually racked up eighteen Broadway credits between them.

The two wrote for Broadway only once, and it was for *Mam'selle 'Awkins*, which premiered at the Victoria Theatre in February of 1900. The show tells the tale of a rich man fallen on hard times who has to ditch his current wife in order to marry a wealthier woman. Along the way he calls on many friends to assist with his hijinks.[1]

The Beaumonts played sisters Sally and Sadie Seltzer in *Mam'selle 'Awkins*. They wrote both music and lyrics for their number, "You're Talking Rag-Time."

CECILIA LOFTUS
Actor-Writer

A well-known Broadway performer for the first four decades of the twentieth century, Cecilia Loftus also contributed music and lyrics to three productions.

Loftus was born in Scotland and got her start in the music halls and vaudeville houses of London. She came to America and toured with both vaudeville and legit theatre troupes, making a name for herself with her talent for impressions. Her Broadway debut was in a repertory company that presented six shows at once, including *Much Ado About Nothing*, *Macbeth*, and *Twelfth Night*. She often performed the work of Shakespeare.

Cecilia Loftus, circa 1901, by Apeda Studio. BY APEDA (PHOTOGRAPHY STUDIO) - J. WILLIS SAYRE COLLECTION OF THEATRICAL PHOTOGRAPHS / WIKIMEDIA COMMONS

Later in 1900, the same year as her Broadway debut, Loftus had her second Broadway job when she was invited to write two songs for *The Belle of Bridgeport*. The show is about a young woman fleeing from a false charge of theft, and the white May Irwin, who played the lead, was known for her interpretation of coon songs.[2] Irwin also produced.

---

1. Bordman, Gerald. *American Musical Theater: A Chronicle*. New York: Oxford University Press, 2001.

2. Coon songs capitalized on Black stereotypes and were written and performed by both Black and white artists. They had their roots in the minstrel shows of the early nineteenth century, and experienced peak popularity between 1880 and 1920, at which point the term *coon* became seen as increasingly racist and problematic and fell out of popular use.

The main writers of the show were Black dramatists, J. Rosamond Johnson, Bob Cole, and James Weldon Johnson, and white dramatist Glen MacDonough. Loftus's songs were titled "Bullfrog Ben" and "(I'm Gwine to Marry) Angeline." The show was largely criticized for its blatant commercialism because it actually featured product placement. Certain brands of typewriters and whiskey were promoted within its flimsy plot.

Later that same year, Loftus—in her last job where she was billed as "Cissie Loftus" rather than "Cecilia"—worked on a revamp of *The Belle of Bridgeport*, this time titled *Madge Smith, Attorney*. She had the same two songs included, still sung by May Irwin, but the plot was altered.

Loftus's third and final Broadway writing credit was the only one for a show where she was also on stage: *The Lancers*. The 1907 Shubert production is a military comedy set in Quebec, and its first two numbers feature both music and lyrics by Loftus, sung by the charming character she played, a young Russian woman intent on capturing the heart of a captain. The script was cowritten by Rida Johnson Young and J. Hartley Manners.

Unfortunately, *The Lancers* received very negative reviews and closed after less than two weeks at Daly's Theatre. It even received a *New York Times* review zinger: "*The Lancers* is described as an entertainment, and that merely goes to show how elastic the language is."[3]

Immediately after *The Lancers*, Loftus married for a second time. (Her first marriage, to writer Justin Hartly McCarthy, had ended in divorce when she was very young.) Loftus's second marriage meant that she retired from all stage work in 1908. Her marriage and health were in trouble by 1914, and she returned to the stage, playing Desdemona in *Othello* at the Lyric after six full years away. She later got a divorce, but did not return to Broadway again until 1927. The remainder of her time on Broadway was spent performing only. In 1934, she originated a scene-stealing role in the Kaufman and Hart play *Merrily We Roll Along*, and in 1938, she brought her self-titled one-woman-show to Broadway at the Vanderbilt.

MAE ANWERDA SLOANE
Coon Songs and Working with a Husband

Between May 1901 and June 1902, Mae Anwerda Sloane had five productions on Broadway. They comprised her entire career on the Great White Way.

Sloane was both a composer and a lyricist, and her most famous song, for which she contributed both words and music, was "My Evaline." This song

3. "What *The Lancers* Proved at Daly's." *New York Times*, 6 December 1907, p. 11.

appeared in *The King's Carnival*, a burlesque musical. In 1901, the genre of burlesque was still known for putting a new spin on literary properties. In this case, several well-known stories about royal knights were combined. Sloane's "My Evaline" was billed on its sheet music as a "darkey love song."[4] T. S. Eliot would later reference the song in his poems. *The King's Carnival* opened in spring 1901, closed for the summer, and reopened to play another month in the fall.

While it was still running, Sloane contributed to *The Liberty Belles*. Here, she wrote the music for both the first act closer, "Jack O'Lantern (The Great Will-o'-the-Wisp Song)" and the second act opener, "Shopping (Song of Spring Fashions)." On both, she collaborated with Harry B. Smith, one of the most prolific Broadway writers of all time. One of the other most prolific Broadway writers of all time was Sloane's own husband, Alfred Baldwin Sloane, who also contributed to the musical. A. B. Sloane specialized in coon songs, and M. A. Sloane's "Jack O'Lantern" was one of these. *The Liberty Belles* is about a girls' school where several of the girls stir up some trouble—one is stage-struck Marjery, who closes act one with "Jack O'Lantern." "Shopping" was sung by the entire chorus.

Sloane followed *The Liberty Belles* with *The Supper Club*. The show played at the rooftop venue that was part of the Olympia Theatre complex, at that point briefly known as the New York Winter Garden Theatre. It was so named because its owners tried to convert the summertime venue into a theater for the colder months.[5] *The Supper Club* was the first show to play it as such, and it was a plotless vaudeville attraction. Audience members could wander in and out as they pleased, and there was no song list in the program.

Like *The Liberty Belles* and *The Supper Club*, M. A. Sloane's final Broadway show, *The Hall of Fame*, also featured the work of her husband. This musical was a hit, at the theater just below the roof garden where the previous show appeared. This time M. A. Sloane contributed music to four songs, although the majority of the show's music was written by A. B. Sloane. *Hall of Fame* parodied the current theatrical hits of the season while at the same time providing its own plot. Sloane's songs were titled "Love Is a Jailer," "Nancy," "When Charlie Plays the Slide Trombone," and "My Pajama Beauty."

---

4. Anwerda Sloane, Mae. "My Evaline: Darkey Love Song." New York: Authors & Composers Music Pub. Co., 1901.

5. "New York Winter Garden; The Roof Theatre Prettily and Lavishly Decorated. Well-Known Performers figure in "The Supper Club," a Plotless Medley of Vaudeville Features." *New York Times*, 25 December 1901, p. 2.

MABEL WHEELER DANIELS
A Troubled Theatrical Troupe

Mabel Wheeler Daniels was the first woman to take a score-reading course at the Munich Conservatory. She grew up composing, surrounded by a musical family.[6]

In 1902, Daniels was one of three composers for the new musical *The Show Girl*. Out of town, the show was titled *The Cap of Fortune*, which became its subtitle at Wallack's Theatre in New York. The show tells the tale of a troubled theatrical troupe whose manager finds a magic cap that enables him to bring the goddess Psyche back to earth for guidance. Ironically for a show about a troubled theatrical troupe, the group putting together *The Show Girl* was troubled by countless incidents during its tryout, with many actors and creative team members replaced.

Daniels had three songs in the piece: "We Are Trying to Support Our Only Mother," "Invocation to Pie," and "In Gay Japan."

She continued to write choral and orchestral pieces.

CLARE KUMMER
Hit Songwriter Hustles Hard to Write a Full Show

Clare Kummer was a playwright, composer, and lyricist, who worked on both plays and musicals on Broadway from 1903 until 1945.

Kummer was born into an illustrious family. Her great uncle was Henry Ward Beecher, and her great aunt was Harriet Beecher Stowe. Virtually all the press that noted her early successes as a writer also made note of this familial connection. In 1917, the *Brooklyn Daily Eagle* reported that Kummer's recent Broadway hit *Good Gracious Annabelle* was thought to be a fluke by those in the know on Broadway, but that when her next play, *A Successful Calamity* proved to be a success as well, those in the industry were satisfied

Clare Kummer. BY BAIN NEWS SERVICE, PUBLISHER/ LIBRARY OF CONGRESS CATA- LOG / WIKIMEDIA COMMONS

that there was a new talented writer on the block.[7] This was despite the fact that Kummer actually had six Broadway credits to her name prior to *Good Gracious Annabelle*. They were all musicals for which she contributed some combination of music, book, and lyrics, usually as part of a team of writers, beginning in 1903.

---

6. "Mabel Daniels: 1878–1971." Library of Congress, https://www.loc.gov/item/ihas.200153249/.

7. "Grandniece of Beecher Is Successful Playwright." *Brooklyn Daily Eagle*, 18 February 1917, p. 34.

And despite the fact that her family gave her connections that assisted her later on in her career, they were not overly encouraging about her writing. Her big break came when producer Arthur Hopkins, known for giving female writers opportunities throughout his career, produced *Good Gracious Annabelle*. The *Brooklyn Eagle* piece summarized: "Mrs. Henry tells her friends that she is now at work on two more comedies and also expects to write a musical comedy—book, lyrics, score and everything. These tasks will, she admits, keep her fairly busy until she decides to write a grand opera or something like that for a change."[8] The article throughout refers to Kummer as Mrs. Henry, as a man named Arthur Henry was her husband at the time.

Also in 1917, Kummer was featured in a special article in *Pearson's Magazine*, written by Ruth Pickering. The article opened with a description of Kummer's appearance and then went on to praise her work. But then Pickering gave a frank explanation of Kummer's journey to enter the workforce. According to the piece, Kummer was regretful that she became unhappily married at eighteen, and then was divorced and had a young daughter to take care of. This was what drove her to seek employment as a writer. She had always loved writing songs and lyrics and playing the piano, but it was the need to support her daughter that caused her to knock on producers' doors, hoping to sell her writing.

While she did sell several songs, including "Dearie," which sold over 1 million pieces of sheet music, she could not get any producer to take a chance on letting her write a full show[9] until Hopkins bought *Good Gracious Annabelle*. The article described how she was turned down by Daniel Frohman and other producers. "Writing songs was her talent—she couldn't expect to have more than *one* talent.[10] They would never listen to her pleading. So not to 'show them' exactly, but just to prove it to herself, Clare Kummer began writing *Good Gracious Annabelle*."[11]

Kummer was known for the down-to-earth realism of her dialogue, which presented people as they were. While her plays might include outrageous events, the people who populated her plays spoke without affect, as though they were just average humans one might meet off of the stage.

---

8. Ibid.

9. Although it was never produced on Broadway, Kummer did pen an 1898 musical called *Captain Kidd; or, The Buccaneers* that played London. And in 1907 she had a musical called *Noah's Ark* close out of town.

10. Kummer also at times lied and said songs of hers had two writers since buyers did not believe one person had written both music and lyrics.

11. Pickering, Ruth. "Clare Kummer: The Year's New Playwright." *Pearson's Magazine* 38 (January 1918).

After becoming accepted as a successful writer, Kummer focused on penning plays for several seasons before she took a turn at a musical. And when she did, it was a pair of one-act musicals presented as special matinee engagements in 1921 at the three-hundred-seat house known as the Punch and Judy Theatre. Kummer wrote book, music, and lyrics, and produced as well. *The Choir Rehearsal* and *Chinese Love* made her the first woman to be the sole writer of a Broadway musical production.

In 1924, Kummer wrote a full-fledged musical, penning book, music, and lyrics for *Annie Dear*, based on *Good Gracious Annabelle*, which was produced by Florenz Ziegfeld. The show did have some additional song contributions by Sigmund Romberg, Clifford Grey, and Jean Schwartz, as Ziegfeld insisted upon these in the show he produced as a vehicle for his wife Billie Burke. It was not a happy collaboration for Kummer.

The week after *Annie Dear* opened at the Times Square, Kummer had *Madame Pompadour* open at the Martin Beck, produced by Beck himself with Charles Dillingham. In this case, Kummer adapted the book for the operetta, which was originally a hit in Berlin. The show opened the Martin Beck Theatre, now the Al Hirschfeld.

Kummer's final musical credit on Broadway was a show called *Three Waltzes*, produced by the Shubert brothers in 1937 at the Majestic. She cowrote with Rowland Leigh the book for this musical. As her work on Broadway tapered off, concluding with a play called *Many Happy Returns* in 1945, Kummer began to work more on film and television projects, and she continued publishing songs. She also worked as a literary agent, selling work by others.

According to a piece written for *Maestra Music* by Sarah Whitfield, there is evidence that Kummer was intended to win the Pulitzer Prize in 1917 for *A Successful Calamity*. The committee selected this show of Kummer's for the award, but, through later deliberations never made public, the show was never recognized. The first woman to win a Pulitzer Prize for Best Play was Susan Glaspell in 1931; Glaspell won for *Alison's House*.[12]

Whitfield also noted a *Chicago Tribune* article from 1917 that commented on female writers, including Kummer: "Although the women may have just as much talent as the men, it is not to be expected that their songs and music numbers ever will become as genuinely popular as are those of the men. The men have this advantage: For the purpose of 'plugging' their new creations, they can go where they please, when they please, and stay out as late as they please without shattering any of the traditions of propriety. The women, however, cannot do this."[13]

---

12. Whitfield, Sarah. "Spotlights on Women Composers in Early Broadway History: Week Three, Clare Kummer." Maestra Music. https://maestramusic.org/blog/spotlights-on-women-composers-in-early-broadway-history-week-three-clare-kummer/.

13. Ibid.

MAUDE NUGENT
"Sweet Rosie O'Grady"

Many musical theatre fans know the work of Maude Nugent without knowing they know it, because her most famous composition made its way into the enduring 1964 musical *Hello, Dolly!*

Nugent wrote "Sweet Rosie O'Grady" in 1896. At the age of twenty-three, she traipsed through the male-dominated Tin Pan Alley, trying to sell her song. When she did, it became a huge popular hit. Nugent performed it herself at vaudeville venues, encouraging its notoriety with a trick whereby she planted another performer in the gallery to take up the second verse. The catchy waltz was so enduring that its title was used for a Betty Grable movie in 1943 and in that same decade, Nugent was still performing the number on television—fifty years after she wrote it. In *Dolly*, set in the late 1800s, the character of Ernestina sings the tune off-key, to great comic effect. "Sweet Rosie O'Grady" was one of the first American songs to sell over a million copies of its sheet music.

Nugent was married to songwriter William Jerome, who attained dozens of Broadway credits in his lifetime, and like a significant number of female writers of the early twentieth century, her limited place at the table was granted to her largely because of her husband's presence. Many critics did not believe that Nugent had written her big hit, and claimed that Jerome must have written it, an allegation that he constantly corrected in the press. They were engaged at the time that she sold the song.

Nugent's two Broadway credits came a decade after her "Sweet Rosie O'Grady" fame. In 1904, she contributed a number to a musical comedy called *An English Daisy*. Her song, with lyrics by Will Heelan, was called "The Coon, the Moon, and the Little Octoroon." The number was performed by the show's title character, Daisy, played by Christie MacDonald, a white actress, to great audience acclaim; they often sang along with its final choruses. "The Coon, the Moon, and the Little Octoroon" is categorized as a coon song.[14]

An English Daisy premiered less than a decade after *A Trip to Coontown*, the first mainstream entertainment written, directed, and performed by Black artists, who, in choosing this title, claimed the word for their own. Two of the writers of *A Trip to Coontown* were Bob Cole and J. Rosamond Johnson—the two Black men who wrote the song that followed Nugent's "The Coon, the Moon, and the Little Octoroon" in *An English Daisy*. Cole and Johnson's song was "Big Indian Chief," not a coon song but a number capitalizing on Native American stereotypes.[15]

---

14. See note 2.

15. Cole, Robert; Johnson, J. Rosamond; Myers, J. W. "Big Indian Chief." Library of Congress. https://www.loc.gov/item/ihas.100010701/.

In 1904, at one of Broadway's most popular venues, the Casino Theatre, a new book musical could feature a songwriting roster including both female and Black artists. While the majority of contributors to *An English Daisy* were white, the fact that the team was diverse overall was not entirely unheard of. Just like Fanny Brice and Bert Williams could share the bill in *The Ziegfeld Follies* a few years later, race and gender did not have to be uniform in the melting pot that was Broadway in the early decades of the twentieth century. Here an audience might see a coon song written by a white woman followed by a Native American pseudo-love call written by a Black male team. These instances were certainly accompanied by distinct challenges for creatives who were not male and white, but they did occur.

Nugent's other credit came the following year in *Fritz in Tammany Hall* (1905). This time she was hired to write the show's 11 o'clock number. It was called "My Irish Daisy," and the production's wish to capitalize on the popularity of "Sweet Rosie O'Grady" was clear. Her collaborator on "My Irish Daisy" was Jean Schwartz, her husband's most frequent collaborator.

Liza Lehmann
A Successful Vocalist Has Her Writing Replaced

In 1905, Liza Lehmann, one of England's most acclaimed turn-of-the-century female composers, achieved her sole Broadway credit, a musical farce called *Sergeant Brue*.

Lehmann started out as a successful vocalist in London in the 1880s. After marrying in the 1890s, she did what almost all female performers did then, directly following their weddings: she politely retired from the stage. But Lehmann was unique in that she decided to begin composing instead. Soon she was writing song cycles, art songs, parlor songs, children's songs, light opera, and more; she became one of Britain's most beloved female composers.

By the early 1900s, Lehmann expanded her reach to both sides of the pond, as she toured America and Europe, singing her own compositions. She became the first president of the Society of Women Musicians and a professor of singing at the Guildhall School of Music. By 1904, when she was invited to compose a new musical farce, audiences were excited to see how the writer of hit song cycles like *A Daisy Chain* and *The Persian Garden* would approach this new style.

It wasn't just any musical Lehmann was commissioned to make her Broadway debut with; she was chosen to compose a new musical with a story by Owen Hall. Hall was known for the smash hit *Florodora*, one of the longest-running shows in Broadway history at the time. His story for *Sergeant Brue* involves a policeman who inherits a great fortune but can't retire and has to stay on the force even though he is a millionaire. Before the musical opened at the Strand Theatre on the West End in 1904, Lehmann told the press, "I could never have believed it would be so easy. I really think I must in a previous existence, let us say on Mars, have been writing musical comedies before. The task has been the greatest fun imaginable."[16]

One can imagine what kind of reaction such confidence may have elicited; for many readers, writing musicals was just not something that women did, and this woman didn't even think the task was difficult! The same article called her "the pioneer of women composers, so far as comic opera is concerned."

Lehmann continued: "Yet dramatic work cannot be said to be entirely out of my line, for I wrote the incidental music to the *Twin Sister* at the Duke of York's, and also the music to a charming fairy play of Teresa Haupt, called *Kleine Else*, which has had a great vogue in Germany. I wrote too, several little musical duologues. My husband, Herbert Bedford, who is also a composer in his spare time, has been very interested in the progress of the work. I have often pulled the piano up to the telephone and played him bits on which I wanted an opinion."

Sergeant Brue was a hit at the Strand and the following year, in 1905, opened on Broadway at the Knickerbocker Theatre.

One magazine, the *Reader*, was particularly condescending. "Perhaps the most disappointing feature of *Sergeant Brue* is its lack of any distinctive music; the composer, Liza Lehman [*sic*] is capable of delicate composition, but she has here struck the level—the musical comedy vein—a combination of flaunting tune and inspired sentiment."[17] The critic went on to praise Frank Daniels in the role of the policeman.

Most reviews were mixed. Some critics did have praise for Lehmann's music, but many thought the work did not live up to the anticipation and was a disappointment. The critical reception was not solely responsible for Lehmann's lack of subsequent Broadway credits, though. She reported that she was uninterested in returning to legitimate theatre in New York because her score had been altered greatly by *Sergeant Brue*'s Broadway producer, Charles Dillingham. By the time the show opened, less than half of the score was written by Lehmann. In fact, in the three-act musical, her first song didn't even show up until act two.

The interpolations were meant to Americanize the production for a New York audience. Over a dozen writers contributed material, including Clare Kummer and Anne Caldwell. This kind of cut-and-paste job was common at the time. Producers owned their writers' work and could do whatever they wanted with it. More than a decade later, those canonical musical theatre writers Richard Rodgers and Lorenz Hart would experience a very similar theatrical trauma when half their material for *Poor Little Ritz Girl* was thrown out and replaced with songs by Sigmund Romberg and Alex Gerber.

16. "Liza Lehmann's Musical Comedy Score." *Courier-Journal*, 24 April 1904, p. 14.

17. *Reader* 6 (June 1905–November 1905), p. 339.

Even with most of her score excised, Lehmann still received praise by many, with her work on *Sergeant Brue* heralded as being as unique as her eclectic career. But she was turned off by the system of creating musical comedy. She continued to write prolifically in many genres including opera. Her book, *Practical Hints for Students of Singing*, became a popular text for vocal students in the 1910s. She never returned to Broadway.

EVELYN BAKER
A British Cinderella

Sergeant Brue opened in the spring of 1905 and closed when the theaters shut down for the summer. Prior to the advent of air conditioning, nearly every production went on hiatus or permanently closed for the summer, when it was too hot to continue. *The Catch of the Season*, with music by Evelyn Baker, opened on the other side of summer in 1905. Like *Sergeant Brue*, *The Catch of the Season* premiered in London, where it was a huge hit the prior year.

Evelyn Baker was listed as one of the show's two main composers, and at least four of the songs in *The Catch of the Season* were written by her. The show was a new twist on the classic Cinderella tale. Cinderella here was called Angela Crystal, and she fell in love with the Duke on his twenty-first birthday in a modern-day setting. Edna May, known as "the Belle of New York," played Angela, and the show opened at Daly's Theatre, a premiere Broadway venue.

One of Baker's four numbers was the second in the show. Titled "We've Become the Great Attraction," it was performed by the Gibson Girls. A "Gibson Girl" was the standard of beauty for American women in the last decade of the nineteenth century and first decade of the twentieth. The term was inspired by the drawings of artist Charles Dana Gibson. Noted traits of a Gibson girl were a feminine hourglass figure, a hairstyle piled on top of one's head, and a confident attitude (but not too confident as to challenge current social norms). *The Catch of the Season* called its chorus of women "Gibson Girls," and eight of these Gibson Girls had been brought to Broadway from France, amid great fanfare.

Jerome Kern marked his third Broadway credit on the show. He wrote both music and lyrics for one number, called "Molly O'Halloran," sung by the heroine. *The Catch of the Season* was Baker's sole Broadway credit.

ANNE CALDWELL
Over Thirty Broadway Shows

One of the most prolific female writers of musical theatre in the first three decades of the twentieth century, Anne Caldwell staked a claim for women in the profession. She wrote book, music, and/or lyrics for over thirty Broadway shows between 1905 and 1928.

Caldwell is an outlier among the female writers of this chapter in several ways. She didn't make her Broadway debut until age thirty-seven. She was self-made and rose within the writing profession without inherited wealth or taking the stage as a performer first. She managed to become the sole writer of many of her productions, rather than one writer within a large group.

Caldwell was one of the first female "career Broadway writers." She collaborated with major players like Jerome Kern and wrote several significant hits. She was a charter member of ASCAP and was eventually inducted into the Songwriters Hall of Fame.

Although she grew up composing music, Caldwell didn't make her professional debut until after she married James O'Dea in 1904. O'Dea was already a musical theatre writer, and for his first job after marrying, he brought Caldwell along. O'Dea was invited to contribute a number to *Sergeant Brue*, and he wrote music to Caldwell's lyrics for "Saturday Afternoon." For many of the women seeking to write on Broadway in the first half of the century, the only way to get a seat at the table was if a spouse or male relative brought them along, and in this regard, Caldwell was indeed part of a pattern.

But Caldwell managed to plant her feet and refuse to leave. Caldwell kept her name, had two children with O'Dea, and continued to churn out Broadway shows. Some were written in collaboration with her husband, and some were not. She wrote both plays and musicals, and in the case of musicals, she wrote both book and lyrics.

Her first big hit was *The Lady of the Slipper*, a modernized Cinderella that opened at the Globe (today the Lunt-Fontanne) in 1912. She cowrote the book with Lawrence McCarty, Victor Herbert wrote the music, and O'Dea wrote the lyrics. It chalked up 232 performances, but two seasons later she had an even bigger hit with *Chin Chin*, a modernized take on the Aladdin story, which ran for 295 performances, also at the Globe. A great majority of Caldwell's shows played the Globe, since it was managed by impresario Charles Dillingham, whom she had a long professional association with.

Caldwell's first shared Broadway credit with Jerome Kern came in 1918, with *The Canary*. She contributed only the act two opener, written to music by Ivan Caryll. Kern and also Irving Berlin contributed elsewhere. The following season, Caldwell and Kern officially collaborated. She was the singular lyricist and librettist and he the singular composer on *She's a Good Fellow*.

The intriguingly titled *She's a Good Fellow* followed a young couple who got married. But with the bride underage and her family disapproving of the groom, the young man had to dress in drag as a woman in order to win acceptance. The wacky plot was a hit with audiences, but the show's run was halted by the

1919 Actors Equity strike, and it never regained its momentum. Nevertheless, Caldwell and Kern wrote a hit song: "The First Rose of Summer." And they soon wrote together again, on *The Night Boat*.

The Night Boat achieved Caldwell's longest run to date—313 performances—and was also about a fascinating subject, well known to many of its audience members but rarely commented upon publicly. At the time the musical opened at the Liberty in 1920, there was a boat that traveled nightly from New York City to Albany, and was notorious for its onboard affairs. Men would tell their wives they were traveling on business, and then climb aboard for an overnight river ride upstate with another woman. The musical was light in tone, but theatrical audiences were titillated by the subject. Although a significant hit in 1920, *The Night Boat* has never received a full theatrical revival; its inherent misogyny makes it a hard sell for modern audiences.

Another Caldwell-Kern hit was *Good Morning Dearie* in 1921. While it achieved an even longer run than *The Night Boat*, it too is un-revivable, not just because of misogynist plotting, but because of racist script moments, stereotyping Asian and Italian characters. Yet another Cinderella reinvention, *Good Morning Dearie* proved that audiences continued to have an appetite for these tales.

Caldwell's Broadway career was long and successful, and she followed it with a career writing movie musicals in Hollywood. While she never created a musical that entered the canon in a significant way, her songs were still heard on Broadway as late as 1975, when the *Very Good Eddie* revival, with music by Jerome Kern, interpolated several of their collaborations. Caldwell thrived in the era when very few musicals were more than just a diversion for a season. Still, many of her individual songs are still known and heard today.

GERTRUDE HOFFMAN
A Pioneer of Choreography

During her long, pioneering Broadway career as a performer and choreographer, Gertrude Hoffman was not usually known as a writer. But she did contribute songs to three Broadway shows.

Hoffman started out as a vaudeville performer and was discovered by impresario Oscar Hammerstein I. He invested in her training and sent her to Europe where she learned about popular dance styles, including interpretations of the Salome dance[18] that were proliferating in the late nineteenth and early twentieth century. In 1903, Hoffman made her Broadway debut, performing and choreographing at Hammerstein's Paradise Roof Garden on 42nd Street.

---

18. In the New Testament, Salome dances before King Herod. This became an iconic moment to depict via different manners of dance.

In those days, dancers often choreographed their own pieces, so women had a better shot at a choreographer position than at most other creative team positions on Broadway. Hoffman parlayed her renowned Salome dances into work plotting the dances for other productions.

Her Salome dances, with their sexually suggestive content, weren't without their detractors. She was arrested for public indecency because of the content of her dance while performing it on Broadway in 1909 and was banned from performing it in several cities on tour.[19]

Hoffman was one of the first feminist choreographers on Broadway. She believed the female form could be used physically to assert power. She was fascinated by the art of imitation and by feminist philosophy, and had ambition to push the potential of what movement could achieve on stage.[20]

Hoffman's first Broadway writing credit was in 1905, for a show called *When We Were Forty-One*. For this vaudeville-burlesque combination, performed at the rooftop theatre at the Olympia, Hoffman contributed music to two songs and co-choreographed. One of her songs had the intriguing title, "Kindly Pass the Chloroform Along." The show was a take-off on a popular play called *When We Were Twenty-One*, with a switch in age. This time, the protagonist tries to poison everyone over the age of forty-one. Elsie Janis made her Broadway debut in the show.

Hoffman next contributed a song to a musical called *The Duke of the Duluth*, her first time working on a Broadway show as a writer without also laboring in another capacity. She penned music for the finale of this vehicle for star Nat M. Wills, which ran for only three weeks.

The following year, after several more Broadway choreography jobs, Hoffman wrote lyrics and collaborated on music for the 11 o'clock number of *The Man from Now*, a new musical at the New Amsterdam Theatre that takes place in both 1906 and a millennium later, in 2906. The science fiction musical dreams up a futuristic world where women are in charge, and after the male characters travel there, they are happy to return to the climate of 1906. The show's original title during its pre-Broadway tour was *2905 or To-Morrow Land*.[21]

Hoffman worked on Broadway until 1927. During her career, she presented Russian ballet on Broadway, before the art form was popularized in America. She performed in male drag, playing opposite Ziegfeld's star and wife Anna Held in

19. Stevens-Garmon, Morgen. "Gertrude Hoffman and the Dance That Offended Public Decency." Museum of the City of New York, 1 August 2017. https://www.mcny.org/story/gertrude-hoffman.

20. "Gertrude Hoffman." University of South Carolina. https://www.broadway.cas.sc.edu/content/gertrude-hoffman.

21. Bordman, Gerald. *American Musical Theater: A Chronicle*. New York: Oxford University Press, 2001.

the show *A Parisian Model*.[22] She created choreography for the large-scale Shubert revues, *Artists and Models*, *A Night in Paris*, and *A Night in Spain*. She became a teacher and dance instructor.

In 1912, Hoffman performed in a show called *(From) Broadway to Paris*, one of the first shows to ever play the current Winter Garden Theatre, that even featured her own theme song. "The Gertrude Hoffman Glide" was one of those pop songs built around a dance craze, and this one was performed by Hoffman, with music and lyrics by her husband. The song capitalized on Hoffman's public persona, with references to Salome and Russian ballet.[23]

CLARA DRISCOLL
She Saved the Alamo

Clara Driscoll was best known for saving the Alamo. She was a wealthy philanthropist who purchased the land occupied by the historic Alamo Mission in San Antonio, Texas, site of one of America's most famous battles. In 1903, it was in danger of being turned into a bank before twenty-two-year-old Driscoll stepped in.[24] After she purchased the Alamo, she turned it over to the state of Texas.

Born into a family of great means, their fortune made in cattle and oil, Driscoll used her wealth to fund political causes she believed in as well as artistic projects. She was also a writer of short stories and novels. Her first book, *The Girl of La Gloria* attained success in 1904. Driscoll often crafted patriotic stories set in her native Texas.[25] She was the hostess of

Clara Driscoll. BY BAIN NEWS SERVICE, PUBLISHER - LIBRARY OF CONGRESS CATALOG / WIKIMEDIA COMMONS

the Texas Building during the World's Fair and the press noted that she was just a regular Texas "girl" who "handles a rifle . . . with as much ease as she wields the pen."[26]

---

22. Hoffman's own spouse, Max Hoffman, was a composer and musical director who worked with Ziegfeld.

23. Stalter-Pace, Sunny. *Imitation Artist: Gertrude Hoffmann's Life in Vaudeville and Dance*. Evanston, IL: Northwestern University Press, 2020.

24. "Clara Driscoll, 64, a Leader in Texas: Chairman of Pro-Roosevelt Convention There in '44 Dies—Preserved Alamo Site President of Bank." *New York Times*, 19 July 1945, p. 23.

25. "Miss Driscoll's New Light Opera, Mexicana." *Austin American-Statesman*, 23 August 1905, p. 3.

26. "Texas Girls Comic Opera Makes a Hit at Nation's Capitol." *St. Louis Post-Dispatch*, 28, January 1906, p. 44.

In 1906, at the age of twenty-four, Driscoll wrote the book and lyrics for *Mexicana*, a musical produced by the Shubert brothers at their Lyric Theatre on 42nd Street. Unlike many musicals at the time, *Mexicana* had only three writers. Driscoll collaborated with Robert B. Smith on book and lyrics, and Raymond Hubbell wrote the book. There was not a single interpolation by another author. It's likely that Driscoll would not allow it, and she held the production's purse strings.

Mexicana, a comic opera about a gold mine, is set entirely in Mexico, and populated entirely by Mexican characters. Driscoll felt passionate about dramatizing this world, as she lived right on the Texas-Mexico border. The show tried out in Buffalo, New York, and Washington, D.C., before making its way to the Shuberts' flagship on 42nd Street. In D.C. and in Manhattan, *Mexicana* was attended by a plethora of politicians, including many with a tie to Texas, so powerful was Driscoll's reach.[27]

Before *Mexicana* even opened on Broadway, the Shuberts announced that they would be getting another new musical from Driscoll. This was thwarted—perhaps by her marriage later that year.

ELLA WHEELER WILCOX
A Poetess Adapts the Story of Queen Esther

Ella Wheeler Wilcox came to Broadway from the world of poetry. Born in Wisconsin in 1850 to a poor family, literary fan Wilcox began writing poetry just so she could get a copy of the periodicals it was printed in. Her most enduring poem was published in 1883 and featured the still-familiar stanza: "Laugh, and the world laughs with you / Weep, and you weep alone." For several decades, Wilcox was one of the most acclaimed poets in America.

Wilcox's one theatrical venture was a play with music called *Mizpah*, worthy of mention even though not technically a musical. *Mizpah* premiered at the Academy of Music in Union Square in 1906, and is a poetic adaptation of the biblical story of Esther. Wilcox wrote the script with Luscombe Searelle, and wrote the songs herself.

About the show's tryout in San Francisco, critic Ashton Stevens wrote: "As for the love scenes . . . you have heard nothing like them in the modern theatre. Give Ella Wheeler Wilcox her rhyme and she can make the strongest dramas of Stephen Phillips[28] sound pulseless. You may or may not care for Mrs. Wilcox'

---

27. "Washington Society Approves Mexicana." *Montgomery Times*, 26 January 1906, p. 7.

28. Stephen Phillips was a popular poet and writer of theatre.

philosophic prose contributions to the newspapers, but when she sings and sings at her best, as she does in *Mizpah*, the music is irresistible."[29]

Mizpah achieved great success on tour for over a year, all over the country, before its twenty-four-performance run in New York. It was highly anticipated, and received positive reviews, but ran for less than a month.

PATRICK BIDWELL
Working under a Male Pseudonym When Tragedy Strikes

In 1908, a new Broadway musical called *Peggy Machree* opened at the Broadway Theatre, located at Broadway and 41st Street. It had one song with lyrics by Denis O'Sullivan, and seventeen lyrics by his wife—whose real name no one knew. She used the pseudonym Patrick Bidwell due to prevailing sentiment that it wasn't appropriate for a married woman to be a stage dramatist.

O'Sullivan was a popular Irish actor, born in California, who rose to fame in London, playing a series of Irish roles.[30] *Peggy Machree* was a vehicle for him, to be performed on an American tour. After landing in cities like San Francisco and Chicago, the Irish-infused musical comedy planned on a New York City debut.

Peggy Machree received rave reviews in local papers, especially for the dynamic performance of O'Sullivan. In February of 1908, while playing *Peggy Machree* in Columbus, Ohio, O'Sullivan became ill with appendicitis and died.

His *New York Times* obituary stated that his wife was with him on tour when he passed, and also stated that his current project, *Peggy Machree*, was written by Patrick Bidwell.[31]

Irish tenor Joseph O'Mara was chosen to pick up the mantle and lead *Peggy Machree*, continuing with the 1908 tour and opening the show on Broadway that December.

Even in the show's rave *New York Times* review, readers did not find out the real identity of Patrick Bidwell. While she was responsible for the majority of the show's lyrics and all of its script and story, she remained essentially nameless. "*Peggy Machree* is a tuneful comedy," the *Times* declared. "It is also funny and differs from the regular machine-made musical play."[32]

29. Stevens, Ashton. "Splendid Material Needs Genius of Belasco." *San Francisco Examiner*, 10 January 1905, p. 5.

30. "Denis O'Sullivan Appears at the Bijou." *Star Tribune*, 5 January 1908, p. 6.

31. "Denis O'Sullivan Dead: Actor Dies in Columbus, Ohio, Following Operation for Appendicitis." *New York Times*, 2 February 1908, p. 9.

32. "*Peggy Machree* A Tuneful Comedy: Is Also Funny and Differs from the Regular Machine-Made Play." *New York Times*, 22 December 1908, p. 9.

NORA BAYES
One of the Top Pop Stars of the Twentieth Century

Nora Bayes has the distinction of being one of the only women in history with a Broadway theater named for her. Currently, our only Broadway houses with female namesakes are the (Helen) Hayes, half of the Lunt-Fontanne (named for Alfred Lunt and Lynn Fontanne), the (Ethel) Barrymore, the Lena Horne, and the Vivian Beaumont.

Nora Bayes. BY BAIN NEWS SERVICE, PUBLISHER - LIBRARY OF CONGRESS CATALOG / WIKIMEDIA COMMONS

The Nora Bayes was a Broadway house on 44th Street, once right in the heart of the theatre district. It was a roof-garden theater on top of another Broadway house. The Broadway house on the ground floor was called Weber and Fields' Music Hall and the theater on the roof was called Lew Fields' 44th Street Roof Garden until the 1910s when the names were switched to the 44th Street Theatre and the Nora Bayes Theatre, respectively. For a time, the Stage Door Canteen was located on the basement level.

The Nora Bayes Theatre was named such in 1918 and held its last show in 1939. In 1945, the entire building was demolished to make way for more space for the *New York Times* building. During its two decades, the Nora Bayes was host to many shows that were part of the Federal Theatre Project, as well as the first edition of the *Greenwich Village Follies*, among other productions. New shows by Victor Herbert, George Gershwin,[33] Irving Caesar, and Mark Hellinger premiered at the Nora Bayes.

In addition to the distinction of being the first woman with a Broadway theater named after her, Nora Bayes occupied a unique place in pop culture. In 2016, *Vanity Fair* published a list of top fashion icons of the last 103 years, titling their article "From Nora Bayes to Rihanna: Behold the Top Pop Stars of the Last 103 Years."[34]

Bayes is still a part of the cultural conscience. In fact, the book *Smash*, on which the television show *Smash* was loosely based, revolved around the making of a Nora Bayes musical, later reconfigured as a Marilyn Monroe musical.

---

33. Bayes collaborated with Gershwin when he was still a teenager.

34. "From Nora Bayes ... to Rihanna: Behold the Top Pop Stars of the Past 103 Years." *Vanity Fair*, 18 May 2016. https://www.vanityfair.com/style/2016/05/top-female-pop-stars-of-the-past-103-years.

Bayes starred in Broadway shows and also wrote music and lyrics for them, as well as produced. Her first Broadway writing credit was for the show *Miss Innocence* in 1908. For that musical extravaganza, she penned a number titled "I'm Learning Something Every Day." She also contributed writing to the musicals *Ziegfeld Follies of 1909*, *The Jolly Bachelors* (1910), *Little Miss Fix-It* (1911), *Roly Poly/Without the Law* (1912), *Maid in America* (1915), *Odds and Ends of 1917*, *Ladies First* (1918), *Queen O'Hearts* (1922), *Lucky* (1927), and posthumously, *Ziegfeld Follies of 1931*.

Three of Bayes's Broadway writing credits were on the best-known theatrical revue in town: *The Ziegfeld Follies*. Florenz Ziegfeld Jr. revolutionized American show business with his Broadway revues, which were presented under his management between 1907 and 1931.[35] The revues featured top stars from diverse cultural and racial backgrounds, lavish scenic and costume designs, magnificent displays of chorus girls known for their beauty, and an overall clash of upper-class glamour and lower-class allure that made the *Follies* the must-see entertainment of every season.

Bayes's first time writing for the *Follies* was in 1908, the first time that the revue boasted Ziegfeld's name in its title. In 1911, the show was still being performed at the Jardin de Paris, the roof garden that was part of the Olympia Theatre complex. In fact, the lush rooftop venue was renamed the Jardin de Paris by Ziegfeld himself, when he took over its management and began the Follies in 1907. He was heavily influenced by French revues, and sought to bring their artistry to Broadway.

In addition to writing for the revue, Bayes also appeared in *Ziegfeld Follies* and tangled famously with Florenz Ziegfeld, at one point walking out of the show. He was forced to pay her more handsomely and woo her back to the production, since Bayes was such an audience darling.

Bayes cowrote the song "Shine On, Harvest Moon" with her husband, Jack Norworth,[36] and made it famous in her performance of it as well. She was the first to popularize the George M. Cohan song "Over There," which became an international smash. Bayes entertained the troops during World War I with "Over There" and spent time overseas with the War Department. In addition to being a star of the stage, she was also a hit recording artist.

Born as Rachel Goldberg, Nora Bayes did not hide her Jewish identity. In fact, she often included Jewish humor in her acts, alongside jokes about her many failed marriages. She poked fun at all of the scandal she was involved with.

---

35. Mordden, Ethan. *Ziegfeld: The Man Who Invented Show Business*. New York: St. Martin's Press, 2008.

36. Bayes was married five times and her many marriages provided tabloid fodder.

According to the *Jewish Women's Archive*, "Known as a ... temperamental star, Bayes relied on her own ... popularity as she resisted managerial control and ignored ... legal contracts. ... In these battles with male businessmen and in her unconventional personal life, Bayes provides some flamboyant ... examples of the broad social changes happening in the United States in the early twentieth century, namely the questioning of traditional roles for women as well as the challenges to male political and economic power that marked the women's movement of the time."[37]

37. Kibler, M. Alison. "Nora Bayes." Jewish Women's Archive. https://jwa.org/encyclopedia/article/bayes-nora.

3

1910s

Operettas and Specialty Material

Rida Johnson Young

Ah! Sweet Mystery of Life: From Naughty Marietta *to* Maytime

One of the prolific and successful female dramatists of the 1900s, 1910s, and 1920s, Rida Johnson Young wrote over thirty shows and over five-hundred songs in a career that included collaborations with many of the major players of her time.

Today, Young is perhaps best known for her lyrics to the songs "I'm Falling in Love with Someone" and "Ah! Sweet Mystery of Life," which have been interpolated into *Thoroughly Modern Millie* (2002). These were originally written with composer Victor Herbert for *Naughty Marietta*, a hit 1910 show that received several Broadway revivals and a film adaptation.

Before this, Young started out as an actor. She later said in interviews that she was not a great actor but that being on stage gave her the experience she needed to understand how to be a great writer. She also worked for a music publisher and as a press agent.

A 1903 article by Alice W. Mortimer was titled "Women Press Agents and What They Do" with the subtitle: "The Work of Rida Johnson Young and Others Who Have Succeeded." Young was only twenty-eight when she was the subject of this piece, which called her "a versatile young lady [who] is both actress and playwright besides press agent." The article went on to describe a farcical mishap during a production of *Hamlet* where Young was the press agent and then summarized.

"Even now when she thinks of it Rida Johnson Young laughs as she sits at her desk in New York writing anecdotes, paragraphs, historic information—anything that will read interestingly concerning operas, songs and music of all kinds. And while she laughs and writes she also dreams—dreams of a time when Rida Johnson Young will be better known as a dramatist than in any other capacity."[1]

Between 1900 and 1909, Young had six plays produced. Several of these featured songs as well. The first was *Lord Byron*, a vehicle for her husband at the time, James Young. In 1906, she wrote a play with music called *Brown of Harvard*, which she also wrote a song for. Her first Broadway musical proper was *Ragged Robin* in 1910, for which she cowrote the book with Rita Olcott. Directly following came the smash hit *Naughty Marietta*.

In 1912, Johnson's *The Red Petticoat* had a humble but respectable run of two months. She cowrote the book with Paul West and wrote lyrics for this show, based on her play *Next*. It had music by Jerome Kern. She continued to write both plays (often including music) and musicals, including shows where she contributed both music and lyrics such as *Lady Luxury* (1914), *Her Soldier*

---

1. "Women Press Agents and What They Do." *Knoxville Sentinel*, 1 August 1903, p. 14.

Boy (1916), *His Little Widows* (1917), *Maytime* (1917), *Sometime* (1918), *Little Simplicity* (1918), and *The Dream Girl* (1924).

In addition to cowriting Victor Herbert's greatest success and collaborating with Jerome Kern, Young also counted Sigmund Romberg and Rudolf Friml among her collaborators. After *Naughty Marietta*, *Maytime* was Young's greatest success. The show, with music by Romberg, played five different Broadway houses over the course of its 492 performances. It was the second-longest-running book musical of the 1910s. The *New York Times* raved about *Maytime*, which is about star-crossed lovers whose descendants end up marrying years later. The opening lines of the review read: "Romantic stories that combine delicate charm and the native aroma of youth with those larger visions in which the tragedy of the individual blends with the eternal comedy of living come very rarely to any generation. Now in *Maytime* the two are combined in a musical setting. Most fortunately, the production is in every way worthy of the material, the acting being really noteworthy and the result is an evening that rises whole regions above the conventional Broadway musical comedy."[2]

When asked in 1922 what advice she'd give to women who wanted to follow in her footsteps, she said, "All [a girl] has to do is to write. In my day every girl wanted to go on the stage. Today every girl wants to write a play. And I think she could do it if she wouldn't try to write it all in one day or one week. My advice to the novice in playwriting is to take your time. Don't write but an hour or so a day until you get the run of things. The next thing to do is to get your acts together and have a surprise or turn in every one."[3]

Young died in 1926, in the midst of her thriving Broadway career, after a long battle with breast cancer. She was fifty-one.

---

2. "Maytime Scores at the Shubert." *New York Times*, 17 August 1917, p. 17.

3. "Dramatist Gives Rules for Success." *The Lima Gazette and the Lima Republican*, 7 December 1922, p. 8.

33

MABEL HITE

Controversial Autobiographical Song

Mabel Hite was a musical comedy and vaudeville performer who also dabbled in writing. She died tragically at age twenty-nine of intestinal cancer.

Her career included many tours, of both legitimate theatre and vaudeville, as well as three Broadway ventures. In her final Broadway show, *A Certain Party*, she wrote her character's big number, which was also the final song in the show. "You're Going to Lose Your Husband" has both music and lyrics by Hite. The song was noted in gossip columns when Hite had marital troubles with her second husband Mike Donlin, a professional baseball player. The two had often made stage appearances together.

Mabel Hite, as seen on the cover of the sheet music for "Do You Think You Could Learn To Love Me" circa 1900. BY UNKNOWN PHOTOGRAPHER, NEW YORK PUBLIC LIBRARY / WIKIMEDIA COMMONS

FRED DE GRESAC

A Nom de Plume

A 1912 article outed Fred De Gresac, telling the public the name was a cover for a female writer. De Gresac responded that she thought her plays would be better received by the public if they thought she was a man.[4]

Between 1903 and 1929, De Gresac wrote about a dozen plays and musicals for Broadway, including her biggest hit *Sweethearts*, which was revived twice. Originally from Paris, her real name was Frederique, and she began writing in France—where she also hid her identity. Spanning the worlds of Broadway, international theatre, and film, De Gresac collaborated with the top writers of her field, including Harry B. Smith and Reginald De Koven.

In 1903, De Gresac's Broadway debut came with the play *The Marriage of Kitty*. She had cowritten a French play, *La Passerelle*, which was adapted into English. *La Passerelle* itself made its Broadway debut the following year. De Gresac's first musical was *The Enchantress* in 1911 for

Fred De Gresac, by Jean Reutlinger. BY JEAN REUTLINGER / GALLICA DIGITAL LIBRARY / WIKIMEDIA COMMONS

---

4. "Woman Playwright Says Public Prefers Men's Work." *Indianapolis Star*, 21 January 1912, p. 36.

which she cowrote the book with Harry B. Smith, who also wrote the lyrics. The music was written by Victor Herbert for this modest hit about the royals in the fictional country of Zergovia. Her next show *The Wedding Trip* was also a collaboration with the same team, and with *The Purple Road* she cowrote book and lyrics with a new team for this adaptation of a Viennese piece.

In 1913, *Sweethearts*, with book by De Gresac and Smith, music by Herbert, and lyrics by Robert B. Smith made a splash at the New Amsterdam. The show is a comic operetta about a royal family and mistaken identity, in the style of many light musicals of the 1910s. In addition to two Broadway revivals, *Sweethearts* also received an MGM screen adaptation, its first all-Technicolor film. A studio cast recording was released in 1947, making this 1913 musical one of the earliest Broadway shows with a pseudo-cast album.

ELSIE JANIS
The War Sweetheart and Her Gang

Elsie Janis, circa 1906, in a promotional photo for the play *The Vanderbilt Cup*. BY BAIN NEWS SERVICE, PUBLISHER - LIBRARY OF CONGRESS CATALOG / WIKIMEDIA COMMONS

Elsie Janis was one of the most prominent multi-hyphenates on Broadway in the 1900s through the 1930s.[5]

Janis starred in several Broadway musicals beginning in 1905. Her first Broadway credit as a writer was a show called *Over the River* in 1912, where she contributed a portion of the music and lyrics.

During World War I, Janis performed in London, incorporating patriotic American numbers into her act, which was part of a variety show. She gained a reputation as a performer fighting for the war effort, and began singing for the troops on the front in France. Janis was nicknamed "Sweetheart of the American Expeditionary Force" and worked tirelessly to raise funds for the war.

In 1915, the Princess Theatre musical *Very Good Eddie* opened on Broadway and included additional lyrics by Janis. Her number "Some Sort of Somebody" was a part of the 1975 revival of the show as well.

After World War I ended, Elsie Janis headlined *Elsie Janis and Her Gang* on Broadway, starring in and writing the book, music, and lyrics for this revue, which featured out-of-work soldiers who had just come back from the war. Much like

---

5. "Elsie Janis." Ohio State University Libraries, https://web.archive.org/web/20080509123343/http://library.osu.edu/sites/exhibits/Janis/.

This Is the Army, Irving Berlin's World War II Broadway revue, *Elsie Janis and Her Gang* was lauded for its authenticity, using real soldiers and incorporating material about wartime. While *This Is the Army* gained fame for this, Elsie Janis actually did it first.

Janis's war-themed revue returned in 1922 as well. Her core audience consisted of veterans and these shows were highly praised. As time went on, this audience dwindled, and Janis experienced a decline in fans. She went to Hollywood where she wrote several songs for films and acted as production manager for others.

In the 1930s, Janis returned to Broadway, staging *New Faces of 1934*, appearing in a special solo engagement, and performing in a vaudeville-style revue.

In 1934, Janis became the first female radio announcer on NBC. This was the same season she was the sole director of a Broadway musical!

The 1930s also found Janis the subject of several gossip columns when she married a man sixteen years her junior. In a piece titled "Why I Waited for Love until I Was 42," Janis told the *Daily News*, "Who's going to be boss? There isn't any bossing in marriage any more. He knows I am always going to work and work hard. I love work. Gilbert [Wilson] will have to make up his mind about what he wants to do and do it in his own way."[6] When asked about children, she cracked that her young husband could be her child.

In 1940, Janis was one of the directors of *Women in War*, which depicted women on the front lines in the Battle of France. The film came out the year after the battle, at the start of World War II.

Janis has a star on the Hollywood Walk of Fame. Her legacy also lies in the entertainment that proliferated during World War II to entertain soldiers; Janis was a pioneer in the way she brought live performance right to the front lines and continued entertaining those fighting for the country once they returned home as well.

BLANCHE MERRILL
Specialty Material Expert

Blanche Merrill turned out popular hit songs in the 1910s and 1920s, which appeared in dozens of Broadway shows including several editions of *The Ziegfeld Follies*.

In 1910, Merrill, an avid theatergoer, saw popular performer Eva Tanguay in a show, inspiring Merrill to write her first song. After submitting this song to Tanguay, Merrill was engaged to write several numbers for the star. Merrill began

---

6. "Why I Waited for Love: Elsie Janis Reveals Real Reason for Her Hesitation Up to Now." *Daily News*, 24 January 1932, p. 40.

contributing to vaudeville acts and signed with a music publisher. She wrote songs for specific performers who would then use these in their acts, including major Broadway revues.

Merrill found her calling when she teamed up with Fanny Brice. The two understood each other's sensibilities. Brice was a unique talent, and Merrill wrote numbers specifically for her, which was just what Brice needed to launch herself to the next level of stardom. She wasn't the kind of performer who could sing just anything, and Merrill had a knack for specialty material that achieved its apex when she wrote songs for Brice such as "The Yiddish Bride," "Becky Is Back in the Ballet," and "I'm an Indian." She wrote for Brice's infamous Baby Snooks character, and their collaboration was long and fruitful.

In addition to writing for Tanguay and Brice, Merrill also wrote for Nora Bayes, Willie Howard, Bert Williams, Evelyn Nesbit, Elsie Janis, and at least four dozen other actors. She became so well known for the skillful way in which she wrote to specific personalities that in 1916 *Variety* published a full-page caricature of Merrill writing for her various star clients. She was prolific in her specialty work, and in doing so, found her way into not just *The Ziegfeld Follies* but also *The Greenwich Village Follies* and *Earl Carroll's Vanities*. In 1917, she was reportedly receiving $20,000 per song.

Merrill also wrote material for artists for vaudeville, plays with music, cabaret, and other projects. Her specialty material found its way into many different kinds of shows, and she was considered the top of her field.

Merrill worked steadily from the 1910s through the 1960s, and in later years her specialty material talents found their way into film and television, including Sid Caesar's *Your Show of Shows*.

No one could write for a personality the way that Merrill could during her years of practice. She would shape each song around a given performer's persona, vocal skills, and energy. Numerous accounts from performers relate that Merrill pinpointed talents they didn't even know they had themselves, and brought these out through the specificity of the material she crafted for them.

AGNES MORGAN
Leader at the Neighborhood Playhouse

Agnes Morgan was a theatrical impresario best known as a director and as one of the leaders of the Neighborhood Playhouse, an alternative theater that acted as an off-Broadway of sorts in the early twentieth century. She was also a playwright, lyricist, book writer, performer, and producer.

Morgan made her Broadway debut in 1913 as a cowriter on the book for a musical called *The Man with Three Wives*, which played Weber and Fields' Music Hall. This was followed by a Theatre Guild project called *Back to Methuselah*.

Morgan staged part of this Bernard Shaw piece in collaboration with Alice Lewisohn, who would become her longtime collaborator.

After getting her start as a performer, including in *The Grand Street Follies*, Morgan's first directing job on Broadway was the hit science fiction play *R.U.R.* She codirected this for the Theatre Guild, which she worked with regularly.

In 1924, Morgan not only appeared in an edition of *The Grand Street Follies*, but she also contributed book and lyrics, and sometimes directed the productions as well. She would go on to work on editions of this revue in 1925, 1926, 1927, 1928, and 1929 as well, before the Great Depression put an end to the tradition.

"The Neighborhood Playhouse producing organization was unique in that it was completely controlled by women," according to the NYCLPC Landmark Designation Report. "The Lewisohns were joined by Agnes Morgan, a playwright and director who had graduated from George Pierce Baker's famous classes in playwriting at Radcliffe College and Helen Arthur, a lawyer who was a playreader and secretary to the Shuberts. Sarah Cowell Le Moyne, a well-known actress, was one of the directors until her death in July 1915. Aline Bernstein and Alice Beer managed the costume workshop."[7]

In 1937, Morgan directed and wrote lyrics for a show called *A Hero Is Born*, with book by Theresa Helburn and music by Lehman Engel. This was a project for the Federal Theatre Project.

"[Agnes Morgan's] technical facility was such that she was everywhere in the theatre, combining a collection of functions the mere mention of which would drive any 'self-respecting' member of the theatre union of today into a decline. Skilled as an actor, she played an occasional role; she developed the technical side of lighting, and had an instinctive gift for direction, as for the function of stage manager. As an amateur she responded to any production need while pursuing her professional career as playwright," wrote Alice Lewisohn Crowley in *Neighborhood Playhouse: Leaves from a Theatre Scrapbook*.[8]

CATHERINE CHISHOLM CUSHING
Pollyanna *and* Glorianna

Catherine Chisholm Cushing was equally adept at writing plays and musicals, and often created vehicles for the greatest stars of her day. She adapted several pieces of source material successfully for the Broadway stage.

---

7. "Grand Street Playhouse" 2011 NYCLPC Landmark Designation Report, http://home2.nyc.gov/html/lpc/downloads/pdf/reports/2433.pdf.

8. Crowley, Alice Lewisohn. *Neighborhood Playhouse: Leaves From a Theatre Scrapbook*, New York: Theatre Arts Books, 1959.

After writing three Broadway plays, Cushing's first Broadway musical was a 1914 operetta called *Sari*. She cowrote book and lyrics with Eugene Percy Heath for this show which played through winter and spring at the Liberty and then the New Amsterdam. *Sari* is an adaptation of a popular 1912 German operetta that was hailed as a sensation overseas, and the reaction wasn't much less enthusiastic in New York. The *New York Sun* wrote that *Sari* was "so fresh, so finished, so thoroughly tasteful in every respect that it hits the bulls-eye of public favor fair and square."[9] The show was brought back for a 1930 revival also at the Liberty.

Cushing's next two projects were a vehicle for Billie Burke and an adaptation of the beloved book *Pollyanna*. She followed this with a 1918 musical that was actually an adaptation of her own play called *Widow by Proxy*, a hit on Broadway in 1913. The musical version has the more festive title of *Glorianna*, and Cushing was the sole writer of both book and lyrics. *Glorianna* has music by Rudolf Friml and was produced by John Cort, back at the Liberty—a high-profile production. The plot about a society woman masquerading as a widow is thin and was typical of its time, and reviews praised leading lady Eleanor Painter as the brightest part of the production even while saying that she could not carry off the character or songs.

In 1920, Cushing adapted another of her hit plays into a Broadway musical. This time the play was *Kitty MacKay*, and the musical was *Lassie*. An even bigger hit than *Glorianna*, *Lassie* also boasts Cushing as the sole book writer and lyricist, this time to music by Hugo Felix. The "lassie" of the title is a young woman who has been adopted into a Scottish family and discovers her roots and true love in London—only to find that her beau might indeed be related to her. He isn't, and the show ran up 159 performances. *Brooklyn Life* called it "an entertainment unsurpassed by any musical comedy in town."[10] The show opened in April at the Nora Bayes Theatre, where it continued to play through the summer months since that house had a movable roof and could be essentially converted into a rooftop theater. In the late summer, *Lassie* transferred to the Casino.

For Cushing's final two Broadway musicals, she wrote only the book. These were *Marjolaine* (1922) and *Topsy and Eva* (1924). *Marjolaine* was another collaboration with Felix, but this time Brian Hooker wrote the lyrics. Star Peggy Wood played the title character, a British woman whose love can't marry her because of the objections of his widower father—who it turns out was once jilted by Marjolaine's mother. It had a respectable run at the Broadhurst.

---

9. Dietz, Dan. *The Complete Book of 1930s Broadway Musicals*. Lanham, MD: Rowman & Littlefield Publishers, 2018.

10. Ibid.

C. V. Kerr
The Dancing Duchess

In 1914, Caroline V. Kerr was billed as C. V. Kerr when she wrote the book and lyrics for a Broadway musical called *The Dancing Duchess*. The *Evening World* review assumed the writer was of the male persuasion, weighing in that, "the book and lyrics were by C. V. Kerr who is said to reside in the Viennese quarter of Cleveland, Ohio. To his efforts were added those of R. H. Burnside."[11] For whatever reason, perhaps a gesture of allyship, the cowriter of the book and lyrics, a man named Robert Hubberthorne Burnside, took on the same billing pattern as his female collaborator.

The show opened in Long Branch, New Jersey, before transferring to Broadway's illustrious Casino Theatre. In ads, it was billed as having the "first and fairest beauty chorus of the season."[12] The show lasted only thirteen performances on Broadway. The *Winnipeg Tribune* review put it in most dire terms, stating, "Of *The Dancing Duchess*, nothing need be said. It came, was seen and died. Among those who died with it were C. V. Kerr who was responsible for the text."[13] And indeed, she did not produce another work of theatre known to the public thereafter.

Dorothy Donnelly
Writer of Two of the Biggest Broadway Hits of the 1920s

Dorothy Donnelly was one of the most successful writers of the 1910s and 1920s on Broadway—of any gender. Among her credits were the book and/or lyrics for such hits as *Fancy Free, Blossom Time, Poppy, The Student Prince*, and *My Maryland*.

Starting out as a performer, Donnelly was markedly successful in that arena as well. She had a family connection, as her father was the manager of the Grand Opera House,[14] but she met expectations with her great talent on stage. Her Broadway debut was playing the title role in the play *Nell Gwyn* in 1901, and in 1903 she notably played the title role in the original production of *Candida* by George Bernard Shaw. Among her two-dozen-plus Broadway performance credits between 1901 and 1915 was also a hit play titled *Madame X*, a melodrama that was made into a 1916 silent film also starring Donnelly. She was nicknamed "The First Actress of the Three-Handkerchief Drama."[15] *Three-Handkerchief Drama*

---

11. "Dancing Duchess Very Largely a Tango Contest." *Evening World*, 21 August 1914, p. 7.

12. "The Dancing Duchess." *Daily Record*, 8 August 1914, p. 6.

13. Hines, Dixie. "New York Review." *Winnipeg Tribune*, 5 September 1914, p. 22.

14. In addition, her mother was an actress, her uncle directed several theatrical venues, and her brother was a New York City senator and judge.

15. Hammond, Percy. "News Notes of the Theater." *Chicago Tribune*, 24 February 1918, p. 57.

was a colloquialism of the time that could now be translated as "tearjerker." During World War I, she performed for troops overseas and directed as well.

For a marquee-name actress to transition to a career as a hit theatrical writer was incredibly rare in the 1910s. Donnelly had no writing credits to her name at the time she signed on to adapt the book to an operetta titled *Flora Bella* for a 1916 production. Unlike many of the other women who made a Broadway career in writing in the early twentieth century, she did not contribute small bits of material to several shows until given more hefty assignments. She abruptly left the world of performing on stage in order to write words that would appear on stage instead.

The following year, Donnelly revised the script for a play called *Johnny, Get Your Gun* (which would later inspire the title of the musical *Annie Get Your Gun*). Also in 1917, Donnelly produced a short-lived play called *Six Months' Option*.

In 1918, Donnelly's first shot at writing the book to an original musical, *Fancy Free*, achieved a 116-performance run. *Fancy Free* starred beloved Broadway performer Marilyn Miller. The *Baltimore Sun*, trying to understand Donnelly's career transition, wrote, "The book must have been written by Miss Donnelly as a sort of mental antidote to the complicated emotional roles she plays so well, for the plot is said to be absolutely devoid of continuity, but full of diverting incidents."[16]

In 1921, Donnelly teamed up with Sigmund Romberg for the first time and was the sole book writer and lyricist for *Blossom Time*, one of the biggest hits of the decade. The original production played 516 performances on Broadway, an outrageously long run at the time. Within four months of closing in 1923, it was revived in extraordinary fashion—at two Broadway theaters simultaneously. *Blossom Time* was presented at the now-demolished 44th Street Theatre, and also directly across the block at the Shubert Theatre, at the same time. The show was considered so popular that it could sustain two revivals at once. The Shuberts allowed audience members with tickets to one production to attend the other on the same night. According to the Internet Broadway Database, "At intermission, the audience cast ballots as to who played the roles best (most had seen the original cast members); the performers with the most votes would be cast in the London premiere of *Blossom Time*."[17]

Blossom Time also received Broadway revivals in 1924, 1926, 1931, 1938, and 1943, and was constantly touring during these years as well. The birth of *Oklahoma!* and the modern book musical, swerving away from the genre of operetta, meant that *Blossom Time* by the 1940s was considered somewhat of a relic,

---

16. "Through Our Own Opera Glasses." *Baltimore Sun*, 27 January 1918, p. 18.

17. "Blossom Time.," Internet Broadway Database, https://www.ibdb.com/broadway-production/blossom-time-523186.

relegated to stock and amateur productions. But it made a significant mark on Broadway during the last hurrah of the operetta.

Blossom Time is a fictional dramatization of the life and work of Franz Schubert. Romberg actually adapted Schubert's work into this book musical which included songs like "Three Little Maids," "Song of Love," and "Love Is a Riddle."

In 1923, Donnelly followed up *Blossom Time* with a new musical comedy called *Poppy*. This time she wrote book and lyrics and also directed. *Poppy* was a W. C. Fields vehicle built around all of the typical elements of musical comedy in the mid-1920s. Fields played a circus man who tries to pass his adopted daughter off as an heiress—and it turns out she actually is one. *Poppy* was a hit at 346 performances, but without the staying or revivable power of Donnelly's other major hits, as it depended on Fields's performance.

In 1924, Donnelly made a major splash to equal that of *Blossom Time* with another Romberg collaboration: *The Student Prince*. The original production ran for 608 performances at the now-demolished Jolson's 59th Street Theatre and featured a cast of 150 performers. This made it the longest running Broadway musical of the 1920s. The romantic musical is about a German prince who follows his heart to experience life as an average student, and along the way falls in love with a waitress named Kathie. In the end, he marries the royal Princess Margaret anyway, but not until after he discovers himself through his exploration of a normal life. Along with *Blossom Time*, *The Student Prince* became one of the last operettas to enter the canon, and was revived in amateur, stock, and regional productions throughout the following decades.

Donnelly's 1926 musical *Hello, Lola* was adapted from the Booth Tarkington play *Seventeen*, which in 1951 became another Broadway musical, this time also called *Seventeen*. *Hello, Lola* closed after forty-seven performances but Donnelly's next Broadway venture, *My Maryland*, again with Romberg, played an entire season. This was based on a Clyde Fitch play about the Civil War and features many patriotic numbers. Less than a month later, in late 1927, Donnelly and Romberg opened the similarly titled *My Princess* on Broadway, based on an original play cowritten by Donnelly.

Donnelly died of pneumonia at the age of forty-eight, in 1928.

HELEN TRIX
International Piano Songwhistleress

Helen Trix was a vaudeville, concert, cabaret and recording artist who first became popular in London and Paris. Although she was American, her drawing room entertainer style translated well in Europe in the late 1910s and early 1920s, and soon she was starring on European stages. Her early career took on a unique form as she had songs she wrote released as recordings, and toured internationally.

Trix, whose real last name was Yeiser, gained popularity in America after pairing with her younger sister Josephine and becoming the Trix Sisters. The two began appearing on the Orpheum circuit, as well as in legitimate theatre ventures in New York. In 1916, Trix contributed music and lyrics to two Broadway shows: *The Century Girl* and *Follow Me*. In 1921, they traveled to London to appear in *From A to Z*, a revue for which Trix wrote some of the music.

According to *Jazz Age Club*, "The Trix sisters had established a reputation as a temperamental pair who were constantly at each other's throats but their good looks and snappy style fitted [their work] perfectly. Off stage the Trix Sisters were considered as daring in the extreme when they wore beige stockings (considered suggestive of flesh) when lunching at the Ritz."[18]

Helen Trix, circa 1913. BY UNKNOWN PHOTOGRAPHER/ UNIVERSITY OF WASHINGTON SPECIAL COLLECTIONS/ J. WILLIS SAYRE COLLECTION OF THEATRICAL PHOTOGRAPHS/ WIKIMEDIA COMMONS

A show called *Tricks* had the majority of its songs written by Trix, and this toured England in 1925. Trix also released more recordings that sold well in Europe. Two of her most famous songs, "You'd Love to Live In Paris" and "London Town" nodded to her international existence.

Helen Trix continued to perform with and without her sister and write material for theaters, cabarets, and clubs, throughout the 1920s and 1930s. Often performing her own material at the piano, she was nicknamed "the piano songwhistleress."

GRACE TORRENS
One Song in the West End's Biggest Hit

Chu Chin Chow was the longest-running musical in West End history for nearly four decades. The 1916 musical ran for five years, a length of time unheard of in that era. In 1917, it made its way to Broadway, achieving a more-than-respectable 208-performance run.

The hit musical is based on *Ali Baba and the 40 Thieves*, and has book, lyrics, and original direction by Oscar Asche and music by Frederic Norton. Once

---

18. "Tricks and the Trix Sisters." Jazz Age Club. http://www.jazzageclub.com/the-trix-sisters/115/.

it became clear that *Chu Chin Chow* had such significant staying power, Asche decided he would need to keep the show fresh by occasionally adding in new scenes and songs. This was sometimes done at the time so that audiences would return to a show to see different material.

One interpolation into *Chu Chin Chow* was a lively song called "At Siesta Time" that had music by Grace Torrens and lyrics by Arthur Anderson. After a few performances, Asche kept Torrens's music but threw out Anderson's lyrics and replaced them with lyrics of his own. The song appeared in *Chu Chin Chow*'s productions on both the West End and Broadway.[19]

Torrens largely worked as a pianist and accompanist in the London concert scene.

ALMA M. SANDERS
Three Decades of Writing

Alma M. Sanders's career as a Broadway composer-lyricist spanned three decades. Her biggest hit was the 1921 musical *Tangerine*, where she cowrote the music with her husband and frequent collaborator Monte Carlo. She also had the distinction of coauthoring the music and lyrics for *Mystery Moon*, which closed on opening night in 1930 under unique circumstances.

A 1921 article in the *Evening News*, around the time *Tangerine* premiered, proclaimed about Sanders, Dorothy Donnelly, and Ann Nichols:

> *Here are three women who have just taught Broadway a new trick and inci-*
> *dentally shattered at least three sacred traditions of the great thoroughfare.*
> *Each has written a musical comedy for the tired business man so successfully*
> *that the trio are the season's musical comedy headliners. Thereon hangs a tale:*
> *In previous seasons T. B. M. [tired business men] musical comedies were all*
> *done by men. Producers accepted plays from women, but when it came to*
> *musical comedies they said "let George do it" and he did. If any courageous*
> *woman did write a musical comedy Mr. Producer always courteously rejected*
> *it, explaining that none but a man could possibly know what would appeal*
> *to the tired business man. As if foresooth [sic], woman in her antique role of*
> *homemaker hadn't cherished this secret since cave days.*[20]

19. Zon, Bennett. *Music and Orientalism in the British Empire, 1780s–1940s*. New York: Taylor & Francis, 2017.

20. "Versatile Actress Blazes Trail for Feminine Contemporaries." *Evening News*, 2 December 1921, p. 19.

The three writers were said to agree that writing a musical was "as easy as it is for any woman to marry the man she wants . . . any woman knows more about what a man wants today than he does himself."

Tangerine's tired businessman plot involves an island where ex-husbands who won't pay alimony are sequestered, along with their ex-wives who start their own businesses and take on the roles ordinarily occupied by men.

Mystery Moon closing on opening night at the Royale in 1930 was ironic, considering the show's original title: *One Night Only*. *Mystery Moon* tells the story of a touring show (called *Mystery Moon*) that plays one-night engagements until it reaches its venue in North Dakota and the company discovers a mystery. The mystery in *Mystery Moon* is that the North Dakota theater is being used for drug smuggling, but the criminals rumor that the house is haunted in order to keep folks at bay.

Reviews of the show were negative, with many critics focusing on the banality of the show-within-the-show, but it was a dispute with the musicians' union that was the real reason for the production playing one performance rather than closing after a weekend or so. As the second performance of *Mystery Moon* was about to begin at the Royale, the entire audience was sent home. The producers and the theatre owners were embroiled in a dispute about who had to pay a bond for four of the sixteen musicians, and it couldn't be settled before show time, so the union refused to let the musicians play. *Mystery Moon* never happened again.

Dan Dietz commented on the overall career of Sanders and Carlo, who always worked together:

> *The songwriting team of Monte Carlo and Alma M. Sanders never had much luck on Broadway.* Tangerine *was of course an undisputed success, but its hit song "Sweet Lady" wasn't written by them. Their second musical* Elsie *(which included songs by Eubie Blake and Noble Sissle) managed 40 performances, and from there and throughout the decade they were associated with a string of disappointments:* The Chiffon Girl *(103 performances),* Bye, Bye, Barbara *(16),* Princess April *(24),* Oh! Oh! Nurse *(32), and* The Houseboat on the Styx *(which managed 103 performances and at least gets credit for a bizarre plot). The team also contributed a song to the 1926 edition of* Earl Carroll Vanities. . . . *Their 1947 musical* Louisiana Lady *crashed after four showings.*[21]

21. Dietz, Dan. *The Complete Book of 1920s Broadway Musicals*. Lanham, MD: Rowman & Littlefield, 2019.

Sanders and Carlo had a long duo career and marriage, but Sanders's first marriage hadn't worked out as well. A 1921 *Buffalo Enquirer* article about her divorce stated:

> *Although Mrs. Ernest Benjamin, under the name of Alma M. Sanders, is the author of more than 30 published love songs, she failed to hold the affections of her husband. Benjamin, who has brought suit for divorce, told Judge Dingeman that "music broke up his home." He testified in court that Mrs. Benjamin kept late hours and often did not return home until 3 a.m. She refused to cook his breakfast, he charged."*

The article, with the headline "Music Hath Charms, but Not for Him" went on to list Sanders's most popular song hits.[22]

---

22. "Music Hath Charms, but Not for Him." *Buffalo Enquirer*, 11 March 1921, p. 2.

4

1920s

Vaudeville Origins, One-Show Wonders, and Pop Hits

ZELDA SEARS
Show Doctor, Journalist, and Secret Writer

Zelda Sears's entrance into the theatre had more twists and turns than most. Sears needed to go to work at age twelve to support her family, and landed a job working in a store in her hometown in Michigan, because she won an essay-writing contest about the store's opening day. After a while, the store's owner recognized her writing talent and transferred her to work on his newspaper.

Sears continued working as a journalist until she interviewed Sarah Bernhardt during an engagement in Chicago. Sears wound up playing an extra in the production that she interviewed Bernhardt about, and her theatrical career began there. She worked her way up in the theatre through her stage roles,[1] and at the same time she began running a stenography and typewriting business in the New York theatre district.

She started acting as a play doctor, helping fix scripts for producers. After over a dozen performing credits on Broadway throughout the 1900s and 1910s, Sears's first official Broadway writing credit came with the show *Lady Billy* in 1920. This began a string of four musicals within four years, which Sears would write both book and lyrics for, also including *The Clinging Vine*, *The Magic Ring*, and *Lollipop*, which she also performed in.

Her start as a full-fledged Broadway writer came about in a roundabout way, but during her next era, Sears was behind the twists. Sears began working for the producer Henry Wilson Savage as a script doctor and became involved with the vice president of his company, Louis C. Wiswell. Sears and Wiswell were eventually married. But in order to get Savage and Wiswell to produce her full musical, *Lady Billy*, Sears submitted the script under a false name.[2]

As the *Detroit Free Press* reported it, Sears followed *Lady Billy* with several Broadway hits. "Add to these achievements Miss Sears's interesting two years of scenario writing and directing for Cecil de Mille, and the fact that she has been a marvelous wife and done not a little farming on the Wilton, Connecticut, farm she and her husband call '"home."'"

After *Lollipop*, Sears wrote one more Broadway play before packing it up for Hollywood, where she became active as a writer for film.

---

1. The stage role Sears became best known for playing in multiple productions was an Old Maid archetype: a wise older woman who wanted to get married despite not having any prospects.

2. "Was Zelda Sears Born under a Lucky Star?" *Detroit Free Press*, 3 June 1928, p. 82.

FRANCES NORDSTROM
Vaudeville and Broadway Multihyphenate

Many multihyphenate artists came out of the vaudeville circuit, since performers often had to craft their own material. Writer-actors developed their voices writing material for themselves and this led to their writing material for others as well.

Frances Nordstrom was one such artist. She developed work for both vaudeville and the legitimate stage. Of her five shows on Broadway, two were musicals: *Snapshots of 1921* and the 1921 *Music Box Revue*. Her lyrics were found in *Snapshots* and for the *Music Box Revue*, she contributed sketch material.

Nordstrom was mostly known as an actor and a non-musical playwright, but her work in a musical was seen by many, as the 1921 edition of Irving Berlin's *Music Box Revue* ran for 440 performances.

LILY HYLAND
A Female Director of Music

The Grand Street Follies was one of several topical revues popular during the 1920s in New York theatre. Presented by the Neighborhood Playhouse, the shows were first presented downtown before moving to the theatre district.

For the first edition, Lily Hyland acted as music arranger and pianist. The Neighborhood Playhouse was run by Agnes Morgan and Helen Arthur, who often hired women in positions other theaters did not. Hyland's official job at the Neighborhood Playhouse was director of music. For the 1922 *Grand Street Follies*, she led an all-male band (other than herself).

The next edition of the *Follies* in 1924 found Hyland composing all the music, to a book and lyrics by Morgan. She went on to contribute music to three more editions of the *Follies* as well as several other shows. She also performed as a classical musician and played harpsichord in the Broadway show *Mixed Bill*.

A review of the 1924 edition of the *Grand Street Follies* stated, "Lily Hyland, who has done admirable musical service before at this theatre, composed and arranged the music, which included delightful bits from standard works and an excruciatingly funny burlesque."[3]

---

3. Holt, Roland. "Revues That Review: *The Grand Street Follies* and *The Beggar on Horseback* Revisited." *News Journal*, 5 July 1924, p. 6.

HAZEL M. ARCHIBALD
Revue Writer Goes Missing

Hazel M. Archibald was a performer and writer who worked in theatre and vaudeville. In 1922 she contributed both music and lyrics for three songs in the Broadway revue *Michio Itow's Pin Wheel*, billed as "a midsummer revel in two acts." Archibald also performed in the show.

Later Archibald became a journalist under the pen name Dora Dean and campaigned for her husband Eben S. Draper, a state senator. She made the news in 1936 when she went missing for ten days. Archibald had stowed away on an ocean liner, but she eventually cabled her husband that she was "happy now" and would return soon.[4]

ANNELU BURNS, ANNA WYNNE O'RYAN, MADELYN SHEPPARD, AND HELEN S. WOODRUFF
All-Female Creative Team and a Legal Squabble

In 1922, an all-female team consisting of librettist Anna Wynne O'Ryan, composer Madelyn Sheppard, and lyricist-librettist Helen S. Woodruff were credited for a new Broadway musical titled *Just Because*. *Just Because* is the first known full-length Broadway musical with an all-female writing team.

An additional female collaborator was also part of the creation of *Just Because*. Annelu Burns did not receive a credit on the show on its opening night in New York, but she did write the original lyrics for the show. When she was unable to be a part of the process either during *Just Because*'s out-of-town tryout or subsequent Broadway run, O'Ryan took over on the lyrics and Woodruff bought out Burns's share on the show.

Just Because ran for forty-six performances at the Earl Carroll Theatre. Its plot involves a young man who swears off marriage and runs a home for orphans. A woman who wants to romance him disguises herself as an orphan in order to win him over—and does. Song titles include "It's Hard to Be a Lady," "Widow's Blues," and "Here's to the Bride."

Impresario Carroll built his theater that year and its first attraction went bust, so he quickly scheduled *Just Because* as his Broadway house's second show. *Just Because* received largely positive notices, with many journalists noting the show was written by women who were "amateurs" before going on to say they were pleasantly surprised by its quality. "*Just Because* turned out to be so delightful an entertainment that it aroused the enthusiasm of even [the] hard-boiled band of first-nighters. The music and the dancing are its chief features. The melodies are of intoxicating loveliness."[5]

---

4. "Mrs. Draper Will Return." *Windsor Star*, 30 April 1936, p. 11.

5. Allison, James M. "New Play Charms Broadway." *Cincinnati Times-Star*, 10 April 1922, p. 6.

The women of *Just Because* were far from inexperienced. Sheppard and Burns had had several songs published, including one popular World War I anthem. And O'Ryan had written several previous Broadway shows: two plays, and in 1922, a John Murray Anderson revue.

Just Because met an early demise due to conflict between Woodruff and the show's producers, Benjamin Berg and George T. Brokaw. Woodruff protested when Berg's name appeared in type as large as hers in the advertising for the show. The conflict led to Berg throwing a tantrum in front of the entire cast at a rehearsal and declaring the show would be a failure, after which Brokaw fired him. Berg sued, alleging that he was the reason the cast was being paid appropriately, in a way that would allow the show to sustain a run. Brokaw had wanted to pay every company member at least $75 weekly, since he felt this was fair. (Ensemble members were typically paid $35 weekly at the time.)[6]

Just Because did go on tour after its Broadway production, where it received praise in several local papers.

An earlier show with music and lyrics by Burns and Sheppard, and book by Woodruff, called *Hooray for the Girls*, was performed as a benefit in 1918.

TOT SEYMOUR
Specialty Writer for Fanny Brice and Sophie Tucker

Tot Seymour was known for her specialty lyrics, written for specific performers. Her Broadway credits included the three revues, *Topics of 1923*, *Innocent Eyes* (1924), and *The Ziegfeld Follies of 1936*. Over the course of her career she wrote for Fanny Brice, Sophie Tucker, and Mae West, among others, frequently collaborating with Vee Lawnhurst. In the 1930s, she had a prolific decade writing songs for movies.

THE DUNCAN SISTERS
Adapting Uncle Tom's Cabin

Topsy and Eva, with book by Catherine Chisholm Cushing, opened on Broadway in 1924. The show is an adaptation of the novel *Uncle Tom's Cabin* by Harriet Beecher Stowe, and has music and lyrics by its two original stars, Rosetta and Vivian Duncan.

The Duncan Sisters were a vaudeville duo who had a popular act playing the two characters from *Uncle Tom's Cabin*. Rosetta played Topsy, a slave, in blackface, and Vivian played Eva, a white girl. The anti-slavery tome was turned into a rollicking musical that was a hit in Chicago for almost a full year before opening in

---

6. "Selma People Watch Play *Just Because*." *Montgomery Advertiser*, 11 March 1922, p. 2.

New York at the Sam H. Harris Theatre. *Topsy and Eva* received largely negative reviews in New York, but not only did it run 159 performances, it was also turned into a film. Songs written by the Duncan Sisters for the show that gained popularity at the time included "Rememb'wring," "Um-Um-Da-Da," and "I Never Had a Mammy."

With its source material, book, music, and lyrics the work of four women, *Topsy and Eva* is one of the first Broadway musicals with an all-female writing team. Part of the reason it is little remembered today is because of the racial stereotypes employed and the problematic use of blackface.

NORAH BLANEY
"Ready to Work"

During World War I, Norah Blaney and her performing partner Gwen Farrar entertained the troops with their act, which they later toured with. Blaney and Farrar were immensely successful as a vaudeville duo. Blaney's one Broadway credit was a song for which she wrote the music, "Ready to Work" that appeared in the hit show *Andre Charlot's Revue of 1924*. Blaney's work as a writer and performer was more so seen on the road and in London.

ELEANOR MARUM AND JANE KERLEY
Regional Acts Come to Broadway

The Marsyas is a 1925 play by Jane Kerley with music by Eleanor Marum. Kerley also directed. The show, based on the Greek myth about a faun that tries to become a God, played one performance at Wallack's Theatre as part of a Little Theatre tournament that was presented regularly for several years. Plays from local regional areas got to present original work for one performance on Broadway as part of the program.

RUTH WHITE WARFIELD AND EUNICE TIETJENS
Middle Eastern Musical

Arabesque is a 1925 play with music that is set in the Middle East. It features music by Ruth White Warfield and words by husband-and-wife team, poet Eunice Tietjens and Cloyd Head. The production at the National Theatre on Broadway ran only twenty-three performances and was notable because it was an early entry by historic designer Norman Bel Geddes and his first time producing and directing on Broadway in addition to scenic designing.

GRACE HENRY
Contributor to Earl Carroll's Shows

As a writer, Grace Henry contributed to three Broadway shows in the 1920s: two editions of *Earl Carroll's Vanities* in 1926 and 1928, and the operetta *Fioretta* in 1929.

For the 1928 edition of *Vanities*, Henry was the main lyricist. About half of the songs were hers, with music by Morris Hamilton, and the other half were written by a slew of others.

Fioretta was Carroll's first attempt at producing a book musical, and he brought Henry along to collaborate again. This time she contributed four songs, written with a few different composers. The show was reportedly the most expensive flop in history at the time, losing $350,000, even though it ran 111 performances.

HELENA PHILLIPS EVANS
Happy Go Lucky

Helena Phillips Evans was largely a performer, appearing on Broadway and in films from the early 1900s through the 1940s. In 1926, she achieved her sole Broadway credit as a writer, on the show *Happy Go Lucky*.

Evans wrote the book and lyrics in full for this show about a millionaire who learns to be more affable. The *Daily News* generally praised the show and introduced Evans's contribution as such: "Helena Phillips Evans, the wife of Charles Evans of the old comedy team of Evans and Hoey, is responsible for the story and the rhymes."[7]

DOROTHY SANDS
Theatre Historian, Actor, and Writer

Dorothy Sands occupies a unique place in the canon, as she was a theatre historian, performer, and writer, who chronicled theatre history through live performance.

Sands began her career as a performer in plays, acting in dozens of productions on Broadway. Her first forays into musicals were as part of *The Grand Street Follies*. She appeared in the revue in 1926, and in 1927 she contributed lyrics as well.

In 1932, Sands presented *Styles in Acting*, where she performed canonical stage works from the Restoration era and later, in the styles of important stage

---

7. Mantle, Burns. "*Red Blinds* Looks Like a Bust; *Happy Go Lucky* New Musical." *Daily News*, 1 October 1926, p. 136.

stars of the past and present.[8] She followed this with *Our Stage and Stars*, a 1933 show she created where she chronicled theatre history from the American Revolution through the days of modern cinema.[9]

According to a *Baltimore Sun* article, Sands first discovered she had a talent for impersonation while working at the Neighborhood Playhouse under Agnes Morgan and Helen Arthur. "I began to worry about this thing called style in acting," Sands told the publication. "I wanted to go back into definite periods in history and recreate acting as it existed in each age and country. So I began to bury myself in the literature and art of different periods. . . . Then I began doing scenes from plays of each period—just for myself, at home alone. I did a few of my favorite scenes one night for Rosamund Gilder, and she liked them. She asked if I would do them for the Cosmopolitan Club."[10]

After a few seasons of presenting her one-woman shows in New York and all over the country, Sands was exhausted and largely went back to playing roles in work by others. Her Broadway credits as an actor numbered almost forty between 1924 and 1970, and her television credits were numerous as well.

ALBERTA NICHOLS
Writer for Ethel Waters and Frank Sinatra

Alberta Nichols worked with her husband Mann Holiner as a songwriting team. She made her Broadway debut in 1926 with the show *Gay Paree*, for which she wrote music to Holiner's lyrics for two numbers. This was followed by *Rhapsody in Black* in 1931, *Hey Nonny Nonny!* in 1932, and *Blackbirds of 1933*. In 1953, three of Nichols's songs were sung by Ethel Waters in Waters's self-named special revue.

Among Nichols's most famous songs were "Until the Real Thing Comes Along," "A Love Like Ours," and "Why Shouldn't It Happen to Us?" In addition to Waters, many other notable performers regaled audiences with Nichols's songs, including Frank Sinatra and Billie Holiday.

---

8. She not only performed this show on Broadway but also at colleges all over America, as well as overseas in Germany at the end of World War II, as part of a rehabilitation program meant to share American culture.

9. Kaplan, Jeffrey. "A Show of One's Own: Dorothy Sands and the Rise of Solo Performance in America." University of Maryland Digital Depository, 2017.

10. "One-Woman Show Led to Unusual Role." *Baltimore Sun*, 1 March 1942, p. 48.

EVELYN ADLER
Tales of Rigo

In 1927, actor Evelyn Adler contributed music and lyrics to a song for the Broadway musical *Tales of Rigo*.

IDA HOYT CHAMBERLAIN
"If She Can Sew and Cook as Well as Write"

In 1927, the musical romance *Enchanted Isle* opened at the Lyric Theatre with book, music, and lyrics all solely written by Ida Hoyt Chamberlain. She also collaborated on the scene design.

The *Daily News* review headline read: "*Enchanted Isle*: One Woman's Work, Ida Hoyt Chamberlain Took On Big Job." It followed to read: "Miss—or is it Mrs.?—Ida looks quite attractive in her pictures so generously distributed to the public gazettes, and if she can sew and cook as well as write, she could certainly make a fine all-around girl."[11] The review went on to give a mostly positive notice to the show.

While Chamberlain never returned to Broadway, she did continue to write. In the 1930s, she spent four years in China studying music and worked to present it to American audiences using Western instruments in various performances.[12]

NORMA GREGG
A la Carte

In 1927, Norma Gregg contributed both music and lyrics to three songs for the Broadway revue *A la Carte*. Her songs were "Never Again," "Sunny Spain," and "Who Is This One?" The show was produced by Rosalie Stewart, one of the only female producers of her era, and ran for forty-five performances at the Martin Beck.

DOROTHY PARKER
Writer and Critic of Legendary Wit

Dorothy Parker, like several of her peers at the Algonquin Round Table, was a theatre critic. And like several others, was a theatre maker as well. She bridged the gap between worlds in more ways than one.

Parker got her start as a poet and a journalist. She was working at *Vanity Fair* when she, Robert E. Sherwood, and Robert Benchley began their mealtime

---

11. *"Enchanted Isle*: One Woman's Work." *Daily News*, 26 September 1927, p. 29.

12. "She Spans a Music Gap." *Kansas City Star*, 12 May 1935, p. 22.

revels at the Algonquin Hotel, where they would discuss everything from theatre to politics. Parker had a knack for wit and poetry, chronicling everyday life. This manifested in accounts of the so-dubbed Algonquin Round Table making their way into the magazine.

Parker's words were often controversial. Throughout the late 1910s, 1920s, and 1930s, her published work included personal revelations, political activism, pointed criticism of those in the theatre industry, incisive book reviews, and dark poetry. She was outspoken, sardonic, and unapologetic.

Dorothy Parker, circa 1934. PHOTOFEST

At the same time, Parker was also represented on Broadway with several musicals and plays. In 1922, *The '49ers*, a revue, features sketches by Parker as well as by several of her Algonquin Table mates. Parker was the only female writer in a lineup that included George S. Kaufman, Marc Connelly, Ring Lardner, Morrie Ryskind, Howard Dietz, and Robert Benchley. The *New York Times* noted that Parker and Benchley chose to burlesque the art of historical drama in their sketch, poking fun at everyone from Queen Victoria to Robert E. Lee.[13]

In 1931, Parker contributed sketches again to a revue, called *Shoot the Works*. As the *Chicago Tribune* described her sketch: "a young man with a hangover learns from a girl all the horrible things he has done the night before." The paper criticized the sketch for being too light, but also elsewhere in the review called Parker an excellent writer, noting that she could bring more to the commercial stage than she had, and producers should stop relying on the same three writers for each project.[14]

Parker's sole contribution to a book musical came far later in her career, with *Candide* in 1957. According to Marion Meade in *Dorothy Parker: What Fresh Hell Is This?*, Parker recalled: "I had only one lyric in it. . . . Thank God I wasn't there while it was going on. There were too many geniuses involved." Parker was irritated by Leonard Bernstein's presumption that he knew how to write lyrics. She complained to *Candide* book writer Lillian Hellman that he clearly wanted to handle the whole show himself. Some years later she was still shaking her head over his mania "to do everything and do it better than anybody, which he does, except for lyrics. The idea was, I think, to keep Voltaire, but they didn't."[15] Parker's song for the show was "The Venice Gavotte."

---

13. Corbin, John. "The Play." *New York Times*, 7 November 1922, p. 14.

14. Chapman, John. "New York Wits Unite Abilities in Brown Show." *Chicago Tribune*, 2 August 1931, p. 44.

15. Meade, Marion. *Dorothy Parker: What Fresh Hell Is This?* New York: Penguin Books, 1989.

After her death in 1967, Parker's work was utilized for the song cycle *Hate Songs*, based on her poetry.

In 1970, the *Kansas City Times* called her "the cynical belle of the '20s, the unromantic other side of the coin of Edna St. Vincent Millay, the match for any of the knights of the Algonquin hotel's round table, as sophisticated as the *New Yorker* and as au courant as *Vogue*, and seemingly as vulnerable as a pit viper."[16]

DOROTHY FIELDS
A Versatile Writer of Hits with Longevity

Dorothy Fields wrote the lyrics to more than four hundred songs, many of which entered not just the hit list but the zeitgeist.

She wrote the book and/or lyrics for Broadway musicals actively from the 1920s until the 1970s, and her work has continued to be heard on Broadway since her death.

Born into a theatrical family, Fields was the daughter of Lew Fields, famed performer and producer. Her brothers Joseph and Herbert went into the family business as well, with Herbert collaborating with Dorothy on several projects.

Dorothy Fields, circa 1951. BY *NEW YORK WORLD-TELEGRAM* AND THE *SUN* STAFF PHOTOGRAPHER: ALBERTIN, WALTER, PHOTOGRAPHER/ LIBRARY OF CONGRESS PRINTS AND PHOTOGRAPHS DIVISION/ WIKIMEDIA COMMONS.

Fields made her Broadway debut in 1928 when she was just twenty-two years old. Although her father was in the theatre, he would not allow his daughter to become a performer. So she focused on writing, and penned some songs with composers J. Fred Coots and Jimmy McHugh.[17] McHugh hired her to write lyrics to his music for some songs in *Blackbirds of 1928*, which ran for a whopping 518 performances.

Fields's first book musical was next: *Hello, Daddy*, produced by and starring her father, with music by frequent collaborator McHugh and book by brother Herbert. Fields wrote lyrics for this show about three men who each think they're the father of the same illegitimate child. The show was notably co-choreographed by Busby Berkeley and Buddy Bradley. Berkeley was white and

---

16. Haas, Joseph. "Beyond the Humor an Unhappy Woman." *Kansas City Times*, 5 December 1970, p. 42.

17. Coots helped Fields get a job with a music publisher, Mills Music, Inc. where she was paid $50 per lyric.

Bradley was Black; white and Black citizens couldn't sit next to each other on a bus in 1929 but they could co-choreograph a big Broadway show. Fields spent the following decade contributing to half a dozen Broadway revues and writing songs for films. Before the age of forty, Fields wrote the lyrics for "I Can't Give You Anything but Love," "On the Sunny Side of the Street," "The Way You Look Tonight," "A Fine Romance," "I'm in the Mood for Love," "Never Gonna Dance," "Pick Yourself Up," and many more. Her main collaborator was Jerome Kern.

In the 1940s, Fields began writing books for musicals. With Herbert, she cowrote book (but not lyrics) for *Let's Face It!* (1941), *Something for the Boys* (1943), and *Mexican Hayride* (1944), all with scores by Cole Porter. In 1945, in addition to cowriting the book, Fields wrote lyrics for the hit *Up in Central Park*, with music by Sigmund Romberg.

Annie Get Your Gun, the canonical 1946 musical, was originally Fields's idea. She brought the idea of a musical about sharp shooter Annie Oakley to Oscar Hammerstein II, who loved it. Fields and Kern were originally supposed to write the score, but when Kern passed away, score duties went to Irving Berlin, who wrote the music and lyrics himself. Fields cowrote *Annie Get Your Gun's* book.

According to PBS's profile on Dorothy Fields for *Broadway: The American Musical*, "Fields' work habits were highly disciplined. Typically, she would spend eight weeks researching, discussing, and making notes on a project, before settling into an 8:30 a.m. to 4:00 p.m. daily work routine."[18] Fields was also known for her musical expertise, which made her a better lyricist, and for her ability to adapt to changing trends in musical theatre. The shows she wrote at the end of her career would have been inconceivable on Broadway at the beginning of her career.

In the 1950s, Fields cowrote the book and wrote all of the lyrics for *Arms and the Girl* (1950) and the lyrics for *A Tree Grows in Brooklyn* (1951). Then she cowrote the books and wrote all of the lyrics for *By the Beautiful Sea* (1954) and *Redhead* (1959). *Redhead*, a Bob Fosse and Gwen Verdon musical, was the big Tony Award-winner of its season. *A Tree Grows in Brooklyn* in particular led to some beloved songs like "Make the Man Love Me," "I'll Buy You a Star," and "He Had Refinement," written with Arthur Schwartz. Fields was adept at writing a lyric brimming with emotion and romance or a lyric filled with comedy or wit. During the earlier part of her career, songs were mostly one or the other, but as she moved into her later collaboration with Cy Coleman, she would write both in one song, for characters that were increasingly realistic.

---

18. "Dorothy Fields." *Broadway: The American Musical*, https://www.pbs.org/wnet/broadway/stars/dorothy-fields/.

Fields's two final Broadway shows were *Sweet Charity* and *Seesaw*, both with Coleman. *Sweet Charity*, another Fosse-Verdon project, features a legendary score with lyrics by Fields. Telling the story of a dance hall hostess with a heart of gold and her adventures searching for love, *Sweet Charity* is subversive, feminist, intelligent, and irresistible, and became a hit on Broadway. This was in no small part due to Fields's contribution, penning lyrics including "Big Spender," "If My Friends Could See Me Now," "There's Gotta Be Something Better Than This," "The Rhythm of Life," "Baby, Dream Your Dream," and "I'm a Brass Band." Every song in *Sweet Charity* was a winner and the combination of Fields and Coleman created a new, electric sound for musical theatre.

Seesaw was not as successful, with no blame to be placed on the outstanding contributions of Fields and Coleman. The show adapted William Gibson's two-person play *Two for the Seesaw*, about an ill-fated romance between a straight-laced lawyer and a zany dancer, into a musical. Fields and Coleman penned several excellent character songs for the leading lady and show-stopping group numbers like "My City" and "It's Not Where You Start," but the original production never quite got its footing, despite being taken over by Michael Bennett. *Seesaw* was however nominated for seven 1974 Tony Awards, including Best Musical and Best Original Score, and won two, for Best Featured Actor in a Musical for Tommy Tune and Best Choreography for Michael Bennett. It was Fields's final musical.

Fields was the only woman who received honors during the inaugural Songwriters Hall of Fame vote in 1971. She was an Academy Award winner and a member of the Theater Hall of Fame. About Fields's legacy, Betty Comden wrote in a foreword for Deborah Grace Winer's Fields biography, "She was THE woman songwriter. The marvelous thing about the way Dorothy wrote is that her lyrics were inventive without being tricky. She could do it—but she never compromised her direct, fresh manner of expressing a thought."[19]

ELISABETH HAUPTMANN
Brecht and Weill's "Silent" Collaborator

A frequent collaborator of Kurt Weill and Bertolt Brecht, Elisabeth Hauptmann's name is far less known, although she worked on many of the same landmark shows.

Hauptmann translated John Gay's *The Beggar's Opera* from English to German so that Weill and Brecht could create *The Threepenny Opera*. *The Threepenny Opera* premiered in Berlin in 1928 before premiering on Broadway in 1933, where

---

19. Winer, Deborah Grace. *On the Sunny Side of the Street: The Life and Lyrics of Dorothy Fields*. New York: Simon & Schuster, 1997.

it made history, changing the idea of how political and social change could be addressed in musical theatre. The show had an acclaimed revised off-Broadway production in 1956 that ran for 2,707 performances.

While she is credited with the German translation any time *The Threepenny Opera* is produced, Hauptmann is not often credited for her work on *The Little Mahogany*, another Brecht-Weill project. Allegedly, some of the writing on that show is hers.

After *Threepenny*, Hauptmann, Brecht, and Weill also collaborated on the musical *Happy End*. This show was not a success in Berlin and didn't receive a Broadway production until 1977. When *Happy End* ran on Broadway in 1977, it starred Meryl Streep and was nominated for the Tony Award for Best Musical. Hauptmann was credited with the original German play, although it was adapted by Michael Feingold. The show, involving a gang of criminals and a group of Salvation Army do-gooders, has been compared to *Guys and Dolls*.

Hauptmann's erasure from the narrative as far as the Brecht-Weill place in the theatrical canon goes has been addressed in works such as *Elisabeth Hauptmann: Brecht's Silent Collaborator*, by Paula Hanssen.

Hauptmann traveled to America to escape the Nazis and often published works under a pseudonym. After World War II, she continued to work in both Germany and America, as a writer and dramaturg.

GLADYS ROGERS
A Shuffle Along *Follow-Up*

The 1928 show *Keep Shufflin'* was one of several attempts to capitalize on the success of the 1921 historic smash hit *Shuffle Along*. *Shuffle Along*'s book writers Flournoy Miller and Aubrey Lyles wrote the book to *Keep Shufflin'*, and also played the same beloved characters in the same setting. *Keep Shufflin'* even opened at Daly's 63rd Street Theatre, where *Shuffle Along* had originally played.

Keep Shufflin''s grand finale is a song called "Harlem Rose" with lyrics by Gladys Rogers and music by Con Conrad, originally performed by leading lady Maude Russell, a prolific Black actor who earlier had introduced the Charleston on Broadway.

Rogers's name was also attached as a composer to a comedy with music called *Cease Firing*, about wartime hospitals, that never wound up being produced.

KAY SWIFT
First Woman to Be Sole Composer of a Hit Full-Length Broadway Musical

Kay Swift was the first woman to be the sole composer of a hit full-length Broadway musical: *Fine and Dandy*, which played the St. James in 1930.[20] She was also the namesake of *Oh, Kay!*, the Gershwin musical.

Swift grew up well-off in Manhattan. Her father was a music critic, so she was introduced to music at a young age. But after her father died when she was young, Swift and her mother struggled to make ends meet. She played music with a trio, and taught lessons in order to support her family. She was hailed as an incredibly talented pianist and went to Juilliard on a full scholarship.

Kay Swift, circa 1930, working on *Fine and Dandy* with James P. Warburg. PHOTOFEST

It was at a society party where Swift was playing that she first met James Warburg, heir to the throne of a massively wealthy banking family. His family objected, but the two married in 1918. They would eventually have three daughters.

Swift didn't change her name, and she didn't stop composing and playing music. In fact, Warburg wrote lyrics to her music for a few projects. He was the one who changed his name, as he didn't think it was appropriate for someone of his position to work in the theatre and didn't want to disgrace his family name by doing so. And so, songs by Kay Swift and Paul James appeared in the revues *Say When* in 1928 at the Morosco, *The Little Show*[21] in 1929 at the Music Box, *The 9:15 Revue*[22] in 1930 at the Cohan (now demolished), and *Garrick Gaieties* in 1930 at the Guild (now the August Wilson), and finally in their hit book musical *Fine and Dandy*.

Now it was Swift and James who threw and attended elegant society parties, with giants of the performing arts world present, and it was at one of these

---

20. This section was significantly inspired by the incredible book, *The Memory of All That: George Gershwin, Kay Swift, and My Family's Legacy of Infidelities*, by Katharine Weber, which I highly recommend. It has also been largely excerpted from *The Untold Stories of Broadway Volume 4*.

21. This featured one of Swift and James's most enduring songs, "Can't We Be Friends?," which was later recorded by Frank Sinatra, Bing Crosby, Linda Ronstadt, and Ella Fitzgerald.

22. This show only ran for seven performances but featured contributions from both the Gershwins and from Swift and James. The *New York Times* review said that Kay Swift's "Up among the Chimney Pots" was "the most memorable number": "'Nine Fifteen Revue' Is Noisy and Speedy: Ruth Selwyn's New Show Has Succession of Scenes, but Is Lacking in Originality," *New York Times*, 12 February, 1930.

parties in 1925 that Swift met the up-and-coming genius composer George Gershwin. Swift and Gershwin connected immediately and became inseparable. Since Warburg was often out of town on banking business, Gershwin would escort Swift to parties and shows, galleries and concerts. They went horseback riding in the country and had Manhattan adventures.[23] She taught him how to mingle with the upper crust, which neither of them had started out with, and from her formal music education, she taught him about elements of orchestration and counterpoint. He coached her in good old-fashioned Broadway music, more down-to-earth than the hoity-toity composition world she knew about. Gershwin recommended Swift as rehearsal pianist for Rodgers and Hart's new musical *A Connecticut Yankee* in 1927, a job that changed her life and launched her into the professional theatre. The two became best friends and closest confidantes—she was the first person whose opinion he sought musically. And in 1927, they began an affair.

The affair became even easier to carry on in 1929 when the stock market crashed and Warburg, who had become a well-respected economist, became part of President Franklin Delano Roosevelt's brain trust, eventually becoming his financial advisor. While Warburg was in D.C. trying to help save the American economy, Swift and Gershwin exchanged private jokes, secret gifts, and musical knowledge.[24] Gershwin was a notorious playboy and Swift was not the only woman he was with. But after all, she was the one who was married.[25]

Swift and her husband still found time to collaborate on *Fine and Dandy*. "Some couples, when faced with a marital crisis, have a baby. My grandparents had a Broadway musical," Katharine Weber wrote in her book about Swift.[26]

Fine and Dandy played the Erlanger, now the St. James, in 1930, right after the stock market crash. It was quite a time to launch a book musical by a team that had never written one before. When *Fine and Dandy* got into financial trouble, Warburg and his banker friends came to the rescue, and, with some help, the

---

23. Much of Gershwin's *An American in Paris* was written in the guest house at Swift and Warburg's country home, between horseback riding sessions with Swift. When it premiered, they celebrated on opening night at Carnegie Hall, and the day after that, they returned to see the matinee just the two of them, sneaking in and standing in the back of the theater. Afterward, as they walked down 57th Street together, Gershwin bought Swift two bracelets she would keep for decades.

24. Swift gave Gershwin a watch fob of a dove with gems for eyes: one her birthstone and one his. He wore it when he played concerts and conducted shows. When his songbook was published in 1932, he dedicated it to her.

25. By various accounts, Swift and Warburg had a mutually agreeable open marriage, and he willingly looked the other way about Gershwin, or he became increasingly jealous, leading to the Swift-Warburg divorce.

26. Weber, Katharine. *The Memory of All That: George Gershwin, Kay Swift, and My Family's Legacy of Infidelities*. New York: Broadway Books, 2012.

show ended up becoming a hit. The fact that Swift was breaking new ground as a female composer of a full Broadway musical was not written about in the press. It was considered a nonevent at the time.

Fine and Dandy is set in a factory, a male-dominated environment. It is generally a typical musical comedy centered around a romance between two young people: Maribelle, the factory owner's daughter, and George, who is working his way up in the factory in order to be worthy of her hand. The show satirizes the social classes and intergenerational conflict.

After *Fine and Dandy*, rather than going on to pursue her next projects as a composer, Swift dedicated herself to assisting Gershwin musically with three projects, one of which was *Porgy and Bess*. Much of the original score and orchestrations are in her hand, which is true for a lot of Gershwin's work. She was an especially indispensable part of Gershwin's process in composing his most innovative musical. Gershwin and Swift also performed his work together. One of the pieces they performed most often was from *Pardon My English* and consisted of the song "Tonight" from the show, followed by a countermelody, followed by both together.[27] Ira Gershwin referred to it as "Her Waltz, His Waltz, Their Waltz."[28] In 1935, George Balanchine offered Gershwin a job scoring his first ballet set in America, and Gershwin recommended Swift instead. She composed *Alma Mater*, and it played the Adelphi on Broadway.

When *Alma Mater* was out-of-town for its tryout in New Haven, Swift found out it was a hit from Gershwin on the phone. She was stuck in Reno, Nevada, since she had to wait there for her divorce from Warburg to become final.

Gershwin had never been married; he was a known womanizer who many doubted would ever settle down. But he did consider marrying Swift, although he came up with reasons not to. His family might object to him marrying someone who wasn't Jewish. Swift's three daughters at times adored him and at other times were horrified by their mother's scandalous affair.[29] He didn't want to give up the dynamic they had and his bachelor lifestyle. Still, he considered.

In 1936, Gershwin and Swift decided that he would go to Hollywood for one year. During this time, they would not correspond at all. At the end of the year, they would decide about their future. Some of their friends thought that after the year, they would be married. Swift tearfully watched Gershwin's plane

---

27. Jablonski, Edward. *Gershwin*. Cambridge, MA: Da Capo Press, 1998.

28. This is very similar to a sequence that would occur at the Imperial in 1978 in *They're Playing Our Song*.

29. On opening night of the Gershwins' *Strike Up the Band* in 1930 at the now-demolished Times Square Theatre, Gershwin turned around to Swift in the front row as he was conducting the orchestra to acknowledge a song that her daughters loved dancing to.

take off at Newark Airport and wondered if they could keep their promise not to speak.

They did keep it. Although, Gershwin's correspondence reveals that he did constantly ask others about Swift. How was she doing? Who was she spending time with? What was she working on?

Gershwin was struck down with a mysterious illness that year. It turned out to be an undiagnosed brain tumor. He died in Hollywood in 1937 at the age of thirty-eight.

Three weeks before Gershwin died, he had cabled Swift. "I'm coming back for both of us."[30]

Two years after Gershwin died, Swift met a cowboy at a rodeo and eloped to his ranch in Oregon. She wrote a book about this, which was made into a movie called *Who Could Ask for Anything More?*: a lyric from a Gershwin song. She became composer-in-residence at Radio City Music Hall for a time, and then created music for the 1939 New York World's Fair.

In 1952, Swift returned to Broadway for the first time since the 1930s, to write music for a one-woman show featuring Cornelia Otis Skinner. Swift also wrote lyrics this time. The show was *Paris '90*, about multiple women who lived in France in 1890. The songs in the show are based on paintings by French painter Henri de Toulouse-Lautrec.

But Swift spent the majority of the fifty-six years following Gershwin's death carrying on his work. She lived to be ninety-five years old and spent much of her time overseeing Gershwin productions, arranging Gershwin scores, playing Gershwin in concert, speaking to music students about Gershwin, and generally overseeing much of his legacy alongside Ira Gershwin and others.

In 1926, the Gershwins had crafted a new show with book by Guy Bolton and P. G. Wodehouse. It was called *Mayfair*. And then it was called *Cheerio*. And then the final title came: *Oh, Kay!* While Gershwin never explicitly stated it, it was understood that the musical's title was a tribute to Swift.

But the tribute didn't stop with the title. *Oh, Kay!* which opened at the Imperial on November 8, 1926, is a racy Prohibition-era farce about bootleggers of booze. The character of Kay—of British ancestry just like her namesake—and her brother use the wealthy Long Island home of rich American Jimmy Winter to carry off their schemes. Kay and Jimmy eventually fall in love. Gertrude Lawrence played Kay and brought the house down introducing the Gershwins' "Someone to Watch Over Me." It became one of their most enduring songs.[31]

---

30. Weber, Katharine. *The Memory of All That: George Gershwin, Kay Swift, and My Family's Legacy of Infidelities*. New York: Broadway Books, 2012.

31. In the 2012 production *Nice Work If You Can Get It*, Kelli O'Hara sang "Someone to Watch Over Me."

MURIEL POLLOCK
Acclaimed Pianist and Writer

Muriel Pollock was known as a writer and also as a pianist. She struck out to create musicals at a young age and began getting produced at a young age, which set her apart from the women of her generation who had to wait many years to break through.

In 1929, Pollock was featured in a *News-Palladium* article titled "Gifted Girls Who Write Songs."The article opened: "In the American Society of Authors and Composers are 600 members, 25 of whom are women. . . . This explains how these feminine pioneers won fame where men said they could not succeed."

Muriel Pollock, circa 1932. BY UNKNOWN, (1932) RADIO ALBUM / WIKIMEDIA COMMONS

The article went on to describe Pollock as one of the youngest in her field. Her first musical *Mme. Pom Pom*, written with Marie Wardall, was produced when she was only nineteen years old. It was an amateur production and since the writers knew nothing about copyright, they did not register their show. Several of the songs from *Mme. Pom Pom* were pilfered and placed in Broadway productions under other writers' names.

In the 1929 article, Pollock expounded on her advice for female writers. "She tersely writes an entire score through feeling. 'It's the gorgeous spontaneity that brings out the best,' she says. 'Too much study, or too great musical knowledge, takes away the natural musical instinct, and the finished product resolves itself into an attempt, rather than a result. Write from the emotions, rather than the head,' is Miss Pollock's advice."[32]

In 1923, Pollock made her Broadway debut when she wrote the music for two songs featured in *Jack and Jill*. In 1927, she gained attention playing piano for the mega-hit *Rio Rita*. Pollock already had a career as a concert, radio, and recording pianist when Florenz Ziegfeld gave her a job as a dueling pianist alongside Constance Mering in the orchestra pit of the musical that would run for nearly five hundred performances. Ziegfeld had an elevated platform put in the pit so that audience members could see the two pianists. Pollock and Mering also played dueling pianos for the Broadway show *Ups-a-Daisy* the following year.

In 1929, Pollock was the sole composer for a Shubert-produced revue called *Pleasure Bound*. *Pleasure Bound* received positive reviews and ran for several months at the Majestic. In 1931, Pollock was one of a large group of writers who

---

32. "Gifted Girls Who Write Songs." *News-Palladium*, 18 January 1929, p. 24.

contributed a song to the revue *Shoot the Works!* Pollock's song, "(Let's Go) Out in the Open Air" was cowritten with Ann Ronell, with both sharing credit for music and lyrics.

Pollock toured successfully as a jazz pianist, wrote compositions for two pianos, was a regular on several radio programs playing her own work, and performed piano rolls including with George Gershwin. In later years, she wrote music for children's shows under the name Molly Donaldson.

CHARLOTTE KENT
College Girl Writes for Broadway

Charlotte Kent was the stage name of Charlotte Hochman, who had a song debut on Broadway the year after she graduated Hunter College. This was especially notable because the song Kent penned for *The Little Show*, that notable revue at the Music Box, was "Stick to Your Dancing, Mabel," which, according to Walter Winchell's column, she had actually written for her senior class day in college.[33]

The Little Show was one of five major revues that Kent would contribute to; four played Broadway and one closed out of town.

After *The Little Show* in 1929 came *Sweet and Low* in the fall of 1930. This revue was put together by impresario Billy Rose and its stars included his wife Fanny Brice. The lineup of other contributors included George M. Cohan, Harry Warren, Ira Gershwin, and Rose himself, whom Kent collaborated with. The song "Overnight" had lyrics by Rose and Kent and music by Louis Alter, and Winchell heaped it with loads of praise in his column.[34] Brice brought down the house with "Overnight" and continued to sing it, even after *Sweet and Low* closed. Kent was also the sole writer of music and lyrics for a song called "Mr. Jessel" that appeared in the show, and another song that she wrote with Rose and Alter was added for Brice to sing after the show opened: "I Wonder Who's Keeping Him Now."

Kent helped musicalize some radio presentations in the 1930s. She contributed original songs to radio plays based on existing newspaper stories and comic strips. This was the first time that original theme songs were heard for a program like this, and Kent wrote twelve that wound up airing.

This led to a feature article in *The Marshall News Messenger.* A large caption above a photo of Kent read, "Girl Becomes Famous by Three Days' Work.... Charlotte Kent, Just One of the Thousands of Job-Hunters in Broadway Agencies for Year and a Half, Flooded by Offers Following Success of 12 out of 13

33. Winchell, Walter. "Walter Winchell on Broadway." *Tribune*, 5 July 1929, p. 5.

34. Winchell, Walter. "Walter Winchell on Broadway." *The Tampa Daily Times*, 5 August 1930, p. 8.

Radio Theme Songs She Wrote."[35] But the article itself lent more credence to the actual facts and challenges of her rise to success.

After noting that Kent was only twenty-four, the article stated: "One has to be familiar with Broadway, its pitfalls and its heartlessness toward the aspiring newcomer, to appreciate the difficulty of the task that the young girl had mapped out for herself. The only other members of her sex who had ever succeeded in scratching the surface of 'Tin Pan Alley' were Dorothy Fields and Mable Wayne [sic], so there was no track which she could follow."

The article further commented on Kent's gender as compared to that of most in her field. When the call went out for writers to audition for the radio gig, Kent worked without stopping for three days. She was described as "not daunted that among the other composers were men who had left their mark on the musical world, whose compositions have sold into millions of copies and are known wherever orchestras or phonographs are heard." Kent was the first to turn in her submission.

Kent hadn't been able to make a big enough name for herself with her contributions to two Broadway revues to get more work, but this significant radio event put her on the map. She now received offers to write full scores for Broadway shows rather than just submit a few songs. Her radio work was performed by well-known stars and was immensely successful.

Alas, Kent's writing of a full Broadway score did not come to pass. Her next show on the boards was *The Illustrators' Show* in 1936. This time she wrote music and lyrics for three of her own songs, but they were only heard for five performances at the now-demolished 48th Street Theatre. In the lineup with her this time were two writers whose songs were heard on Broadway for the first time in the show: Frank Loesser and Frederick Loewe (each collaborating with other writers). The revue, with a concept that musicalized alongside images from the Society of Illustrators, received poor reviews and closed quickly during the depths of the Depression.

Indeed, Kent may have seen more work had she been treading the boards during another decade. Her next opportunity came from the Works Progress Administration's theatre department, the Federal Theatre Project. *Sing for Your Supper* was to be their first musical of sorts presented on Broadway, and the topic to be tackled was the work of the WPA on Broadway. Newspapers continually covered that the show was in rehearsals for a year and a half. In 1939, developing an all-new large-scale Broadway revue without the usual resources of Broadway, under government terms, was a different kind of venture that somewhat imitated today's lab and workshop process, albeit extended. This time, Kent wrote songs and sketches for the revue with ambitious aims that most critics claimed fell flat.

---

35. "Girl Becomes Famous by Three Days' Work." *Marshall News Messenger*, 31 March 1931, p. 7.

Unimpressed by the contrast of how long the process had taken and the final product, the critical consensus was that *Sing for Your Supper* had tried and failed to do something it took the biggest Broadway stars and producers to pull off. The duration of development time and cost involved, plus the notices, likely prevented the Federal Theatre Project from attempting more musicals of this sort.

In 1952, Kent contributed to a revue called *Curtain Going Up*, which closed in Philadelphia and also included in its lineup the work of a young Mel Brooks.

5

1930s

Musicals of the Great Depression

NANCY HAMILTON AND MARTHA CAPLES
All-Female Revue Writing Team

Martha Caples wrote the music to Nancy Hamilton's lyric for the theme song of the *New Faces* revues. First used to open the show in its 1934 edition at the Fulton, the song was also used in the 1936 edition. The women wrote a few other pieces for the 1934 show as well. One was cleverly called "Six Managers in Search of an Actress—As They Never Are."

Caples and Hamilton began collaborating in 1930 with a revue they put together called *And So On*, which was presented in association with Smith College and had an all-female cast. Hamilton wrote book and lyrics and Caples music. This all-female writing team toured their show, putting it together with different young casts associated with colleges and clubs in each town.

Nancy Hamilton, circa 1926. BY NATIONAL PHOTO COMPANY COLLECTION / UNITED STATES LIBRARY OF CONGRESS / WIKIMEDIA COMMONS

In a joint interview with the *Montclair Times* while the show was being done the following year with Montclair's Junior League, they said: "The reason why we have called our intimate revue *And So On* is because we have a theory that life is a two-a-day vaudeville show that goes on and on, so on and so on."[1] *And So On* opens in the middle of a number, to further drive this home—that the audience is joining in the middle of the action, which is unending.

While Caples's only Broadway gig was *New Faces*, Hamilton had a varied Broadway career from 1932 to 1946. She actually appeared in *New Faces of 1934* as well as in several other Broadway shows. As a performer and a writer, she contributed to the three-show Shubert series with the titles *One for the Money*, *Two for the Show*, and *Three to Make Ready*. The smart revues were interrupted by World War II, which Hamilton spent writing radio scripts and performing with Katharine Cornell's company in Europe.

Hamilton and writing partner William Morgan Lewis Jr. wrote one number that was put into Mary Martin's production of *Peter Pan* but dropped during its pre-Broadway tryout in 1954. This was an act two opener for Captain Hook called "The Old Gavotte." They got the gig because of Hamilton's friendship with Martin.

---

1. "League Show Is New Departure." *Montclair Times*, 22 April 1931, p. 2.

The Hamilton-Lewis song "How High the Moon," which is in the Song-writers Hall of Fame, appeared in *Motown: The Musical* on Broadway in 2013.

DOROTHY HEYWARD
And Bess

Dorothy Heyward was a playwright who had six plays produced on Broadway between the 1920s and 1940s. She also wrote the book of one musical and adapted the book for another musical from a play she'd previously written. The former was called *Jonica*, and the latter was called *Porgy and Bess*.

Heyward met her husband, DuBose Heyward, at the MacDowell Colony, and they frequently collaborated. In 1925, DuBose Heyward wrote a novel called *Porgy*. His wife felt the book would make a great play, and in 1927, *Porgy* premiered on Broadway, adapted for the stage by the couple. The Theatre Guild produced this work at the Guild Theatre, now known as the August Wilson. It was notable because the story about Black citizens of a tenement in South Carolina was performed by Black actors—a rare occurrence at a time when blackface was frequently employed by white performers to tell such stories. The use of Black actors was insisted upon by the Heywards. It was also Dorothy's idea to adjust the novel's ending, making it more optimistic for the stage in that Porgy followed Bess to New York before curtain. The show became a huge hit, running 367 performances.

In 1930, Heyward wrote the book for an original musical based on her own short story. This was *Jonica*, about a young woman who travels to New York for a wedding and gets into a bit of innocent trouble along the way. *Jonica* was the Broadway debut of Moss Hart as a writer. However, he never included the show in interviews or biographies after he became famous; the show's forty performances and silly plot were seemingly an embarrassment to him. The *New York Times* review read: "*Jonica* proved to be a fairly lively show ... of musical comedy cliches ... and of a knowing, slightly insane humor that sprang out in unexpected places and made some of the soggier portions endurable. ... The story, as related by Miss Heyward and Moss Hart, is fully as complicated as any ordinary musical comedy libretto should ever be allowed to be."[2]

Five years later, Heyward's next musical *Porgy and Bess* premiered on Broadway and forever altered the art form. George Gershwin had read the original novel the year after it was published and the idea for a musical stage adaptation had been percolating in his head ever since. The Theatre Guild presented the musical, which Gershwin thought of as a folk opera, at the Alvin with book by

---

2. "*Jonica* Involves Girl in Many Tangels: Musical Comedy Based on Story by Dorothy Heyward Is Given in Craig Theatre." *New York Times*, 8 April 1930, p. 34.

DuBose Heyward, music by George Gershwin, and lyrics by Heyward and Ira Gershwin. While Dorothy was technically not credited with work on the musical adaptation, she was very involved with the process.

A 1935 *New York Times* piece told readers how nine years earlier, George Gershwin had picked up a copy of the book *Porgy*, by DuBose Heyward, in an effort to read until he fell asleep after a tiring day of rehearsal. Gershwin was so inspired by the book, and the idea of turning it into an opera, that he immediately wrote Heyward a letter. When Heyward received the letter, in Charleston, South Carolina, he and his wife Dorothy Heyward were actually in the middle of adapting the book into a play for the Theatre Guild.

The article shared: "An opera seemed very far away indeed. Mr. Heyward replied that he would be glad to talk with Mr. Gershwin when he came to New York."

"Mr. Gershwin didn't wait for Mr. Heyward to come to New York. He went to Charleston."[3]

STELLA UNGER
"Camille, Colette, Fifi"

Stella Unger wrote one lyric for a song in the 1930 Broadway operetta *Three Little Girls* and contributed to *Earl Carroll's Vanities* the same year. The next year found her performing in a play called *Papavert*. This was followed by a contribution to *Belmont Varieties*. When the show was revised as *Manhattan Varieties*, her song was dropped.

Unger's main Broadway gig was writing the lyrics and cowriting the book for *Seventh Heaven*, the 1944 musical now mainly known for boasting the first featured role for the previous ensemble player Chita Rivera. As prostitute Fifi, Rivera performed the showstopper "Camille, Collette, Fifi" with two other women. This was a song she continued to perform throughout her career, including in her 2005 Broadway career retrospective, *Chita Rivera: A Dancer's Life*. *Seventh Heaven*'s leads were Gloria DeHaven and Ricardo Montalban. They played impoverished lovers on the streets of 1920s Paris in the piece based on the hit 1922 play by Austin Strong.

In 1958, the *New York Times* announced Unger was working on a Broadway musical about outer space called *Twinkle, Twinkle*. This never materialized.

She composed songs for movies and worked for *NBC* in later years. Unger's best-known songs include "Don't Cry, Baby" and "Have You Met Miss Fandango?" "Camille, Colette, Fifi" was used during a sequence on the reality television program *Dance Moms*.

---

3. "On the Genesis of a Folk Opera." *New York Times*, 6 October 1935, p. 157.

MARY COHAN
George M. Cohan's Daughter

Mary Cohan was the daughter of George M. Cohan, one of the most legendary entertainers and entrepreneurs in theatre from the 1880s through the 1940s. The senior Cohan started out as a vaudeville performer and became one of the most powerful director-producer-writer-stars on Broadway, creating hit songs such as "Give My Regards to Broadway" and "The Yankee Doodle Boy."

Born in 1909 to George Cohan and Agnes Mary Nolan, Mary Cohan grew up around show business, so it was no surprise when she wrote music for a revival of her father's play *The Tavern* at the age of twenty-one. *The Tavern* was written by Cora Dick Gantt and had been a hit vehicle for George M. Cohan as star and producer.

Cohan was twice disowned by her father, each time for marrying a musician. The first was in 1927 when she married a banjo player and the second was in 1940 when she married an accordion player. Reporting for the *International News Service*, a 1940 article stated that the elder Cohan barricaded himself at home and refused to see anyone after his daughter eloped. He said he was "too busy writing a play." In response Mary said, "Father is stubborn, and so am I. I adore him, but we're both too Irish, I guess."[4]

The elder Cohan had a reputation for having a roaring temper. Mary Cohan captured all of this and more in 1968 when she collaborated with Francine Pascal, John Pascal, and Michael Stewart to create *George M!*, a new Broadway retrospective about her father's life. *George M!* ran for over a year and introduced a new generation to the influence of Cohan's work. Mary revised the music and lyrics to fit the storyline where needed.

In 1939, Cohan dabbled in nightclub performing. On the night of her debut, attendees included John Barrymore, Sophie Tucker, George S. Kaufman, Ethel Merman, and Jimmy Durante. Her set list included "Mary Is a Grand Old Name" a song her father often performed in her honor.

DANA SUESSE
Girl Gershwin

Dana Suesse was a busy and popular songwriter, mainly active in the 1930s, 1940s, and 1950s. At times nicknamed "Sally of Tin Pan Alley" and "Girl Gershwin," Suesse wrote music and lyrics for songs and musicals, penned straight plays and acted, composed concertos and incidental music for projects.

---

4. "Mary Cohan Finally Elopes and Marries George Ranken." *Tampa Bay Times*, 7 March 1940, p. 1.

Suesse got a big break when band leader Paul Whiteman commissioned her to write an original piece for his orchestra in 1931. This was the same way that George Gershwin's "Rhapsody in Blue" premiered, so comparisons were inevitable. At this point, Suesse had already written songs for one Broadway show: *Sweet and Low*, produced by impresario Billy Rose. Suesse and Rose worked together often—both as songwriter and producer and as cowriters. Suesse composed the music for *Billy Rose's Diamond Horseshoe Revues*, *Billy Rose's Casa Mañana Revues*, and *Billy Rose's Aquacade* at the 1939 New York World's Fair.

Dana Suesse, circa 1930s. PHOTOFEST

In addition to *Sweet and Low*, Suesse's other Broadway shows where she contributed music or lyrics included *Chamberlain Brown's Scrap Book* (1932), *Ziegfeld Follies of 1934*, *You Never Know* (1938), *A Case of Youth* (1940), *Crazy with the Heat* (1941), *The Seven Year Itch* (1952), and *Golden Fleecing* (1959).

In a 1939 article for *Screen & Radio Weekly*, Annemarie Ewing and Jack Sher wrote about women in the songwriting business. "Breaking into Tin Pan Alley is the toughest thing in the world. And if you think it's tough for the men—well, it's 10 times tougher for women. Of the 1,006 members of the American Society of Composers, Authors and Publishers, only 72 are women. And of these 72, there are probably not more than half a dozen of whom you've heard." The article went on to discuss the contributions of Mabel Wayne, Kay Swift, Ann Ronell, and finally Suesse.

"In the long run, though, leave it to the red-heads. It was a red-headed girl, Dana Suesse, who found out when she came to New York from Louisiana with a briefcase full of Etudes and Preludes in the classic vein that writing music was one thing and getting it published was another. Especially if you're a girl. But you can't stop a red-head."[5] The piece went on to praise some of Suesse's best-known work, including her songs "Whistling in the Dark" and "You Ought to Be In Pictures." The latter, written with Edward Heyman, has lived on in many movies, and is often called one of the anthems of Hollywood. It has been recorded by everyone from Doris Day to Ann-Margaret. Suesse's work has continued to be featured in popular media, from animated programs like *Daffy Duck* to blockbusters like *Robin Hood: Men in Tights*.

While Suesse gained popularity on Tin Pan Alley, Broadway, and in Hollywood, she was through and through interested in classical music in the concert

---

5. "The Girls." *Screen & Radio Weekly*, 30 July 1939, p. 56.

world. She made a big comeback with a 1974 Carnegie Hall concert, after many years in retirement, and a large amount of her overall work was composed for symphonies and concert halls.

Suesse wrote several full musicals, where she contributed both music and lyrics, in her lifetime, but none were produced.

ANN RONELL
First Woman to Write a Full-Length Broadway Score Alone

Like Kay Swift, Ann Ronell also benefitted from the friendship and mentorship of George Gershwin. She met him while she was a student at Radcliffe when she had the opportunity to interview him for a project.

Gershwin encouraged Ann Rosenblatt to change her name to Ann Ronell. After all, he himself had been born Jacob Gershowitz. He also suggested she get training by acting as rehearsal pianist for a show, and then hired her for his own musical *Rosalie* in 1928. She was twenty-one years old.

Ann Ronell, circa 1953, by Walter Albertin. BY *NEW YORK WORLD-TELE-GRAM* AND THE *SUN* STAFF PHOTOGRAPHER: WALTER ALBERTIN / WIKIMEDIA COMMONS

In 1931, she made her Broadway debut as a writer when she collaborated with Muriel Pollock on a song for *Shoot the Works!* This show was an effort by Heywood Broun to get actors and writers working, just after the Great Depression hit and people were in a panic. *Shoot the Works!* featured the contributions of many well-established writers alongside brand-new folks. Ronell got to be one of them after she heard about the project and just showed up at the theater, trying to get her songs heard and considered. The one that ended up being picked, "Let's Go Out in the Open Air," was performed by rising star Imogene Coca.[6]

Ronell hit Tin Pan Alley and began to sell her songs there. In the early 1930s she became successful with "Baby's Birthday Party," "Rain on the Roof," "Give Me Back My Heart," and "Willow Weep for Me." Then she began writing songs for films and achieved her most enduring song, "Who's Afraid of the Big Bad Wolf" cowritten with Frank Churchill, which was featured in 1933's *Three Little Pigs*. This became the first hit song from a Disney film. She started composing for projects overseas as well.

A 1933 article captured Ronell's rise to success. "Tin Pan Alley still is man's domain. But sunny, smiling, determined little twenty-three-year-old Ann Ronell,

---

6. Zimmers, Tighe E. *Tin Pan Alley Girl: A Biography of Ann Ronell.* Jefferson, NC: McFarland, 2001.

from Omaha, Nebraska, has crashed it! She has made good in a big way with four popular song hits and a score of others. Even the most anti-feminist old member of Tin Pan Alley had to relent and with one accord she has been acclaimed as one of its own."[7]

Ronell was quoted in the article by Julia Blanshard about first meeting Gershwin when she interviewed him as a student. She shared that it was their conversation that made her resolved to make it as a songwriter herself. She also spoke about getting her start in the business.

"I found that it is impossible to even have your songs heard by the right people, unless you have a pull. Let a girl try to crash into the song-writing game and men will say, 'Isn't she cute,' 'When can I have a date,' or 'This is too tough a game for a nice girl like you!'" The article went on to describe Ronell's indefatigable perseverance in show business and her entry to the professional world which was prescribed once Gershwin, Vincent Youmans, and Irving Berlin heard her work and helped her get a start. The article concluded with a paragraph about her physical appearance and manner of dress. Ronell spent much of the 1930s in Hollywood, not only writing songs but also music directing, one of the first women to do so for major Hollywood movie musicals.

Ronell's second Broadway venture, a decade after her first, was even more distinguished. She was the sole writer of both music and lyrics for *Count Me In* in 1942 at the Barrymore. In this, she became the first woman to write the full score of a full-length Broadway musical by herself. Kay Swift had broken ground as the first woman to write all the music of a full-length Broadway musical by herself, and now Ronell added lyrics to that distinction as well.

Count Me In started as a college musical. Future theatre critic Walter Kerr met Leo Brady who was a professor at Catholic University, when Kerr took classes there. The two wanted the college students to have a theatre experience as close to professional as possible, so they decided to write a show for them to perform. They enlisted Ronell to write the songs. Musicals involving patriotic wartime themes were increasingly popular, so they decided to do another one of those. *Count Me In*'s plot involves a shy businessman who wants to help the war effort at home and how he tries to enlist his family and community to do so. Before long, the Shuberts were interested in bringing the show to a professional stage, and the college students were replaced by Broadway actors.

George Abbott was enlisted to direct the show in its next steps, and immediately clashed with Ronell. He eventually left the show, stating that the score was inferior and that he doubted Ronell's abilities to better it.[8]

---

7. "She Crashed Tin Pan Alley." *Wisconsin Rapids Daily Tribune*, 15 February 1933, p. 8.

8. Zimmers, Tighe E. *Tin Pan Alley Girl: A Biography of Ann Ronell.* Jefferson, NC: McFarland, 2001.

The show tried out in Boston, where Ronell's score received excellent reviews, the show overall less so. Many thought the book was overly busy. *Count Me In*'s cast included Gower Champion, as one of the children of the lead character. Another future Broadway choreographer, Danny Daniels, was also in the cast. The rest of the illustrious company included Luella Gear, Charles Butterworth, and Jean Arthur.

Count Me In received mediocre reviews on Broadway and ran sixty-one performances. In an interview years later, Ronell commented, "It was a terrific experience writing a show at last, and I understand now why there have been so few women who ever got a hearing on Broadway."[9]

In 1944, Ronell adapted the 1847 Friedrich Wilhelm Riese operetta *Martha* for Broadway, with Vicki Baum. It played several performances at City Center. Her last Broadway gig was composing a lullaby for the original Broadway production of *The Crucible* in 1953.

Separate from Broadway, Ronell continued to work busily in the following decades. Her song for the 1945 movie *Story of G.I. Joe*, which was Academy Award nominated, was the first theme song to ever play over film credits. She scored a Marx Brothers movie. She worked on a project with Judy Garland to musically adapt beloved songs into Garland's style.

In a 1950 interview, Ronell said "Some day I intend to compose the first American opera for film production." The final line of the piece was "Ten to one she does."[10] She never did, but her accomplishments are nevertheless impressive.

ZORA NEALE HURSTON
Folklore and Ethnographic Research

Zora Neale Hurston was a cultural icon whose many titles included novelist, essayist, playwright, anthropologist, educator, folklore historian, filmmaker, and musical theatre writer.

Among the work Hurston is best remembered for is her 1937 novel, *Their Eyes Were Watching God*. The book is about the journey toward self-discovery of Janie Crawford, a Black woman in her forties in early twentieth-century rural Florida. Considered a masterwork of American literature as well as an important work about the Black experience and about the female experience, *Their Eyes Were Watching God* was not as appreciated in its time as it became later on. Initial reviews, including in publications for and by the Black community, were

---

9. Ibid.

10. Perrigo, Lucia. "Girl Composer of Hits Hopes Some Day to Do Score of First U.S. Film Opera." *Circleville Herald*, 28 November 1950, p. 5.

negative, and it took time for Hurston's unique voice to be recognized. Starting in the 1970s, the book was rediscovered and became beloved by new generations, given rave reviews by critics, added to many academic reading lists, and made into a 2005 television movie executive-produced by Oprah Winfrey and with a screenplay that counted Suzan-Lori Parks among its writers.

Hurston was an expert in Caribbean and African American folklore, and these greatly influenced her work. She was a pillar of the Harlem Renaissance, and her short stories were included in important works of that era. She founded a school for dramatic arts within Bethune-Cookman University, a Black college in Florida, where she was from.

In the 1930s, Hurston made several forays into the live theatre world. A few of these were musicals.

In 1930, Hurston collaborated with Langston Hughes on *Mule Bone: A Comedy of Negro Life*. The two gifted writers, who were close friends, had a difficult experience working on the play together. Not only did it end their friendship, but the play was never produced. They sought to craft a work about Black people that did not employ tropes or stereotypes. *Mule Bone* is based on a folkloric tale of a love triangle that leads to an alleged crime that is resolved unpredictably. The problems between Hurston and Hughes stemmed from differing views about whether a third collaborator should be credited, their shared patron, and rumors about the play being submitted to theaters by one without the other's permission. *Mule Bone* debuted more than sixty years later, after the deaths of both authors, when it was produced by Lincoln Center on Broadway.

The year 1931 marked Hurston's only official run of a Broadway musical that she contributed to. *Fast and Furious* is a revue that played the New Yorker Theatre (today Studio 54) and ran only seven performances. It features sketches by Hurston, and she also performed in the show. *Fast and Furious* was unique for its time in that it featured a creative team that included both male and female artists and both Black and white artists. Other writers who contributed to the piece included Forbes Randolph, Lottie Meaney, Jackie "Moms" Mabley, Mack Gordon, and Harry Revel. *Fast and Furious* received overall negative reviews.

In 1932, *The Great Day*, billed as "A Program of Original Negro Folklore," was presented by Hurston at Broadway's Golden Theatre for one special performance. Hurston put her whole self into this evening full of song, dance, and authentic representation of Black history, but despite some good reviews, the show was not picked up by a producer to continue. A program note by Alain Locke observed that most work put on stage about Black people involved secondary imitations. But, he said,

"Great Day" is a strange arrangement of a part of a cycle of Negro folk-song, dance and pantomime collected and recorded by Miss Zora Hurston

over three years of intimate living among the common folk in the primitive privacy of their own Negro way of life. It is thus a rare sample of the pure and unvarnished materials from which the stage and concert tradition has been derived; and ought to show how much more unique and powerful and spirit-compelling the genuine Negro folk-things really are.[11]

Hurston attempted to revise *The Great Day* under the new title *From Sun to Sun.*

Singing Steel, Hurston's 1934 musical piece about railroad workers, premiered in Chicago. Another work where Hurston utilized ethnographic research and folklore to create a show, *Singing Steel* was part of the WPA Federal Theatre Project.

BERENECE KAZOUNOFF
Concert Pianist to Writer to Manager

In 1932, concert pianist and acclaimed musician Berenece Kazounoff contributed to the Shuberts' new book musical, *A Little Racketeer*, which played at the 44th Street Theatre. *A Little Racketeer* was a vehicle written for star Queenie Smith about a woman who wants to become a popular career criminal. The show ran forty-eight performances at the large theater that used to be on the south side of 44th Street near Broadway.

Next, Kazounoff contributed to *The Illustrators' Show* in 1936. In 1939, she wrote several songs with John Latouche and one with Sylvia Marks for an intimate revue called *Two for Tonight* that played the Cherry Lane. At the time, before the birth of off-Broadway as we know it, this production was considered by many a Broadway show.

Kazounoff's final Broadway credit and biggest hit was *Reunion in New York*, another intimate revue but this time at the Little Theatre (now the Helen Hayes) in 1940. *Reunion in New York* was put together by The American Viennese Group, Inc., a group of Austrian immigrants who had escaped violence in their country and wished to present work both celebrating their land and also looking to their future in America. Current theatre was satirized as it was in nearly all revues at the time, and Kazounoff's contribution to the proceedings was a take on William Saroyan called "A Character in Search of a Character."

Kazounoff became a manager for young musicians and spent the rest of her career advocating for them and guiding their careers.

---

11. Program for Zora Neale Hurston's *The Great Day*: a program of original negro folklore, New York, 1932, Smithsonian Collection, https://ids.si.edu/ids/deliveryService/?id=AAA-AAA_taylpren _20694&max=1300.

MILDRED KAUFMAN AND HELEN LEARY
Two Ill-Fated Showcase Revues

The fall of 1932 found two musical revues opening on Broadway that each had contributions from largely male teams—plus Mildred Kaufman and Helen Leary. The shows were *Belmont Varieties* (at the Belmont) and *Manhattan Varieties* (at the Cosmopolitan). *Manhattan Varieties* was actually a retooled version of the earlier show, but neither caught on, and they ran a total of seventeen performances.

Kaufman wrote lyrics to her husband Alvin Kaufman's music for several of the numbers and Leary contributed sketches alongside her husband Nolan Leary.

The two variety shows were both meant as sort of auditions for out-of-work actors struggling through the Great Depression. Reviews praised the performers who were given material meant to impress and gain them more long-standing employment.

GENEVIEVE PITOT
One of the Top Dance Arrangers

Genevieve Pitot got her start as a classical pianist giving recitals before beginning to accompany dance classes, including at Martha Graham's company, and then parlaying this into arranging for dance within theatrical work.

A prolific dance arranger for Broadway musicals, Pitot eventually counted among her many credits the original Broadway productions of *High Button Shoes, Kiss Me, Kate, Miss Liberty, Call Me Madam, Two on the Aisle, Two's Company, Can-Can,* and *Li'l Abner*. As the dance arranger for *The Body Beautiful* and *Milk and Honey*, she had the distinction of creating the dance music for the Broadway breakthroughs of the team of Jerry Bock and Sheldon Harnick as well as Jerry Herman.

As a composer in her own right, Pitot created the music for two full-scale dance productions on Broadway: *Candide* in 1933 and *Adelante* in 1939, as well as an important work of the Federal Theatre Project that played Broadway.

Candide was billed as a "dance drama" and Pitot wrote the music with John Coleman. The libretto was by Charles Weidman who also starred in this adaptation of Voltaire's beloved eighteenth century novel. The notices were negative, and many were confused by the ideas put forth in the show. This was much like the reaction that the musical theatre version of *Candide* received when it premiered on Broadway in 1956.

The *Candide* with Pitot's music got a revival with the Federal Theatre Project in 1937. Oddly, in this revival at the Nora Bayes, only Pitot's part of the score remained, and the other composer was Wallingford Riegger. This time the show was presented as a double bill with a dance show called *How Long, Brethren?* based on "Negro Songs of Protest." Pitot wrote the music for this Federal Theatre Dance Project production which utilized Black singers and white dancers, a casting decision extremely unique at the time. After *How Long, Brethren?* played the Nora Bayes, it moved to the Maxine Elliott's by popular demand. In her obituary, the *New York Times* mentioned Pitot's contribution to this show and called it "one of the earliest black American protest dances."[12]

Pitot's collaborator Donald Saddler praised Pitot's brilliance as a composer and arranger, noting that he and other dancers would tell her that although she was a musician, she had "the soul of a dancer."[13]

About her busy career, including *Shangri La* and *Li'l Abner* back-to-back, Pitot once told the press, "I went from Tibet to Dogpatch in one week."[14]

ESTELLE MORANDO
A Shady *Underdog Summer Musical*

The 1933 Broadway musical *Shady Lady* found newcomer Estelle Morando cowriting the book with well-established Broadway writer J. Fred Coots (*Sons o' Guns*). At least this is what was announced in April of that year. By the time the show reached the Shubert Theatre in July, Coots was nowhere to be found, and Morando was sole book writer, with uncredited contributions and consulting by Irving Caesar.

Harry Meyer apparently had a lot of trouble assembling his creative team, because between April and July several writers were announced who never actually reached the rehearsal room. In addition, Morando and Coots were at one point said to be writing the score as well. It was eventually penned by Sam H. Stept and Jesse Greer (music) and Bud Green and Stanley Adams (lyrics).

When the show opened in July in 1933, there were low expectations. Nearly everyone deserted the city for the summer, so barely any shows opened then due to the heat. Modern air conditioning changed this, but at the time, the fact that *Shady Lady* appeared during July sent the message that this was a lower-tier production. Nevertheless, the show had some star wattage because it starred Helen Kane. Kane was known as the "boop oop a doop" girl for the phrase she uttered while singing "I Wanna Be Loved By You" in the popular show and movie *Good Boy*. Kane was an iconic personality and a much-admired starlet of the flapper

---

12. Dunning, Jennifer. "Genevieve Pitot, Dance Composer. *New York Times*, 9 October 1980, p. B19.

13. Ibid.

14. "Woman's World." *Somerset Daily American Newspaper*, 27 June 1959, p. 5.

style. *Shady Lady* was intended as a vehicle for her, but not even Kane's popularity could get 1933 audiences to pay attention to this summer starter.

GERTRUDE STEIN
A 1934 Broadway Musical with an All-Black Cast

Gertrude Stein was a zeitgeist-shifting writer, a lesbian icon, a Jew living in Nazi-occupied France, a skilled art collector, and the center of a generation of artists who transformed the worlds of visual and written work in the mid-twentieth century. Stein had an original, complex style and is often quoted and referenced today.

Although she is not best known for her contributions to musical theatre, musicals with her words were influential and significant—one on Broadway and two off-Broadway, one prior to her death and two after.

Gertrude Stein, circa 1935, by Carl Van Vechten. BY CARL VAN VECHTEN/ VAN VECHTEN COLLECTION AT LIBRARY OF CONGRESS/ WIKIMEDIA COMMONS

The first was *Four Saints in Three Acts*, which premiered at the now-demolished 44th Street Theatre in 1934. Despite playing on Broadway, the show is actually an opera, with words by Stein and music by Virgil Thompson. *Four Saints in Three Acts* revolves around Stein's two favorite saints, Saint Therese of Avila and Ignatius Loyola. The show is an surrealist depiction of a group of about forty saints in total, who recollect their time on Earth.

The show featured an all-Black cast, and the music director was Eva Jessye, a Black female choral conductor. The concept of having an all-Black cast was chosen by Thompson and Stein, who felt that Black performers delivered the work best. *Four Saints in Three Acts* had initially been written for an all-white cast and Thompson told the *New York Times* that if audiences had an adverse reaction to the all-Black cast, they would just "have them play in white-face."[15]

In Circles is a 1967 off-off-Broadway musical that transferred to off-Broadway in 1968 and was inspired by Stein's 1920 work, *A Circular Play*. Al Carmines put Stein's words to music in a collage celebration of her philosophy and style. As historian Thomas Hischak wrote in *Off-Broadway Musicals Since 1919: From Greenwich Village Follies to The Toxic Avenger*: "No efforts were made to explain or even thematically tie the various pieces together (which was true to

---

15. "Four Saints in Three Acts: Gertrude Stein and Virgil Thomson Collaborate on Opera for Hartford." *New York Times*, 31 December 1933, p. x8.

Stein), though the audience was told that each of us lives in a separate circle."[16] *In Circles* won an Obie Award and received an original cast album.

In the *New Yorker*, Edith Oliver wrote: "Miss Stein's quirky lines glitter with meaning—for everybody. They are, of course, terribly funny, and the comedy is rooted in wisdom and poetry and pureheartedness [*sic*]. Non sequitur they may be but never nonsense. There is nothing trivial or silly here, and there is always the awareness that tragedy is just a hairbreadth away."[17]

Gertrude Stein's First Reader is a 1969 family musical where young performers interpreted Stein's words.

JUNE CARROLL
The Face of New Faces

One of the most integrally involved female writers on the theatrical revue scene consistently from the 1930s through the 1960s was June Carroll. Sister of revue impresario Leonard Sillman who created the indelible *New Faces* revues, Carroll was a book writer, a composer, a lyricist, a performer, and a creative hub around which other artists flourished.

New Faces, a witty, intimate revue series focused on presenting new talent both on stage and off, premiered in 1934. For this edition, Carroll provided several lyrics. In fact, many of the writers involved with the first edition were women, also including Viola Brothers Shore, Nancy Hamilton, and Martha Caples. Carroll, who wasn't married yet and still went by June Sillman at that point, had originally been in the cast, but had stepped out of it to focus on writing.

"It has always been my practice to avoid appearances in the shows which I have written and particularly those with which my brother is identified as producer," she later told the press. "When it came to *New Faces'* 1952 edition, our backers actually asked that I appear, and while I demurred, they kept insisting. So I finally agreed and I have enjoyed the experience, but I will be concentrating on writing again in the future."[18]

Later in 1934, Carroll provided some of the book for the quick-lived *Fools Rush In*, also staged by her brother. She followed this up with book, music, and/ or lyrics for the 1936 and 1943 editions of *New Faces*, as well as the revues *Who's Who* (1938) and *All in Fun* (1940). In *Who's Who*, she was found on stage as well.

---

16. Hischak, Thomas. *Off-Broadway Musicals Since 1919: From Greenwich Village Follies to The Toxic Avenger*. Lanham, MD: Scarecrow Press, 1911.

17. Oliver, Edith, "Off Broadway: Perfect Circles," *New Yorker*, November 18, 1967, pp. 131–33.

18. McLellan, Dennis. "June Carroll, 86; Lyricist, Singer Best Known for 'New Faces' Revue." *Los Angeles Times*, 21 May 2004.

The year 1946 found Carroll as the librettist, penning book (with Robert Duke) and lyrics for *If the Shoe Fits*, a modern take on Cinderella. The show was Sillman's first time producing a book musical. *If the Shoe Fits* only lasted twenty-one performances but was notable for several reasons. The scenic designer Edward Gilbert pioneered several technological advances for *If the Shoe Fits*. He set out to "build a device that would turn the pages of a book and change the sets at the same time . . . decided he'd [also] like to have pop-ups as are used in children's books . . . [and crafted] a very complicated machine [enabling] scenes [to] be changed sideways." A patent was even obtained for this scenic advancement.[19]

If the Shoe Fits also found Carroll collaborating with a young writer who would later be known under the name Cy Coleman. Coleman was a high school senior when he got a job as a rehearsal pianist on the show, and he ended up doing some writing and vocal arrangements as well.[20]

If the Shoe Fits received markedly negative reviews including several scathing notices for Carroll's work.

Her next outing was *New Faces of 1952*, the biggest hit edition, which even spawned a film adaptation. Carroll wrote and starred, and appeared in the film as well. The numbers she wrote included "Monotonous," which was sung and made famous by Eartha Kitt. She received acclaim for writing songs like "Penny Candy," which she also performed, as well as for performing songs she *didn't* write, like "Guess Who I Saw Today," which was penned by Elisse Boyd and Murray Grand. Carroll's talent as a multifaceted artist was on great display in *New Faces of 1952*, which ran for a year at the Royale (now the Jacobs).

Carroll also contributed as a writer to *New Faces* in 1956, 1962, and 1968, to the 1957 Broadway revue *Mask and Gown* and the 1963 off-Broadway revue *Tour de Four*, and to several projects for film and television.

VIOLA BROTHERS SHORE
Serial Mystery and Revue Writer

Viola Brothers Shore was a writer of short stories who broke into Hollywood and began writing silent films in the 1920s before working in theatre as well. As the *Kansas City Kansan* wrote, "Viola Brothers Shore is a successful author, wife and mother and playwright—isn't that rather an establishment of new precedents?

19. Funke, Lewis. "News and Gossip of the Rialto: *If the Shoe Fits* Will Bring to Town Novel Scene Technique 'If the Shoe Fits.'" *New York Times*, 1 December 1946, p. x1, https://www.nytimes.com/1946/12/01/archives/news-and-gossip-of-the-rialto-if-the-shoe-fits-will-bring-to-town.html.

20. Propst, Andy. *You Fascinate Me So: The Life and Times of Cy Coleman*. Essex, CT: Applause, 2015.

Mrs. Shore has proved again that a woman can have a professional career as well as successfully manage the domestic side of her life."[21]

A 1924 special guest piece that Shore wrote for the *Brooklyn Daily Eagle* had the successful writer pen a full-page piece titled "Viola Brothers Shore, Writer, Discusses What Children Should Be Told about Marriage."[22]

By the 1930s, Shore had added mystery writer of serials to her job list. She made her Broadway debut writing a decent amount of the sketches and lyrics for *New Faces of 1934*, which lasted 149 performances. Here she collaborated often with June Sillman, who she again worked with on the 1934 revue *Fools Rush In*.

Shore opened both *Fools Rush In* and a straight play she cowrote, *Piper Paid*, on Christmas Day 1934. They both lasted less than two weeks on Broadway. Shore continued to have an immensely successful career writing off of the stage.

MARY SCHAEFFER
The Provincetown Players' Revue

The Provincetown Players was an experimental theatre group who were part of the invention of modern off-Broadway, at the time called the Little Theatre movement. Starting in 1915, the company revolutionized theatre, introducing the work of Eugene O'Neill and Susan Glaspell, laying groundwork for a less commercial theatre scene, and gaining attention for Greenwich Village as a hub for uncompromising art. Much like the off-Broadway nonprofit scene that would flourish starting in the second half of the twentieth century, the Provincetown Players produced more female writers than were being produced on Broadway.

The Provincetown Follies was the first attempt of the Provincetown Players to get into the revue scene, and present a musical entry in their roster. And much like that same off-Broadway nonprofit scene in current day, the declared goal of *The Provincetown Follies*, before even opening, was to move the show to Broadway proper after the show's planned success off-Broadway.

This never happened, nor did other future iterations of the revue, because this one was just moderately successful. Reviews were negative, but audiences did turn out for about a month at the end of 1935.

Mary Schaeffer composed music and lyrics for "Riverman" and "Dancing Dream," two songs in the lineup.

---

21. "Author Does Things She Hadn't Intended." *Kansas City Kansan*, 21 October 1921, p. 20.

22. Tarleau, Ellen. "Viola Brothers Shore, Writer, Discusses What Children Should Be Told About Marriage." *Brooklyn Daily Eagle*, 13 July 1924, p. 73.

MARIANNE BROWN WATERS
Right This Way

Marianne Brown Waters got her start as a radio singer before turning to writing and having a play produced by the Shuberts on Broadway in 1933. *The Blue Widow* played only a month at the Morosco, and afterward, Waters honed her craft as a song writer and began writing lyrics for nightclub and recording artists.

Her sole Broadway musical was *Right This Way* for which she wrote book and lyrics in 1938. The show is about an American journalist and French stylist who fall in love. While Waters was credited as the main lyricist, the show wound up with half a dozen interpolated songs by Sammy Fain and Irving Kahal, and also had credits for additional dialogue.

Of the pre-Broadway tryout, the *Cincinnati Enquirer* thought the music and lyrics were "tuneful and clever" but thought "the plot intrudes and is taken too seriously." About Waters's work, the critic wrote that "her lyrics surpass the story. Miss Waters elected to follow formula for the structure, but her lyrics depart from the conventional."[23]

ELEANOR FARJEON
British Bouquets

Eleanor Farjeon was born into a Jewish literary family in England in the 1880s. This combination of facts alone makes her stand out among Broadway writers of the 1930s. Farjeon's brothers were both writers, and she collaborated with them on stage shows that were produced in England. She also wrote poems and books, and she was a journalist for a time.

Farjeon's one foray to Broadway was *Two Bouquets*, an operetta she wrote book and lyrics to along with her brother Herbert. *Two Bouquets* had already run for a year in London when Marc Connelly decided to bring it to America, inspiring Eleanor's first visit to New York City since she was a teenager thirty-four years prior.

Two Bouquets employed the music of many well-respected operetta writers and the Farjeons fashioned a new story with new words about a Victorian romance around it. In the *New York Times*, Brooks Atkinson advised that the old-fashioned musical "deserves the attention of theatergoers who are not deranged by swing-band orgies."[24] Two of the stars of *Two Bouquets* were Patricia Morrison and Alfred Drake, future original leads of *Kiss Me, Kate*, a decade later.

---

23. Bernfeld, Herman J. "Right This Way." *Cincinnati Enquirer*, 16 November 1937, p. 2.

24. Atkinson, Brooks. "THE PLAY: The Two Bouquets' Revives Some Victorian Music in Light Opera Form." *New York Times*, 1 June 1938, p. 19.

Joseph Jefferson, Farjeon's maternal grandfather, was one of the most famous American actors of the nineteenth century.

Bella Spewack
The Real-Life Kiss Me, Kate

The Tony Awards began in 1947, but it wasn't until 1949 that the categories of Best Musical and Best Book of a Musical premiered. That year, Bella Spewack won both, with her collaborators, for *Kiss Me, Kate*. The first Best Musical has a score by Cole Porter and a book by husband-wife team Bella and Samuel Spewack.

Bella Cohen grew up in poverty on the Lower East Side. Her mother made sure she finished high school, which was a rare occurrence for a poor Jewish immigrant girl in the 1910s, and this was the thing that changed her life and gave her a future. She wrote about all of this in a 1922 memoir titled *Streets: A Memoir of the Lower East Side*, which wasn't published until after her death seven decades later.

Cohen got her start in journalism in the 1920s. At age nineteen, she met Samuel Spewack, also a nineteen-year-old journalist. They spent several years working as news correspondents in Russia together. Upon returning to America, Samuel wrote novels, and the pair wrote movies, until 1928, when they made their Broadway debut with a play called *The War Song*.

The War Song was written by the Spewacks with George Jessel, who also starred. The show is a serious take on World War I from the point of view of an American soldier held as a prisoner of war in France, while the female members of his family and his girlfriend suffer in various ways, back in the states. The Spewacks used their experiences as journalists to write the show. This dark work was a far cry from the lightness of their later shows.

Just a few months later, the Spewacks were back on the boards with *Poppa*, a show they wrote to be directed by George Abbott. This show is about a Jewish family and relevant social issues that Bella encountered during her youth. Again, the sociopolitical atmosphere influenced the Spewacks' plays. Their next two Broadway shows, *Clear All Wires* (1932) and *Spring Song* (1934) also fell into this category.

According to the *Jewish Women's Archive*, "it is widely accepted that Sam created the plot and action, while Bella wrote most of the dialogue. George Abbott, the legendary Broadway director, said that the Spewacks "know how to write lines which are not only funny to read but which crackle when spoken in the theatre." True, some of their serious dramas received mixed reviews, but the negative response was mostly to the plot, not the dialogue. Anyone familiar with the

Spewack comedies is struck by the liveliness of the text, the witty remarks, the biting irony, and the fast tempo."[25]

In 1935, the Spewacks had a change in fortune and in focus. *Boy Meets Girl*, a zany Hollywood-based comedy, ran for 669 performances, their longest run by far. The show has their trademark wit and intelligence, but treats far less serious subjects than their previous works. This was followed by *Leave It to Me!*, their first Broadway musical in 1938. The show was adapted from their play *Clear All Wires*. *Leave It to Me!* retains the Spewacks' use of social and political themes but throws them into a musical comedy. The plot puts a hapless businessman in the Soviet Union as its newest American ambassador, leading to all kinds of hijinks, from Mary Martin singing "My Heart Belongs to Daddy" at a train station in Siberia, to the character of Stalin performing a dance number at the show's climax. *Leave It To Me!* commented on fascism, Nazism, and Soviet Russia, but the way in which it did so was quickly outdated. In fact, during the show's 291-performance run at the Imperial, Stalin had to be edited out of the show due to the signing of the Nazi-Soviet Pact. The show's political themes have made theaters hesitant to revive it, although they were considered progressive at the time.

Leave It to Me! found the Spewacks collaborating with Cole Porter, with whom they would later write their biggest hit, *Kiss Me, Kate*. First came *Miss Swan Expects* (1939) and *Woman Bites Dog* (1946), both running on Broadway for only single-digit performances. Then in 1948, *Kiss Me, Kate* hit the boards and became a canonical musical theatre work.

Initially, Bella was writing the book of *Kiss Me, Kate* without Samuel, even though they had done every Broadway collaboration together. Ironically, the couple's marriage was on the rocks even as Bella attempted to put together a story about a theatrical couple's relationship troubles while trying to perform *Taming of the Shrew*. But the Spewacks were known for fighting constantly while collaborating on every show. Life imitated art as the Spewacks penned the book of *Kiss Me, Kate*, to Cole Porter's indelible score. About the original 1948 production at the New Century, Brooks Atkinson wrote "Bella and Samuel Spewack have contrived an authentic book which is funny without the interpolation of gags. Cole Porter has written his best score in years, together with witty lyrics."[26]

Indeed, *Kiss Me, Kate* was hailed as an important continuation of the Rodgers and Hammerstein revolution. *Oklahoma!* and *Carousel* had changed the musical from being what it once was when shows like *Leave It to Me!* opened. Now musicals had their elements integrated more meaningfully. *Kiss Me, Kate* did this and in doing so, proved that such a seamless creation had value even when it was

---

25. Taub, Michael. "Bella Spewack." *Jewish Women's Archive*, https://jwa.org/encyclopedia/article/spewack-bella.

26. Atkinson, Brooks. "At the Theatre." *New York Times*, 31 December 1948, p. 10.

a musical comedy rather than a musical play. The Spewacks and Porter avoiding "the interpolation of gags" meant that the musical comedies to come would derive their humor from character and situation.

The Spewacks' next Broadway venture found them in different roles. This time, Samuel wrote a play called *The Golden State* that Bella produced. When the show opened out of town at the Walnut Street Theater, the *Philadelphia Inquirer* wrote a piece about the couple's newest form of collaboration.

"'After I read Sam's play,' Bella explained, 'I thought it was the best thing he had ever done and asked him if I could produce it. He looked doubtful, gave me one week to find backers. . . . Sam broke in, his face still wearing an incredulous expression. 'In one week, she found 41 backers.'"[27] *The Golden State* ran for twenty-five performances on Broadway.

The Spewacks' biggest post–*Kiss Me, Kate* success on stage was *My 3 Angels*, which ran for ten months at the Morosco in 1953. The play is set in French Guiana in 1910 and involves the interactions between three prisoners and a French family. The show was made into a movie in 1954, and joined the ranks of the Spewacks' other screen projects. Several of their plays were made into movies, including *Clear All Wires* and *Kiss Me, Kate*. In addition to several B-movies, they also wrote original theatre-focused movies like *Mr. Broadway*, about George M. Cohan.

Bella Spewack claimed credit for the idea of Girl Scout cookies. The Girl Scouts began selling cookies to raise money in the 1930s, and Spewack said this was due to her influence, having contributed the idea while working for the Scouts in 1920s.

Undeniably, her greatest contribution to the musical theatre was her work on the story of *Kiss Me, Kate*, which was based on her own life-long sparring match with her theatrical collaborator husband.

DORIS HUMPHREY
Creator of Theatrical Ballets

Doris Humphrey was a groundbreaking choreographer. She was a dance theorist who created new techniques in modern dance and employed them in her work on Broadway and on other stages. Her choreography work on Broadway spanned the 1930s to the 1950s and on several of these shows—*The Race of Life*, *With Red Fires*, and *To the Dance*—she was credited as a writer as well. These original theatrical ballets were performed in repertory at the Nora Bayes Theatre, the rooftop venue at the 44th Street Theatre.

---

27. Wilson, Barbara L. "A Pair of Playwrights." *Philadelphia Inquirer*, 5 November 1950, p. 150.

In 1973, a book about Doris Humphrey was released that consisted of half her autobiography, unfinished at the time of her death, and half a biography written by Selma Jeanne Cohen. A *Baltimore Sun* article did a write up: "Both women's libbers and women artists will feel that Doris Humphrey and Selma Jeanne Cohen tell it like it really is. In her own words, Doris Humphrey considered herself *An Artist First* [the book's title] and her other roles as daughter, woman, lover, wife and mother secondary. During the early part of her life, she was anti-marriage and said, 'I knew that I was too committed to dance to be able to give it up and live happily with any man.'"[28]

SYLVIA FINE
Danny Kaye's Secret Weapon

Many theatre aficionados know that Sylvia Fine was married to star actor Danny Kaye. Not many know the full breadth of her career, since she spent so much of it supporting his.

Fine was an aspiring composer during her time at Brooklyn College and she even penned the school song. After graduating, she worked as a rehearsal pianist and composer. In 1939, Fine and Kaye met working on an off-Broadway show called *The Sunday Night Varieties* that ran for three performances. Fine was so impressed by Kaye's performance that she convinced director-producer Max Leibman to hire him to work on shows with them at Camp Tamiment.

Sylvia Fine with Danny Kaye, circa 1945. BY DS PUBLICATIONS / WIKIMEDIA COMMONS

That fall, the group at Tamiment had the opportunity to bring their show to Broadway. With James Shelton, Fine wrote the score for the 1939 musical *The Straw Hat Revue*. The show played at the Ambassador for two months in the fall of that year. Fine and Kaye married the following year and were together until his death in 1987.

Although *The Straw Hat Revue* didn't run for very long, it did not lack for positive reviews overall. It was praised in the *New York Times* and several other publications. In the *Daily News*, Burns Mantle called it the "best intimate revue since the first *Garrick Gaieties*."[29] The show earned struggling actor Kaye his first rave notices.

---

28. Bond, Chrystelle T. "Doris Humphrey Biography Exhibits Honesty, Tact." *Baltimore Sun*, 26 February 1973, p. 16.

29. Mantle, Burns. *Daily News*, 3 October 1939, p. 145.

Within a few months after closing, Fine and Kaye not only were married but also she was writing his material for nightclubs and appearances. Not only did she write for him, but she also often accompanied him at the piano for his performances too. As Kaye grew to become a Broadway and Hollywood success, Fine wrote songs for him for movies and recordings. In 1941, when Kaye appeared in *Let's Face It!* on Broadway with a score by Cole Porter, there were two songs interpolated for him to sing that were written by Fine with Max Leibman.

A 1960 *Pittsburgh Post-Gazette* piece stated: "Rarely in show business has the 'woman behind the man' been as imposing a figure as Sylvia Fine who has spent the past 20 years virtually unidentified in the widening glow cast by the career of her husband, Danny Kaye."[30]

Her *New York Times* obituary stated, "Mrs. Kaye was known for her complex, witty lyrics, and she was often described as a composer of patter songs, which turn on the rapid delivery of tricky lines." The article went on to cite several of her most popular songs, including "Anatole of Paris," "The Lobby Number," and "Soliloquy for Three Heads." Then the article shared that Fine had disagreed with this assessment, stating that she had only ever written two patter songs; the rest were merely songs with patter sections.[31] Over the course of her career, she wrote over one hundred songs for Kaye.

Separate from Kaye's career, Fine produced a television special called *Musical Comedy Tonight* in 1979 that won a Peabody Award. She was a producer and professor who educated about musical theatre.

---

30. "Who Is Sylvia?" *Pittsburgh Post-Gazette*, 30 October 1960.

31. Grimes, William. "Sylvia Fine Kaye, 78, Songwriter; a Proponent of Musical Theater." *New York Times*, 29 October 1991, p. B5.

6

1940s

Hit Tunesmiths with Broadway Flops, Writers with Major Careers in Other Fields, and the Longest-Running Team in Broadway History

DORCAS COCHRAN
Some of the First Mic'd Songs on Broadway

Better known for writing hit pop songs and movies, Dorcas Cochran did write for Broadway once, contributing to *Earl Carroll's Vanities* in 1940. Cochran was the main lyricist of that edition of the revue, and more than half of the songs were hers. This was the last presentation of *Vanities* to play Broadway after a run of seventeen years, having started in 1923. It was not a hit, eking out only twenty-five performances.

What was notable about *Earl Carroll's Vanities of 1940* was the use of body microphones. It is widely assumed that body mics did not come into use on Broadway until the 1960s, but there were actually rare occasions when a show utilized them in the previous decades. The body mics in *Vanities* received a terrible critical lambasting, and most critics felt they couldn't hear Cochran's songs as they were meant to be heard because of the sound issues. Her spirited songs included "The Lady Has Oomph," "Westward Ho!," "Can the Can-Can" and "Song of the Sarong." These were written to music by Charles Rosoff.

Cochran had gotten her start on Broadway, appearing in the ensemble of the musical *You Said It* in 1931. But the majority of her work came from writing pop songs for artists including Eartha Kitt and Dean Martin and contributing to 1940s film musicals like *Juke Box Jenny*, *Swing It Soldier*, and *Swing Out the Blues*.

MARÍA GREVER
Mexican Composer with a Latin-American Broadway Musical

Viva O'Brien was called a Latin-American Broadway musical in the press. The subtitle fit. Its engine and composer was fifty-six-year-old history-making Mexican composer María Grever (sometimes referred to in media as Marie Grever).

The book was by William K. Wells and Eleanor Wells, music by María Grever, and lyrics by Raymond Leveen for this 1941 show at the Majestic with the subtitle: "An Aquamusical."

Viva O'Brien is about a Spanish and Irish man (hence the two clashing words in the title) who has to lead a group of scientists to find a magical wishing stone in Yucatan. The original production boasted a swimming pool and a waterfall on stage—although the waterfall was actually made of granulated sugar. The 1952 musical *Wish You Were Here* famously had a swimming pool on stage at the Imperial—but that pool is remembered because that show ran. *Viva O'Brien*'s swimming pool has been forgotten because the show closed after only twenty performances.

For years, *Viva O'Brien* was used as a punchline because, as historian Dan Dietz wrote, "[It] received some of the most scathing notices of the decade."[1] Critics were absolutely perplexed by this old-fashioned musical that had new-fashioned Spanish and Mexican themes and sounds. (William K. Wells was known for having written many editions of *George White's Scandals*, dating back to 1923.[2]) In the *New York Post*, Wilella Waldorf called the show "childishly trying" and said that the way to tell the Mexican and American characters apart was how they pronounced the word "Mexico." This was typical for the kind of remark made about the Latin-American elements in the show.

There were a small number of nice nods in the press. In the *Daily News* Burns Mantle wrote: "The outstanding personality of the production [is] Marie Grever . . . a Spanish lady of a long line of Castilian somebodies. . . . Her numbers are original and I suspect you will be hearing a good deal from her songs."[3]

The show was the idea of the well-connected Grever, and she was the one who secured the main investor who put up the show's capitalization. At the time of *Viva O'Brien*, she was already the first female Mexican composer to achieve international success with songs like "What a Difference a Day Makes" and "Tippi-Tippi-Tin." Grever was born in Mexico, to a Mexican mother and Spanish father. She married an American oil company executive and spent most of her adult life in New York City.

It was Grever's lifelong goal to bring Mexican music to American culture. She wanted to introduce new audiences to the collision of its Spanish and indigenous elements. The songs in *Viva O'Brien* both embrace this ("Mozambamba," "Carinito," "Yucatana") and also play on the foundations of musical comedy to give the Broadway audience humor they could recognize ("Don Jose O'Brien," "Wrap Me in Your Sarape"). While there are many María Grever recordings, there are no known recordings of *Viva O'Brien*.

---

1. Dietz, Dan. *The Complete Book of 1940s Broadway Musicals*. Rowman & Littlefield Publishers, 2015. With this note, Dietz actually singles out what the most decried musicals of the 1940s were—and three of them are featured in this chapter: *Viva O'Brien*, *The Girl from Nantucket*, and *The Duchess Misbehaves*. With the tiny percentage of Broadway musicals that had female writers, what are the odds that three would make up such a large percentage of the most sieged upon musicals? Were critics and audiences reacting, even subconsciously to the fact that the shows had women at the helm? Or was it something else?

2. Eleanor Wells was only twenty-four years old when she cowrote the book to *Viva O'Brien* with her husband who was in his late sixties.

3. Mantle, Burns. "'Viva O'Brien' Has Nice Score, No Wit." *Daily News*, 19 October 1941, p. 18.

MARION JONES FARQUHAR
Olympic Tennis Champion

Marion Farquhar was first represented on a Broadway stage with her libretto for a new version of *Princess and the Pea*, titled as such, and presented by the WPA as part of its opera initiative. This was more than two decades before *Once Upon a Mattress*, also based on that story, hit Broadway. In 1936, the WPA presented a few of its operas at the Biltmore, and Farquhar was one of their writers.

The 1866 Jacques Offenbach operetta *La vie parisienne* was revived on Broadway in 1941 and 1942 with new translated lyrics by Farquhar. At the helm was the New Opera Company. When they presented *The Maid as Mistress* and *The Secret of Suzanne* as a double bill on Broadway for two performances in 1944, Farquhar was on hand for lyrics as well.

Farquhar tops the list as far as Broadway writers with striking careers in other fields. She was an award-winning tennis player who won the US championship for Women's Singles Tennis in 1899 and 1902. In 1900, she became the first woman to win an Olympic medal.

MOLLY PICON
The First Lady of Yiddish Theatre

Molly Picon was a Yiddish theatre and film star who became a marquee name and one of the top celebrities in her field.

Picon, a daughter of Jewish immigrants from Poland, got her start as a child actor of the Yiddish Theatre in Philadelphia in the 1910s. In the early twentieth century, Yiddish Theatre was notably separate from mainstream theatre productions. Professionals might have entire careers in the Yiddish Theatre without ever setting foot in an English-speaking venue. Jewish citizens, many first-generation Americans, flocked to these theaters, seeking a connection with their heritage by consuming relevant cultural entertainment with like-minded patrons.

Molly Picon, circa 1958. BY UNKNOWN PHOTOGRAPHER/ WILLIAM MORRIS AGENCY (MANAGEMENT)/ WIKIMEDIA COMMONS

Picon thrived as a performer and eventually writer and celebrity personality during the hey-day of the Yiddish Theatre and also in the era where the genre became integrated with mainstream theatre projects.

While she didn't make her Broadway debut until 1940 when she was forty-two years old, appearing in a play called *Morning Star*, Picon technically had a presence in Broadway theaters earlier than that. Her Yiddish musical comedy film *Yiddle with His Fiddle* was a headliner event at the Ambassador Theatre in 1937, when it was a movie house. Later, one of her most famous film appearances would be as Yente the Matchmaker in *Fiddler on the Roof*, adapted from the landmark Broadway musical.

Up until the 1940s, Picon never appeared on the English-language stage. But after *Morning Star*, she appeared in several Broadway shows up until 1977. For her second, *Oy Is Dus a Leben!* in 1942, she not only starred but also wrote lyrics. The show is an autobiographical musical that tells stories first about the legends of the Yiddish stage, and then about Picon's own career and life. Her husband, Jacob Kalich, wrote the book and also directed and performed, and their frequent collaborator Joseph Rumshinsky wrote the music. The three had created many shows together for the Yiddish theaters on Second Avenue but this was their first venture together uptown. It was a success, in the midst of World War II in 1942, and Jewish theatergoers flocked to see a Picon appearance on 58th Street and 7th Avenue.

The theater that *Oy Is Dus a Leben!* played at was actually named the Molly Picon Theatre, one of the few Broadway houses to be named for a woman throughout theatre history. The house, which originally opened in 1921 as Jolson's 59th Street Theatre for Al Jolson, had a short life, only active as a Broadway theater from 1921 until 1954. It was only known as the Molly Picon Theatre while *Oy Is Dus a Leben!* played there. The theater was best known as the New Century Theatre, which was its final name and what it was called when it housed its biggest hit, *Kiss Me, Kate* from 1948 to 1950.

In the *New York Times*, Brooks Atkinson commented on Picon's crossover moment, performing for the Broadway audience after an already extensive career downtown on the Yiddish stage. He noted that audiences loved her and that "although Broadway is not Second Avenue, Yiddish can be understood uptown, too."[4] Atkinson hypothesized that the decrease in demand for Yiddish theatre might be because of American immigration quotas. But he also thought another reason could be that former Yiddish theatre patrons were now attending Broadway shows instead, due to attractions including Picon.

It was reviews like this that paved the way for Picon's continuing crossover efforts, bringing the legacy of Yiddish theatre more into the mainstream. While she was largely labeled a performer and not a writer, her creative fingerprint was always present when she was headlining a show. Because so much of her comedy and variety material was in her own voice, she collaborated with the writers of her

---

4. Atkinson, Brooks. "Molly Picon in *Oy Is Dus a Leben*, Musical Comedy about Her Career." *New York Times*, 13 October 1942, https://timesmachine.nytimes.com/timesmachine/1942/10/13/85055270.html?pageNumber=19.

shows in a fluid way. She also hosted radio shows, wrote books, and made count-less appearances as herself, in addition to continuing to perform in film, theatre, and television until she was in her nineties. She was a pioneer as a female Jewish comedian, and she paved the way for many others.

MARJERY FIELDING
Sixteen Shows a Week on Broadway

Marjery Fielding was a Broadway choreographer who worked on five Broadway musicals between 1935 and 1944 including the infamous spectacle *Jumbo*.

On one of these shows, she also worked as composer and lyricist. This was *Priorities of 1942*, a surprise hit at the 46th Street Theatre that combined vaude-ville and variety and ended up running 353 performances. Of course, it racked up showings at twice the rate of a regular Broadway production since *Priorities of 1942* played sixteen shows a week. There were two shows every day plus an extra matinee every Sunday and a midnight show on Saturdays. This meant an eight-show weekend!

Fielding wrote the songs for The Versailles Beauties with Charles Barnes. The Versailles Beauties was the name for the ensemble of women in the show.

Fielding had gotten her start writing as well as choreographing local shows in Miami, Florida, for Milton Berle.

BETTY COMDEN
The Longest-Running Writing Team in Broadway History

One of the most prolific, successful, and bril-liant musical theatre writers of the twentieth century, Betty Comden was a musical comedy icon. With Adolph Green, Betty Comden was responsible for many beloved musicals on stage and screen from the 1940s through the 1990s. Comden and Green, who were inducted into the Songwriters Hall of Fame

Betty Comden with Adolph Green, circa 1945. PHOTOFEST

in 1980, were called by the organization "the longest running creative partnership in theatre history."[5]

Comden was a first-generation American whose parents were Jewish immi-grants from Russia. She graduated from NYU in 1938, having studied drama,

---

5. "Betty Comden." Songwriters Hall of Fame, https://web.archive.org/web/20101023061431/http://songwritershalloffame.org/exhibits/C59.

and that same year she met Green. Together with Leonard Bernstein, John Frank, Alvin Hammer, and Judy Holliday (then credited as Judith Tuvim), Comden and Green formed a group called The Revuers who performed a club act at the Village Vanguard downtown. Their original comedy and songs gained notice and they had a small role in a 1944 movie called *Greenwich Village*. Later that year, Comden and Green made their Broadway debut and quite a splash with the landmark musical *On the Town*.

On the Town, about three sailors on leave for one day in Manhattan and the three captivating women they meet, is a fresh and dynamic musical that introduced Comden and Green to New York as both musical theatre writers and actors. Vividly relatable for theatergoers who had spent the past few years with loved ones at war, and some who had been at war themselves, *On the Town* is an uplifting and thrilling musical comedy that also plumbs the depths of what it meant in 1944 to be living in the moment, treasuring each experience since time might be limited.

Comden and Green wrote both book and lyrics to the music of Leonard Bernstein, and they starred as Ozzie and Claire, who fall for each other in comedic fashion at the Museum of Natural History but are kept apart by Claire's esteemed fiancé for the bulk of the story. Songs that Comden and Green wrote for *On the Town* included "New York, New York," "Come Up to My Place," "I Can Cook Too," and "Some Other Time." The show was a major hit, if a scrappy one, and was adapted for Hollywood in 1949, including only part of the score, and with Comden and Green writing the screenplay. *On the Town* remains one of the most revived shows from the 1940s.

Comden and Green's next Broadway venture, *Billion Dollar Baby*, opened in 1945 and was not a smash, running for half a year. Their next Broadway show *Bonanza Bound* closed out of town, so Comden and Green spent much of the rest of the decade on the West Coast. In addition to adapting *On the Town*, they were also responsible for writing the film versions of *Good News* (1947) and *The Barkleys of Broadway* (1949). Comden and Green had wildly successful careers in film in addition to their Broadway careers. They also wrote *Singin' in the Rain* (1952), *The Band Wagon* (1953), *It's Always Fair Weather* (1955), *Auntie Mame* (1958), and *Bells Are Ringing* (1960).

The seven films above found Comden and Green writing for some of the biggest stars of their day including Fred Astaire, Ginger Rogers, Frank Sinatra, Gene Kelly, Cyd Charisse, Donald O'Connor, Debbie Reynolds, June Allyson, Peter Lawford, Rosalind Russell, Judy Holliday, and Dean Martin. For their film work, they would win multiple Screenwriters Guild Awards and be nominated for multiple Academy Awards. Of course, their work was seen on screen also in multiple made-for-television movies like *Wonderful Town* (1958) and *Peter Pan* (1960). Their writing for film was notably personal; they based the characters in the backstager *The Band Wagon* on themselves and often incorporated real-life events that they had heard about or experienced into their writing, especially when they were creating stories about show business. While Comden and Green spent their career writing largely for characters in book musicals or plot-driven films, they built a bridge between the variety revue elements of the last era and the importance of story in mid- and late twentieth-century musical entertainment.

Comden and Green's first Broadway show since *Billion Dollar Baby* in 1945 was *Two on the Aisle* in 1951, a spirited revue where they collaborated with Jule Styne for the first time in the theatre. It was to be their only true variety revue on Broadway. They were the sole book and lyric writers for the show, which starred Dolores Gray and Bert Lahr. Gray gained acclaim for her showstopper "If," which showed off Comden and Green's talents for rapid-fire lyrics paired with quirky character details, wedded perfectly to the music of their collaborator.

In 1953, Comden and Green wrote the lyrics for *Wonderful Town*, with book by Joseph A. Fields and Jerome Chodorov, and music by Leonard Bernstein. The show, based on Fields and Chodorov's play *My Sister Eileen*, was itself based on the autobiographical stories of Ruth McKenney. McKenney shared tales of her adventures with her younger sister Eileen. The two move to New York City from Ohio, Ruth to be a writer and Eileen an actress. The Broadway musical version of their story, starring Rosalind Russell, won the Best Musical Tony Award. Again, Comden and Green got to show off their skill for writing for characters who were young, contemporary New Yorkers following their dreams. Their wit was a distinctive trademark, but they could also capture a certain melancholy and longing in their lyrics that humanized their characters.

Comden and Green, who collaborated for sixty years, functioned as one unit. Throughout their career, there were no theatrical projects that one would do without the other. They were always a duo. Comden did write an autobiography called *Off Stage*, a fantastic personal tome that chronicles her career and personal life—with a significant focus on the latter. About the book, the *Democrat and Chronicle* noted, "Her adult life, [Comden] writes in *Off Stage*, has been a constant struggle to balance the demands of family and career. She and her husband had two children, Susanna and Alan, but Comden was often away. Perhaps the two greatest losses of her life were the deaths of Steven and Alan: her husband to pancreatitis in 1979 and her son to drugs when he was still in his twenties."[6]

Comden navigated her personal struggles and tragedies, while never taking a full step back from writing or her creative partnership. When it came to musicals, films, songs, and any other form of entertainment writing, Comden and Green were an inseparable team.

---

6. Lasser, Michael. "On the Town." *Democrat and Chronicle*, 13 January 1996, p. 21.

In 1954, Comden and Green contributed lyrics to *Peter Pan* starring Mary Martin. The show, rare for a 1950s book musical, essentially had two writing teams. With Jule Styne, Comden and Green wrote "Neverland," "Distant Melody" and several other tunes, and the other half of the score was written by Moose Charlap and Carolyn Leigh. In 1955, *Peter Pan* became the first full-length Broadway production shown on color TV, breaking records as far as viewership.

Comden and Green's next major musical after *Peter Pan* was *Bells Are Ringing*. They reunited with their Revuers buddy Judy Holliday, who led the show as Ella, an answering service operator. The spirited, funny Ella was inspired by Green's own answering service operator. Many of Comden and Green's characters feel like real New Yorkers that one might meet on the street or at a party, and many of them have elements that were pulled from real life. For *Bells are Ringing*, Comden and Green wrote book as well as lyrics. With their frequent collaborator Jule Styne, they came up with beautiful ballads like "Long Before I Knew You," "Just in Time," and "The Party's Over"—although the show is largely an upbeat romp, with many comedic character numbers. It was in *Bells Are Ringing* that theatergoers first got a major glimpse of one Comden and Green trademark: an unbreakable heroine declaration 11 o'clock number, which in this case was "I'm Going Back." This would later recur in moments like *Fade Out—Fade In*'s "Go Home Train" and *Hallelujah, Baby!*'s "I Wanted to Change Him," among others.

In 1958, Comden and Green wrote lyrics for songs that appeared in the hit play *Say, Darling*. All of their songs are diegetic, as the show is about the making of a musical. Richard Bissell wrote the book that the musical *The Pajama Game* was based on. Then he wrote a book about the experience of adapting *The Pajama Game* into a musical from his book—and this was made into the show *Say, Darling!*

Later that year, Comden and Green made a splash on Broadway in *A Party with Betty Comden and Adolph Green*. In this intimate revue featuring the two as themselves, Comden and Green regaled audiences with sketches and songs from throughout their career so far. The show actually began off-Broadway, but even on Broadway, in a bigger house, the two made the theater feel like a living room cocktail party. They returned to Broadway with the show in 1977, updating it with new material they'd written in the interim. In performing their own work, most of which they'd written for actors, they gave rise to a new era of musical theatre writer-performer hybrids. They weren't the first musical theatre writers to commercially perform their work—on the contrary, there were many of their contemporaries who did this, such as Cy Coleman, who often gave concerts with himself on keys and vocals. But Comden and Green were pioneers in crafting entertainment personalities that were an indelible part of their public persona as writers.

In the 1960s, Comden and Green wrote four Broadway musicals. None were smash hits, none were outright flops, and all were filled with hilarious writing, lovable characters, and memorable songs. There was *Do Re Mi* (1960) about a con man who goes into the jukebox business, filled with swinging tunes and Borscht Belt cracks. In 1961 came the unique *Subways Are for Sleeping*, best remembered now for its David Merrick advertising stunt. When the show received mediocre reviews, Merrick took out an ad with rave critics' quotes—from a slew of men who happened to have the same names as the major critics, and who were wined and dined at *Subways Are for Sleeping* before being asked to sign their name to positive reviews. The show had a Tony Award-winning performance by the brilliant Phyllis Newman, Green's wife and later mother of musical theatre writer Amanda Green. *Fade Out—Fade In* in 1964 was a star vehicle for Carol Burnett as Hope Springfield, a would-be starlet trying to make it in glamorous 1930s Hollywood. The show was dependent on Burnett and stymied by an injury she incurred and her subsequent absences. Unlike almost all of Comden and Green's other musicals, flops and hits alike, *Fade Out—Fade In* is almost never revived. This is not for any substantial reason, as the material is superb, with the heroine's numbers particularly rousing. Comden and Green's last musical of the 1960s was *Hallelujah, Baby!*, a musical that has the odd distinction of being the only Broadway show to ever win the Best Musical Tony Award prize after having already closed. The exploration of race in America and the fight for equality is told through the lens of one character who remains the same age even as the decades of the twentieth century move forward around her. This role was originally played by the great Leslie Uggams, and the show catapulted her to stardom. It had a book by Arthur Laurents and was directed by Burt Shevelove. Jule Styne wrote the music for all four of Comden and Green's 1960s musicals.

Often asked about their writing process as a team, Comden and Green would share that typically, Green would arrive at Comden's apartment in the morning and the two would stare at each other until they came up with a good idea. A 1976 *Philadelphia Daily News* article, on the cusp of their new production of *A Party with Betty Comden and Adolph Green*, shared, "Betty Comden is, you learn, the tough cookie, the steadfast plugger of the partnership. She can rationalize away a flop, or inactivity, faster than you can raise the sore subjects. 'We've developed the philosophy that nothing's ever a waste of time, and that there are never any guarantees in this business. The more ambitious the project, the bigger its risks. . . . And in the theater, you never know what the public's going to like tomorrow. You can only write what you are, what you express,' [Comden said]. The article goes on to describe Green as 'the comparative softy, the romantic of the team.'"[7]

The 1970s were kicked off with *Applause*, a musical adaptation of the beloved film *All about Eve* which found Comden and Green again hitting it out of the

---

7. Takiff, Jonathan. "Song Writing's a Party for Comden and Green." *Philadelphia Daily News*, 17 December 1976, p. 44.

park with a behind-the-scenes show biz story. Their songs for leading lady Lauren Bacall capitalized on what Bacall could do well, which wasn't sing like a typical musical comedy star but rather carry songs on personality. The show won Best Musical at the Tony Awards. By the end of their career, this was a distinction that four of their shows would receive (*Wonderful Town, Hallelujah, Baby!, Applause,* and *The Will Rogers Follies*). They won Best Score for all four of those, and won it for *On the Twentieth Century* as well.

The year 1971 saw the first major Comden and Green revival. *On The Town* received its second Broadway production, with a stacked cast including Donna McKechnie, Phyllis Newman, Bernadette Peters, and Marilyn Cooper. The revival had only a short run. A 1998 Broadway revival, a transfer from the Public's Delacorte Theatre off-Broadway in the park, ran for about the same amount of time, but was more publicly acclaimed, featuring performances from Lea DeLaria, Jesse Tyler Ferguson, Jose Llana, Annie Golden, Mary Testa, Jonathan Freeman, Robert Montano, and Perry Laylon Ojeda. The most successful Broadway revival came in 2014, running for a year at Broadway's mammoth Lyric Theatre and starring Jay Armstrong Johnson, Tony Yazbeck, Alysha Umphress, Clyde Alves, Megan Fairchild, Allison Guinn, Jackie Hoffman, Michael Rupert, and Elizabeth Stanley. Other major revivals of Comden and Green shows on Broadway include *Peter Pan* (1979, 1990, 1991, 1998, 1999), *Bells Are Ringing* (2001), *Wonderful Town* (2003), and *On the Twentieth Century* (2015).

In 1974, Comden and Green contributed lyrics for a small handful of songs to *Lorelei*, a stage musical remake of *Gentlemen Prefer Blondes*. They then conceived, with Norman L. Berman, an off-Broadway musical tribute to their collaborator Leonard Bernstein, called *By Bernstein*. It was Comden and Green's first of two times working on a new musical for off-Broadway. The other instance was in 1985 when they contributed two songs written with Cy Coleman to Hal Prince's revue about baseball, *Diamonds*.

On the Twentieth Century, Comden and Green's second and only other original Broadway musical in the 1970s after *Applause*, is a 1920s screwball farce, art deco in musical form, with music by Cy Coleman and original direction by Hal Prince. It follows the Twentieth Century Limited train on a cross-country journey as the dramatic personalities inside clash with comic opera style. The show largely concerns egocentric producer Oscar Jaffe and mercurial actress Lily Garland, former lovers and idiosyncratic personalities.

Comden and Green were also represented on Broadway in the 1970s with the one-woman show *The Madwoman of Central Park West*, starring Phyllis Newman. They wrote the opening number, "Up! Up! Up!" for this revue where Newman played a fictional version of herself.

Comden and Green's biggest flop to date came in 1982: *A Doll's Life*. This musical sequel to *A Doll's House* was a concept that many thought the team ill-suited for. The Hal Prince–directed musical received negative reviews, and all elements of the show were blamed for its short run of only five performances. With composer Larry Grossman, the team tried to tell a story of Nora during a new era for feminism, but the pieces did not come together satisfactorily.

In 1983, Comden appeared as an actor in the Wendy Wasserstein play *Isn't It Romantic* off-Broadway. Comden did start out as a performer and in fact won a Theatre World Award for her performance in *On the Town*, but *Isn't It Romantic* was one of only two major New York appearances she made performing words that were not her own. The other happened in 1985 when she and Green sang "Rain on the Roof" in the New York Philharmonic special concert performance of Stephen Sondheim and James Goldman's *Follies*.

In 1985, *Singin' in the Rain* was adapted for the Broadway stage. For the first time, Comden and Green found themselves working on a theatrical property that they had created first for film. For this show, Comden and Green adapted their screenplay into the musical's book, while the only lyric that was theirs was "Moses Supposes." The show ran for about a year.

The final original musical Comden and Green premiered on Broadway was a smash: *The Will Rogers Follies*. The team was in their seventies when this Cy Coleman–composed retrospective celebration of Will Rogers's life opened in 1991 and won the Best Musical Tony Award during a competitive year that also included *Miss Saigon*, *The Secret Garden*, and *Once on This Island*. Comden and Green wrote spirited lyrics and collaborated with book writer Peter Stone and director Tommy Tune to bring the humorist, performer, and politician who exemplified Americana to life. The show was originally written for John Denver, but wound up starring Keith Carradine. Comden and Green and Coleman won the Tony for Best Score for their work with numbers like "Will-a-mania," "Give a Man Enough Rope," "Our Favorite Son" and "Never Met a Man I Didn't Like." The show ran for nearly one thousand performances. That year, Comden and Green also received Kennedy Center Honors.

Green died in 2002 and Comden in 2006. Their work has lived on powerfully ever since. Their songs are still in the public conscious and often heard in new movies and television. "Some Other Time" and "Just in Time" are two of the most oft used, leading one to realize just how well Comden and Green wrote about time itself: seizing the moment, making each day glorious, and the sweet sadness that comes with knowing it's all fleeting.

Revivals of their work continue to be seen in New York and all over the globe, and of course their original recordings and media live on. Comden and Green's legacy is also felt in the theatre industry via the proliferation of writer-performer personalities that emerged in the generations that followed them. Green's daughter, musical theatre writer Amanda Green is just one example of a musical theatre writer who does not only sit in the back of the theatre but is also known for skilled and spirited performances of their own work. Comden and Green are also often used as an archetype, whether conscious or not, when fictional writing teams for musicals are being dramatized.

Betty Comden and Adolph Green can't be separated as far as their contributions go. They functioned as a successful and unbreakable team for many decades, to the credit of them both. They were sometimes mistaken for a couple, although they were never romantically involved and both were happily married to others. They were creative partners and close friends, two halves of the same storytelling brain.

KAY TWOMEY
Misunderstood Show about a Captain's Painting

Kay Twomey was mostly known for her 1947 hit song "Serenade of the Bells," which spent sixteen weeks on the charts, as well as for her work writing songs for Elvis Presley, from his 1960 film *G.I. Blues* onward. These successes came after a great personal disappointment: the twelve-performance run of her 1945 Broadway musical *The Girl from Nantucket*.

Twomey, who had always dreamed of writing songs, was the main lyricist on *The Girl from Nantucket*. Twomey wrote the majority of the lyrics for this musical about a Captain whose past heroics are supposed to be immortalized on a sophisticated town mural—only a house painter is accidentally hired. Most critics didn't bother to describe the plot, which also involved the Captain's nieces and their love interests.

In the *Daily News*, John Chapman wrote, "To a lover like myself of the American musical comedy, this show is 90% torture. Its lyrics, by Kay Twomey, are so desperately smart, they hurt."[8]

David Camelon dramatized the final day of *The Girl from Nantucket* in a piece about Twomey. "Kay Twomey walked slowly from the deserted theatre for the last time—into the raw November cold of a Broadway night. Overhead, workmen stripped from the marquee the last of the lights that had spelled *The Girl from Nantucket*—the musical comedy into whose lyrics she had poured her heart. . . . About her . . . swirled friendly, laughing crowds. But Kay . . . could think only of failure—of the barbed words that had torn the life out of the show, and, in doing so, had torn away something of her heart, her hopes, her courage—until she had nothing left."[9]

The article went on to explain Twomey's troubled childhood, where she had almost died of rheumatic fever, her inability to write after the disappointment of

---

8. Chapman, John. "*Girl from Nantucket* Is Season's Low for Musicals, and That's Low." *Daily News*, 10 November 1945, p. 99.

9. Camelon, David. "The Faith of Kay Twomey." *Pittsburgh Sun-Telegraph*, 26 September 1948, p. 82.

The Girl closing, meaning that she could not support her sister and mother who depended on her, and the fact that publishers began turning her down because of her flop Broadway show. She went to Florida, where she had previously recovered from her rheumatic fever, pulled herself together, came back to New York, and wrote "Serenade of the Bells."

While Twomey never returned to Broadway, her songs were performed by everyone from the Beatles ("Lend Me Your Comb") to Frank Sinatra ("Hey! Jealous Lover").

TRUDE RITTMAN
Golden Age Arranger

The right-hand woman of Rodgers and Hammerstein's music team, Trude Rittman was one of the top arrangers during the Golden Age of Broadway. She created arrangements or music for all of the following shows in their original productions: *Carousel, Finian's Rainbow, Allegro, Gentlemen Prefer Blondes, Peter Pan, The King and I, Paint Your Wagon, My Fair Lady, The Sound of Music,* and *Camelot.* She was also credited varyingly on other shows as assistant to Richard Rodgers (*South Pacific*), music assistant to Agnes de Mille (*Brigadoon*), rehearsal pianist (*Billion Dollar Baby*), musical continuity (*Wish You Were Here, Fanny, On a Clear Day You Can See Forever*), and more.

And, in fact, Rittman wrote for several Broadway musicals as well.

A refugee from Nazi Germany, Rittman was an immensely talented composer in her own right. While her credits may not reflect it at first glance, she created the "Small House of Uncle Thomas" sequence for *The King and I* and the vocal sequence in "Do Re Mi" for *The Sound of Music.* The majority of Rodgers and Hammerstein's brilliant Broadway musicals were bolstered and improved musically by her hand.

"Rodgers sometimes chafed at Trude Rittman's elaborations on his melodies in her dance and vocal arrangements, insisting at one point, "It's *Rodgers* and Hammerstein, not Rittman and Hammerstein," according to *Something Wonderful: Rodgers and Hammerstein's Broadway Revolution* by Todd Purdum.[10]

Rittman entered the collaborative kingdom of the two most popular writers on Broadway through choreographer Agnes de Mille, whom she first worked with on a concert in 1941. Rittman and de Mille worked in tandem to craft the dance sequences for many shows. They were not always credited originally for their work, in which they were often the only women in the room. To Rodgers

---

10. Purdum, Todd. *Something Wonderful: Rodgers and Hammerstein's Broadway Revolution.* New York: Henry Holt and Co., 2018.

and Hammerstein's credit, many creative. teams on Broadway had no women in the room at all.

Later in life, Rittman told the *Boston Globe* a story about a later collaboration with Richard Rodgers, *Two by Two*, in 1971. She was vocal and dance arranger, and a new male orchestrator was treating her poorly in creative meetings. Richard Rodgers said to Rittman, "He's afraid of you. Sometimes I'm afraid of you too."[11]

"Isn't that cute?" a then eighty-nine-year-old Rittman commented to the *Globe*.

GLADYS SHELLEY
Misunderstood Show about Goya

Known as The First Lady of Tin Pan Alley, Gladys Shelley actually started out as a poet. Her poetry gained some attention at the New York World's Fair in 1939, and soon she was writing songs as well.

With over three-thousand songs penned in her lifetime, Shelley worked with everyone from Nat King Cole to Fred Astaire. She wrote the theme song for Palisades Amusement Park, which was owned by her husband Irving Rosenthal. While she was writing, Shelley also had a career as a Broadway actor.

Her one Broadway musical credit as a writer came in 1946 with the musical *The Duchess Misbehaves*. Shelley wrote both book and lyrics to the music of Frank Black for this show about Francisco Goya, the famous Spanish painter of the eighteenth and early nineteenth centuries. The plot of *The Duchess Misbehaves* follows a modern-day man hit over the head at an art exhibit, inspiring an adventure where he thinks he is Francisco Goya.

Jackie Gleason quit the night before opening and was replaced by journeyman actor Joey Faye in the lead role of Goya. The show was served abysmal reviews all around and closed after five performances at the Adelphi.

Shelley wrote the lyrics to the finale number for a play with music about Prohibition called *Johnny 2 x 4* that played the Longacre in 1942. She also wrote lyrics for a revue that closed out of town in 1944: *Vincent Youmans' Fiesta*. The show, which had a different title in each town it played before closing on the road, had one of the largest losses of capital for a musical to date.

---

11. Hartigan, Patti. "A Lifetime of Stories from Musical Theater." *Boston Globe*, 3 October 1997, p. 51.

SYLVIA DEE
"Chickery Chick" Writer Pens Teen Show

Sylvia Dee was a songwriter whose hits included "The End of the World" and "Bring Me Sunshine," still heard on film soundtracks and in popular culture otherwise, today. But perhaps her most well-known contribution was "Chickery Chick," a tune many children still learn in their first music classes.

Dee's one foray into Broadway writing was *Barefoot Boy with Cheek*, where her lyrics were set to music by Sidney Lippman. The 1947 musical was produced and directed by George Abbott and starred Nancy Walker and Red Buttons. Based on book writer Max Shulman's stories about college life at the University of Minnesota, the show was in many ways a typical Abbott affair; a musical about young people is a regular occurrence on Broadway now, but in the 1940s, this was an Abbott specialty. *Barefoot Boy with Cheek* was predated by *Babes in Arms* and *Too Many Girls*. This was before the cult of the teenager took over American culture and Broadway was transformed in the 1960s by hits like *Bye Bye Birdie* and *Hair*.

Barefoot Boy with Cheek received lukewarm reviews. Brooks Atkinson concluded his by saying: "In his association with embryo citizens Mr. Abbott has had more real fun in the past."[12] The show played out 108 performances at the Martin Beck (today the Al Hirschfeld).

MIRIAM BATTISTA
The Sleepy Hollow Musical

Miriam Battista appeared in more than fifteen Broadway shows as a performer before her sole credit writing book and lyrics for a Broadway musical. Only two of the productions she appeared in were musicals: *Hot-Cha!* (1932) and *Fools Rush In* (1934). She started life as a child actor both on stage and screen and gained fans through movies where she was dubbed "Little Miriam." Her Broadway debut came at the age of three when she appeared in *A Kiss for Cinderella* starring Maude Adams.

Miriam Battista, circa 1932. BY MURRAY KOR-MAN/ WIKIMEDIA COMMONS

In 1948, Battista penned *Sleepy Hollow* with her husband, Russell Maloney, who joined her in writing the words, and George Lessner, who composed the

---

12. Atkinson, Brooks. "The New Play: *Barefoot Boy with Cheek*: Abbott's Musical Comedy at the Martin Beck Seen as Another Class Reunion on a Dear Old College Campus." *New York Times*, 4 April 1947, p. 20.

music. The show was the first production to play the St. James after *Oklahoma!* closed, having achieved a five-year run. The adaptation of the classic Washington Irving story about Ichabod Crane is as spooky and spirited as its source material, but it didn't manage to run. Despite praise for the score, most reviews were not pleased with the show overall and it only played twelve performances. *Sleepy Hollow* was followed into the St. James by *Where's Charley?* which ran for two years.

Battista and Maloney also cohosted a television talk show called *The Maloneys*.

EUDORA WELTY
A Skit about the Breevort

Eudora Welty was a Pulitzer Prize–winning writer and photographer. She won the Presidential Medal of Freedom and was the first living writer to have her work cataloged by the Library of Congress.

Welty's best-known contribution to the musical theatre is *The Robber Bridegroom.* Her 1942 debut novel of the same title became the 1975 Broadway musical. As far as a hands-on contribution to musical theatre, Welty had only one of those on Broadway. In 1956, a sketch that she wrote appeared in *The Littlest Revue*. In her biography about Welty, *Eudora: A Writer's Life*, Ann Waldron explained how that came about.

"One evening when she was in New York, Eudora was sitting in Schrafft's at Fifth Avenue and Thirteenth Street with Hildegarde Dolson. . . . The two women agreed that the current Broadway musicals were so bad they could do better, and they decided to spend the summer of 1948 collaborating on their own musical."

"Writing a musical with a plot was 'too much trouble,' they decided, so they settled on a series of skits, each to be written by only one of them."[13]

The revue they wrote was called *What Year Is This?* They couldn't get the show produced, but one of Welty's skits did make it into a 1949 revue called *Lo and Behold* that played the Red Barn Playhouse in Massachusetts. This was "Bye-Bye, Breevort" about the hotel on 8th Street and 5th Avenue that had once been a haven for Bohemians and artists and had recently been demolished amid much fanfare. *Lo and Behold* did not move on but "Bye, Bye, Breevort" found its way into *The Littlest Revue* at the Phoenix.

---

13. Waldron, Ann. *Eudora: A Writer's Life*. New York: Anchor Books, 1999.

ANITA LOOS
Gentlemen Prefer Blondes

Anita Loos is best remembered today as author of the 1925 novel *Gentlemen Prefer Blondes*, which has been adapted numerous times for stage and screen. She was also an amazingly prolific writer for stage and screen otherwise. She was the first female staff scriptwriter in Hollywood. Between the 1910s and 1950s, Loos racked up over two hundred movie credits as a writer.

On Broadway, Loos wrote seven plays. One of these was the original play version of *Gentlemen Prefer Blondes* in 1926, another was 1931's *The Social Register*, which she also staged, another was the long-running hit *Happy Birthday* in 1946, and a fourth was *Gigi* in 1951, which gave Audrey Hepburn a big break.

In 1949, Loos made her one foray into the Broadway musical when she collaborated with Joseph Fields on the book for the *Gentlemen Prefer Blondes* musical, with music by Jule Styne and lyrics by Leo Robin. The show was revived on Broadway in 1995, but not before receiving a Broadway remake as *Lorelei* in 1974—with new lyrics by Betty Comden and Adolph Green and a new book by Kenny Solms and Gail Parent. The musical introduced the song "Diamonds Are a Girl's Best Friend" and made a star of Carol Channing.

JEAN KERR
Successful Theatre Writer, Successful Book Writer, and Partner of Critic

Like many female writers, Jean Kerr was often referred to both publicly and privately as being best known for her attachment to a male writer. The wife of longtime *New York Herald Tribune* and *New York Times* theatre critic Walter Kerr, Jean Kerr was very much a successful writer in her own right, who wrote Broadway shows as well as comedic essays.

Kerr's biggest hit on the stage was *Mary, Mary*, the record-breaking play that ran 1,572 performances after premiering in 1961. *Mary, Mary* is a comedy about a recently divorced couple who have to deal with their taxes together and wind up locked in an apartment during a snowstorm with a farcical cast of characters. Kerr was the show's sole playwright.

Prior to *Mary, Mary*, Kerr made her Broadway debut with a short-lived play called *The Song of Bernadette* when she was only twenty-three years old, in 1946. She had already been married to Walter for two years—they met when he was her professor at the Catholic University of America and were married soon after. The Kerrs eventually had six children, and Kerr stayed very active as a writer throughout her time raising children—a definite rarity among women who wrote for the theatre in the 1940s.

Kerr's debut as a writer for musical theatre came in 1949 when she collaborated with Walter on both lyrics and sketches for the revue *Touch and Go*. Unlike almost every other major theatre critic of the twentieth century, Walter Kerr not only wrote *about* theatre, but he also *wrote* theatre. In this instance, he also directed the successful production which played the Broadhurst and then the Broadway for a total of five months and starred Nancy Andrews and Helen Gallagher. Rare for a revue, the Kerrs were the show's only lyric and sketch writers. The music was by Jay Gorney, and ballet music was by Genevieve Pitot. *Touch and Go* largely focused on spoofing current show business hits and was additionally memorable because it marked the Broadway debut of Hal Prince, who acted as the show's stage manager and even went on for a performance as an understudy.

Kerr wrote seven plays that landed on Broadway between 1946 and 1980, and was involved in the writing of three musicals. After *Touch and Go* came *John Murray Anderson's Almanac* in 1953, for which Kerr was one of a handful of sketch writers. This was a venture without Walter. Kerr's two sketches for the show, titled *My Cousin Who?* and *Don Brown's Body* were part of a lineup that also included work from Harry Belafonte (who also appeared), Cy Coleman, Sheldon Harnick, and Richard Adler and Jerry Ross, all at the beginning of their careers.

Kerr's one book musical on Broadway was *Goldilocks*, for which she cowrote both book and lyrics with Walter (who also directed) in 1958. The show was not a success and is mainly remembered for the presence of its star, Elaine Stritch.

Goldilocks came right on the heels of Kerr's successful book *Please Don't Eat the Daisies* in 1957, a collection of comedic essays about life in the suburbs from a former woman of the city. *Please Don't Eat the Daisies* was the first of four books that Kerr would author. It would be adapted into a film in 1960.

It was *Please Don't Eat the Daisies* that led to Kerr getting attention in her own right as cowriter of *Goldilocks*. The *Albany Democrat-Herald* noted that Walter and Jean Kerr were relatively unknown until Jean Kerr wrote her first book. Then "they became known to everybody, as everybody near died in screams while reading" personal stories about the Kerrs' domestic life, raising their four sons. The piece called Jean Kerr "the drama critic's irrepressible frau."[14] The headline was "Those Kerrs Again—The Daisy Eaters Throw a Neat Fit." Because Jean Kerr wrote autobiographically about her family life married to a well-known fellow writer, and the essays performed so well, she was written about rather uniquely among theatre writers.

While *Goldilocks* was playing its pre-Broadway tryout in 1958, it received a *Boston Globe* profile on cowriter Kerr, choreographer Agnes de Mille (billed in the article as "dance instructor"), and Virginia Whitehead. The article by Elizabeth

---

14. Alexander, Charles. "Those Kerrs Again—The Daisy-Eaters Throw A Neat Fit." *Albany Democrat-Herald*, 21 February 1959, p. 6.

Bernkopf began by describing the three women working on *Goldilocks* as fitting well into the categories of big, middle-sized, and little bear. "Jean Kerr, coauthor with her husband Walter, is a nice husky size 18. Agnes DeMille, in charge of the dances, wears a pleasant 12 (or 11 or 13). And Virginia Whitehead, wife of producer Robert, who is a sort of gatherer-upper-of-loose-ends . . . tips the scales at 100 pounds, soaking wet, and fits cozily into a size 5."[15] Kerr wrote often in her essays about her own weight and body image.

The first two columns of the article covered the women's eating and drinking habits while working on shows out of town, and the next two covered their family lives, before getting into work habits. Kerr explained to the journalist that when writing alone, her office was "an old car parked several blocks from the house," so that she could have privacy and time away from Walter and their sons.

The oddly titled *Goldilocks* is not a musicalization of the fairy tale, but rather a story about the silent film era. Several stories in a few of Kerr's books were about the challenges and hilarity of creating this new musical.

15. Bernkopf, Elizabeth. "Women Authors Pick Craziest Spots for Writing." *Boston Globe*, 21 September 1958, p. 101.

7

1950s

Comedians, Radio Personalities, and Women at the Piano

LUCILLE KALLEN
The Only Woman Writing for Your Show of Shows

Lucille Kallen got her start writing radio plays. Then she worked her way up on the nightclub circuit, writing songs and sketches and playing the piano. She worked for several years putting together entertainment at Camp Tamiment, one of the main adult vacation spots that employed aspiring professionals in their theatre ventures. Over the years Camp Tamiment provided a training ground for Neil Simon, Carol Burnett, Jerome Robbins, and many more.

Kallen made history on television as the only female writer on Sid Caesar's *Your Show of Shows* staff from 1950 to 1954. When interviewed about the show later in life, she shared that her work was discovered at Camp Tamiment and the producers of a new TV show wanted to hire her, Sid Caesar, and Imogene Coca. "'At which point,' said Ms. Kallen, 'we all asked, "What is TV?"'"[1]

Right around the time her work on *Your Show of Shows* was beginning, Kallen also worked on two Broadway revues.

Alive and Kicking only eked out forty-six performances at the Winter Garden in 1950, but it is an important footnote in a lot of musical theatre history tales. The main reason is that the revue starred Gwen Verdon and was choreographed by Jack Cole, her influential early mentor and collaborator. Another is that the large group of writers involved included Sammy Fain, Hoagy Carmichael, Harold J. Rome, Jerome Chodorov, Joseph Stein, and many others. There were two women on the show's large writing staff: Irma Jurist, an arranger and composer, and Lucille Kallen.

Kallen only had one song in *Alive and Kicking*, and it was not presented at all performances, but she fared better on the next Broadway revue she worked on, *Tickets, Please!* which opened only three months later. *Tickets, Please!* starred revue stalwarts Grace and Paul Hartman and ran for 245 performances. Songs with lyrics by Kallen in the show include the title song, and the numbers "Washington Square," "Back at the Palace," "Symbol of Fire," and "Maha Roger." Among the topics *Tickets, Please!* spoofs are a Senate investigation, a musical comedy ballet, and a women's club lecture on cooking dumplings. The opening sketch is about how they'd originally called the show *South Pacific* but realized they had to change it when another show with that title opened; this leads directly into the title song of *Tickets, Please!* for which Kallen was one of the writers. The show's staff included a young assistant stage manager named Hal Prince.

Kallen's third and final Broadway credit was a play called *Maybe Tuesday* that she cowrote with her frequent musical theatre collaborator Mel Tolkin. Brooks Atkinson told *New York Times* readers how he felt: "[The writers assume] that

1. Bass, Milton R. "The Lively World." *Berkshire Eagle*, 10 July 1980, p. 10.

seven bachelor girls living together in a common apartment is hilarious and fraught with piquancy." Atkinson admitted that opening night audience members seemed to concur with the authors, based on their laughter and reactions. Kallen told a journalist on opening night, "Humor based on truth makes for audience identification." Atkinson overheard this and countered: "This department, lacking personal identification, believes that the nubility pangs of seven temporary spinsters are not ... funny."[2] *Maybe Tuesday* closed after only five showings.

In addition to many other television credits, Kallen was also a best-selling author of mystery novels. She was a book doctor on the 1963 Broadway musical *Sophie* and in 1969 she wrote the book when the Rodgers and Hammerstein musical *State Fair* made its stage debut at the MUNY.

JOAN EDWARDS
A Radio Star

Also contributing lyrics to *Tickets, Please!* was Joan Edwards. Edwards contributed music as well, and her songs in the revue were "Darn It, Baby, That's Love," "Restless," "You Can't Take It with You," "Television's Tough on Love," and "The Moment I Looked in Your Eyes." "Darn It, Baby, That's Love" was recorded by Eydie Gormé and Steve Lawrence as well as by Robert Goulet and Phyllis McGuire.

Edwards gained fame on the radio. She had her own show, *Girl about Town*, on CBS. She was also a soloist for *Your Hit Parade* for five years. She worked with Paul Whiteman and his orchestra and toured vaudeville houses as well as played nightclubs. While *Tickets, Please!* marked her only time working on Broadway, she also wrote songs for television, radio, nightclubs, and advertising.

DOROTHEA FREITAG
Woman at the Keys

Dorothea Freitag had a long theatre career as a dance arranger, music arranger, music coordinator, music director, conductor and musician. In these capacities, her credits included the original Broadway productions of *Tovarich*, *Golden Boy*, *I'm Solomon*, *Zorba*, *Dear World*, *70, Girls, 70*, and *Raisin*, as well as *Mod Donna*, off-Broadway. From 1948 to 1978, she was an in-demand woman at the keys in theaters on and off Broadway.

---

2. Atkinson, Brooks. "Theatre: Bachelor Girls: *Maybe Tuesday* New Playhouse Comedy." *New York Times*, 30 January 1958, p. 18.

In addition, Freitag wrote for a few shows. In 1950, she composed several of the songs for the Broadway dance revue *Katherine Dunham and Her Company*. In 1956, she composed, arranged, and played the music of a one-woman show called *Autobiography* starring Irene Hawthorne. In 1957, Freitag wrote several songs for a Leonard Sillman two-piano revue on Broadway called *Mask and Gown* and also acted as music director, arranger, and pianist. While it only ran for thirty-nine performances, *Mask and Gown* did receive a cast album.

In a write-up of *Mask and Gown*, the *Chicago Tribune* called Freitag "a kind of 'Girl Friday' who does the conducting."[3]

MILLIE ALPERT
She Writes Her Husband's Material

Bagels and Yox was a Yiddish theatre revue that played Broadway in 1951 and ran for a respectable 208 performances. The show played the Holiday Theatre, a Broadway house that was once on the southwest corner of 47th Street and Broadway. During intermission of *Bagels and Yox*, the Holiday's lobby was filled with people handing out bagels to audience members.

Millie Alpert wrote additional lyrics for *Bagels and Yox*. The other songwriters involved were Sholom Secunda and Hy Jacobson.

Alpert wanted to be a journalist but couldn't get a job at a newspaper, so she started her own jewelry business. On a trip to a Catskills resort, she met her future husband Larry Alpert, and the first writing she ever did was for him to perform on stage. Larry was a failed cartoonist turned comedian.

A 1952 *Boston Globe* article during the post-Broadway tour of *Bagels and Yox* started with the headline "Larry Alpert's Wife, Millie, Writes Most of His Material." Marjory Adams's story went on to say: "'The only way Larry could sign me up to a contract was to marry me,' giggled pretty Millie Alpert. Her Chinese-slanted eyes sparkled and her poppy-rouged lips parted in a smile at her husband's expense.[4] 'That's not true,' sputtered the tall young comedian from *Bagels and Yox* at the Shubert Theatre. 'Don't say that.'"[5]

---

3. "Tuesday Night Set Aside for Benefit Show." *Chicago Tribune*, 31 August 1958, p. 90.

4. As previously noted, this is one of many times in this work where the goal is to reprint problematic critical language as it originally appeared, in order to question its impact.

5. "Larry Alpert's Wife, Millie, Writes Most of His Material." *Boston Globe*.

ELISSE BOYD
A Criminal Case

Leonard Sillman's New Faces revues were a special kind of recurring theatrical event. While most revues presented stars and well-known talent, *New Faces*, as its name announces, intended to introduce audiences to fresh talent, both on and off stage.

One of the writers chosen as new talent was Elisse Boyd, who wrote songs for the 1952 and 1956 editions of the show. While she had been writing songs for decades, she was forty-two when she made her Broadway debut. In 1952, Boyd's song "Guess Who I Saw Today" became a runaway hit. It was eventually recorded by everyone from Eydie Gormé to Eartha Kitt to Toni Tennille. Boyd wrote the haunting lyrics for the song about a woman who slowly reveals a story about a couple she saw who were very much in love. In the end, the audience finds out the man in the couple is actually the singer's husband. The music was by Murray Grand.

In 1956, Boyd penned the lyrics for "Hurry," also written with Grand.

In 1957, Boyd was one of the many writers for the off-Broadway revue *Kaleidoscope*, a breezy topical show that played the Provincetown Playhouse and lasted the summer. Historian Thomas Hischak compared it to the rooftop revues that used to occur on Broadway in the early 20th century.[6]

Boyd made the news the year before her Broadway debut for her connection to a criminal case. She was assaulted and beaten in her home. The accused was a city detective named Robert M. Hinds who had been visiting her home with other friends. This was the topic of several news stories since Boyd's husband, who had been out of town, was a government adviser of the Federal Munitions Board.

ANNA RUSSELL
Back-Stabbing Bitch

Anna Russell was an English-Canadian singer and comedian, extremely popular for her parodist skills set to music. She sold out stages all over the world, appeared in opera houses, created best-selling albums and published books. Russell was of a feminist ideology and humor somewhat ahead of her time: When asked once how to be a successful singer, she acknowledged that vocal skill was important but then noted, "It helps to be an independently wealthy, politically

---

6. Hischak, Thomas. *Off-Broadway Musicals Since 1919: From Greenwich Village Follies to The Toxic Avenger*. Lanham, MD: Scarecrow Press, 1911.

motivated, back-stabbing bitch."[7] *Anna Russell's Little Show* was this firecracker female's singular foray onto Broadway; in 1953, she hit the Vanderbilt Theatre for a short run.

Anna Russell's comedic style offended everyone from her parents to the patrons who protested at her sold-out performances at Town Hall. Her humor was bawdy, and she never pulled punches. She pounded beers during interviews. She wrote both music and lyrics and starred in this *Little Show,* which also featured dancers and pianists to back her up. *New York Times* critic Brooks Atkinson admitted the show was professional but that he was exhausted by Russell's exuberance. As she skewered everyone from Cole Porter to Gilbert and Sullivan, Russell was wild and wicked and not everyone's taste—but for those who loved her, she occupied a place that no other comedian did, unique and unapologetic and altogether musical.

The Vanderbilt Theatre lasted for less than a year more after *Anna Russell's Little Show* closed. When you pass a series of new buildings next to the James Earl Jones Theatre on 48th Street, you are where Anna Russell once played.

In 1964, Anna Russell gave off-Broadway a shot with *All by Myself* at the 41st Street Theatre, for which she wrote music, lyrics and book and also performed.

Elizabeth Miele
I Gotta Hit the Trail

Elizabeth Miele had a most unconventional path for any woman working on Broadway in the 1920s through the 1950s. She started out writing plays, and her *City Haul* and *Did I Say No?* were produced on Broadway in 1929 and 1931, respectively. In 1932, she began producing and between that year and 1937, she presented seven productions—all straight plays. Her final Broadway credit was the 1954 *Hit the Trail,* where she both produced and wrote the lyrics.

Hit the Trail was one of those Broadway musicals that inspires critics to list all of the other worst Broadway musicals they've ever seen. The show was hit with slamming notices. Even two years later, critics were still disparaging *Hit the Trail* in conjunction with other musicals. In his *My Fair Lady* review, Walter Kerr wrote about hearing the first few songs in the show: "After that, you couldn't have stopped *My Fair Lady* if you'd invited the authors of *Buttrio Square, Hit the Trail* and *Carnival in Flanders* to work over the second act."[8]

---

7. Wierzbicki, James. "Comedy: Anna Russell has staying power." *Cincinnati Post,* 6 February 1978, p. 13.

8. Filichia, Peter. "The First Hit Broadway Musical from A Movie." MasterWorks Broadway, 21 February 2012, https://www.masterworksbroadway.com/blog/the-first-hit-broadway-musical-from -a-movie/.

Like *My Fair Lady*, *Hit the Trail* opened at the Mark Hellinger Theatre, but unlike *My Fair Lady*, it only played four performances there. *Hit the Trail*, which was called *On with the Show* during its tryout, is about a struggling opera company in the 1890s that becomes stranded in a town in Nevada. The remainder of the plot involves the opera's leading lady having to take over a beauty emporium and choose between marrying a local banker or the opera's manager.

The out-of-town tryout was very troubled. Miele was a champion of the show's leading lady Irra Petina and had written *Hit the Trail* as a vehicle for her. When Petina became ill, her understudy, Vera Brynner (sister of Yul) had to go on, and when Brynner wasn't sufficiently prepared, she and Miele got into a backstage squabble so dramatic that it became physical. They had to be separated and the scandal made the papers. Brynner was one of several actors who left the show out of town and whose parts were written out, not necessarily in that order. Another scandal happened in town when reportedly, during opening night, leading man Robert Wright was singing a ballad and looked at his watch. After *Hit the Trail*, Miele retired from the professional theatre.

CAROLYN LEIGH
Lyricist of Peter Pan *and* Little Me

One of the first prominent and successful female musical theatre writers to enter the permanent canon of the art form, Carolyn Leigh was a lyricist whose work for Broadway includes *Peter Pan*, *Wildcat*, *Little Me*, and *How Now, Dow Jones*. She wrote often with Cy Coleman, and their best-known songs together include "Witchcraft," "The Best Is Yet to Come," "Hey, Look Me Over," and "I've Got Your Number." In addition to Leigh's work on Broadway, she wrote extensively for television, film, and recordings.

Carolyn Leigh, circa 1976. PHOTOFEST

Leigh started out as an advertising copywriter. She then worked at a radio station and at a talent agency for TV. One day at the agency, she was on the phone with a song publisher when he asked if she wrote songs. She lied and said she did, went home and wrote some, submitted them to him, and he contracted her.

In a 1954 piece on *Peter Pan* by the *Fort Worth Star-Telegram*, Alice Hughes noted that in the last three years, lyricist Carolyn Leigh had written five-hundred songs, with "Young at Heart," as performed by Frank Sinatra, serving as her big break. *Peter Pan* was another big break, as Leigh's lyrics for "I Won't Grow Up," "I'm Flying," "I've Got to Crow" and "Tender Shepherd" would go on to become immortal. Leigh had actually gotten the job because Mary Martin, one of the biggest stars on Broadway at the time, and her husband, manager, and producer, Richard Halliday, were fans of "Young at Heart" and asked if she'd like to write *Peter Pan*. She was twenty-seven years old at the time.

Hughes wrote: "On dress rehearsal day I sat with Carolyn Leigh at the back of the Winter Garden. . . . Listening spellbound to the singing of the words she had composed, she kept repeating to herself, 'I can't believe it.'. . . And, as if that were not enough, when we left the theater, three-sheets announcing the play had just been put up. Pausing, we read 'Story of *Peter Pan* by Sir James Barrie. Words and lyrics by Carolyn Leigh.' Again she muttered, 'I don't believe it.'"[9]

Peter Pan, starring Mary Martin in one of the legendary performances of her career, was initially fraught with problems. Director-choreographer Jerome Robbins brought in his better-known collaborators, lyricists Betty Comden and Adolph Green and composer Jule Styne to augment the score that Leigh had written with Moose Charlap. This was purportedly due to conflicts between Robbins and Leigh.

Leigh also famously sparred with directors Bob Fosse and Cy Feuer during *Little Me*. When Fosse and Feuer cut her act one finale, "Lafayette, We Are Here," she was so furious that she left the theater and returned with a policeman, demanding that Fosse, Feuer, and the entire rest of the creative team be arrested for violating her contract with the Dramatists Guild. When much of the *Little Me* team reunited a few years later for *Sweet Charity*, they replaced Leigh with Dorothy Fields.

In between *Peter Pan* in 1954 and *Little Me* in 1962, Leigh penned some lyrics for the final edition of the *Ziegfeld Follies*, long after the death of the man who made the revues. The 1957 *Follies* played the Winter Garden and Leigh's two songs were "The Lover in Me" and "Salesmanship." This was followed by *Wildcat* (1960), a vehicle written for Lucille Ball where she played an oil prospector in 1910s Texas. The show was not a success but became legendary on its own terms when beset with drama from Lucille Ball's public divorce from Desi Arnaz, and her acquiescence to playing Lucy Ricardo for excited audiences who came to the Alvin wanting just that. The show was her only appearance in a Broadway musical.

The 1963 *Daily News* feature "Songwriting Is Now A Hit and Mrs. Trade" by Patricia O'Haire spotlighted the work of Leigh as well as that of Anne Croswell and Mary Rodgers, and stated: "Three of Broadway's newest musical comedies are proof that you should never underestimate the melody power of a woman."

---

9. Hughes, Alice. "A Woman's New York: Those Broadway Cheers Are for Mary and Pan's Music." *Fort Worth Star-Telegram*, 28 October 1954, p. 21.

The article also opened with the quote, "Everybody knows you can't stage a musical comedy without girls. But it's beginning to look as if you can't write musicals without girls, either."[10]

The piece continued to remind readers that Betty Comden, Dorothy Fields, Rida Johnson Young, and Dorothy Donnelly had all written prominent Broadway musicals. A photo of Leigh and Coleman working on *Little Me* was accompanied by the caption: "Ladies' Day in Tin Pan Alley: Whoever said tunesmithing was a man's job hasn't heard about lyricist Carolyn Leigh."[11]

For *Little Me*, Leigh, Coleman, and book writer Neil Simon adapted Patrick Dennis's book about fictional star Belle Poitrine into a zany musical comedy vehicle for Sid Caesar. *Little Me* has had some lasting power, including two Broadway revivals. It provides great opportunities for two leading actors as the male lead plays all of Poitrine's love interests throughout her varied and comedic adventures and Poitrine herself has juicy scenes and numbers.

In 1967 came Leigh's final Broadway musical, *How Now, Dow Jones*, a show she came up with the idea for. A fascination with the stock market led to this 220-performance production at the Lunt-Fontanne, and Leigh received a Tony nomination for Best Score (as she also did for *Little Me*). *How Now, Dow Jones* has a beloved cast album and aficionados over the years have particularly admired the torch song "Walk Away" as well as the bouncing "Step to the Rear" which gained fame when Marilyn Maye recorded it, and later sang it in a car commercial. For *How Now, Dow Jones*, Leigh collaborated with composer Elmer Bernstein and book writer Max Shulman.

A 1972 interview with Leigh for the *Courier-Journal* found interviewer James Doussard running down Leigh's credits in anticipation of a new television musical comedy special she wrote about sports. His first few questions to her were about the program in question and then he said: "You seem to like men a lot. Describe yourself." He followed this up with the question: "Are you sexy?" Leigh quipped back: "Hmm, well, let's say three darned attractive guys thought enough to marry me."[12]

On Broadway, Leigh's songs have also appeared in *The American Dance Machine* (1978), *Jerome Robbins' Broadway* (1989), *Mostly Sondheim* (2002), and *Come Fly Away* (2010).

---

10. O'Haire, Patricia. "Songwriting Is Now a Hit and Mrs. Trade." *Daily News*, 5 May 1963, p. 906.

11. Ibid.

12. Doussard, James. "Carolyn Leigh Spoofs the Spectator." *Courier-Journal*, 25 January 1972, p. 20.

PORTIA NELSON
Nightclubs and Nuns

Musical theatre aficionados know Portia Nelson's name because she was the original Miss Minerva Oliver in the original production of the cult musical *The Golden Apple*. But Nelson actually worked on as many productions on and off Broadway as a writer as she did as an actor.

Nelson first wrote songs and sang in Los Angeles, trying to get a break while performing in nightclubs. Her first big break was performing at the Blue Angel nightclub in New York.

In 1955, the year after *The Golden Apple* opened on Broadway, Nelson was one of the three main songwriters for *Almost Crazy*, a musical revue that was put together in a more haphazard way than most Broadway fare. A millionaire from Oklahoma financed the show on a whim. An out-of-town tryout was skipped in favor of New York previews, which was untraditional at the time. The show closed quickly, after receiving poor reviews.

Nelson's contributions to *Almost Crazy*, which mainly features pieces that take aim at movies, television programs, and shows, are "Always Tell the Truth," "Mother's Day," and "Don't Bait for Fish You Can't Fry." "Mother's Day" is reprised multiple times and has a lyric by Joyce Geary. The *Daily News* called it the best number in the show.[13] Nelson wrote the other two songs on her own.

In 1958, Nelson's irresistible song "Sunday in New York," a swinging anthem to the city, premiered in off-Broadway's *Demi-Dozen*, a Julius Monk revue performed at Upstairs at the Downstairs. The following year Nelson had her own radio series with the same title. "Sunday in New York" became one of Nelson's most popular and beloved songs. She continued to write, record, and perform cabaret for the next several decades. Her song "Make a Rainbow" was performed by Marilyn Horne at President Bill Clinton's 1993 inauguration.

She also appeared on dozens of musical theatre albums in her lifetime, including several of the theatre compilations Goddard Lieberson created before it was customary for each show to receive its own cast album. She played Sister Berthe in the *Sound of Music* film.

JOYCE GRENFELL
A Comedians' Comedian

A British multihyphenate, Joyce Grenfell largely found her fame in her native country. But she did make two appearances on Broadway, in 1955 and 1958, with self-titled shows. In *Joyce Grenfell Requests the Pleasure* ... she wrote book and

---

13. Iams, Jack. "Almost Crazy Has a Lot of Zest." *Daily News*, 22 June 1955, p. 17.

lyrics and also starred. In *Joyce Grenfell (Monologues and Songs)*, she added directing into the mix as well.

Grenfell was known as a comedian who wrote and performed her own material, satirizing the mores and foibles of everyday life. Some called her brand of comedy too tame and bland, not suited to American audiences. Others adored her style, which never verged on cruelty, but which often had something serious to say underneath.

For *Joyce Grenfell Requests the Pleasure* . . . , she was joined by three other performers who took the stage when she needed a break. For her return show, she was all alone. Nearly all songs were the work of Grenfell and her collaborators, but in 1955, she did interpolate a number from the 1910 edition of *The Ziegfeld Follies* which was by Jean C. Have and Harry Von Tilzer. It was quite an event for a woman to have written the majority of two Broadway scores, within three years of each other, in the 1950s.

Grenfell was related to both Lady Nancy Astor and Ruth Draper. In 2005, a poll was conducted among comedians to find out who "the Comedians' Comedian" was, and she landed in the top fifty of comedy legends.[14]

LILLIAN HELLMAN
Candide *Was Her Idea*

The successful playwright Lillian Hellman, best known for her plays, including *The Children's Hour* (1934), *The Little Foxes* (1939), *Watch on the Rhine* (1941), and *Toys in the Attic* (1960), also collaborated on one musical: *Candide*, in 1956.

Hellman wrote the original book for *Candide*, which has music by Leonard Bernstein, lyrics by Richard Wilbur, John Latouche, and Dorothy Parker, and was based on the novel by Voltaire. The original production of *Candide* ran for only seventy-three performances, but was widely regarded as a would-be masterpiece that just fell short of meeting its potential. It has been revised and revived numerous times in the decades since, including a Hal Prince–helmed immersive production in 1974, with a new book by Hugh Wheeler, and some new lyrics by Stephen Sondheim. Wheeler's book was also used in a 1997 revival. Indeed, Hellman's book for the musical is no longer used in productions of *Candide* today, but was partially responsible for the cult hit status awarded the show after its initial bow. The idea to adapt the novel for the stage was Hellman's initially, as she conceived it as a play with music. When the show evolved into a full-fledged musical, she found creating a musical to be a far less favorable experience than creating a play.

---

14. Thorpe, Vanessa. "Cook Tops Poll of Comedy Greats." *Guardian*, 1 January 2005, https://www.theguardian.com/uk/2005/jan/02/arts.artsnews.

Hellman's book for the original production was praised in several reviews, including in the *Daily News*. They wrote, "Lillian Hellman has made the libretto, and has made it strong and sound. Her scenes and characters are clear as she takes *Candide* on his fantastically imaginative tour."[15]

A musical version of *The Little Foxes*, called *Regina*, was based on Hellman's play, and ran on Broadway in 1949.

JOAN FORD
Friend-Collaborator of the Kerrs

Goldilocks was a rare 1950s book Broadway musical that had two women on its writing team. The show, set in the era of silent pictures, has a book by Walter and Jean Kerr, music by Leroy Anderson, and lyrics by the Kerrs and Joan Ford.

Ford was a personal friend of the Kerrs who was invited to collaborate on the musical by them. She had no other professional musical theatre writing credits. While the writers collaborated fully on most songs, some lyrics were done by individuals on the team. Ford did the lyric for "Who's Been Sitting in My Chair?," one of the show's best remembered tunes, as well as "Heart of Stone."[16]

DOROTHY REYNOLDS
Wrote the Longest Running Musical of All Time, for a Time

Dorothy Reynolds and Julian Slade had a long-term writing partnership throughout the 1950s and 1960s. The British team was best known for their musical *Salad Days*, which for a time was the longest running musical in all of musical theatre history.

They first met while working together as employees in a pub. Slade was in his twenties and was the resident pianist, and Reynolds was in her forties and worked as a waitress. They made up songs for fun on breaks, and this eventually turned into *Salad Days*.

Salad Days is a light-hearted 1954 musical about a young 1920s couple who come into possession of a magical piano that makes everyone who hears its music need to dance. A group of zany uncles fills out the plot of this inherently British show which held the title of longest running musical ever, until surpassed by the Broadway production of *My Fair Lady*.

---

15. Chapman, John. "*Candide* a Fine Musical." *Daily News*, 9 December 1956.

16. Wright Briggs, George, Jr. "Leroy Anderson on Broadway: Behind-the-Scene Accounts of the Musical *Goldilocks*." *American Music* 3. no. 3 (Autumn 1985), pp. 329–36.

Salad Days originated as a commission for the Old Vic's resident company in Bristol, and was meant to run for only a few months. But it was so successful that it transferred to the West End.

After debuting in the West End, where it would eventually rack up 2,288 performances, *Salad Days* came to New York four years later in 1958. It played only eighty performances at the Barbizon Plaza Theatre off-Broadway, and its premature closing was blamed on a newspaper strike that prevented the show from being properly reviewed.

In London, Reynolds and Slade continued to work together on musicals including *Free as Air*, *Hooray for Daisy*, *Vanity Fair*, *Sixty Thousand Nights*, and *The Pursuit of Love*, between 1957 and 1967. None came close to matching the success of *Salad Days*.

Reynolds also worked as an actress both before and after her musical theatre writing career. She appears on the original cast album of *Salad Days*.

FRAN LANDESMAN
Writer of the Beatnik Generation

Fran Landesman got her start as a journalist. Then, when her husband Jay Landesman began managing the Crystal Palace nightclub in St. Louis in the 1950s, she was inspired to turn her passion for writing into work as a lyricist. In 1955, she wrote what would become her most famous song, "Spring Can Really Hang You Up the Most," to music by Tommy Wolf. It was recorded by singers from Ella Fitzgerald to Barbra Streisand.

In 1959, the Landesmans wrote a musical called *The Nervous Set*, and they placed "Spring Can Really Hang You Up the Most" in the score, even though it had been written several years earlier. The show was based on an unpublished novel by Jay Landesman, and he cowrote the book with Theodore J. Flicker. Fran Landesman wrote the lyrics, and Tommy Wolf wrote the music. *The Nervous Set* premiered at the Crystal Palace nightclub before landing on Broadway at Henry Miller's Theatre.

Describing the show, Brooks Atkinson wrote: "The point of view is sharp in *The Nervous Set*. . . . In both words and music it has a shrewd slant on contemporary attitudes. . . . Nothing on the local music stages this season has been so acid and adult as the wry portrait of Greenwich Village beatniks it offers."[17] Atkinson had one of the most positive reviews for *The Nervous Set*; most critics were perturbed by the concept of exploring the beatnik generation in a Broadway show.

---

17. Atkinson, Brooks. "Theatre: Beatnik Picnic." *New York Times*, 13 May 1959.

As John Chapman opened his review: "*The Nervous Set*, an intimate and friendly musical, makes me wonder if I really am an old poop."[18]

The Nervous Set found two squares, much like the average middle-aged couple, out on the town in New York, exploring the counterculture world in Greenwich Village. Even though the culture was seen through the eyes of comfortable outsiders, some audience members were unhappy that the revolutionaries of the show seemed to win out in the end.

Landesman and Wolf's *Nervous Set* song "The Ballad of the Sad Young Men" was another standout and has gained in popularity over the years. The score was played by a jazz combo, a surprising musical choice for 1959 Broadway, and one that lent credence to the beatnik theme. The show closed after twenty-three performances.

The Landesmans considered themselves beatniks in real life; Jay had published *Neurotica*, a magazine that put out work by Jack Kerouac and Allen Ginsberg, and Fran was a poet who described their open marriage and other lifestyle choices in her work.[19]

Landesman continued to write musicals but never returned to the professional New York theatre. In 1964 she moved to London, where the majority of the rest of her shows were produced, including *London Days and New York Nights* which played the Park Royal Theatre in 1983.

The Landesmans remained members of the counterculture. When they moved to London they became well known on the beatnik scene and were referred to as Fran Fabulous and Stan Stunning. At one point Fran appeared on a BBC program and told the audience she would bring cannabis to a desert island; the station received letters of complaint.

Their nephew is producer and former National Endowment for the Arts chairman Rocco Landesman.

MARY RODGERS
A Complicated Legacy

Many female theatre writers who should be known in their own right are instead known for their relation to a man in the industry; Mary Rodgers has the distinction of being known for her relation to three. The daughter of Richard Rodgers, mother of Adam Guettel, and lifelong close friend of Stephen

---

18. Chapman, John. "Beatnik Musical, 'Nervous Set,' Rouses Memories of an Old Poop." *Daily News*, 14 May 1959, p. 37.

19. Sams, Craig. "Fran Landesman Obituary." *Guardian*, 10 August 2011, https://www.theguardian.com/theguardian/2011/aug/10/fran-landesman-obituary.

Mary Rodgers with Rich-
ard Rodgers, circa
1959. PHOTOFEST

Sondheim was a talented composer in her own right who led a fascinating life and created indelible work.

In the musical theatre world, Rodgers is perhaps best known for composing *Once Upon a Mattress*, a show that found success on Broadway and then immense continuing popularity in stock and amateur productions for over half a century. Otherwise, Rodgers's best known work is the novel *Freaky Friday*, which has lived on past its original form, with subsequent generations discovering it through new adaptations on stage and screen.

Rodgers was born in 1931, in the midst of her father's acclaimed collaboration with Lorenz Hart. She was on the cusp of teenager-hood when her father began his groundbreaking work with Oscar Hammerstein II, which would revolutionize musical theatre. Young Mary Rodgers was present for the Rodgers and Hammerstein musicals that would shape the art form, and she was part of the next generation of artists who would take the baton and run with it. In fact, in 1949, it was Mary Rodgers who introduced aspiring director-producer Hal Prince to fledgling writer Stephen Sondheim at opening night of *South Pacific*. She was only eighteen years old and the company she kept consisted of the brightest past, present, and future lights of the American theatre.

Rodgers began composing as a teenager and her first professional ventures found her creating songs for recordings for children, some with Sammy Cahn. In 1957, her *Ali Baba and the 40 Thieves 40* received a recording featuring Bing Crosby. Rodgers had several songs published while in college, before dropping out to get married. Rodgers studied music but not composition at Wellesley; Wellesley, a college for women, did not even teach composition then, believing it was an area closed off to women.

When Rodgers visited Sondheim out of town for the pre-Broadway tryout of *West Side Story*, a collaboration with Leonard Bernstein struck up. Rodgers helped write and produce Bernstein's New York Philharmonic Young People's Concerts in the 1950s and 1960s. It was their years of coming up together in these decades that Sondheim would later cite as inspiring the "Opening Doors" section of his musical *Merrily We Roll Along*. About writing *Merrily* in general, Sondheim wrote, "In truth, like the characters in the show, I was trying to roll myself back to my exuberant early days, to recapture the combination of sophistication and idealism that I'd shared with Hal Prince, Mary Rodgers, Jerry Bock and Sheldon Harnick, John Kander and Fred Ebb, and the rest of us show business supplicants, all stripped back to our innocence."[20]

In 1961, Sondheim composed a song for Rodgers as a birthday gift. Titled "Mommy on the Telephone," the song's lyrics were published in Sondheim's compendium *Look I Made a Hat*. In the song, Sondheim chronicled Rodgers's balancing of motherhood and professional life as a writer with her passion for gabbing on the telephone.

Once Upon a Mattress, which Rodgers composed while still in her twenties, was to be her most enduring work for the stage. While writing it, she consulted her father for his opinion, an experience she realized she must not repeat, as it blurred the line between her writing and his. She wanted to be sure to compose in her own voice.

The musical, based on the fairy tale *The Princess and the Pea*, started out in 1958 as a project written for Camp Tamiment, a popular resort getaway for adults that boasted professional entertainment and was a stomping ground for several musical theatre writers at the beginning of their careers. Rodgers wrote the music, Marshall Barer the lyrics, and Barer, Jay Thompson, and Dean Fuller the book for this tuneful, pleasurable, comedic romp. *Mattress* is about a kingdom where no citizen can get married until the prince does. An unlikely spousal candidate named Winnifred shows up and surprises everyone with her flair, outspokenness, and individuality. The show is chock full of great comedic roles, from the overbearing Queen Aggravain to the mute King to the soft shoe-dancing Jester.

Mattress opened in New York at the Phoenix Theatre in 1959, and wound up playing five houses during its Broadway run. The show was considered a scrappy underdog, and seen as a youthful and silly project. So, in the days where productions were often ousted to make way for the next show the theater owner desired, *Mattress* trouped from the Phoenix to the Alvin to the Winter Garden to the Cort to the St. James. While moving theaters during a Broadway run was much more common in the 1950s and 1960s than it is now, to play five theaters in one year was unheard of. *Mattress*'s run might have been longer if theatergoers knew where it was consistently playing!

At the 1960 Tony Awards, the show was only nominated for Best Musical and Best Actress for Carol Burnett as Winnifred, not winning either prize. The 1960 Tony Awards were dominated in the musical categories by *The Sound of Music*, *Gypsy*, *Take Me Along*, and *Fiorello!*

---

20. Sondheim, Stephen. *Finishing the Hat: Collected Lyrics (1954–1981) with Attendant Comments*. New York: Knopf, 2010.

Somewhat dismissed on Broadway for its youth appeal and otherwise,[21] *Mattress* found that it was its youth appeal that gave the property great longevity. The show became one of the most performed musicals in America with endless summer camps, schools, community theaters, and more regularly singing Rodgers-composed songs like "In a Little While," "Shy," "Normandy," "Happily Ever After," and "Very Soft Shoes."

Rodgers was active in the revue and variety scene; her father had been also, when first starting out. But while the elder Rodgers's involvement in shows like *The Garrick Gaieties* led to bigger opportunities, Mary's work on productions like *Red Hot* (1959), *From A to Z* (1960), *The Mad Show* (1966), *Davy Jones' Locker* (1972) and *Working* (1978), while high quality, tended to lead in the other direction. Revues consisting of original material during the second half of the twentieth century were often relegated to off-Broadway semi-obscurity or received quick non-lucrative Broadway runs. Some professionals involved did go on to long writing careers—but the revues themselves did not tend to breed major opportunities as often, since they were less successful.

The Mad Show, a stage musical version of *Mad Magazine*, found Rodgers as the sole composer. The show is a cult favorite, and in particular the song "The Boy From ..." lives on, in part because Rodgers collaborated on it with Sondheim, credited at the time as Esteban Ria Nido. Rodgers's tuneful and comedic chops are on fine display in the show. For *Working*, the Stephen Schwartz–led revue based on Studs Terkel exploring how people feel about their professions, Rodgers composed "Nobody Tells Me How," a song about a late-career teacher that has lyrics by Susan Birkenhead.

Largely by choice, Rodgers's career composing for the stage petered out as she focused on being chair of Juilliard, maintaining her father's legacy, writing children's books, including the *Freaky Friday* series, and being with her family. She felt that writing books for young people allowed her much more flexibility than working on musicals, giving her time to raise her children and be actively involved in her family life.

Some considered the Broadway musical *Hot Spot* the event that truly put an end to Rodgers's ambitions to continue a career as a theatre composer. The 1963 star vehicle for Judy Holliday had a troubled process, unpleasant in all regards, culminating in a one-month run. The show, about a Peace Corps volunteer who stirs up trouble in a fictional foreign country, saw multiple directors come and go, as well as multiple show doctors take a crack at the tricky script. The humor was dull-edged, the plot was slight, and the score wasn't special enough, most critics

---

21. For instance, the *Daily News* called it "lumpy" and spent the entire second paragraph of the review comparing Rodgers's work to that of her father. (Watt, Douglas. "'Once Upon a Mattress' Is Lumpy; Judy Still Great but Pixie's Gone." *Daily News*, 12 May 1959, p. 215.)

thought. (*The Daily News* did say, "The music, by Mary Rodgers, stands up and stands out"[22]—but they were the exception to the rule.) Rodgers's pal Sondheim came in to ghost write two numbers with her and with lyricist Martin Charnin, including the opening, "Don't Laugh," the only song that has lived on in concert performances. Ken Mandelbaum noted in *Not Since Carrie* that *Hot Spot* only premiered at the Majestic because Richard Rodgers's musical adaptation of *I Picked a Daisy*, which had booked the theater, was stalled.[23]

Even in her obituaries, Rodgers could not escape the legacy she was part of. The *Washington Post* obit for Mary Rodgers reminded readers of her father's influence.[24] Her *New York Times* obit was topped by a photo of her at the piano in 1959 with her father leaning over her.[25]

A 2003 *New York Times* feature by Jesse Green about Mary Rodgers's son Adam Guettel heavily explored the legacy he was part of, in addition to his own career and life. The article shared that in the 1960s, Mary Rodgers brought the idea for a musical adaptation of the film *The Light in the Piazza* to Richard Rodgers, who said it was not for him. Decades later, she brought the same idea to her son, and Guettel created what is widely considered to be a masterpiece; *The Light in the Piazza* premiered at Lincoln Center and won many accolades, with many considering it to be one of the finest Broadway musicals of the century so far. The article wondered why Mary Rodgers hadn't composed *Piazza* herself.

"I had a pleasant talent but not an incredible talent," she told *the Times.* "I was not my father or my son. And you have to abandon all kinds of things."[26]

There are several pointed revelations in the article, which plumbs the depths of family history and its intersection with musical theatre. "The gap between [Richard Rodgers's] secret reality and the beautiful world of his very public art almost swallowed up everyone standing nearby. Possibly as a reaction, his daughter Mary Rodgers Guettel has developed a personal style you might call knee-jerk transparency, except that you do not need even a tiny rubber mallet to get the goods from her."[27]

---

22. Chapman, John. "'Hot Spot' Runs into Plot Trouble." *Daily News*, 21 April 1963, p. 49.

23. Mandelbaum, Ken. *Not Since Carrie*. Griffin, 1992. The show *On A Clear Day You Can See Forever*, with a score by Alan Jay Lerner and Burton Lane, was originally called *I Picked a Daisy*, with a score by Lerner and Richard Rodgers. That version never came to fruition.

24. Langer, Emily. "'Mattress' Composer Followed Father's Lead." *Washington Post*, 3 July 2014.

25. Weber, Bruce. "Mary Rodgers, Author and Composer in a Musical Family, Dies at 83." *New York Times*, 27 June 2014, https://www.nytimes.com/2014/06/28/nyregion/mary-rodgers-author-and-composer-and-daughter-of-richard-rodgers-dies-at-83.html.

26. Green, Jesse. "A Complicated Gift." *New York Times*, 6 July 2003, https://www.nytimes.com/2003/07/06/magazine/a-complicated-gift.html.

27. Ibid.

In 2022, *Shy: The Alarmingly Outspoken Memoirs of Mary Rodgers*, written by Rodgers and Jesse Green, was published. Although Rodgers died in 2014, she had a posthumous triumph when her revelatory book became the must-read of the year in theatre circles.

Rodgers inherited her father's legacy in multiple ways. She represented his interests with the Rodgers and Hammerstein Organization, helping to oversee new productions, movies, recordings, the usage of older recordings, and much more.

"In perhaps any other family Ms. Rodgers would have been the star. But along with a series of men in her life, she belonged to the Windsors of the musical theater," the *New York Times* wrote in Rodgers's obituary.[28]

---

28. Weber, Bruce. "Mary Rodgers, Author and Composer in a Musical Family, Dies at 83." *New York Times*, 27 June 2014, https://www.nytimes.com/2014/06/28/nyregion/mary-rodgers-author-and -composer-and-daughter-of-richard-rodgers-dies-at-83.html.

8

1960s

Family Musicals, Musical Families, and Conceiver Credits

ANNE CROSWELL
Oscar Wilde, Vivien Leigh, and King Solomon

A favorite of off-Broadway musical aficionados, *Ernest in Love* is a creation from librettist-lyricist Anne Croswell and composer Lee Pockriss that adapted Oscar Wilde's *The Importance of Being Earnest.* The stage show began its life as a television project in 1957 and was expanded for its premiere at the Gramercy Arts Theatre.

The musical only had 111 showings, so its marvelous reputation is very much the result of its original cast recording, which has allowed it to find new fans continuously since 1960. It was revived at the Irish Repertory Theatre in 2009.

Critics during both the original production and revival agreed that the musical was a strong and reliable adaptation, delightfully expanding upon the spirit of Wilde's original play.

Croswell and Pockriss had such a successful time collaborating that they joined again in 1963, this time on Broadway, for *Tovarich.* Now they were adapting a French play, with Croswell taking on lyrics and Pockriss music, plus David Shaw on book. *Tovarich* was highly anticipated for being the musical debut of Vivien Leigh, who wound up winning the Tony Award for Best Actress in a Musical. The plot revolves around a former Russian noble (originated by Leigh) who finds herself working as a servant to an American family in the 1920s, following the Russian Revolution. *Tovarich* played 264 performances on Broadway.

In 1965, Croswell contributed to the off-Broadway revue *Wet Paint*, which also featured writing from Martin Charnin, Sheldon Harnick, and Paul Lynde, and starred Linda Lavin.

In 1968 Croswell was on Broadway again, with *I'm Solomon*, for which she cowrote the libretto with Dan Almagor, and penned the lyrics. Music was by Ernest Gold, and the piece was based on a play by Sammy Gronemann, which had been turned into a hit musical in Israel several years earlier. The subject was King Solomon, as played by Dick Shawn. *I'm Solomon* only managed seven performances at the Mark Hellinger (today the Times Square Church).

Part of the reason *I'm Solomon* closed so quickly, making it one of the most expensive flops to date, was its enormous production expense. Advertisements boasted "a cast of 60," and the show was given the grand treatment, eclipsing its entire thesis: Do King Solomon's subjects love him because of his status or because of himself? He disguises himself as a poor cobbler to find out.

In *Not Since Carrie*, Ken Mandelbaum notes that the show "featured a memorably tacky song about the frequency with which Solomon's many wives got to sleep with their husband ("Once in 2.7 Years") [as well as] a couple of nice songs and an extremely silly book."[1]

---

1. Mandelbaum, Ken. *Not Since Carrie.* New York: Griffin, 1992.

Croswell was visibly relieved to be working outside New York in 1974, during an interview she gave to Jean Dietrich of the *Courier-Journal*. "On Broadway you usually work three years on a show, then come the out-of-town tryouts and as soon as the reviews come out panic sets in." Reflecting on her current project, a musical adaptation of *She Stoops to Conquer* called *Chips 'n' Ale* that was set to premiere at Actors Theatre of Louisville, she commented, "But at Actors Theatre of Louisville all is calm. This is the way a show should be done, then take it to Broadway."[2] At this time in 1974, it was almost unheard of to present a show regionally before Broadway. Within a few decades, a commercial producer partnering with an established regional nonprofit would be one of the main ways that musicals were steered to Broadway.

Croswell got her start working as a copywriter for an ad agency. Her contributions to jingles and political benefit performances led to work writing songs for television and recording artists, which led to musical theatre.

JEANNE GARGY
A Greenwich Village Revue

In 1960, a topical revue called *Greenwich Village, U.S.A.* opened at One Sheridan Square. Its music and lyrics, satirizing all topics relevant to Village residents, were by Jeanne Gargy. Gargy tackled topics from beatniks to NYU students, and the show found an audience for eighty-seven performances. The sweet style of the show likened it to revues of the 1950s; topical off-Broadway shows like this one were about to move in increasingly more sexual and political directions. *Greenwich Village, U.S.A.* did receive a cast recording and one can observe that Gargy's score was clever and fun. The show's final number was titled "Save the Village," sung just as the Village—and the theatre it contained—were about to change in a huge way.

MARGUERITE MONNOT
A French Musical Theatre Writer Who Collaborated with Edith Piaf

Edith Piaf has proven an ideal candidate for live musical interpretation over the years, whether in musicals, one-woman shows, or other entertainments. And thus, Marguerite Monnot is often part of the proceedings since Monnot was responsible for several of Piaf's most significant songs.

Since Piaf cowrote her own material, when she began writing with Monnot, they were declared the first all-female French writing team. Monnot's most remembered Piaf collaborations are "Milord," "Hymne a l'amour," and "La vie en

---

2. Dietrich, Jean. *Louisville Courier-Journal*, 21 April 1974.

rose," on which they collaborated with Louiguy (Louis Guglielmi). From Josephine Baker's concert at the Palace in 1973 to the off-Broadway bio-show *Piaf ... A Remembrance* in 1977, Monnot's work with Piaf showed up on theatrical stages.

In one instance, Monnot wrote a Broadway musical, and this made history as well. *Irma La Douce* was a hit in France, and then a hit in London, and then a 1960 hit in New York at the Plymouth (now Schoenfeld) and later Alvin (now Neil Simon) Theatres, where it ran 524 performances and was nominated for seven Tony Awards, winning Best Actress in a Musical for Elizabeth Seal. Monnot was not nominated, nor were her fellow writers, Alexandre Breffort (original book and lyrics), Julian More, David Heneker, and Monty Norman (English book and lyrics). There was no award for Best Score or Book given, during a break in this category being included, although other musicals that season included *Bye Bye Birdie, Do Re Mi*, and *The Unsinkable Molly Brown*.

Irma La Douce unceasingly embraces Parisian culture. Not only had Broadway not had a hit French musical in many years, this one was *very* French. Signs outside the Plymouth assured potential audience members that they could understand the show even if they didn't speak the language. (While the show was basically in English, many of the terms used were not.) The plot of the show is about a prostitute who is beloved by a man who can't afford her—and commits crimes and farcical hijinks in order to try to keep her for himself. Many attributed *Irma*'s success to the way it took a scandalous premise and made it feel wholesome. Indeed, Howard Taubman wrote in his *New York Times* review: "The saucy, sentimental music by Marguerite Monnot, as French as the Place Pigalle, casts a wholesome glow over sin."[3]

Upon the success of *Irma*, Monnot was sent offers for new American musical projects, but she rejected them, preferring to live in France. She died of a ruptured appendix only a year after *Irma* opened on Broadway, while it was still running, at the age of fifty-eight. *Irma* was later made into a film with Shirley MacLaine and Jack Lemmon, but Monnot's music was banished to the background, as the film was not a musical.

HELEN DEUTSCH
Hi, Lili

Helen Deutsch wore a lot of hats during her career. She managed the off-Broadway theatre troupe, The Provincetown Players. She worked as a theatre critic and wrote reviews for the *New York Times* and the *New York Herald-Tribune*.

---

3. Taubman, Howard. "The Theatre: Place Pigalle Genially Satirized: *Irma La Douce* Has Debut at Plymouth, Gallic Musical Turns Vice into Innocence." *New York Times*, 30 September 1960, p. 31.

She was a Broadway press representative in the 1930s and a Hollywood screen-writer in the 1940s.

Working in Hollywood, Deutsch wrote the script for the film *Lili*, and the lyric for its famous song "Hi-Lili Hi-Lo." When the musical *Carnival!* (1961) was made with *Lili* as source material just a few years later, Deutsch was credited with "based on original material by Helen Deutsch."

Deutsch also wrote poetry, a book about the history of the Provincetown Players, and the screenplays for *The Unsinkable Molly Brown* and *Valley of the Dolls*.

JOAN JAVITS
Writer of "Santa Baby"

In a fashion more prevalent in pre-1940s Broadway musicals, *Tovarich*, in 1963, had one interpolated song by another writing team; Joan Javits penned music and lyrics with Philip Springer to Vivien Leigh's first big number in the show, called "You'll Make an Elegant Butler (I'll Make an Elegant Maid)."

Javits and Springer were best known for the popular song "Santa Baby," which was released a decade earlier in 1953. They were hired to write a Christmas tune for Eartha Kitt to record. "Santa Baby" is now one of the most performed and recorded songs in the American songbook.

Prior to *Tovarich*, Javits had been represented on and off Broadway with *The Young Abe Lincoln* in 1961. The show tells the story of Abraham Lincoln's childhood, up until the time he runs for Illinois legislature, in the style of a musical the whole family can enjoy. This kind of effort to get young audiences hooked on musicals was ramping up in the early 1960s.

The Young Abe Lincoln opened off-Broadway, transferred to the Eugene O'Neill Theatre for a brief run, and then returned off-Broadway. The show's songs were preserved on an original cast album.

The more adult-themed *Hotel Passionato* had Javits working again off-Broadway in 1965, collaborating again with Springer, as well as book writer Jerome J. Schwartz. Based on a flop 1957 Broadway play, *Hotel Paradiso*, which had starred Angela Lansbury and Bert Lahr, the plot found a modern couple attempting to check into a hotel but coming upon a series of obstacles in the form of people they know. The show received negative reviews and closed in a little over a week. Among its stars were Linda Lavin and Jo Anne Worley.

In 1952, Javits worked on a revamped version of *Shuffle Along* that intended to have Pearl Bailey headlining. Bailey dropped out before the show reached Broadway, but Javits still had one song in the piece: "It's the Gown That Makes the Gal That Makes the Guy."

She is the niece of the late New York Senator Jacob Javits.

LOLA PERGAMENT
Adapting She Stoops to Conquer

Lola Pergament started out as a poet and then built a career as a theatre publicist throughout the 1950s, including at off-Broadway's Greenwich Mews Theatre. Not long after she took over publicity work at that house, she was also employed there as a playwright.

Her main musical credit came in 1961 when her musical adaptation of the famous eighteenth-century Oliver Goldsmith play *She Stoops to Conquer* played The Gate Theatre. Pergament contributed book and lyrics to Robert Kessler's music. The dizzy story about a man who can only be himself among lower-class women, inspiring his high-bred fiancée to masquerade as a poor maid so she can meet the real him, was played by a cast that included Elly Stone. *O Marry Me!* was not well received and closed after twenty-one performances.

In her later years, Pergament managed the sale of vintage Betty Boop dolls.

FAY KANIN
The Gay Life *and* Grind

Some women were able to get a writing position on a show because of family connections, but not many could say they had as *many* family connections as Fay Kanin. Her husband was Michael Kanin, a producer and writer, and Michael's brother was Garson Kanin, a prolific performer, director, and writer who worked on the following Broadway productions as director, writer or both: *Born Yesterday*, *The Diary of Anne Frank*, *Do Re Mi*, and *Funny Girl*. He also wrote *Smash*, the novel that inspired the television series. Even her sister-in-law was a Broadway costume designer. But while a spot at the table was only allowed to some women if their father, brother, or spouse was there, they did have to pull their own weight and then some, once they were there—and Fay Kanin certainly worked her way up herself.

Kanin got her start writing for radio and local news before landing a job as a Hollywood story editor and script reader. She rose through the ranks at RKO, and it was there that she met Michael Kanin. After they married, they began selling screenplays. Their first Broadway project was *Goodbye My Fancy*, a 1948 play with feminist themes that were radical for the time. The show was a hit, running for over a year, and its glossy, comedic texture allowed its more progressive ideas to get across to its audience. The story concerns an influential female politician returning to her alma mater and coming in conflict with its more conservative systems.

Kanin continued to write plays and screenplays, as she delved into the world of musical theatre as well. Her two Broadway musicals were more than two decades apart: *The Gay Life* in 1961 and *Grind* in 1985. For the former, she cowrote the book with her husband and for the latter, she was the sole librettist.

The Gay Life is beloved by musical theatre enthusiasts even though it only ran for three months. The show is about a womanizer and all of his current and former flames. He eventually settles down with the sister of his best friend, who was played by Barbara Cook in the original production. Initially, the conceit had one woman playing all of the love interests of the main character, but this was abandoned. The show is largely admired for its score by Arthur Schwartz and Howard Dietz.

Grind was based on an unproduced screenplay Kanin had written. It is a controversial, risky piece addressing issues of race and class in America, with the backdrop of a burlesque theatre. Characters include struggling immigrants and Black performers battling racial injustice. The show's plot about violence resulting from these class and race issues has similarities to that of the musical *Ragtime*, which would come a decade later (based on the 1975 E. L. Doctorow book).

The fact that *The Gay Life* and *Grind* were Kanin's two Broadway ventures speaks volumes about her career. She could write in different genres, she evolved with the times, and she tried to tell new stories.

Kanin was president of the Academy of Motion Picture Arts and Sciences from 1979 until 1983, and was the second woman to ever hold this position.

ANN CORIO
Queen of Burlesque

Ann Corio's big moment on Broadway was a show she created called *This Was Burlesque*, which opened off-Broadway at the Casino East Theater in 1962 and ran for 1,509 performances before transferring to Broadway at the Hudson in the spring of 1965. Corio toured the show, then brought it back to New York for an off-Broadway stint in 1970. A new version was revived on Broadway at the Princess in 1981, where it lasted a few weeks. *This Was Burlesque* was even filmed for HBO.

Corio was one of the most enduring burlesque stars and striptease artists of the 1920s and 1930s. For years she was the most beloved stripper on the bill on the burlesque circuit, combining humor and sexuality. Her act even inspired a slogan in Boston: "You can't graduate from Harvard until you've seen Ann Corio."[4] In 1937, burlesque was banned from New York and Corio had to search for a new path. After two decades as a headlining artist on stage, she made her way to Hollywood, where her persona won her roles in B-films, and she also

---

4. Van Gelder, Lawrence. "Ann Corio, a Burlesque Queen on Broadway Is Dead." *New York Times*, 9 March 1999, p. C27.

modeled as a pin-up girl during World War II. As burlesque faded from popularity, Corio found work as an actress, touring in theatre roles.

The next chapter of Corio's career found her parlaying her burlesque expertise and longevity into her own retrospective stage show. *This Was Burlesque* utilized Corio's recollections about her life and career to present a nostalgic celebration of the art form, with dancers and comedians in the old style. Despite the fact that many of the reviews were negative and condescending, claiming stage entertainment had moved on from such types of show, *This Was Burlesque* became a long-running hit Off-Broadway. Corio was the book writer, director, and narrator of sorts.

After three years off-Broadway and transferring to Broadway for its last three months in New York, *This Was Burlesque* toured, playing all over America. A new version at the Princess Theatre in 1981 utilized additional material that Corio had crafted for her tell-all book of the same name that had since been published. This production was meant to capitalize on the popularity of the Broadway show *Sugar Babies*, a 1979 Broadway hit that was also intended to celebrate burlesque. *Sugar Babies* was the work of big Broadway and had stars and sparkle; *This Was Burlesque* was a more realistic version of the burlesque genre, and this desire to capture *Sugar Babies*' run-off audience was unsuccessful.

"What is called burlesque today isn't that at all. Those girls aren't artists," Corio told the press in the 1960s. "They just take clothes off, and they don't even do that very well. Burlesque is exactly what it says it is. It's from the Italian word *burlare*, to satirize, to laugh. That's what we do, and we are not offensive."[5]

Of the 1981 revival, the *New York Times* wrote, "Miss Corio, who looks radiant, does it all by the book and, whether you like the book or not, it is to her credit that she catches the flavor of the old burlesque with little attempt to ennoble or elevate it. This is close to the real thing."[6]

ANNA MARIE BARLOW
Rumpelstiltskin *and* Ambassador

In 1962, a new musical called *Half-Past Wednesday* with book by Anna Marie Barlow, music by Robert Colby, and lyrics by Colby and Nita Jonas, opened at the Orpheum Theatre off-Broadway. It had a planned run of two performances and then was brought back for four more a few weeks later. The five-person cast included Dom DeLuise.

---

5. Van Gelder, Lawrence. "Burlesque Shows 'Bawdy but Never Vulgar.'" *New York Times*, 14 March 1999.

6. "Ann Corio." *Sydney Morning Herald*, 15 May 1999, p. 47.

Half-Past Wednesday was an adaptation of the fairy tale "Rumpelstiltskin," and the authors later tried to more strongly brand their musical by changing its title to *Rumpelstiltskin*. It did receive a cast album. This kind of adaptation of a classic fable meant for both adult and child audiences proliferated in the years following *Once Upon a Mattress*'s success.

Barlow's next major project was *Ambassador*, which played less than a month at the Lunt-Fontanne in 1972. Barlow cowrote the book with Don Ettlinger for this musical based on Henry James's novel about an American man who finds romance in Paris. *Ambassador* had played London first, where it was also not a hit. Barlow joined the show for its New York run. *Ambassador* was judged to be bland, the kind of musical that was pleasant enough that it could have had a modest run in a previous decade but was not able to survive the more challenging theatrical economics of the 1970s.

Barlow was also a playwright, and was produced starting in 1953 with her play *On Cobweb Twine* which starred Mildred Natwick. Her play *Taffy* starred Kim Stanley. Both shows closed out of town. In 1967, she was showcased as an emerging writer in a play festival at the Theater de Lys (today the Lucille Lortel) and Dan Sullivan in the *New York Times* wrote: "[Barlow's plays] showed her to be a good craftsman who may someday be more."[7] Her other work includes *Ferryboat*, which is published, and *Hallelujah!* which received a television airing in 1969.

NAOMI CARYL HIRSHHORN
Spoon River Anthology

A folk singer, Naomi Caryl Hirshhorn was at the helm of the theatrical adaptation of Edgar Lee Masters's *Spoon River Anthology*. The written work, which was published in 1915, espouses in poetry the obituaries of residents of a small town, revealing their lives and the true nature of their community.

In 1963, the stage version opened at the Booth before moving to the Belasco. Hirshhorn was credited as composer, and was part of the on-stage cast as well, playing guitar. Following the show's Broadway bow, it received a television dramatization. It was also revived off-Broadway in 1973 at Stage 73.

---

7. Sullivan, Dan. "Theater: New Playwright: *Double Play* Offered at ANTA Showcase." *New York Times*, 13 December 1967, p. 55.

VINNETTE CARROLL
First Black Woman to Direct on Broadway

Vinnette Carroll is more often recognized for her outstanding contributions to theatre in the second half of the twentieth century as a director, but she was also a writer.

Carroll holds the distinction of being the first Black woman to direct a Broadway show. This was Micki Grant's *Don't Bother Me, I Can't Cope* in 1972. Carroll also conceived this musical about the Black experience.

Vinnette Carroll, circa 1979. BY *LOS ANGELES TIMES*, CC BY 4.0 / WIKIMEDIA COMMONS

Carroll made her Broadway debut in the role of Negro Woman in *A Streetcar Named Desire* in 1956. She acted throughout the 1950s and early 1960s. She won an Obie Award for *Moon on a Rainbow Shawl* in 1962, in which she appeared in both London and New York. James Earl Jones won an Obie as well for this work, which was groundbreaking in several ways. Written by Black British playwright Errol John, *Moon on a Rainbow Shawl* commented on systemic racism in a way that had not often been seen before.

In 1963, Carroll adapted a series of sermons by James Weldon Johnson into a new musical called *Trumpets of the Lord*. Johnson's sermons had the uniting theme of telling Bible stories from a Black point of view. Carroll took these words along with existing popular gospel songs and threaded them together to become *Trumpets of the Lord*. Three reverends, originated by Al Freeman Jr., Cicely Tyson, and Lex Monson led the presentation of the tales, and Theresa Merritt led the singing. The show ran for 160 performances at the Astor Place Playhouse. In 1969, it was brought to Broadway for a special one-week engagement.

In 1965, Vinnette Carroll founded the Urban Arts Corps, a theatre company focused on bringing arts to underserved communities and getting artists of different races together to create new productions. The Urban Arts Corps produced over one-hundred plays including *Don't Bother Me, I Can't Cope*, which went on to play over one-thousand performances on Broadway.

In 1976, Carroll returned to the Bible for inspiration again when she used the first book of the New Testament, the Book of Matthew, to craft a new theatre piece called *Your Arms Too Short to Box with God*. Carroll conceived the show, wrote the book, and directed, receiving two Tony Award nominations. The musical ran for a little over a year and later returned for two Broadway revivals.

But Never Jam Today was Carroll's other venture on Broadway as director, writer, and conceiver. This is a Black version of *Alice in Wonderland* that Carroll first conceived for City Center in 1968. It took over ten years for the show to get picked up and brought to Broadway, where it lasted only eight performances at the Longacre.

A 1976 interview with Carroll appeared in the *New York Times* and complimented her multihyphenate artistic achievements before diving into her career in a questionable manner. The interviewer's first question, referring to *Your Arms Too Short to Box with God*, was simply "Is it like *Godspell* or *Jesus Christ Superstar?*" Carroll replied, "I didn't even see *Godspell* until I'd finished it," and the interviewer countered with "But it is another black version of a white story?"

Carroll said no, the musical wasn't consciously that, and went on to describe her inspiration for the show, including the idea of Christ as Martin Luther King Jr. She spoke unapologetically about her take on Black theatre makers of the time. When the interviewer asked point blank why she hadn't done more straight plays she shared that she felt white producers would only put their money behind musicals with Black creators, not plays.

The interviewer asked, "Isn't there an implied anti-intellectualism in this form of theater that gets by without a book, that whites enjoy seeing blacks do?"

"There's a simplicity that is really sophisticated in the way that Picasso's simple lines are sophisticated," Carroll explained. "And there was a time when black audiences were ashamed of having it done out of Harlem. But anyone who looks down on this form shouldn't be dignified with an answer."[8]

PATRICIA TAYLOR CURTIS
Youth Musicals About Racial Issues

In 1964, Patricia Taylor Curtis and her husband Norman Curtis collaborated on a musical called *Unfinished Business*, which was remarkable for its time in that it featured teenagers of all races singing about contemporary topics including civil rights.

In 1968, they made a bigger splash with their first Equity production, *Walk Down Mah Street!*, book and lyrics by Patricia and music by Norman, which similarly featured teenage actors, all either Black or Puerto Rican. This time the show's themes were almost all related to race. In his book *Off-Broadway Musicals*, Thomas Hischak noted that

> *The prejudices against African Americans were looked at in a wry rather than bitter manner. There was both pride and satire in "Basic Black." The sketches looked at crime-ridden neighborhoods, jobs closed to Black Americans,*

---

8. Mason, Clifford. "Vinnette Carroll Is Still in There Swinging: Vinnette Carroll." *New York Times*, 19 December 1976, p. X4.

and the efforts of some African Americans to behave like white people. Perhaps white audiences felt a bit uncomfortable as they laughed. It was a volatile time, with urban race riots and the assassination of Martin Luther King Jr. two months earlier, thus a show that made light of racial inequality was treading dangerous ground.[9]

The Curtises noted that most of their actors came from performing arts high schools, where they had sent audition notices.[10] During a WNYC interview, a journalist asked Norman about his beginnings and the beginnings of *Walk Down Mah Street!* Then he turned the questions on Patricia and asked if she was a playwright or if it was just a whim of the moment for her, and questioned what other talents she had.

Patricia noted that she was putting the question on her level, and spoke eloquently about how important it was for anyone interested in theatre to explore all production elements of it so that they could do their own job better. She emphasized that while she wrote the words and directed, the actors contributed greatly because everyone in the room was part of the process, and so much improv was employed.

The *New York Times* review of *Walk Down Mah Street!* was significantly positive, opening with "As lovely a group of people as have ever voiced social protest in revue format danced and sang their way through *Walk Down Mah Street!* last night at the Players Theater in Greenwich Village." The show was immersive, with actors venturing into the audience.

Walk Down Mah Street! returned for a special engagement at Town Hall in 1969. The Curtises other works included *If We Grow Up!!!*, also about young people and social and racial issues. They ran Next Stage Theatre Company for many years.

ISOBEL LENNART
Funny Girl

Isobel Lennart was largely a screenwriter, and had only one work produced on Broadway—and yet she wrote the book for one of the most indelible stage musicals of Broadway's so-called Golden Age. She also wrote its subsequent screenplay adaptation.

Funny Girl was written by Lennart several decades into her own show business career, when she was forty-eight years old. Lennart's career was made in Los

---

9. Hischak, Thomas. *Off-Broadway Musicals Since 1919: From Greenwich Village Follies to the Toxic Avenger.* Lanham, MD: Scarecrow Press, 1911.

10. "Walk Down Mah Street!" The NYPR Archive Collections. 22 July 1968, https://www.wnyc.org/story/walk-down-mah-street/.

Angeles, where she started out as a script assistant for MGM. She maneuvered this into a career writing, and her films included *Anchors Aweigh*, *Love Me or Leave Me*, *Please Don't Eat the Daisies*, and *Two for the Seesaw*.

In 1952, Lennart was called before the House Un-American Activities Committee, and she gave them the names of fellow communists in the entertainment industry in order to avoid being blacklisted herself.

Although Lennart worked largely in film in Los Angeles, she also helped run her husband's theater, The Stage Society. The Stage Society produced the Los Angeles premieres of many hot New York shows.

In the early 1960s producer Ray Stark had several false starts in commissioning a Fanny Brice biopic. He eventually ended up with Lennart after she wrote a screenplay called *My Man* that impressed. This became *Funny Girl*, the show that launched Barbra Streisand's career and made Fanny Brice an even more immortal part of show business history.

Funny Girl had a famously troubled development period. In fact, original director Jerome Robbins left following untenable disagreements with Lennart about the vision for the show. According to the *Los Angeles Times*, Lennart rewrote every scene for *Funny Girl* hundreds of times.[11]

While Lennart wasn't nominated for a Best Book Tony Award for *Funny Girl*, she did win a Writers Guild of America Award for her screenplay for the film. It's Lennart that gave audiences Fanny Brice quotes like "Hello, gorgeous" and "I'm a bagel on a plate full of onion rolls!" She turned the legend that was Brice into the legend that was Streisand and crafted a story for all time.

JOAN LITTLEWOOD
Groundbreaking Collective Environmental Theatre

Joan Littlewood revolutionized theatre and the way it was made in Britain, starting in the 1940s.

Joan Littlewood. BY STRATFORD-EAST/ WIKIMEDIA COMMONS

The *Guardian* called her "for several decades not only the most important woman in the English-speaking theatre but also the most vital person in the English stage."[12]

After World War II, there was a call for big changes to happen in the theatre—for theatre to change from a conventional middle-class genre of entertainment to a more collective art form. Littlewood seized the opportunity and

---

11. "Isobel Lennart—In Memoriam." *Los Angeles Times*, 7 February 1971, p. 473.

12. "Oh What a Lovely." *Guardian*, 25 June 1984, p. 12.

led the charge. She experimented with environmental elements in theatre, from removing the proscenium and curtain to sending actors to interact with audience members. She premiered improvisation techniques in the theatre that would lead to a new form of collaborative play in which all artists participated. In 1945, she cofounded the Theatre Workshop, which employed these techniques, and became a touchstone for theaters in England.

It was these techniques that were utilized to build the piece that became *Oh, What a Lovely War!* The musical premiered at Littlewood's home base in Stratford in 1963, transferred to the West End, and then opened at the Broadhurst in 1964, winning great acclaim. The show is a satire, using World War I to comment on all war. The show received four Tony Award nominations, including one for Best Musical and one for Littlewood, for Best Director. While the songs were preexisting, the book was credited to Littlewood along with the Theatre Workshop. *Oh, What a Lovely War!* was built out of research that the entire company did, under Littlewood's leadership, into World War I. Historic facts and figures were enmeshed with well-known songs to create a commentary on the realities of war.

Littlewood's style of theatre making is much more common now, but in the 1960s, a play or musical devised by a group was a fresh innovation.

MARILYN BERGMAN
Hit Songs, Hollywood Smashes, and Two Broadway Flops

Marilyn and Alan Bergman were married songwriters who had a lengthy career in theatre, television, film, and recorded music. Among their credits are songs for movies as varied as *E.T.* and *The Thomas Crown Affair*. Their most famous lyrics include "The Way We Were" and "Nice 'n' Easy." They won two Academy Awards and were inducted into the Songwriters Hall of Fame. From 1994 to 2009, Marilyn served as president and chair of ASCAP.

The Bergmans were involved in many theatrical productions, sometimes explicitly writing and other times having their previously completed work included in a program. The two Broadway musicals they wrote organically were *Something More!* (1964) and *Ballroom* (1978). While neither show was a hit, the latter has gained countless fans for the Bergmans' songs because of its original cast album.

Something More! found the Bergmans writing lyrics to Sammy Fain's music for a show starring Barbara Cook as the wife of a restless novelist who decides to escape stifling Long Island and take his family to Italy. While tempted by the thrills of a foreign country, in the end, the family decides that home is where the heart is. The show lasted only fifteen performances.

The Bergmans returned to Broadway for *Ballroom*, Michael Bennett's comeback musical after *A Chorus Line*. *Ballroom*, based on a television program by Jerome Kass who also wrote the musical's book, had some songs by the Bergmans as well, who added to their score for the stage version. The show is about an older widow who finds a new lease on life at a dance hall in the Bronx. When she discovers that her lover is married, she decides she'd rather have a compromised version of her dreams than no dream at all. "Fifty Percent" became one of the Bergmans' most beloved and indelible songs. Their lyrics for the show were written to the music of Billy Goldenberg. *Ballroom* had a disappointing run; its reception was largely chalked up to the fact that high expectations were inevitably going to hurt the next musical by the creator of *A Chorus Line*.

At the 1979 Tony Awards, *Ballroom* received eight nominations (and one win, for Bennett and Bob Avian, for Best Choreography). Best Score was not among the nominations—and the Bergmans were in good company as far as Best Score non-nominees that year. *The Best Little Whorehouse in Texas* and *They're Playing Our Song*, each also with a female writer, had not been nominated. All three shows received nominations for Best Musical, but not for Best Score. Those went to *Carmelina*, *Eubie!*, and *The Grand Tour*. The winner in both categories was *Sweeney Todd*.

The Bergmans also had material on Broadway in *André DeShields' Haarlem Nocturne* (1984), *Street Corner Symphony* (1997) and *Come Fly Away* (2010). They wrote a new musical called *Chasing Mem'ries: A Different Kind of Musical* that opened in 2017 at the Geffen Playhouse.

Marilyn Bergman passed away in 2022.

MARIAN GRUDEFF
A Canadian Musical Theatre Writing Team

Marian Grudeff was one half of a Canadian musical theatre writing team with Ray Jessel. Grudeff and Jessel were best known as writers of *Spring Thaw*, an annual Canadian revue that became the longest-running professional satiric revue in North America. Grudeff got her start as a concert pianist and played with the Toronto Symphony when she was only eleven years old. Her first job on *Spring Thaw* was as music director in 1950, but soon she met Jessel, and they began writing hit material for the show.

While Grudeff and Jessel had material being performed in off-Broadway revues, they remained in Canada until they became acquainted with the producer Alexander Cohen. In his travels to Canada, Cohen met the writing team, who performed their calling-card-material for him. They had written six songs about the life of P. T. Barnum, because they were told this was the kind of standard, inspired by the B.M.I. Workshop, that musical theatre writers needed in order to get hired by a producer for a new project. Cohen actually came on board to produce their Barnum musical itself, and he planned on opening it on Broadway.[13]

At the same time, he was working on a musical called *Baker Street*, about Sherlock Holmes. The Barnum musical never came to fruition (there would be a Broadway musical about P. T. Barnum in 1980 by another team and a movie musical by a different team in 2017). But because of Grudeff and Jessel's relationship with Cohen he hired them to score *Baker Street*. One of the show's pre-Broadway tryouts was in Toronto. The show opened on Broadway in 1965 and played 311 performances at the Broadway, directed by Hal Prince.

Grudeff and Jessel were unique among Broadway writing teams in that they both wrote music and they both wrote lyrics.

SYLVIA YOUNIN
Bringing Yiddish Theatre to the Masses

On the 1966 Broadway musical *Let's Sing Yiddish*, Sylvia Younin and Naomi Hoffman had one of the most unique credits in Broadway history: "Shtetl Envisioned by." The two women helped conceive this Jewish musical based on Yiddish folklore and humor that played the Brooks Atkinson for three months. After its first two numbers, "Once Upon a Shtetl" and "Let's Sing Yiddish (Hassidic Melodies)" it was clear the musical was attempting to appeal to the Jewish theatre party crowd, which was prominent in that era.

Papers reported that the show was only coming to Broadway because there were so many flop productions in the first part of the season that the theatre owners were seeking out any stop-gap booking, no matter how unconventional. Indeed, *Let's Sing Yiddish* lasted longer than the previous four productions at the Brooks Atkinson combined: 107 performances.

Four years later Younin returned to Broadway with another Yiddish musical, helmed by director Mina Bern and which also featured writing by her husband Wolf Younin. This was *Light, Lively and Yiddish*, which played the Belasco. Sylvia Younin wrote both lyrics and text this time.

In 1970, Ben Bonus, who produced *Let's Sing Yiddish*, and Sol Dickstein, who produced *Light, Lively, and Yiddish* gave an interview to Louis Calta at the *New York Times* about their decision to bring Yiddish theatre to Broadway. They explained that the Yiddish Theatre district, previously located on Second Avenue, was now overrun by the homeless, and the theaters were now showing rock musicals. They did not think the area once known as Jewish Broadway would ever return. Bonus said, "The Yiddish theatre has always been like a wandering star. It

---

13. Atkey, Mel. *Broadway North: The Dream of a Canadian Musical Theatre*. Ontario, Canada: Natural Heritage, 2006.

goes from country to country, from town to town, which we are still doing. It's a question of moving from the shtetl to Broadway."[14]

The Younins continued to work in the Yiddish theatre scene, away from Broadway, and in 1970, hosted the first radio course in conversational Yiddish.

MEGAN TERRY
Laying the Groundwork for the Rock Musical

Viet Rock laid the groundwork for the rock musical as we know it today, and specifically inspired *Hair*. Megan Terry wrote the book and directed, and Marianne de Pury[15] composed the music for this 1966 protest musical, one of the first theatre pieces to speak out against the Vietnam War, one of the first musicals to employ full company improv techniques and interactions with the audience, and one of the first shows to utilize rock music in such a way. One of the reasons *Viet Rock* has not gained a significant place in musical theatre history is because it's often considered a play with music rather than a musical,[16] and another is that it closed after sixty-two performances.

Terry was a playwright, director, and technical director, who received a Rockefeller Foundation Grant to study theatre. *Viet Rock* was developed at Yale, where she sought to create a theatre piece that could "[give just as valid a picture of the war as] the bombardment of impressions we get from the mass media."[17]

Most critics were horrified by *Viet Rock*, with Walter Kerr expressing himself thus:

> *The one truly distressing thing about* Viet Rock *is that it is never aware for one moment that it is behaving precisely as mindlessly as the conduct it means to mock. In fact, it simply adapts the tools of warmongering to the uses of the theater. In all of the linguistic and physical writhing, the tortured mime, the atonal song and the clash of hard heels against the floorboards that "playwright"[18] Megan Terry has put together in the name of theatrical adventurousness and political common sense, not one cogent thing is said*

14. Calta, Louis. "Yiddish Theater Moves to Broadway." *New York Times*, 25 September 1970, p. 32.

15. De Pury also wrote incidental music for *America Hurrah*, a play that opened off-Broadway four days prior to *Viet Rock*, and for a time managed the Washington Square Methodist Church, a theatrical venue.

16. *Viet Rock* does lean more toward identification as a play, but because of its use of music, dance, and chant, as well as its influence on *Hair*, inclusion was merited here.

17. Sullivan, Dan. "Play on Vietnam to Open at Yale: Work Follows 7 Soldiers from U.S. to the Front." *New York Times*, 26 September 1966, p. 48.

18. Yes, he put "playwright" in quotations.

about our involvement in Vietnam, about how we got there or about how we are possibly ever to get out.[19]

Gerome Ragni was one of the cast members of *Viet Rock*, and shortly after, he used what he learned from the experience to create *Hair,* where he was one of the writers as well as the original actor to play Berger.

Viet Rock and *Oh, What A Lovely War!*, which opened in their respective countries within a year of each other, employ some similar techniques to address war theatrically but are very different musicals.

In 1973, Terry contributed additional lyrics to the musical *Thoughts,* which played the Theatre de Lys (today the Lucille Lortel). Her work was mostly on plays rather than musicals.

Historian David Savran wrote of Terry: "The work of no other contemporary American playwright can boast the extraordinary scope of that of Megan Terry. In the course of over thirty years her collected plays have become a virtual compendium of the styles of modern drama, ranging from collaborative ensemble work to performance art to naturalism. . . . Beginning with her earliest work, she has devised a politically and socially activist theater, using a diversity of nonrealistic forms to challenge a culture which has systematically disparaged nonlinear drama. Megan Terry remains a key figure in the development of the American alternative theater."[20]

KETTI FRINGS
Pulitzer Prize–Winning Writer of Look Homeward, Angel

Ketti Frings was better known for her plays and films than for her two Broadway musicals. The writer who was named Woman of the Year by the *Los Angeles Times* in 1958 was also the recipient of the Pulitzer Prize for her play *Look Homeward, Angel,* based on the Thomas Wolfe novel.

After three stints writing plays for Broadway—two quick flops and the hit *Look Homeward, Angel*—Frings attempted a musical with *Walking Happy* in 1966. *Walking Happy,* while forgotten now, was one of the most prominent musicals of its season. Nominated for Best Musical, the show is a nineteenth-century romp set in England with a thin plot about a boot shop owner and his three daughters' journeys to the altar for marriage. Frings penned the book based on the hit play *Hobson's Choice* by Harold Brighouse. She cowrote it with Roger O.

---

19. Kerr, Walter. "The Theater: *Viet Rock*: Play by Megan Terry at the Martinique." *New York Times,* 11 November 1966, p. 38.

20. Savran, David. *In Their Own Words: Contemporary American Playwrights.* New York: Theatre Communications Group, 1993.

Hirson. Critics largely praised their work in bringing the much-loved story to the stage in musical form.

Frings's other Broadway musical was *Angel*, the 1978 adaptation of her own play, *Look Homeward, Angel*. Frings cowrote the book for *Angel* with Peter Udell. Udell also wrote the lyrics, and Gary Geld wrote the music; the two had previously collaborated on the hits *Shenandoah* and *Purlie*.

Like *Shenandoah* and *Purlie*, *Angel* was to be a hearty look at Americana through the lens of one small sliver of community—in this case, the Gants of North Carolina. As Ken Mandelbaum wrote in *Not Since Carrie*:

> *While the musical book eliminated two characters, it otherwise followed Frings' play very closely, and most of the musical's dialogue was taken verbatim from the play. But* Angel *was another case of "chop and drop": the songs added nothing, were not up to the level of the original dialogue, and failed to make the characters vivid or real. What remained was a diluted version of Frings' play, with sometimes pretty songs that were not even on Frings' level, let alone Wolfe's, during the musical numbers, one waited for what was left of the original play to return.*[21]

Angel closed after only five performances at the Minskoff.

"When I was 18, I had to make a momentous decision—whether to be an actress or a writer," Frings told the *Los Angeles Times* in 1959. "I chose writing because it seemed to be that as an actress grew older, she would find more problems—lines and sags and bulges would worry her, that sort of thing. But a writer, I thought, should get better as he[22] grew older. He should know more and understand more."[23]

In addition to the 1972 television adaptation of *Look Homeward, Angel*, Frings's other screen credits included *The Company She Keeps* (1951), *Come Back, Little Sheba* (1952), and *Foxfire* (1955).

MARY BOYLAN
A Shirley Temple Parody Musical Hit
Mary Boylan was an actor and writer who worked in several different capacities on off-Broadway musicals in the 1960s and 1970s.

21. Mandelbaum, Ken. *Not Since Carrie*. New York: Griffin, 1992.

22. The interview did indeed quote Frings as using the pronoun *he* here.

23. Smith, Cecil. "Ketti Frings Studies Life." *Los Angeles Times*, 22 February 1959, p. 81.

The 1967 off-Broadway musical *Curley McDimple* is mainly remembered today only as a footnote in the career of Bernadette Peters, who briefly starred. This is despite the fact that the show, a spoof of Shirley Temple movie musicals from the Great Depression, was a huge hit, racking up 931 performances at the Bert Wheeler Theatre. Mary Boylan cowrote the book with Robert Dahdah, and Dahdah also wrote music and lyrics and directed.

Curley McDimple was part of the same trend as the better-known *Dames at Sea* that found 1960s off-Broadway musicals lovingly satirizing show business tropes of the earlier decades of the twentieth century with bright and snappy pastiche tunes and performances. *Curley McDimple* is filled with tap dance, and includes songs like "Love Is the Loveliest Love Song" and "Swing-a-Ding-a-Ling." A 1972 revival of the musical played out the summer shortly after the original production closed, and this time, Boylan was in the cast as well. *Curley McDimple* was published but not recorded, and thus is rarely if ever seen.

Boylan continued to collaborate with Dahdah. In 1976, their musical *Those Darn Kids* played Theatre for the New City. The original musical about kids just like those in *The Little Rascals*—but who go to outer space—was presented for two weeks. They followed this up with *Clara Bow Loves Gary Cooper* at the same theater in 1978.

Boylan's work without Dahdah included *Blood*, a musical devised by its cast that played the Public Theater's Martinson Hall in 1971. *Blood* is an anti-Vietnam piece that uses Aeschylus's Greek trilogy *The Oresteia* as a jumping off point.

Boylan's credits as an actor included Broadway, off-Broadway, and film, from Tom Eyen's legendary *Women Behind Bars* to the movie *Annie Hall*.

GRETCHEN CRYER AND NANCY FORD
Long-Running All-Female Team

Gretchen Cryer and Nancy Ford, circa 1980s. PHOTOFEST

Gretchen Cryer and Nancy Ford hold a spectacular and unique place in musical theatre history as the first well-known long-term female team.

Cryer and Ford met at DePauw University in 1955 and began writing musicals together. At DePauw they presented two musicals: *For Reasons of Loyalty* and *Hey Angie!* They had a show called *Rendezvous* produced at Boston University in 1960.

Ford wrote music and Cryer book and lyrics, and both women also held other positions on their shows and those of others. Ford got her start in New York as a pianist, playing for *The Fantasticks* among other shows. She also worked as a secretary and a writer of soap operas. Cryer was a performer, who appeared in the original Broadway casts of shows including *Little Me*, *110 in the Shade*, and *1776*.

Ford's connection to *The Fantasticks'* writers, Tom Jones and Harvey Schmidt, helped the team get their first production off-Broadway: *Now Is the Time for All Good Men*. The show premiered in 1967. *Now Is the Time for All Good Men* has a contemporary story with anti-war themes, and it introduced Cryer and Ford's socially conscious, piano-heavy, equally-folk-and-musical-theatre-influenced style to audiences. Cryer played the lead role and Ford understudied all of the women in the cast.

Now Is the Time for All Good Men was panned by critics, but did receive an original cast album. Cryer and Ford's next show, *The Last Sweet Days of Isaac*, was the opposite in terms of critical reception. The musical, which played the Eastside Playhouse in 1970, was critically acclaimed. *The Last Sweet Days of Isaac* won the Obie Award for Best Musical, the Outer Critics Circle Award for Outstanding Off-Broadway Musical, and a Drama Desk Award. This show is an abstract statement about mortality and human connection that revolves around the character of Isaac, age thirty-three in act one and nineteen in act two.

The *New York Times'* Walter Kerr, known for his rampant dislike of rock musicals, called the show "my favorite rock musical thus far." Further, he wrote, "Gretchen Cryer, it turns out—has succeeded in writing a book that is not only as good as the music but walks right into the music without hemming and hawing about it."[24] Austin Pendleton originated the role of Isaac, and the show was directed by Word Baker, who had also directed *The Fantasticks* as well as *Now Is the Time for All Good Men*.

Shelter was Cryer and Ford's next musical and their only Broadway venture as writers. The show comments on the growing human obsession with technology, specifically with computers and televisions. While it only ran for a month at the Golden, its kooky style, relevant story, and unmistakably contemporary score left an impression.

To begin with, as Ken Mandelbaum notes, *Shelter* was the first musical in postwar history to be fully written by women. It was also about a decidedly contemporary topic: a television ad writer who has controlled his life by living on a studio set under the oversight of a computer named Arthur. The show was labeled as a bit too weird, and a bit too intimate for a Broadway focused at the time on *Grease* and *Pippin*, both less than a year old.

A cast album of the 1997 York Theatre revival is available, and an original cast album was recorded but never released—although it's widely circulated among the theatre aficionado crowd. "Woman On The Run" is like nothing heard

---

24. Kerr, Walter. "My Favorite Rock Musical So Far." *New York Times*, 8 February 1970.

on Broadway before or since—a driving folk-rock anthem infused with the sound of 1970s computer technology.

In 1974, Cryer and Ford began performing together as an act, starting at Manhattan Theatre Club (MTC). With Ford at the keys and Cryer at the mic, they delivered their own material.

In 1978, Cryer and Ford premiered the show they are perhaps best known for: *I'm Getting My Act Together and Taking It on the Road*. Somewhat an apotheosis of their three earlier off-Broadway musicals, *I'm Getting My Act Together* is semiautobiographical and fights for women to have the right to equality in multiple arenas. The show began at the Public Theater where it gradually caught on thanks to word of mouth and the championing of Joe Papp. It then transferred to the Circle in the Square off-Broadway. It did not receive positive reviews, but became Cryer and Ford's biggest hit based on audience opinion. It went on to play over one thousand performances in New York.

"Theater is for sharing our common human experience, and saying to somebody else, 'I've been through this and I'm showing it to you,'" Cryer told the *Associated Press*.[25] *I'm Getting My Act Together* revolves around Heather, a thirty-nine-year-old singer-songwriter rehearsing to go on tour. She is dealing with her divorce from an ex-husband who expected her to play the role of child-wife in their marriage, a manager who does not want her to reveal her real age or her angry side, and her own creative and personal demons.

"It takes a long time to change. Intellectually we may make certain life decisions about the way we want relationships to be, like men and women being equal.... If you're questioning those ways and intellectually arriving at a new position, that doesn't mean your feelings have arrived," Cryer also remarked. The article went into detail about how the show had received many letters from audience members who had been moved. Some accused the show of not being feminist enough, and Cryer and Ford stated that they wanted to tell a truthful story about a woman who had not arrived at a conclusion about her role in society yet, but was on a journey. The piece also referred to both women's divorces. Cryer and Ford stated that much of their work was at least semiautobiographical, so as a result, press always tended to dive into their personal lives in stories.

In 1985, Cryer and Ford's *Hang On to the Good Times* was produced at Manhattan Theatre Club. The show is a contemporary song cycle, much like the one that the show's director, Richard Maltby Jr., had created at MTC of his and collaborator David Shire's work, several years prior: *Starting Here, Starting Now*. *Hang On to the Good Times* was the idea of MTC artistic director Lynne Meadow, who wanted Cryer and Ford to have an avenue to present a collection of songs in a similar way. The show was unfortunately never recorded.

---

25. "Cryer-Ford Team Feel Current Show Communicates Best." *Paducah Sun*, 22 July 1979, p. 27.

Cryer and Ford took a crack at tackling a historic figure with *Eleanor*, a 1986 musical about the life of Eleanor Roosevelt. The show premiered at Williamstown Theatre Festival but did not continue to New York. Cryer directed this production of the show, which is a concept musical about Eleanor's life, set at her birthday party. The show received a negative review in *Variety* that killed its future, according to the writers.[26]

The American Girls Revue is a 1998 show that played multiple cities including New York, depicting the beloved American Girl Dolls on stage. The show played at American Girl Doll flagship stores and adapted stories from the different historic eras written about in the books. The show received a cast recording.

Circle of Friends is a 2000 sequel to *The American Girls Revue*, by Cryer and Ford. The *Chicago Reader* wrote that they were surprised at the meaningful quality of the piece, given its venue: the basement of American Girl Place. They said, "Theater that empowers girls doesn't come along very often—what could have been a commercial instead celebrates the complexity of girls' friendships."[27]

The 2007 TheaterWorks USA adaptation of *Anne of Green Gables* was the work of Cryer and Ford. The show opened at the Lucille Lortel, previously called the Theatre de Lys, where the writers' off-Broadway debut, *Now Is the Time for All Good Men*, had opened four decades earlier.

A 2007 review by Stephen Holden in the *New York Times* of Cryer and Ford's cabaret act noted: "*I'm Getting My Act Together* . . . triumphed at the moment when the winds of feminist self-determination were whistling through American pop culture. . . . Then the wind changed."

"Ms. Cryer and Ms. Ford are exemplars of the spirited but polite keyboard-based 1970s folk-pop that refuses to despair."[28]

In 2011, Cryer and Ford debuted a sequel to *I'm Getting My Act Together and Taking It on the Road*. Titled *Still Getting My Act Together*, the show was played in rep with the original. The two were later combined into one evening and performed in Los Angeles. Cryer described the show as such: "Act one was dispelling the old set of stereotypes about what it was to be a woman. Act two is about dispelling the stereotypes of what it's like to be older." She also said about the potential dated nature of the original: "Even though a lot of the barriers have

26. Kerns, Nancy Jane. "Gretchen Cryer and Nancy Ford: Elevating the Female Voice in American Musical Theatre." University of Hawai'i, 2018. https://scholarspace.manoa.hawaii.edu/bitstream/10125/62576/Kerns_hawii_0085O_10075.pdf.

27. Vanasco, Jennifer. "Circle of Friends: An American Girls Musical." *Chicago Reader*, 17 January 2002, https://chicagoreader.com/arts-culture/circle-of-friends-an-american-girls-musical/.

28. Holden, Stephen. "Sure, Times Have Changed, but Optimism Stays in Style." *New York Times*, 17 April 2007, https://www.nytimes.com/2007/04/17/arts/music/17crye.html.

been broken and we have women who are doctors and CEOs, the emotional underpinning of the sexual politics hasn't really changed. So the core of it is still valid." She told *LA Magazine* that mothers and daughters were attending the production together and feeling that the "emotional reality" of both parts of the story resonated with both generations.[29] One of the producers of the show was Cryer's son, actor Jon Cryer.

The Cryer and Ford song "Old Friend" is one of the team's most lasting legacies, having been performed or recorded by everyone from Betty Buckley to the New York Gay Men's Chorus. The title of *I'm Getting My Act Together and Taking It on the Road* has also entered the cultural lexicon, and often receives friendly parody. The show had a high-profile revival starring Renee Elise Goldsberry at Encores! Off-Center in 2013.

FRANCINE PASCAL
Sweet Valley High *Creator*

Francine Pascal created one of the most popular teenage book series of all time: *Sweet Valley High*. Many know Pascal's name because it has appeared on millions of volumes that have been devoured, mainly by young women, since 1983 when they were first published. The tales of Jessica and Elizabeth Wakefield and their friends and family members have been the basis of hundreds of books, multiple spin-off series, a television show, a board game, and endless other pieces of work.

Wakefields aside, Pascal spent significant time in the theatre before becoming the queen of teen dreams with *Sweet Valley*. With her brother, prolific Broadway librettist Michael Stewart, and her husband John Pascal, Francine Pascal penned the book to *George M!*, the 1968 Broadway musical about George M. Cohan. The hit show ran for a year.

In 1999, Pascal revised the book for the beloved flop musical *Mack and Mabel*, originally written on Broadway by her brother. The show had a disappointing run in 1974. Pascal's revisal of the show tried out in Massachusetts. Her work on tweaking the show to try to bring it to new audiences has been present in several productions since. *The Berkshire Eagle* wrote of the 1999 production: "Francine Pascal, sister of the show's librettist, the late Michael Stewart, has taken a thin, poorly plotted and crafted book and given it substance."[30]

---

29. Byrd, Craig. "Curtain Call: 35 Years Later, Gretchen Cryer Creates a Sequel to *I'm Getting My Act Together and Taking It on the Road.*" *LA Magazine*, 14 October 2015, https://www.lamag .com/culturefiles/curtain-call-35-years-later-gretchen-cryer-creates-a-sequel-to-im-getting-my-act -together-and-taking-it-on-the-road/.

30. Borak, Jeffrey. "*Mack and Mabel* Comes of Age in Sheffield." *Berkshire Eagle*, 29 June 1999, p. 15.

JOSEPHINE JACKSON
A Black Experience in Song

Josephine Jackson and Joseph A. Walker cowrote the book for the off-Broadway musical *The Believers*, which played three-hundred performances at the Garrick Theatre in 1968. They also both appeared in the show and contributed some of its music and lyrics.

The Believers was subtitled "A Black Experience in Song," and the show sought to dramatize Black history from just prior to the Atlantic slave trade right up to the current day. There were scenes set in Africa and scenes set at riots that had happened so recently that some audience members may well have been present at them. Like *Hallelujah, Baby!* which had happened a year earlier, *The Believers* fit a lot of years of Black history into one evening, but unlike its predecessor, *The Believers* was more in revue-type format.

The show received an original cast album and was subsequently produced regionally throughout the late 1960s and early 1970s.

MARÍA IRENE FORNÉS
Influential Experimental Theatre Maker

María Irene Fornés was one of the most influential experimental theatre makers of the twentieth century. Her work off-off-Broadway and off-Broadway has been characterized as feminist for the way that it centers women's thoughts, needs, and ideas. She was a nine-time Obie Award winner.

Fornés's most famous work is *Fefu and Her Friends*, a play that employs the experimental technique of having its audience divided in four, and the same scene played out four separate times as the audience shifts from location to location, until everyone has seen them all. Her new ideas for both content and form shifted the art form of the off-Broadway play.

María Irene Fornés, circa 1966. PHOTOFEST

Fornés was born in Cuba. She began writing in her thirties when her romantic partner Susan Sontag was having writer's block and Fornés tried to demonstrate to her how easy it was to put something down on the page.

Fornés's prominent musical theatre work was *Promenade* (1969). She wrote book and lyrics (to Al Carmines's music) and directed this absurdist musical comedy, which opened off-Broadway's Promenade Theatre.[31] The show is about a

---

31. It has never been made clear whether the show was named for the theater or vice versa.

Black convict and a white convict who escape prison, fight the establishment, and wind up back in jail. *Promenade* inspired comparisons to Brecht and *Candide*, but it was essentially unlike anything else. The score is unbelievably eclectic, and the characters have names like 105, 106, Miss I, Mr. R, Mr. T, and so on.

Promenade's relentless anti-war, anti-establishment, anti-capitalist views and its intense manner of expressing them inspired rave reviews from many of the critics, including Clive Barnes in the *New York Times*. It ran for 259 performances and won the Obie Award for Distinguished Play. The cast recording is a favorite among connoisseurs. The show received an Encores! Off-Center production in 2019.

Fornés's one Broadway venture was a play called *The Office* that closed in previews in 1966. The show, directed by Jerome Robbins and starring Elaine May and Doris Roberts, is a social commentary about life as a modern secretary.

Patti Jacob
Big Hollywood Money in a Big Broadway Musical about a Big Mayor

The husband-and-wife team of Patti and Bill Jacob wrote music and lyrics for the 1969 Broadway musical about the life of Mayor Jimmy Walker, which played the Winter Garden for eighty-four performances.

Together, Bill and Patti had written scores, a 1968 Motorola television special, and shows in Las Vegas and at the Latin Quarter. They also created nightclub and recording material for artists including Frank Sinatra, Diahann Carroll, Florence Henderson, Steve Lawrence and Eydie Gormé, and Bobby Rydell. *Jimmy* was their only legit musical.

Because the show was produced by Jack Warner, millionaire movie mogul of Warner Brothers, it was one of the first instances of big Hollywood money bringing an original musical to Broadway. *Jimmy* was such a big deal for this reason that it actually booted *Mame* out of the Winter Garden and to the Broadway Theatre.

Jimmy was partially inspired by *Fiorello!*, which had been a hit musical about a New York City mayor a decade earlier. The show starred Frank Gorshin, Anita Gillette, and Julie Wilson. Some of the reasons that *Jimmy* didn't quite catch on were that an attempt to make it fun and palatable eliminated the most interesting events of Walker's life, the bouncy 1960s score didn't fit the 1920s time period, and in the last year of the 1960s, Broadway was pointed in a more alternative direction.

One of the Jacobses' more impressive numbers was "The Walker Walk" which featured all thirty-six ensemble members singing, dancing, and playing kazoo. Their score was orchestrated by a team that included emerging orchestrator

Jonathan Tunick, called in to do a patch job in between *Promises, Promises* and *Company*.

Barnes outdid himself with cruel one-liners in his review, calling *Jimmy* "a musical with only three flaws—the book, the music, and the lyrics." He said that Gillette and Wilson "were so good that while they couldn't stop the show, they often threatened to start it."[32]

ANN STERNBERG
Gertrude Stein: Now Starring Kids

Gertrude Stein's First Reader, with music by Ann Sternberg, setting words by Stein, was the final musical to open off-Broadway in the 1960s, on December 15, 1969. The show was performed at the Astor Place Theater, which since 1991 has been known as the home of *Blue Man Group*.

While Stein's work has inspired many musicals over the years, this one was unique in that it was created for children. Sternberg, who was also known as an actor, radio personality, composer, pianist and dance arranger, was on stage at the piano, interacting with all of the young performers as they interpreted Stein's poetry.

Sternberg's other credits included work composing and music directing at the O'Neill, a 1961 off-Broadway musical called *All in Love* where she was dance arranger, as well as both music and lyrics for a stage musical version of *Sleeping Beauty*.

---

32. Suskin, Steven. "On the Record: Cast Albums of *Jimmy* and *Let It Ride*." *Playbill*, 26 April 2009, https://playbill.com/article/on-the-record-cast-albums-of-jimmy-and-let-it-ride-com-160239.

9

1970s

Protest Musicals, Female Teams, and Writers of Color

Myrna Lamb
The First Women's Liberation Musical

Mod Donna is perhaps one of the most revolutionary forgotten musicals in the canon. Many times throughout musical theatre history, a show that displays great innovations and opens new doors for expression is not fully understood or appreciated by the public in its time—but musicals that come after often adapt its innovations and are more successful at integrating them into the art form because of the shows that paved the way. A typical example of this is *Allegro*, the 1947 Rodgers and Hammerstein musical, directed and choreographed by Agnes de Mille, which introduced many new elements of the concept musical to audiences but does not usually receive credit for doing so, as it perplexed its audiences. Nevertheless, it led the way for many musicals that came afterward. *Viet Rock* could fit into this category as well.

Mod Donna is another example. In 1970, this musical opened at the Anspacher at the Public Theater, with book and lyrics by Myrna Lamb and music by Susan Hulsman Bingham. It was considered by some to be the first women's liberation musical presented at a mainstream theater.

Lamb spent her early career days in the 1960s working with the New Feminist Repertory Company. Her play, *But What Have You Done for Me Lately* is about a pregnant man who has to beg a panel of women to let him get an abortion. Her work was immediately labeled as feminist theatre, and at the time, she did not disagree.

Mod Donna was part of a slew of protest musicals being presented by the Public Theater in the 1970s. But it was unique in that it was the first from a notably female perspective. Unlike later feminist protest musicals like *I'm Getting My Act Together . . .* , *Mod Donna* was angry and uncompromising. Its extreme perspective has been pointed to as one reason why the show was so misunderstood.

Lamb's plot for *Mod Donna* found a modern woman, Donna, who began sleeping with a married couple. After becoming pregnant by the husband, Donna refuses the couple's offer to adopt her baby. So, the husband retaliates by murdering her. Lamb meant for the show to be an indictment of the toxicity of marriage as an institution. Historian Dan Dietz wrote: "Her catalogue of the wrongs perpetrated against women comes across as a male chauvinist's parody of feminist writing."[1]

Mod Donna's team had a significant number of women on it. Liza Redfield was the music director and orchestrator. Ze-eva Cohen choreographed. Jane Neufield stage-managed. Dorothea Freitag conducted an all-woman band. The

---

1. Dietz, Dan. *Off Broadway Musicals, 1910–2007: Casts, Credits, Songs, Critical Reception and Performance Data of More Than 1,800 Shows.* Jefferson, NC: McFarland, 2009.

show was directed by Joe Papp and he and Lamb butted heads throughout the process, although he started out as a champion of her work, and produced more of it later.

In an interview with Marilyn Bender for the *New York Times*, Lamb said, "There's been a little animosity from some women in the movement because I took a male director. I'm a feminist but I can't be a female chauvinist."[2]

In his program note, Papp claimed *Mod Donna* was "not a show about the feminist movement. Though Myrna Lamb is an activist and an ardent feminist, her work is much too ambiguous, too sophisticated, too comedic, to satisfy the clear-cut political sloganeering required by a mass movement."[3]

Mod Donna was dubbed "A Space-Age Musical Soap" and its over-the-top design was intended to show audiences that this was an unrealistic dramatization, reflecting on real-life themes, *not* telling a story intended to be taken literally. This concept was further enhanced by commercial breaks that appeared throughout the musical, likening it to a soap opera. In her book *Hard Times: The Adult Musical in 1970s New York City*, Elizabeth L. Wollman wrote:

> *The score of* Mod Donna, *like the dialogue and absurdist situations, does well to lighten the mood of the piece and to challenge the conventions of the traditional musical. Bingham's [music] tends toward jazzy dissonances and jagged rhythms; a reel-to-reel recording of the original production indicates that most of the lyrics were either chanted, loudly and bluntly, in unison by the chorus, or begun as solo pieces for principal characters who were then joined by the chorus after a verse of two. The songs, all of which feature Lamb's densely poetic lyrics, are written in a variety of styles, including tango, waltz, vaudeville, striptease, and rock and roll, and the styles don't necessarily match the emotional states of the characters.*[4]

Lamb wrote the libretto for *Apple Pie*, a musical which played the Anspacher in 1976. This show was just as wildly eviscerated by critics. *Apple Pie* is about a woman who escaped Hitler's Germany and all of the ways that she finds the United States just as oppressive and unjust as what she experienced in Europe. Reviews were condescending and overwhelmingly negative, claiming that the style of the show made it impossible to understand. *Apple Pie* never received

2. Bender, Marilyn. "Mod Donna—a Woman's Cry." *Chicago Tribune*, 28 March 1970, p. 117.

3. Wollman, Elizabeth L. *Hard Times: The Adult Musical in 1970s New York City*. New York: Oxford University Press, 2012.

4. Ibid.

a commercially released recording, but a record of the show was distributed to those involved and still exists among collections, today.

Lamb found that based on the space she occupied, it was not possible for her to find space in mainstream theatre. In a 1976 *New York Times* interview with Barbara Crossette, she commented on the critical reaction that both *Mod Donna* and *Apple Pie* received.

> *They don't say "I don't agree with what you've done or how you've done it." They say: "You can't write." I no longer consider myself a doctrinaire feminist. Though the feminist movement nurtured all of us, I am disillusioned with it. What I found after I was savagely attacked by critics for* Apple Pie *was that the women were no different than the men—they are afraid to affiliate with you if you are not an establishment success.*[5]

Of course the great majority of critics who evaluated both of Lamb's works at the Public were men. But a *New York Times* piece by Grace Glueck shared mostly negative thoughts on the show and culminated in saying: "I congratulate Myrna Lamb, the author, and Susan Hulsman Bingham, the composer, for getting this material off their—well, chests, and for getting a man to produce it. It didn't make me want to burn my bra—but did send me back to those early women's libbers who said it all so much better: Ibsen and Shaw."[6] She was not the only critic to negatively compare the work of *Mod Donna*'s female writers to work by male writers labeled as feminists such as Ibsen and Shaw, and also Strindberg and Coward.

In 1970, there was a backlash against the unfairly misogynist reception of *Mod Donna*. In the *Village Voice*, Vivian Gornick wrote that the criticism of the show was "patronizing and unilluminating"[7] and in a letter to the editor of the *New York Times*, Lucy Komisar, vice president of the National Organization for Women and a theatre critic in her own right wrote:

> *The reactions of your reviewers to* Mod Donna *follow the predictable pattern of anti-feminist polemics.* Mod Donna *is a masterful, witty, sardonic and blistering attack on the sexist system that forces women to destroy each other.... Myrna Lamb's lyrics are ... poetry that represents what we feel in our guts.... Lamb is one of us and we are fiercely proud of her and of the*

---

5. Crosette, Barbara. "Women Take the Stage in *Crab Quadrille.*" *New York Times*, 19 November 1976, p. 57.

6. Glueck, Grace. "'I Didn't Burn My Bra.'" *New York Times*, 10 May 1970, p. 89.

7. Kessler, Kelly. *Gender, Sex, and Sexuality in Musical Theatre*. Bristol, UK: Intellect Books Limited, 2022.

contribution Mod Donna *has made to the literature of our movement and to the cause of our liberation.*[8]

Wollman shares a moment that Lamb experienced just after *Mod Donna* closed and she was summarily rejected for a Guggenheim grant. At a National Organization for Women fundraiser, Lamb found herself regaled by a performance from an upcoming musical called *God Bless God (She Needs It)*. At the event, the show's male producer claimed it was to be the first women's liberation musical. When Lamb corrected him that *Mod Donna* had occupied that spot, he corrected himself that *God Bless God* would be the first women's liberation musical to have a successful run. The show's female writer added that it would also be the first one that was actually palatable. *God Bless God* never materialized in a full production.

CAROLE BAYER SAGER
They're Playing Her Song

One of the most successful pop lyricists of a generation, Carole Bayer Sager is well known for her songs which have gone platinum, won countless awards, appeared in films, and experienced endless radio play and concert performances.[9] She wrote or cowrote "Arthur's Theme (Best That You Can Do)," "Don't Cry Out Loud," "The Prayer," "Through the Eyes of Love," "Nobody Does It Better," "That's What Friends Are For" and many more, during a career that has found her collaborating with singers from Barbra Streisand to Michael Jackson. At the beginning of her career, she recorded and performed her own work as well.

While Bayer Sager is not best known for her work in musical theatre, she did pen two musicals for Broadway, and was involved in several others.

In 1970, the musical *Georgy*, very closely based on the movie *Georgy Girl* starring Lynn Redgrave, which had come out only four years earlier, opened on Broadway. This was a rare occurrence on Broadway in 1970: to base a new musical on a recent movie. Even when it did happen, the writers had to distinguish the properties from each other to discourage constant comparisons. They didn't usually capitalize much on the movie's brand. *Promises, Promises*, which was based on the movie *The Apartment*, wasn't called *The Apartment: The Musical*.

Part of what critics didn't like about *Georgy* was that it seemed like a movie that they had just seen—but slowed down. This kind of adaptation wasn't the norm, and critics were sour on it. But the show, about an unlikely young heroine

---

8. "Drama Mailbag." *New York Times*, 31 May 1970, https://www.nytimes.com/1970/05/31/archives/drama-mailbag-drama-mailbag-women-victims.html.

9. This section has been largely excerpted from *The Untold Stories of Broadway Volumes 1 and 4*.

in an unconventional storyline about unexpected pregnancy and the compromises of modern American life, had a lot going for it that critics didn't see.

The lyrics were by a twenty-two-year-old Carole Bayer. (She would add her married name "Sager" later.) The book was by Tom Mankiewicz, who, after an executive from United Artists saw one of *Georgy's* four performances, was whisked off to Hollywood where he wrote many of the James Bond films. The music, by George Fischoff, had a brassy, bouncy, young pop sound that was new to Broadway at the time. It would be done to more acclaim later in the decade, such as in Sager's 1979 musical with Marvin Hamlisch, *They're Playing Our Song*. In 1978, Neil Simon and Marvin Hamlisch had begun work on a musical adaptation of Simon's play *The Gingerbread Lady*. But Simon quickly had another idea. Hamlisch was always telling him stories about his relationship with fellow writer Carole Bayer Sager. Simon thought that would make an even better musical: the real-life foibles of two songwriters falling in love.

Simon wrote the book, Hamlisch wrote the music and Sager wrote the lyrics, as the three fictionalized Hamlisch and Sager's own romance. Ironically, the two were about to break up just as work on the musical began, but creating the show kept them together a bit longer. This made some of the press interviews—where journalists wanted to know about all of the parallels between them and their onstage counterparts, Vernon and Sonia—slightly awkward.

In her memoir, titled *They're Playing Our Song*, Sager shares what the collaboration was like.

"We need a song in the discotheque, Carole," Neil said. "They're out on their first date, what would they dance to?"

"Well, I'm not much of a dancer," I said apologetically. "I mean, I wish I were, but . . . maybe a slow song, I could dance to that."

"It's a discotheque, Carole," Marvin said to me. "Pay attention."

"Well, you're not a dancer either," I said defensively. "What would you dance to?"

"Carole, we're not Vernon and Sonia," he said. "This is fiction based on us. It's not our biography."

Neil laughed. "You're both so crazy," he said. "They're going to have to dance in this scene, so figure out what kind of song you'd dance to."

Bayer Sager's work was also heard on Broadway in the revue *Dancin'* (1978), the Peter Allen show *Up in One* (1979), Phyllis Newman's *The Madwoman of Central Park West* (1979), and the Peter Allen jukebox musical *The Boy from Oz*.

171

PHYLLIS ROBINSON
DDB's First Female Copy Chief Goes Broadway

Phyllis Robinson was the first female copy chief at Doyle Dane Bernbach, one of the world's top advertising agencies. She had worked at DDB for two decades and was one of its vice presidents when she made her professional theatre writing debut as the co-lyricist of *Cry for Us All* in 1970.

The show is an adaptation of William Alfred's hit play *Hogan's Goat* which had premiered only five years earlier and told a story of Irish immigrant struggle in 1890s Brooklyn. A corrupt mayor and an immigrant leader battle for power alongside a twisted love story that leaves both of their wives dead.

Cry for Us All had Alfred collaborating with Robinson on the lyrics and with director Albert Marre on the book. The music was by Mitch Leigh whose mega-hit *Man of La Mancha*, which had opened in 1965, was still playing on Broadway.

The show's plot is as dark as its title and audiences didn't warm to it during a troubled out-of-town tryout. Joan Diener, who was married to Marre, starred, and while she was a highly respected actress, she was both miscast and given increasing amounts of unnecessary material during the process. The score has its fans and has been praised for its ambition in musicalizing a relentlessly bleak story about corruption and death.

ELINOR JONES
A Musical about Colette

Colette was a French writer and actor who lived from 1873 to 1954 and became an icon, winning the Nobel Prize for Literature, penning the novel *Gigi*, and living a life both scandalous and ahead-of-its time. In 1970, her life became an off-Broadway musical, titled simply *Colette*.

The music was by Harvey Schmidt and lyrics by Tom Jones, the men whose off-Broadway hit *The Fantasticks* was already well on its way to breaking records. *Colette's* book, based on the woman's own autobiographical writing, was by Elinor Jones, Jones's wife at the time.

The show ran for a few months, largely on the strength of Zoe Caldwell's performance in the title role. The cast also included Schmidt, Holland Taylor, Mildred Dunnock, Keene Curtis, Charles Siebert, and Barry Bostwick. The production at the Ellen Stewart Theatre was produced by stalwart Broadway producer Cheryl Crawford, who had been working on the Great White Way since the 1920s. Her associate producer was Mary W. John, who would later produce *Dear Oscar*.

The writers continued to revise *Colette*, hoping for the musical to have a well-received comeback. In 1982, a new pre-Broadway production closed out of town and in 1994 the much-revised show was recorded as *Colette Collage*.

Jones continued to write extensively for the theatre, working with John Houseman's Acting Company and creating straight plays.

AMY SALTZ
Auteur of the Youthful Commune Musical

The Village Arena Theatre at 62 East 4th Street was the name of the venue where *Touch* (tag line: "The Communal Musical") played for 422 performances from 1970 to 1971. But the theater has been known by many other names over the years. Just prior to its time hosting *Touch*, the place was called The Fortune Theater and was used by Andy Warhol as both a gay cinema and a live event space.

The events preceding *Touch* at the Village Arena were on-theme, since the musical, with a book cowritten by Amy Saltz who also directed, is about a commune that provides an opportunity for sexual freedom. The show was developed at a summer stock theater in Pennsylvania and almost everyone on or off stage was younger than twenty-four years old.

In the *Times*, Mel Gussow wrote: "At the preview I attended, I wondered if all of [the actors] would get through the show without forgetting their lines or bursting into tears. They made it through to the end and one was pleased for them. There was a certain charm in this threat of stage fright." He went on to call *Touch* artless and amateurish, but claimed this was part of its charm. Audiences agreed and flocked to see this innocent-feeling sexual musical for about a year.

On the commune, the young characters in this rock musical sang songs with titles like "Reaching, Touching" and "Tripping." The gentle approach to the controversial youth culture was part of what drew in audiences. After half a year, the musical transferred to the Martinique Theatre, a better-known and more centrally located off-Broadway spot near Herald Square.

Saltz was one of the only artists involved who actually had professional New York theatre credits; she had assistant directed a production of *King Lear* at the Vivian Beaumont two years prior and was working at the Public Theater at the time *Touch* premiered. She wound up assistant directing *Hair* at the Public, an experience she brought to the table on *Touch*. Saltz's direction for *Touch* was praised as avoiding cliche in some reviews; other reviews claimed the show didn't even seem directed, but rather naturally improvised—which those in the theatre know takes a good deal of elegant and precise direction.

Touch did move forward to have several productions after New York, including a prominent one in Boston, but it was never commercially recorded or licensed and is thus largely forgotten. Saltz went on to direct off-Broadway and regionally. Her work on *Touch* as a cowriter of the book was in conjunction with her auteur work directing the show and she didn't author other musicals.

NAOMI SHEMER
The First Lady of Israeli Song and Poetry

Naomi Shemer contributed music and lyrics to several songs that appeared in the 1971 Israeli musical *To Live Another Summer, To Pass Another Winter*. Shemer was an Israeli singer-songwriter who was called "the first lady of Israeli song and poetry" and worked extensively in her native country, only making this one stop on American theatrical soil.

How many Broadway musicals can say they had their out-of-town-tryout in Tel Aviv? *To Live Another Summer, To Pass Another Winter* is a musical about Israeli life as seen through the eyes of that nation's youth. Modern Broadway style songs and rock songs mixed with traditional Israeli folk music at the old Helen Hayes Theatre for three months and then the Lunt-Fontanne for three months. Critics were split between enjoying the musical's appeal and objecting to what they judged to be a publicity campaign for Israel disguised as a commercial musical. Clive Barnes wrote, "The show has an endearing vitality and an enduring spirit . . . only an Arab could hate [it]!"[10] But his review was not the only objectionable one. Sharing in that honor was *Time* magazine which found "the girls [to be] the [most] good-looking . . . all season . . . and if any one of them opts to stay in the U.S., she can make someone a happy man."[11]

To Live Another Summer, To Pass Another Winter was joined by a second Israeli Broadway musical, *Only Fools Are Sad*, which opened one month later, one block over at the Edison in 1971.

Shemer's song "The Grove of Eucalyptus" achieved great popularity in Israel before being placed in *To Live Another Summer*. She also wrote the music for the show's "Noah's Ark" number.

ADDY O. FIEGER AND CARYL GABRIELLE YOUNG
An All-Female Team and Oscar Wilde

In 1972, a musical entirely written by women opened on Broadway and closed after five performances. This was *Dear Oscar*, an original musical about Oscar Wilde's life, with book and lyrics by Caryl Gabrielle Young and music by Addy O. Fieger.

---

10. Barnes, Clive. "Theater: Pleasant Revue." *New York Times*, 22 October 1971.

11. "The Theater: Hark, the Israeli Skylark." *Time*, 1 November 1971.

Dear Oscar opened at the Playhouse Theatre, a small venue on 48th Street near Ninth Avenue. The Playhouse, also known as the Jack Lawrence in its later years before being demolished in the late 1980s, could be used as a Broadway or off-Broadway house, depending on a show's contracts.

This 1972 Broadway musical revolves around Wilde's relationship with his wife and with his male lover, which leads to his jailing in the 1890s. The reviews were overwhelmingly negative. Unlike the majority of musicals from the late 1960s onward that chose to dramatize a famous personality, *Dear Oscar*'s music was *not* anachronistic; it was English music hall pastiche, meant to closely imitate the music of its setting. Critics used to the likes of *Jesus Christ Superstar* seemed offended that an approach would be taken that musicalized such a figure with a realistic musical style rather than a contemporary, conceptual one.

The show was produced solely by Mary W. John, and it's worth noting that this rare all-female writing team was chosen and employed by a female producer.

Fieger also composed a 1980 off-Broadway musical called *Changes*, and cowrote the book with Danny Apolinar and Dorothy Love. *Changes* played at the Theater de Lys (now known as the Lucille Lortel) and its stars were Kelly Bishop, Larry Kert, Trina Parks, and Irving Allen Lee. The show is a sung-through musical about two adult couples and the relationship challenges they face in modern life, framed from one New Year's Eve to the next. The show closed after only seven performances. Fieger's music appeared in the more successful off-Broadway revue *Secrets Every Smart Traveler Should Know* posthumously in 1998.

EVE MERRIAM AND HELEN MILLER
Inner City

The subtitle for *Inner City*, the 1971 Broadway musical, was "A Street Cantata." The show, with music by Helen Miller and lyrics by Eve Merriam, was based on Merriam's book, *The Inner City Mother Goose*.

The show was conceived and directed by Tom O'Horgan—*Hair*'s director—just a couple years after that musical opened. *Hair* was still playing next door at the Biltmore while *Inner City* was playing at the Barrymore. *Inner City* had nine racially diverse cast members performing over fifty songs (narrowed down from over seventy that were written) in the sung-through musical that takes classic nursery rhymes and updates them to be about modern city life.

In the liner notes for the original cast recording by MasterWorks, Merriam said,

> *[I]nner City is] satire for unadulterated adults, thereby following in the tradition of the original* Mother Goose *rhymes back in the eighteenth century when "Little Jack Horner," "Mary, Mary Quite Contrary," "Who Killed*

Cock Robin" and other characters were invented as sophisticated political and social commentary on the times. I wanted to say something about the urgent concerns of our own age, and so I set my book in the heart of where the liveliest action is—inside the Inner City, for this, as the opening number sings, "This the Nub of the Nation."[12]

The show starred Linda Hopkins, who received the show's sole Tony nomination—and won, for Best Featured Actress in a Musical. She also won the Drama Desk Award. The show was compared unfavorably to *Ain't Supposed to Die a Natural Death*, the Barrymore's previous tenant. *Inner City* ran for three months.

About the overall concept of *Inner City*, Merriam wrote in the show's album liner notes: "We wound up with our show about the perils and pleasures of being alive today and not giving up hope that we can all survive and make our cities safe for living and loving and neighborliness and regreening."

The show is licensed as *Inner City*, although in 1984, it received an off-Broadway reworking where it was retitled *Street Dreams*.

TONI TENNILLE
Future Pop Legend Writes Environmental Protest Musical Produced by Roger Ailes

Mother Earth is a protest musical about saving our planet, a modern pop-rock performance piece presented on the heels of *Hair* that wanted to make audiences feel fired up about air pollution, species extinction, big business, and overpopulation. It played twelve performances at the Belasco in 1972.

Toni Tennille, circa 1976. ABC/PHOTOFEST © ABC

The show played South Coast Rep and American Conservatory Theater out of town before coming to New York. It received nearly all rave reviews in California, with critics remarking that *Mother Earth* was fresh, exciting, and had something to say.

Mother Earth moved to Broadway, produced by Republican media consultant Roger Ailes; the man who would later become CEO and chairman of *Fox News* once produced a Broadway musical about the environment. His sole Broadway credit would always be *Mother Earth*, a show with anti-Vietnam sketches and jokes about fashionable gas masks and a song called "Save the

---

12. Merriam, Eve. "Inner City- 1971." MasterWorks Broadway, https://masterworksbroadway.com/music/inner-city-1971/.

World for Children." Ailes, then thirty-two years old, even wrote additional lyrics for *Mother Earth* in addition to raising the money for it from Nixon supporters who were grateful he had helped Nixon get elected. Ailes's *Playbill* bio was all about his previous work in television and politics and many critics pointed out that *Mother Earth* would be better off on public television than at the Belasco.

Mother Earth has music by Toni Shearer, later known as Toni Tennille. When the show was still in its out-of-town phase, the keyboard player moved on to another gig, and a man named Daryl Dragon came in to sub on keys for *Mother Earth* in between Beach Boys gigs. That's how the duo later on known as Captain and Tennille met.

"The keyboardist had been given a recording of me singing songs from the show and he liked it, so he agreed to fly up from L.A. and audition," Tennille wrote in her memoir.

> *I first saw him in the lobby of the theater, a rail-thin, pale young man with large brown eyes and scruffy dark hair. He was dressed all in black and slumped on a bench, arms crossed in an aloof, bored manner. But when he sat down and began to play, I immediately knew he was perfect for the show. And there was something about him I found intriguing. His long, slender fingers would play the music perfectly note by note, and then suddenly switch to an entirely different tune right in the middle, improvising for a few bars before going back to the first song. It was like he was telling me jokes through the music, and it made me laugh.*[13]

When *Mother Earth* closed at the Belasco, Tennille went to join the Beach Boys on tour and the rest is music history. Within three years, Captain and Tennille had the Record of the Year for "Love Will Keep Us Together."

While *Mother Earth* received only raves on the West Coast (*Variety* even said it was better than *Hair*), it received largely pans on the East Coast. The main complaint of every critic could be reduced to: Yes, but what's your point? Who could possibly be against saving the environment?

Newspapers also said that *Mother Earth* was "too slick to be amateur and too amateur for professional theatre" (Martin Gottfried, *Women's Wear Daily*)[14] and bristled at the show being "a bit [too] collegiate" (*Time*).[15] These young people with something to say about saving the planet just did not belong on Broadway!

---

13. Tennille, Toni. *Toni Tennille: A Memoir*. Essex, CT: Lyons Press, 2016.

14. Dietz, Dan. *The Complete Book of 1970s Broadway Musicals*. Lanham, MD: Rowman & Littlefield Publishers, 2015.

15. Ibid.

In the *New York Times*, Clive Barnes said, "Humorless humor is a form of aural pollution" and then worried that his bad review of *Mother Earth* was like "stealing wheat germ lollipops from kids."[16]

Toni Tennille (Shearer) was very proud of the show, its message, its modern sound. Her regret was that she never had a lawyer look over her contract when Hollywood producer types came to see *Mother Earth* in California and bragged they could bring it to Broadway. She signed away creative control to Ailes and his two collaborators without realizing it. By the time the show opened on Broadway, she did not consider it her own anymore. The show had been cheapened and changed without her consent and it broke her heart. She would not return to Broadway.

The cast of *Mother Earth* included John Bennett Perry, Matthew Perry's father. He was one of several cast members who went on record about how the men who took control of *Mother Earth*, producer Roger Ailes, director Ray Golden and consultant (Broadway's legendary) Kermit Bloomgarden, didn't understand it, and were turning something young and vibrant into an out-of-touch Borscht Belt musical. One of the first things they did was insist the show had to be sexier, and put all of the women in hot pants. Tennille was horrified by this.

When Tennille quit the show, she was replaced as a performer by Kelly Garrett, who would later win a Theatre World Award for her performance. "[Kelly] was striking looking and a hell of a singer, but she had no Broadway experience I knew of," Perry remembered for Gabriel Sherman's book on Roger Ailes.[17] Rick Podell, another *Mother Earth* actor who would later originate a role in *Sunset Boulevard*, contributed, "Roger made sure she had some solos. People go: wait a minute, is the producer fucking the leading lady?"[18] And Frank Coombs, another cast member was supposed to help Kelly catch up on learning the choreography without touching her. "The only reason the show existed was Roger was dating Kelly Garrett and Kelly needed Broadway work."[19]

But Ailes did care about *Mother Earth* for other reasons. One day at a *Mother Earth* rehearsal at the Belasco he bragged, "I sold The Trick to the American people, now I'm going to sell THIS and it's going to be great."[20]

A publicity stunt staged by Roger Ailes found the cast of *Mother Earth*, outside the Belasco, wearing gas masks and riding their bicycles to the theater.

---

16. Barnes, Clive. "Stage: *Mother Earth*, a Rock Revue." *New York Times*, 20 October 1972.

17. Sherman, Gabriel. *The Loudest Voice in the Room: How the Brilliant, Bombastic Roger Ailes Built Fox News—and Divided a Country.* New York: Random House, 2014.

18. Ibid.

19. Ibid.

20. Ibid.

"It's a great show," Ailes said at the time. "I don't know anything about Broadway, but I'm learning. It's much more exciting than politics. Nixon was O.K.—but all those state campaigns—wow! I mean, I finally got bored with South Dakota."[21]

MICKI GRANT
Don't Bother Her, She Can't Cope

In 1981, Micki Grant expressed a frustration to the *Evening Sun*. "A woman or a Black person should be allowed to write about universal themes. It's as if we had no right as women and blacks to get involved in anything other than black and white issues. I want people to get to know each other as people. As long as you don't give me a problem, I don't have a problem. If you get up in the morning and look in the mirror and you have a headache, you don't have a Black headache."[22]

Micki Grant in a production shot from *Don't Bother Me, I Can't Cope*, circa 1972, with Bobby Hill. PHOTOFEST

Grant was an exceptional pioneer in musical theatre who had much attention called to her gender and race over the years because of the barriers she broke. The headache line was one that recurred in her interviews over the years as she sought to make her point about being seen as a writer of universally resonant stories.

Grant started out professionally gaining more attention as a performer, although she was also playing and writing music from a young age. She appeared off-Broadway in four shows in subsequent years in the early 1960s: *Fly Blackbird* in 1962, *Brecht on Brecht* in 1963, *The Cradle Will Rock* in 1964 and *Leonard Bernstein's Theatre Songs* in 1965. She also appeared on Broadway in *Tambourines to Glory* in 1963.

Tambourines to Glory was written by Langston Hughes. About his influence, Grant said, "We had a special relationship because I was a disciple of his poetry, then he became a playwright, so I sort of followed in his footsteps in a way. But that was one of the greatest things in my life: meeting Langston Hughes."[23]

---

21. Ibid.

22. "Lyricist Micki Grant Is That and More." *Evening Sun*, 12 November 1981.

23. Kahn, Erin. "The Irrepressible Micki Grant: Award-Winning Composer, Actor and Trailblazer." *Stage Buddy*, 24 November 2020. https://stagebuddy.com/theater/theater-feature/irrepressible -micki-grant-award-winning-composer-actor-trailblazer.

In 1966, Grant joined the cast of the soap opera, *Another World*, becoming the first Black actor to hold a contract role with a main storyline on a daytime soap. She appeared on the show for seven years. She was also the first Black woman to achieve success at her high level writing commercial jingles for television.

Although Grant's acting career took off in a significant way first, she was a published writer at age twelve, with a book of poetry, and her 1959 song "Pink Shoe Laces" topped the pop charts.

In 1972, Grant's writing career soared when she wrote book, music, and lyrics for *Don't Bother Me, I Can't Cope* (she was the first woman to write all three for a Broadway musical)—and starred in the show too! The show won the Outer Critics Circle Award for Outstanding Musical, the Drama Desk Award for Most Promising Lyricist (for Grant), the Grammy Award for Best Score from an Original Cast Show Album, and many other awards. *Cope* was nominated for four Tony Awards, including Best Musical, Best Book of a Musical, Best Original Score, and Best Direction of a Musical for Vinnette Carroll, Grant's frequent collaborator who, with *Cope*, became the first Black woman to direct a musical on Broadway.

Don't Bother Me, I Can't Cope opened at the Playhouse Theatre and then transferred to the Edison, two theaters that are no longer Broadway houses. The show ran for over one-thousand performances on Broadway. It is an extraordinarily original song cycle about the Black experience in America.

Don't Bother Me, I Can't Cope sets the Black experience to song, in a show that features eclectic musical styles. The musical explores religion, education, prejudice, life in the tenements, student protests, the intersectionality of the struggles for feminism and Black power, and so much more. *Cope* gives a powerful voice to the Black experience, and its message, focused on the absolute need for political change and altogether optimistic that it would happen, is the inspiring work of Grant and Carroll. Since Grant also starred in the show, she was able to share her own words and music, in her own voice. One highlight of *Cope* is a song called "They Keep Coming," where the cast names Black heroes and heroic acts, and a few allies, while chanting the title of the song insistently, a frenetic celebration of Black excellence.

A 1976 *Boston Globe* feature on Grant noted that she constantly said Vinnette Carroll's name in the media, crediting her for conceiving *Cope* and for so much more during their longtime collaboration, in which they clicked from the beginning. She also commented on the current state of theatre for Black artists, and their connection to *Cope*.

A Boston Globe article commented, "Grant says she's feeling good about the number of Blacks who are working in commercial theater today. She says she feels even better that many of the actors or actresses appearing in, say, *Guys and Dolls* or *Bubbling Brown Sugar*, put in some time with one of the *Cope* companies.

But production money is still hard to come by for Black women as she and Carroll have discovered."[24]

Even though *Cope* was a smash hit, Grant and Carroll had trouble finding investors for their next show, *I'm Laughing, but I Ain't Tickled*, a Jamaican folk tale that Grant also starred in, which played Carroll's Urban Arts in 1976. Carroll gave an interview to the *Daily News* when the piece opened and commented on the proliferation of "Black theater" all across America. "In the 60's, Black people suddenly [became] more economically solvent. They could spend money for more than just the bare necessities of life. When that happened, playwrights were encouraged to write, producers were willing to take the risks, and suddenly, Black audiences developed."[25]

Unlike *Cope*, *I'm Laughing, but I Ain't Tickled*, didn't continue past Urban Arts. It never received a cast recording and hasn't been produced since.

Grant's next Broadway venture after *Cope* was *Your Arms Too Short to Box with God*, for which she wrote additional music and lyrics. The show was directed by Carroll and the majority of its score was by Alex Bradford, but Grant wrote five numbers, including the opening. The musical was based on the *Book of Matthew*, and it received a Broadway revival in 1980.

In 1978, Grant was one of several writers who contributed to the Stephen Schwartz–helmed revue, *Working*. Grant's numbers, "Lovin' Al," "If I Could've Been," and "Cleanin' Women" are highlights of the show, chronicling what it was like to be part of the American workforce. "Lovin' Al" is the story of a parking lot attendant, "If I Could've Been" is a central piece for the show, closing act one, and "Cleanin' Women" is Grant's take on domestic house cleaners. The song movingly and spiritedly tells the story of mothers who professionally clean houses so that their daughters don't have to.

Grant's second original musical as sole writer on Broadway was *It's So Nice to Be Civilized*. In 1980, she wrote book, music, and lyrics for this show, which closed after eight performances at the Martin Beck Theatre. *It's So Nice to Be Civilized* is about a white social worker who is tasked with initiating an art project in an impoverished Black neighborhood. The show has more of a plot than *Cope* but is still filled with character portraits and is episodic in a song-cycle-esque style. Critics did not respond to this combination of genres and the show received fairly lukewarm reviews across the board.

The *New York Times*' Mel Gussow compared *It's So Nice to Be Civilized* unfavorably to Melvin Van Peebles' *Ain't Supposed to Die a Natural Death* and wrote further, "Admittedly, Miss Grant is not seeking such a rough-edge grittiness. As we know from her previous musicals . . . she is a cheerful and convivial composer.

---

24. "Micki Grant Can Cope as Star/Composer/Lyricist." *Boston Globe*, 15 October 1976.

25. She Came a Long Way." *Daily News*, 10 May 1976.

Her songs are melodic representations of the winking sunburst that adorns the program of her new show."[26]

Grant had many additional writing credits. In 1974, she cowrote lyrics and wrote music for *The Prodigal Sister*, with book writer and co-lyricist J. E. Franklin. The show played the Theatre de Lys. She also wrote music and lyrics for *Phillis* (1986) and English lyrics for *Jacques Brel Blues* (1988).

Don't Bother Me I Can't Cope has received renewed interest in recent years. This might have happened earlier if the show's cast recording had been reissued on CD, but as it was only on LP for decades, a generation missed out on hearing it. *Cope* received an off-Broadway production at the York Theatre in 2016 and an Encores! Off-Center production in 2018, choreographed and directed by Savion Glover.

Grant also won an NAACP Image Award, the National Black Theatre Festival's Living Legend Award, the Sidney Poitier Lifelong Achievement Award, and a Lifetime Achievement Award from the Dramatists Guild of America. She passed away in 2021.

DIZ WHITE
New York's First Long-Running Musical in Spanish

What was New York's first long-running musical in Spanish? It was *El Grande de Coca-Cola*, which played 1,114 performances at the Mercer Arts Center and at Plaza 9 in the Plaza Hotel from 1973 to 1975.

Diz White conceived *El Grande de Coca-Cola* with Ron House. The show is about a town in Honduras where a would-be impresario promises to present a parade of stars at the local theater. When none of them show up, he attempts to pass off the local town folk as celebrities. The loosely plotted musical was devised by its original group of actors, White included, during an initial European tour. It could be understood by non-Spanish speakers as well, as it capitalized hugely on physical comedy and impressions.

While *El Grande de Coca-Cola* was not recorded, it was licensed, and so it is still presented today. It also received a 1986 revival at the Village Gate.

White has had a long career as an actor and writer, working in television, theatre, film, and books.

---

26. Gussow, Mel. "Stage: *Nice to Be Civilized*, a Musical Neighborhood." *New York Times*, 4 June 1980.

ANNE BEATTS
Pioneering Comedy and Liner Notes

Anne Beatts was one of the original writers for *Saturday Night Live*. But like many television writers, her professional foundation was in the theatre. Beatts was one of the creators of the hit off-Broadway revue *National Lampoon's Lemmings*, which played the Village Gate for 350 performances in 1973. The live show was based on the humor magazine of the same name, which Beatts ended up becoming involved with because she dated one of its writers.

"The only entree to that boys club was basically by fucking somebody in the club," Anne Beatts told the *New Yorker* in 2002. "Which wasn't the reason you were fucking them necessarily. I mean, you didn't go 'Oh, I want to get into this. I think I'll have sex with this person.' It was just that if you were drawn to funny people who were doing interesting things, then the only real way to get to do those things yourself was to make that connection."[27]

Beatts certainly didn't have an easy time getting her work heard and advancing in the comedy systems of the 1970s. She told *Vice* that she quit the magazine after asking one of its cofounders why her pieces were infrequently published and hearing him respond: "I just don't think chicks are funny."[28] She cried into her soup.

Of the ten writers for *National Lampoon's Lemmings* at the Village Gate, Beatts was the only woman. Two years later, in 1975, she was one of the only women writing in the first season of *Saturday Night Live*. She wrote for the show until 1980. She went on to amass many television credits, including creating the beloved series *Square Pegs*.

In 1979, Beatts made her Broadway debut writing material for Gilda Radner's show at the Winter Garden. She did this alongside several fellow *Saturday Night Live* writers, with Lorne Michaels at the show's helm.

In 1986, Beatts received a unique Broadway credit. On the Ellie Greenwich jukebox musical *Leader of the Pack* she was billed with: "Liner Notes by Anne Beatts." The musical was one of the very first to take the songs popularized by an artist and use them to tell the life story of that artist. Before *Leader of the Pack*, most Broadway musicals that used a popular song catalog did so in revue form. But this musicalization of the life of Ellie Greenwich, known for songs like "Be My Baby," "Chapel of Love," and "Do Wah Diddy" was a new kind of show. And Beatts was tasked with the material between the songs, which the 1986

---

27. Gladwell, Malcolm. "Group Think." *New Yorker*, 2 December 2002, https://www.newyorker.com/magazine/2002/12/02/group-think.

28. Cohen, Sascha. "Anne Beatts, Laughter Pioneer." *Vice*, 23 January 2016, https://www.vice.com/en/article/jpy78g/anne-beatts-laughter-pioneer.

production did not consider a "book" but something else. A pioneering Broadway jukebox musical, *Leader of the Pack* labeled its Beatts-written book as liner notes. The original concept for *Leader of the Pack*, which originated off-Broadway at the Bottom Line, is attributed to Melanie Mintz.

While nominated for Best Musical, nearly all critics found the show and its book to be thin. This was decades before the heyday of jukebox musicals, cued by *Mamma Mia!* at the turn of the twenty-first century, and the tone and style of such a show was not to the liking of the theatrical elite.

JILL WILLIAMS
She Wrote All Three

Jill Williams wrote book, music, and lyrics for *Rainbow Jones*, which closed on opening night at the Music Box Theatre in 1974.

The show is about a young woman named *Rainbow Jones* who has decided to drop out of society. She spends her days hanging around Central Park reading *Aesop's Fables* and, oddly enough, talking to many of the animals she finds there. These animal roles are played by human actors in *Rainbow Jones*, and one finds out later that Rainbow's odd behavior is because each of the animals represents one of her dead family members, lost through a tragic accident.

The show was nearly universally panned, and Williams herself received some skewering, condescending reviews. For example, Douglas Watt of the New York *Daily News* wrote that "Williams should, for the common good, henceforth be denied access either to a typewriter or to a musical instrument of any kind."[29]

Williams had previously worked as an advertising copywriter. She penned *Rainbow Jones* because she was inspired by *You're a Good Man, Charlie Brown* to create a musical that could be family fare. She went on to write several books, but did not return to the professional New York theatre scene.

Unlike many of the very-quickly-closed musicals in this book, *Rainbow Jones* is licensed and thus its life continues in other theaters.

CHARLOTTE ZALTZBERG
Bearing Lorraine Hansberry's Legacy

Throughout history, it was often only possible for women to get a seat at the writers' table on Broadway if their male romantic partner, brother, or father was working in the field. Charlotte Zaltzberg had a more unusual connection. Her brother-in-law was one of most skilled musical theatre librettists of all time,

---

29. Watt, Douglas. *"Rainbow Jones." Daily News*.

Joseph Stein. While Stein was writing *Fiddler on the Roof,* he often discussed the process with Zaltzberg, who wanted to work in the theatre.

Zaltzberg's eventual professional entry to the field also came around in a unique way. After Lorraine Hansberry, writer of *A Raisin in the Sun,* passed away, her husband, Robert Nemiroff, hired Zaltzberg as his secretary to help manage Hansberry's legacy and works. She worked on projects for stage and radio, including *To Be Young, Gifted, and Black,* an adaptation of Hansberry's writing. The play had a 380-performance run at the Cherry Lane Theatre in 1969. Zaltzberg also worked as the general manager of the Mayfair Theatre, as part of a Yiddish theatre company, and was active in civil rights work.

Zaltzberg's work with Hansberry's words led to jobs on a 1970 Broadway production of *Les Blancs* and a 1972 Broadway production of *The Sign in Sidney Brustein's Window.* The combined run of both shows didn't add up to a month—but *Raisin* was a different story.

In 1973, the musical adaptation of *A Raisin in the Sun,* with a book by Nemiroff and Zaltzberg, music by Judd Woldin, and lyrics by Robert Brittan, opened at the 46th Street Theatre (now the Richard Rodgers). It won the Tony Award for Best Musical, and was also nominated for eight other awards, including Best Book and Best Score. Virginia Capers won for Best Actress in a Musical, playing Lena Younger.

In the *New York Times,* Clive Barnes wrote: "The present book by Robert Nemiroff and Charlotte Zaltzberg is perhaps even better than the play. It retains all of Miss Hansberry's finest dramatic encounters with the dialogue, as cutting and as honest as ever, intact. But the shaping of the piece is slightly firmer and better."[30]

Lorraine Hansberry, the first Black female playwright to have a play performed on Broadway, died at age thirty-four of pancreatic cancer. Zaltzberg died at age forty-nine of breast cancer, only a few months after *Raisin* opened. She was given her Tony Award nomination posthumously.

JOYCE STONER
An A Chorus Line *Prequel*

I'll Die If I Can't Live Forever is an off-Broadway musical revue that opened in October of 1974 and ran for eighty-one performances. The exact timing of the show's opening is important because of another musical that came soon after.

Karen Johnson conceived the story and Joyce Stoner wrote music and lyrics for this musical about stage struck young people trying to make it in show business. The musical is set at an audition and the characters share their dreams and

---

30. "What's Opened in the Theater?" *New York Times,* 4 November 1973.

struggles. This was all happening in *I'll Die If I Can't Live Forever* while Michael Bennett was still developing what would become the musical *A Chorus Line*, which would open off-Broadway in April of 1975 and go on to become one of the landmark musicals of the canon.

I'll Die If I Can't Live Forever was more satiric and cynical than the later show. As Thomas Hischak noted, the show poked fun at later musicals like *A Chorus Line* and *Fame*, even though it materialized before they did.[31]

Stoner's songs have titles like "My Life's a Musical Comedy," "It's Great to Be Gay," and "Let's Have a Rodgers and Hammerstein Affair." The show played the Improvisation on 44th Street near Ninth Avenue, which is today The Producers Club—and then, was about two blocks from the future home of *A Chorus Line* on Broadway, the Shubert. The reviews were mostly gleefully positive, critics rejoicing over the scrappiness of the concept and how it was executed by talented young people. Stoner was also one of the performers.

Stoner continued to write theatre, and also made a career as an art conservator, directing one of the three fine art graduate conservation programs in the country.

I'll Die If I Can't Live Forever is licensed and published, and while it may not be well- remembered today, in 1974, the *New York Times* called it "the best mini-musical in town."[32]

NITRA SCHARFMAN
The Shortest-Running Best Musical Tony Nominee

The Lieutenant is the shortest-running production to ever be nominated for the Best Musical Tony Award. In 1975, the sung-through rock opera about the My Lai massacre during the Vietnam War played nine performances at the Lyceum. The title refers to the one lieutenant who was scapegoated and arrested, even though multiple U.S. soldiers killed hundreds of unarmed civilians. These events happened only seven years before the musical was produced.

The brainchild of three writers, Nitra Scharfman, Gene Curty, and Chuck Strand, *The Lieutenant* was compared to *Jesus Christ Superstar*, and received mainly positive reviews. The *Daily News* called it a "shattering anti-recruitment poster"[33] and the *New York Times* said: "*The Lieutenant* has a passion and vitality

---

31. Hischak, Thomas. *Off-Broadway Musicals Since 1919: From Greenwich Village Follies to The Toxic Avenger.* Lanham, MD: Scarecrow Press, 1911.

32. "Display Ad 89—No Title." *New York Times*, 2 December 1974, p. 43.

33. Watt, Douglas. "*The Lieutenant* Is Shattering." *Daily News*, 11 March 1975, p. 187.

not often found in musicals these days. It is also, and this may be even rarer, a musical with something to say worth saying."[34]

There were a few bad reviews, including the *New York Post*, which said: "One of the most deplorable aspects of the . . . Vietnam [War] was the way . . . it has spawned so many plays on the subject."[35] And *Women's Wear Daily*, who wrote "Rock musical[s]. . . . Once and for all, this genre is dead."[36]

The *New York Times* reported on the musical's origin story: "In 1967, . . . Mrs. Scharfman, a housewife and mother of three, with only the musical training parents often impose on children, needed someone to sing for demonstration tapes of some songs she had written. The person selected was Mr. Curty's girlfriend Barbara (now Mrs. Curty). She suggested that since Mr. Curty, who had been teaching music and singing in clubs in Queens, also was writing music, Mrs. Scharfman and he collaborate."[37] Strand joined the group after meeting Curty and explained that "1971 was a bad [year] for electrical engineers and Nitra looked like a great source of home-cooked meals." Shortly after, they came up with the idea for *The Lieutenant*.

The Lieutenant is almost completely forgotten today, because even though it was appreciated in its moment, including being nominated for the Best Score Tony Award over *Mack and Mabel* that season, it was never recorded or licensed. Scharfman was the fifth woman to ever be nominated for the Tony for Best Book and the fifth for Best Score as well.

In 2023, *The Lieutenant* returned to New York for the first time since its Broadway run in 1975, as part of the York Theatre Company's Mufti series.

NTOZAKE SHANGE
for colored girls

While not technically a musical, *for colored girls who have considered suicide / when the rainbow is enuf* defies categorization and has been described alternatingly as a play, a musical, a play with music, or a choreopoem. Its author Ntozake Shange was a writer of both stage and literature and she herself described *for colored girls* as a choreopoem. In the show, which started performances at a bar called Demonte's on East 3rd Street, then moved to the Henry Street Settlement, playing free performances, then transferred to the Public Theater off-Broadway before transferring to Broadway's Booth Theatre for a lengthy run from 1976

34. Barnes, Clive. "*Lieutenant* Has Passion, Vitality." *New York Times*, 11 March 1975, https://www
.nytimes.com/1975/03/10/archives/lieutenant-musical-with-something-worth-singing.html.

35. Watts, Richard. "One of the Most Deplorable." *New York Post*, 11 March 1975.

36. Ettorre, Barbara. "*The Lieutenant*." *Women's Wear Daily*, 11 March 1975.

37. "Tony-Award Nominee from Queens." *New York Times*, 6 April 1975, p. 94.

Ntozake Shange, circa 1978. BY UNKNOWN PHOTOGRAPHER/ WIKIMEDIA COMMONS

to 1978, she addressed the lives of Black women in America.

In the *New York Times*, Clive Barnes wrote: "Black sisterhood. That's what Ntozake Shange's totally extraordinary and wonderful evening is all about. It has those insights into life and living that make the theater such an incredible marketplace for the soul. And simply because it is about black women—not just blacks and not just women—it is a very humbling but inspiring thing for a white man to experience."[38]

The show includes music by Diana Wharton for a song contained therein called "I Found God in Myself."

Shange was profiled in the *New York Times* in 1976 and said, "We have to demand the regular-ness of being human; just stop saying being black is a drag. It's really tough and dip-sadeedah, all of which is true. We have always been people. We must be allowed the right to be just regular Joe Blow."[39]

Shange had a long and successful career as a playwright and writer of books, winning a Guggenheim fellowship and an Obie Award among many other accolades, and while she wasn't typically considered a musical theatre writer, her creation of *for colored girls* deserves mention for its use of poetry and music.

In 2010, the show received a starry film adaptation. In 2022, *for colored girls* received a Broadway revival, which was nominated for seven Tony Awards, including two for director-choreographer Camille A. Brown. The revival was positively acknowledged for spotlighting the legacy of such an important piece of work about the Black female experience.

EMME (EMMELYNE) KEMP
"It's Hard to Categorize Pianist-Singer-Composer Emme Kemp"

Emme Kemp is a prolific performer and writer whose career has spanned Broadway, recordings and television. She got her start at nightclubs, both at the piano and in front of the mic as a vocalist. It was rare to see a Black woman headlining

---

38. Barnes, Clive. "Stage: Black Sisterhood: Ntozake Shange's *For Colored Girls* Opens at Papp's Anspacher Theater." *New York Times*, 2 June 1976, p. 42, https://www.nytimes.com/1976/06/02/archives/stage-black-sisterhood-ntozake-shanges-for-colored-girls-opens-at.html.

39. Fraser, C. Gerald, "Theater Finds an Incisive New Playwright." *New York Times*, 16 June 1976, p. 27, https://www.nytimes.com/1976/06/16/archives/theater-finds-an-incisive-new-playwright.html.

as a pianist in 1963, but Kemp consistently did. She also played music with military bands and in cocktail lounges.

A mentee of the legendary musical theatre writer and musician Eubie Blake, Kemp recorded and performed with Blake throughout the 1970s. She arranged an evening of his songs for Harvard University, and it was these musical arrangements that led to her job in 1976, as one of the first Black women to write for a Broadway musical with *Bubbling Brown Sugar*.

In addition to cowriting music and lyrics for *Bubbling Brown Sugar*'s title song, she also performed in the cast. "You could say I got to the Broadway stage through the pit!" she told an interviewer in 1991.[40] For the show she also cowrote the song "Moving Uptown" and was the sole writer of the numbers "Dutch's Song" and "Harlem Makes Me Feel." *Bubbling Brown Sugar* is a musical revue celebrating the contributions of Black artists during the Harlem Renaissance, and Kemp was at the helm of all of the show's new material. It ran for 766 performances at the ANTA Playhouse (now the August Wilson Theatre).

In 1983, *Billboard* announced that Kemp was working on a new musical called *Brassy*, writing book, music and lyrics herself.[41] The show never materialized.

Kemp was still performing, lecturing, and recording in the 2010s.

ROSETTA LENOIRE
She Built a Theatre with No Color Bar

Rosetta LeNoire is perhaps most well known throughout America for her role as Mother Winslow on the hit sitcom *Family Matters*, which aired from 1989 to 1998. She also made theatre history as a multihyphenate and impresario, and worked on Broadway from 1939 to 1983. She was a leader of racial equity in casting, and she founded Amas Repertory Theatre Company, an interracial theatre troupe which presented and advocated for color-blind and color-conscious casting in all productions. Actors Equity eventually created an award in her name for diversifying theatre casting.

Rosetta LeNoire in a publicity shot for *Family Matters*. PHOTOFEST

According to the *Guardian*, LeNoire was born in Hell's Kitchen. "She had a West Indian father who became one of the first black men in New York to work as a licensed plumber and electrician. Her mother died giving birth to her

40. "It's Hard to Categorize Pianist-Singer-Composer Emme Kemp." *Arizona Republic*, 13 March 1991, p. 72.

41. "Musicals Bound for Broadway." *Billboard*, 29 January 1983.

younger brother when a Harlem hospital refused to admit her because she was black. A white policeman who knew her from church forced her admission, but she was treated and left in the hallways, where complications from pneumonia killed her."[42]

LeNoire began her career as a performer. She joined the WPA's theatre troupe and performed in Orson Welles's famous production of *Macbeth*. Her Broadway debut was as Peep-Bo in *The Hot Mikado*, an all-Black reworking of the Gilbert and Sullivan operetta. By her second Broadway show, an all-Black production of *Anna Lucasta* presented by the American Negro Theatre, LeNoire was not only on stage but also choreographing a dance. She had been dancing since she was a little girl—her godfather was the inimitable dancer Bill "Bojangles" Robinson, and he had taught her. She had developed rickets from lack of sunlight and her legs had to be broken and reset; Bojangles taught her how to dance so she could regain use of her legs. She was also mentored musically by Eubie Blake. Blake was highly influential, and she eventually opened a children's theatre group in his name.

In the 1940s, she staged a theatrical benefit for the family of a mother and child who were lynched in Monroe, Georgia. Her first professional job had been touring the country with a Black musical theatre troupe and it opened her eyes to social injustice across America. After seeing the aftermath of a lynching, she decided she wanted to be part of social change and that theatre was a great way to do that. "Theatre techniques are a marvelous implement to bring people of all races, colors and creeds together," she said.[43] She also worked and performed at the Stage Door Canteen, the venue that provided support and entertainment to those serving during World War II. In 1942, she performed a song by Langston Hughes and Emerson Harper at the Stage Door Canteen and brought down the house. She worked with Hughes for decades, also appearing in his work in Harlem theaters.

In 1968, LeNoire founded Amas, which is Latin for "you love." Her leadership in fighting for racial equity in the theatre led to dozens of productions, employing hundreds of artists—and the industry took note. She used her own savings to found the company, which eventually produced over sixty musicals. That savings consisted of $500 which she had squirreled away as "getaway money" in case her marriage didn't work.[44] One of the most successful was *Bubbling Brown Sugar*, which was conceived by LeNoire in 1976, leading to her inclusion here as a theatre writer. *It's So Nice to Be Civilized*, which made it to Broadway in 1980, had book, music and lyrics by Micki Grant and also began at Amas.

---

42. Carlson, Michael. "Rosetta LeNoire." *Guardian*, 26 March 2002, https://www.theguardian.com/news/2002/mar/26/guardianobituaries.

43. "National Medal of Arts Recipient Rosetta LeNoire Dies at Age 90." *Star*, 20 March 2002, p. 19.

44. Holden, Stephen. "Black Musicals Have Cause to Sing." *New York Times*, 7 March 1986, p. C1.

LeNoire's work as a producer and artistic director was mostly on off-Broadway shows, and several, like *Mama, I Want to Sing!*, about the life of singer Doris Troy, had long runs. The show played over 2,500 performances at the Heckscher in Harlem, beginning in 1983, after originating off-off-Broadway in 1980. It is not included in most off-Broadway histories since its venue was located so far uptown, which meant many historians did not consider it technically off-Broadway. In other places, the musical is called the longest running Black musical off-Broadway. Musical theatre writers Ann Duquesnay and Queen Esther Marrow[45] appeared in the show throughout the years. There is a cast recording made with the original off-off-Broadway cast, and the show inspired a sequel called *Born to Sing!* that played the Union Square Theatre in 1996.

Through her founding and leading of Amas, LeNoire arguably had a hand in the creation of more Black-helmed musicals than anyone else during the twentieth century. From 1968 to her death in 2002, Amas produced original musicals by Black writers more than any other theatre company, along with their other achievements in promoting diversity in all areas of the theatre. Many of these shows have been forgotten by the masses since they were not recorded or licensed, but they did happen, and under LeNoire, they did tell stories no one else was telling. Amas continues its mission today.

In 1999, LeNoire was presented with the National Medal for the Arts. President Bill Clinton said, "Rosetta did more than dream of a theatre with no color bar—she actually built one."[46]

BERTHA EGNOS AND GAIL LAKIER
A Mother-Daughter Writing Team

In 1977, a musical opened on Broadway that had book, music, and lyrics by women, a female director and a female choreographer. That musical was *Ipi-Tombi*.

Bertha Egnos wrote the book and music and directed. Her daughter Gail Lakier wrote lyrics, and Sheila Wartski choreographed. *Ipi-Tombi* originated in Johannesburg, South Africa, where Egnos and Lakier had already created many musical revues and musical comedies. It was a huge hit and played London before hitting New York, at the Harkness Theatre.

Located on Broadway near 62nd Street, the Harkness was an undesirable Broadway house with a too-far-north location. It was built in 1905 when theatre impresarios imagined the theatre district would continue to grow northward.

---

45. See chapter 11.

46. Martin, Douglas. "Rosetta LeNoire, 90, Producer Who Broke Color Bar, Dies." *New York Times*, 20 March 2002, https://www.nytimes.com/2002/03/20/arts/rosetta-lenoire-90-producer-who-broke-color-bar-dies.html.

When this didn't happen, the theater languished for decades, even when Lincoln Center became its nearby neighbor in the 1960s. *Ipi-Tombi* was the Harkness's final production; it was demolished soon after.

The musical is purportedly about a Black South African young man who leaves his family to work in the mines, but it is generally understood to be a plotless revue about the culture in the country. The original cast was mainly comprised of Zulu men and women. *Ipi-Tombi* was picketed by anti-apartheid protestors who thought the show gave a false sense of what life in South Africa was really like. There were protestors outside the Harkness for almost every performance of the show's one-month run. At the time of the Broadway closing, the Johannesburg production had been running for three years and was still going strong.

Not only was the show judged to be problematic for its treatment (or lack thereof) of racial issues in South Africa, the translation of *Ipi-Tombi* was found to literally be "bring on the girls," which a few critics found to be misogynist as well. The show might not have received the best reviews, but it also wasn't helped by the fact that the nightly protests scared most audiences away.

An original London cast album exists.

ELIZABETH SWADOS
A Prolific Visionary

Elizabeth Swados was a writer, an educator, a visionary, and a disruptor. She forged her own path in musical theatre, creating experimental work that opened doors for others. She focused on socially conscious work and on serious issues affecting young people. She worked prolifically on new musicals, on Broadway, off-Broadway, in educational settings as a theatre professor at New York University, and beyond.

Swados got her professional start at La MaMa, composing music for several original pieces in the early 1970s, including a version of *Medea*. She studied world music in college and was inspired to create theatre in the way that world music was created: collectively. She also loved the folk music and protest songs of the 1970s, from Bob Dylan to Joan Baez. Seeking to merge these passions, Swados began to develop her unique creative style.

Elizabeth Swados, circa 1978, by Bernard Gotfryd. BY GOTFRYD, BERNARD, PHOTOGRAPHER / WIKIMEDIA COMMONS

In 1977, Swados conceived, directed and wrote music for a show called *Nightclub Cantata* that played 145 performances at the Village Gate. Reporting on the show, the *New York Times* wrote that *Nightclub Cantata* was "a tapestry of poems and narrative (by, among others, Sylvia Plath, Carson McCullers and the composer herself) set to music, which means raga, folk chants, bird call and other exotic sounds. 'I set out to do a piece that would have the seriousness of a cantata and the frivolousness of a nightclub,' she said."[47]

From the beginning of her career, Swados sought to combine pure entertainment with work that was culturally relevant, feeling the two had become diametrically opposed, instead of as integral as they could and should be. Swados was only twenty-five years old when she composed music for Joe Papp's first two shows at Lincoln Center, *The Cherry Orchard* and *Agamemnon*. She believed in creating music based on sounds in the real world.

In 1978, Swados burst into the theatre mainstream in a significant way, when she created *Runaways*. Swados wrote book, music, and lyrics, directed and choreographed, and played off-stage guitar for the show, possibly making her the multihyphenate who worked in the most positions on one show. Also, *Runaways* was based on interviews that Swados conducted with kids who were actual runaways, living on the city streets in the 1970s. Many of the show's original cast members were actual runaways who were among those Swados had spoken to in order to inform the work.

Swados brought the idea for *Runaways* to Joe Papp, who championed it and gave it a premiere at the Public Theater in 1978. After that, the show moved to Broadway, where it received five Tony nominations—four of them for Swados, for Score, Book, Direction and Choreography, plus one for the show for Best Musical. *Runaways* played 274 performances on Broadway. A show consisting of all young people singing about serious topics was incredibly revolutionary for Broadway. There was a specific kind of authenticity and vigor to *Runaways* that was present in all of Swados' work but that made the show an outlier on Broadway.

In 1979, Swados's *Dispatches* premiered back at the Public. It played Joe's Pub, back when that venue was called the Cabaret Theater. The show is a rock musical about Vietnam based on a book by Michael Herr. Swados composed, adapted, and directed.

Her next four productions opened at the Public Theater as well: *The Haggadah, a Passover Cantata* (1980), *The Seagull* (1980), *Alice in Concert* (1980), and *Lullabye and Goodnight* (1982).

The Haggadah, a Passover Cantata is one of several Swados musicals involving Judaism. The show tells the Passover story, using puppets and a young cast. Moses was originally played by the nine-year-old Craig Chang and a nine-year-old

---

47. Gussow, Mel. "Elizabeth Swados Writes Cantata for Cabaret." *New York Times*, 7 January 1977, https://www.nytimes.com/1977/01/07/archives/new-jersey-weekly-elizabeth-swados-writes-cantata-for-cabaret.html.

Martha Plimpton also appeared in the cast. The scenery, costumes, masks, and puppetry were by Julie Taymor.

For *The Seagull*, Swados composed and arranged music to a new adaptation by Jean-Claude van Itallie, directed by Andrei Serban, with whom she collaborated several times.

Alice in Concert, Swados's third production at the Public in the year 1980 alone, has gained appreciation over the years for its taped broadcast starring Meryl Streep. Swados wrote book, music, and lyrics for this modern retelling of *Alice in Wonderland*, which was directed by Joe Papp and choreographed by Graciela Daniele. Swados also conducted.

Lullabye and Goodnight is a "musical romance" about pimps and prostitutes that expanded on a few songs in *Runaways* and actually had Josie de Guzman from the original *Runaways* cast reprising her role in the earlier show. In the *New York Times*, Frank Rich did not respond to the abstract nature of some of the writing nor the style of commentary rather than direct narrative that was employed. The review opened, "When Elizabeth Swados speaks directly from the heart, she writes songs that both haunt and disturb. *Lullabye and Goodnight*, her new musical at the Public's Newman Theater, contains several such songs—the best to be heard from Miss Swados since 'Every Now and Then' and 'Lullabye from Baby to Baby' in *Runaways*. Yet the show itself is a failure, done in by the other, less ingenuous aspects of its author's sensibility."[48]

Swados only came back to Broadway once after *Runaways*: with *Doonesbury* in 1983. The musical was based on the comic strip of the same name by Gary Trudeau, and Trudeau wrote the book and lyrics while Swados composed the music. Audiences experienced Swados in a new kind of form, creating music for comic strip characters come to life, for a musical with more commercial intentions than her previous work. *Doonesbury* has some terrific numbers, infusing an original pop sensibility with traditional musical theatre storytelling. The show did not get the reviews it needed in order to run, and closed after three months.

Swados worked with Trudeau again for *Rap Master Ronnie*, which premiered at the Top of the Gate in 1984. Trudeau was a vocal critic of Ronald Reagan, and in this show, Trudeau and Swados musicalized a satirical fake campaign for the politician. Utilizing rap, hip-hop, and pop, *Rap Master Ronnie* portrays Ronald Reagan and Nancy Reagan trying to get out the Black vote in the inner city by articulating policies about everything from women's rights to drug use. The show was also made into a music video, and a made-for-TV movie that featured Carol Kane, Jon Cryer, and the Smothers Brothers. The multimedia release of the material was innovative.

---

48. Rich, Frank. "Stage: Elizabeth Swados's *Lullabye*." *New York Times*, 10 February 1982, https://www.nytimes.com/1982/02/10/theater/stage-elizabeth-swados-s-lullabye.html.

In the late 1980s, Swados wrote additional music for *Hannah Senesh* (Cherry Lane, 1985), composed music for *Phaedra Britannica* (1988, CSC Theatre), and composed music for *Don Juan of Seville* (1989, CSC Theatre).

In 1989, Swados premiered *The Red Sneaks*, her adaptation of *The Red Shoes*, told through the perspective of city youth, at Theatre for a New Audience. The show played the Perry Street Theatre and Swados also directed. In 1990, she returned to the Public for *Jonah*, a retelling of *Jonah and the Whale* told with a rock sensibility—where the character of Jonah even played drum solos. In fact, in addition to *The Haggadah, a Passover Cantata* and *Jonah*, Swados wrote several other biblical shows, including *Esther, Jerusalem*, and *Song of Songs*.

Swados continued to compose music for plays as well as create original musicals. She composed the music for *The Tower of Evil* (1990, CSC Theatre), *Cymbeline* (1998, Delacorte Theater), and *Hamlet* (1999, Public Theater/Newman).

In 1992, she wrote book and music for *Groundhog* and also directed this original musical about a homeless man dealing with mental illness, which premiered at New York City Center/Stage II. When Swados's mother committed suicide and her brother developed schizophrenia, she became increasingly interested in exploring mental illness and depression in her work. She also lived with depression herself. *The Applause/Best Plays Theatre Yearbook* thought *Groundhog* was the "most daring" musical of the season.[49] *Groundhog* was one of many Swados projects that were called Brechtian, but in reality, there should have been a new term like "Swadosian" used to describe innovations that Swados honed over and over in her work. Historian Dan Dietz noted, "One wishes the ambitious-sounding work had been recorded. *Groundhog* may well be the most personal and heartfelt musical written by Swados, and one hopes she will someday revisit the material."[50] The musical was optioned by Milos Forman, who wished to turn it into a film.

In 2014 Swados delivered her final off-Broadway musical, less than two years before her death. *A Fable*, which played the Cherry Lane Theatre, has a story commenting on the current problematic elements of finance and politics. Alexis Soloski wrote in the *New York Times*: "There is music by the respected composer Elizabeth Swados. The cast sings it without much feeling. Or tunefulness."[51]

Swados was actively working on many shows at the time of her death in 2016. In addition to her musical theatre work, she wrote three novels, three nonfiction books, and nine children's books. She composed music for several films,

---

49. Dietz, Dan. *Off Broadway Musicals, 1910–2007: Casts, Credits, Songs, Critical Reception and Performance Data of More Than 1,800 Shows.* Jefferson, NC: McFarland, Inc., 2010.

50. Ibid.

51. Soloski, Alexis. "Will Jonny Be Good? Hell and Heaven Wager." *New York Times*, 29 May 2014, https://www.nytimes.com/2014/05/30/theater/a-fable-in-two-acts-at-the-cherry-lane.html.

and developed and presented many musicals not listed here in educational settings, regionally, and off-off-Broadway.

Her *New York Times* obituary admitted Swados's unconventional relationship with theatre criticism and with the establishment. "Over the next several decades she poured forth a seemingly endless stream of stage productions that tested the vocabulary of critics, who described them variously as song cycles, mosaics, tapestries and oratorios. . . . 'What I set out to do was make an experimental musical theater,' she told the *Times* in 1991. She added, 'Broadway is a museum that's not moving forward, and musical theater should reflect what and how we are now—our pop culture, our political situation.'"[52]

A 2020 *Forbes* article, a few years after Swados's death, sought to depict the innovations of her legacy in a way that would make readers fully understand their groundbreaking nature. With the headline, "This Visionary Artist Was Mixing Hip-Hop into Musical Theater as Far Back as the 1970s," journalist Jeryl Brunner emphasized that Swados integrated eclectic music forms such as world music, rap, folk, and experimental music into her musicals.[53] The piece came out in conjunction with *The Liz Swados Project*, an album featuring many of Swados's students and collaborators reinterpreting her songs.

Lin-Manuel Miranda has shared that his parents saw *Runaways* on their wedding night, and has emphasized that Swados was mashing up hip-hop and pop with musical theatre, and featuring a diverse cast in her work, back in 1978—almost four full decades before *Hamilton*.

Swados also left behind a strong legacy of students who became theatre makers in a large variety of ways, many of whom appeared on *The Liz Swados Project* album, including Grace McLean and Shaina Taub.

Carol Hall
Singer-Songwriter, Whorehouse *Writer*

Carol Hall started out as a singer-songwriter, and released two albums in the early 1970s. Her second album contained her first hit, "Jenny Rebecca," which was also recorded by Barbra Streisand, Mabel Mercer, and Olivia Newton-John.

In the early to mid-1970s, Hall also contributed to *Free to Be . . . You and Me* and wrote songs for *Sesame Street*. She wrote jingles for commercials and one-off songs with collaborators she met in the BMI Workshop. Her big break in theatre

---

52. Grimes, William. "Elizabeth Swados, Creator of Socially Conscious Musicals, Is Dead at 64." *New York Times*, 5 January 2016, https://www.nytimes.com/2016/01/06/arts/elizabeth-swados -creator-of-socially-conscious-musicals-is-dead-at-64.html.

53. Brunner, Jeryl. "This Visionary Artist Was Mixing Hip-Hop into Musical Theater as Far Back as the 1970s." *Forbes*, 24 July 2020, https://www.forbes.com/sites/jerylbrunner/2020/07/24/this -visionary-artist-was-mixing-hip-hop-into-musical-theater-as-far-back-as-the-1970s.

came in 1978 when she wrote the music and lyrics to *The Best Little Whorehouse in Texas*, an unexpected smash hit on Broadway.

The Best Little Whorehouse in Texas, with book by Larry L. King and Peter Masterson, based on a story by King, started out as an off-off-Broadway workshop, transferred to an off-Broadway production at the Entermedia Theatre downtown, and in 1978, took Broadway by storm at the 46th Street Theatre (now the Richard Rodgers).

Hall was originally from Texas, and her hometown roots were on display in *Whorehouse*. She bridged a gap between country music and musical theatre in a way that only a Texan singer-songwriter also obsessed with Cole Porter, Yip Harburg, and Jacques Brel could. The story about a brothel with an alliance with the local sheriff, and the TV reporter that threatens to bring them down, is served joyously by Hall's songs like "Hard Candy Christmas," "Texas Has A Whorehouse in It," "A Lil' Ole Bitty Pissant Country Place," "The Aggie Song" (a censored version of which was performed on the Tonys).

The Best Score category at the Tony Awards that season took an odd turn. The Best Musical nominees were *Sweeney Todd* (which won), *Ballroom*, *The Best Little Whorehouse in Texas*, and *They're Playing Our Song*. Best Score only had one nominee in common: *Sweeney Todd*, which won, for Stephen Sondheim. The other Best Musical nominees were snubbed for Best Score in favor of *Carmelina* (Burton Lane and Alan Jay Lerner), *Eubie!* (Eubie Blake, Noble Sissle, Andy Razaf, F. E. Miller, Johnny Brandon, and Jim Europe), and *The Grand Tour* (Jerry Herman).

The Best Little Whorehouse in Texas ran for 1,584 performances. Hall stepped into the cast during the run to play stints as both Doatsy Mae and Mona Stangley. While it's not unheard of to find the writer of a Broadway show also starring in it, it's definitely rare to have them playing two different roles at different times! The show spawned a 1982 movie version starring Dolly Parton and Burt Reynolds, a 1982 Broadway revival, an ill-fated 1994 Broadway sequel called *The Best Little Whorehouse Goes Public*, and a high-profile 2001 tour starring Ann-Margret.

Some newspapers at the time of the show's premiere refused to print its title. The show retaliated by hanging a billboard in view of Times Square, on top of its theater, that just said the word: "Whorehouse." Hall told the press: "When you see it, you understand it's not about a whorehouse, but about the hypocrisy and what goes on in the news game."[54]

Whorehouse Goes Public was one of several sequels to beloved hit musicals, also including the sequels to *Annie* and *Bye Bye Birdie*, that came to life in the 1980s and were poorly received. Combined, this pretty much put an end to the excitement for stage musical Broadway sequels.

---

54. "Wonderful People Bring Composer Back." *Tyler Morning Telegraph*, 29 May 1984, p. 32.

Pop Matters wrote of Hall: "She had an ear, not just for melodies that possessed a singular pulchritude, but also for profound turns of phrase.... [Her songs were] witty and with a charmingly bookish sensibility, characterized by pathos that never descend[ed] into mawkishness. This was a woman with world-class songwriting chops."[55]

Indeed, Hall's early two albums point to a great talent for storytelling through folk-pop music that would recur in her musical theater work. They could almost be produced as song cycles themselves. And four songs from her recording days did end up in her 1986 Off-Broadway musical *To Whom It May Concern*.

To Whom It May Concern is a concept musical of sorts, set at a church service, where each churchgoer has a turn to share their story in intersecting songs and monologues. The show premiered at an actual church: St. Stephen's, on the Upper West Side, where audience members were made to feel that they were part of the action. It was an immersive musical during an era where these were rarer. *To Whom It May Concern* was never recorded, and several historians have commented that it really deserved to be. The show might have been performed in community theaters, and particularly with church groups, frequently, had there been a recording. The cast included Gretchen Cryer, Tamara Tunie, Guy Stroman, Kecia Lewis, Dylan Baker, and Becky Gelke—the latter two who met while doing the show and were later married.

In 2010, *A Christmas Memory*, the musical adaptation of the Truman Capote story, opened at TheatreWorks in Palo Alto, with lyrics by Hall, music by Larry Grossman, and a book by Duane Poole. It broke attendance records at the theater.

Hall was heavily involved with the Dramatists Guild Council and was vice president of the Dramatists Guild Fund.

MICHELE BROURMAN
Working *Contributor*

The musical revue *Working* counted several female writers in its stable of dramatists who crafted songs based on Studs Terkel's interviews. One of these was Michele Brourman, who wrote music for "Treasure Island Trio" and "Husbands and Wives" and collaborated on the music for "Nightskate" with Stephen Schwartz, who conceived, directed, and wrote the musical's libretto. None of these songs appear on the musical's original cast album. All three were instrumental pieces accompanied by dance performances in the original production.

Brourman has written music to Amanda McBroom's lyrics for eighteen animated feature films, including the *Land before Time* series. Brourman contributed

55. Donovan, Charles. "Carol Hall: The Final Interview." *Pop Matters*, 1 April 2019, https://www.popmatters.com/carol-hall-the-final-interview-2633063304.html.

additional music to McBroom's 2005 off-Broadway musical *A Woman of Will*. Her songs have been recorded by Michael Feinstein, and she is also a recording artist in her own right.

Brourman's other musicals include *I Married Wyatt Earp* and *Dangerous Beauty*.

GRACIELA DANIELE
Multihyphenate

Masterful and sought-after multihyphenate Graciela Daniele should be mentioned for her writing contributions to several musicals, although she is much better known as an acclaimed director and choreographer. Daniele got her start on Broadway as a performer in the 1960s, collaborated as a dancer with both Michael Bennett and Bob Fosse in the 1970s, and for the past several decades has been a prolific director-choreographer.

Her credits in the writing realm include Spanish lyrics for the song "Un Major Dia Vendra" in *Working* (1978), book and concept for the 1989 musical *Dangerous Games* (which she also directed and choreographed), and book and concept for the 1995 dance musical *Chronicle of a Death Foretold* (which she also directed and choreographed).

Daniele is best known for her long-term collaborations with Lynn Ahrens and Stephen Flaherty, William Finn, and Michael John LaChiusa, and her direction and/or choreography for the original Broadway productions of *The Mystery of Edwin Drood*, *Once on This Island*, *Ragtime*, *Marie Christine*, and *The Visit*. In 2023, LaChiusa musicalized Daniele's own life in the show *The Gardens of Anuncia*, which Daniele directed and co-choreographed.

SUSAN BIRKENHEAD
Five Broadway Musicals, Many Works in Progress with Major Players

With Broadway credits including *Working* (1978), *King of Schnorrers* (1979), *Jelly's Last Jam* (1992), *Triumph of Love* (1997), and *High Society* (1998) and off-Broadway credits including *A ... My Name Is Alice* (1984), *What about Luv?* (1984), *Tatterdemalion* (1985), and *The Secret Life of Bees* (2019), Susan Birkenhead has been a staple in the American musical theatre for several decades.

Her work as a lyricist can be heard on several cast recordings. Her "Watching All the Pretty Young Men" appears on the *A ... My Name Will Always Be Alice* compilation, and her "Nobody Tells Me How," written with music by Mary Rodgers, appears on several *Working* recordings.

Birkenhead's most notable acclaim came from her work on *Jelly's Last Jam*, the long-gestating Broadway musical about Jelly Roll Morton. She was the sole lyricist adapting the work of Morton for the musical alongside composer Luther Henderson, for this show with a book and direction by George C. Wolfe. She was nominated for a Tony Award for Best Score; she was part of *Working*'s nomination for Best Score as well.

Birkenhead has coauthored several musicals with major players that have yet to play New York, including *Pieces of Eight*, *Minsky's*, *Moonstruck*, *Hats!*, *Radio Girl*, *The Flamingo Kid*, and *Fanny Hackabout Jones*.

A 2000 *New York Times* feature titled "Where Have All the Lyricists Gone?" explored a generation of Broadway lyricists exemplified by Craig Carnelia, Susan Birkenhead, Lynn Ahrens, Mark Waldrop, and David Zippel. The piece postulated that Birkenhead might be better known if she had a consistent composer-collaborator and praised her stunning work on the song "Serenity" from *Triumph of Love*.[56]

DORIS WILLENS
Piano Bar

In 1978, an unassuming six-person musical opened at the Westside Theatre upstairs and achieved a four-month run. This was *Piano Bar*, with lyrics by Doris Willens, music by Rob Fremont, and book by both. *Piano Bar* has a simple conceit: a bunch of strangers wander into a New York City piano bar on a rainy night and stay to sing out their hearts to each other, revealing their true life stories. The show's reviews weren't stellar, and most praise was reserved for the cast.

Willens, who was a newspaper journalist and also worked in advertising before *Piano Bar*, continued to write musicals. She authored *Disraeli*, *Spent: A Musical Revue about Growing Older in America*, *Great Books: A Musical Romp*, and *Monkey Business*, all which were developed with the community theater group Primrose Productions in Dix Hills. She also authored two books, including one about her time as public relations director for Doyle Dane Bernbach, where one of her assignments was to write a celebratory show for the agency every five years.

Piano Bar is licensed and performed by theatre groups looking for intimate musicals.

MARY KYTE
Creating a Patriotic Statement

Mary Kyte is largely known as a director and choreographer. Her credits include *Smile*, *Tomfoolery*, *America Kicks Up Its Heels*, and *God Bless You, Mr. Rosewater*.

---

56. Singer, Barry. "Where Have All the Lyric Writers Gone? A Modern Question." *New York Times*, 20 February 2000, p. AR36, https://www.nytimes.com/2000/02/20/arts/music-where-have-all-the -lyric-writers-gone.html.

She also conceived and created musical staging for the Broadway musical *Tintypes*. *Tintypes*, which opened at the Golden Theatre in 1980 after an off-Broadway bow in 1979, is a five-person revue celebrating the music and personalities that converged in America between the turn of the twentieth century and the beginning of World War I. Exploring the first century of American culture through music, *Tintypes* presents songs on patriotism, progress, poverty, love, family, race, and more that was impacting the melting pot of immigrants at that time. The original actors, including Jerry Zaks, Carolyn Mignini, Lynne Thigpen, Trey Wilson, and Mary Catherine Wright, portrayed everyone from Anna Held to George M. Cohan to Emma Goldman during the musical.

When the show was first presented at the York Theatre off-Broadway prior to its Broadway run, the *Christian Science Monitor* wrote: "Mary Kyte has create[d] an authentic, lively, and thoroughly enjoyable piece of Americana.... The mood of *Tintypes* varies as widely as the songs themselves. Miss Kyte's use of them is fresh and inventive.... The well-remembered somehow becomes the newly discovered. Dialogue inserts include soap box speeches, campaign oratory, letters to the editor, and old-timely vaudeville gags."[57]

Tintypes was conceived by Mary Kyte with contributions also made by Mel Marvin (who arranged the music and vocals in addition to conducting) and Gary Pearle who also directed. Kyte created the musical staging. The show was nominated for Tonys for Best Musical and Best Book of a Musical (for Kyte) as well as Featured Actress in a Musical for Lynne Thigpen.

Tintypes was recorded for an original cast album and also received a video recording of a live performance.

ADRIENNE ANDERSON
Collaborated with Peter Allen and Barry Manilow

Adrienne Anderson has been represented on Broadway in three shows: *Up in One* (1979), *The Boy from Oz* (2003), and *Disaster!* (2016). The first two instances were with songs from her collaboration with Peter Allen and the third was with a song from her collaboration with Barry Manilow.

Allen's 1979 tour de force *Up in One* at the Biltmore featured two songs that he and Anderson had previously penned together: "Love Crazy" and "I Go to Rio." These same two numbers were included more than two decades later in the Allen bio-musical *The Boy from Oz*, starring Hugh Jackman. Anderson's song in *Disaster!* was "Daybreak" with Manilow. Manilow's first recording was of a song Anderson wrote: "Amy"; the two have had a long-lasting professional

---

57. Beaufort, John. "*Tintypes*; Musical Review Conceived by Mary Kyte. Directed by Gary Pearl with Musical Staging by Miss Kyte." *Christian Science Monitor*, 9 June 1980.

partnership. Anderson has also written with and for Melissa Manchester and Dionne Warwick.

Anderson did write deliberately for legitimate theatre in 1996, when *City Kid*, for which she contributed book and lyrics, premiered in Seattle, Washington. The show, which opened around the same time as *Rent* on the other side of the country, is also a youthful rock musical addressing contemporary issues, which inspired some comparisons.

PHYLLIS NEWMAN
The Madwoman of Central Park West

The great actress and humanitarian Phyllis Newman was best known for her performances in shows like *Subways Are for Sleeping* (Tony Award) and *Broadway Bound* (Tony Award nomination). The wife of musical theatre writer Adolph Green and mother of musical theatre writer Amanda Green and journalist Adam Green, Newman was enmeshed in musical theatre writing history for her entire life until she passed away in 2019.

She was the namesake of the Phyllis Newman Women's Health Initiative, an important arm of Broadway Cares/Equity Fights AIDS, that she founded in 1995 to help women in the industry. The initiative has raised millions of dollars to help women in the arts.

Phyllis Newman, circa 1966. BY ABC TELEVISION / WIKIMEDIA COMMONS

Newman's significant writing credit came in 1979 with her one-woman Broadway show *The Madwoman of Central Park West*. She played a fictional version of herself in this intimate musical directed by Arthur Laurents. Laurents and Newman collaborated on the book, and the songs were by a slew of high-profile writers, including Leonard Bernstein, John Clifton, John Kander, Jerry Bock, Mary Rodgers, Joe Raposo, Ed Kleban, Peter Allen, Bruce Sussman, Jack Feldman, Barry Manilow, Betty Comden, Adolph Green, Fred Ebb, Sheldon Harnick, Martin Charnin, Carole Bayer Sager, and Stephen Sondheim.

Two of the numbers have lyrics by Newman, to John Clifton's music. These are "My Mother Was a Fortune Teller" (the show's original title when it opened off-Broadway) and "List Song." The show received a cast album.

10

1980s

Jukebox Musicals and a Return to Revues

MIRA J. SPEKTOR AND JUNE SIEGEL
The Housewives' Cantata

Mira J. Spektor wrote the music and June Siegel the lyrics to the 1980 off-Broadway musical *The Housewives' Cantata*. While the show, which also had a book by William Holtzman, only ran twenty-four performances, it has lived on thanks to its original cast album.

The Housewives' Cantata was produced at Theater Four on 55th Street by Cheryl Crawford, the longtime Broadway producer whose work dated back to the 1930s. The show's conceit finds three sisters growing through marriage and motherhood from the 1960s through the 1980s. *The Housewives' Cantata* tackles their lives as seen through their roles as housewives. What did it mean for each of them to be a housewife, and which struggles did this present to three different individuals of this era?

Song titles include "What Is a Woman?," "Dirty Dish Rag," "Song of the Bourgeoise Hippie," "Guinevere among the Grapefruit Peels," "Adultery Waltz" and "Divorce Lament." *The Housewives' Cantata* shows three women navigating their relationships with their spouses and with what is expected of them in their day-to-day lives, during decades that see significant societal evolution about the idea of women's roles in the home.

The *Daily News* wrote: "*Cantata* is a witty, good-natured satire on men who use, abuse, bore and ignore women in the name of married love. The subject is not new but the treatment of it is unpretentious, undoctrinaire, and free from self-conscious rhetoric."[1] The original cast featured Patti Karr, Forbesy Russell, Sharon Talbot, and in the role of all of the men in the sisters' lives, William Perley.

Spektor later wrote a mini-opera based on the Lizzie Borden story, called *The Passion of Lizzie Borden*, and one based on events of World War II called *Lady of the Castle*. She has worked as a composer on many other stage pieces and recordings.

Siegel's other musical stage work includes *A . . . My Name Is Alice*[2] and *Pets!*

LUCIA HWONG
M. Butterfly *Composer*

A woman of many music-related talents, Lucia Hwong has composed music for theatre pieces, television, concert halls, film, and dance. On Broadway, she composed the music, acted as music director, and played the lute during the original

---

1. Nelsen, Don. "Double the Pleasure with Cheryl Crawford." *Daily News*, 19 February 1980, p. 294.
2. Her lyrics for "At My Age" are notable.

Lucia Hwong. BY LUCIA HWONG - OWN WORK, CC BY-SA 3.0 / WIKIMEDIA COMMONS

1988 production of *M. Butterfly*. She composed the music for *Golden Child* on Broadway in 1998 as well. Hwong has a long-term collaboration with David Henry Hwang, author of both of those plays. Her other work with Hwang includes the off-Broadway pieces *FOB* (1980), *The Dance and the Railroad* (1981), *Family Devotions* (1981), and *Sound and Beauty* (1983). All of these were produced at the Public Theater.

In addition to her work with Hwang, Hwong has also composed music for theatrical pieces by Anna Deavere Smith and Joyce Carol Oates. She has worked extensively at Lincoln Center. She often acts as arranger and on-stage musician for pieces she has composed.

Among Hwong's honors are a Citation of Outstanding Contribution by the Board of Public Works of the City of Los Angeles and the Asian American Arts Alliance Artist of the Year Award.

CAROLE KING
A Pop Icon Scores an Off-Broadway Children's Musical

Carole King is popular and well-regarded as a pop icon, singer-songwriter legend, and central figure of one of Broadway's most successful jukebox musicals: *Beautiful*, in 2013. But what was she doing off-Broadway in the 1980s?

King had a unique timeline of events as far as her entry into the musical theatre genre. In 1975, she wrote the score for an animated television special of several of Maurice Sendak's books that was titled *Really Rosie*. Sendak, the popular writer and illustrator of children's stories had several books about a street gang of kids growing up in Brooklyn, including *Chicken Soup with Rice*, *Pierre*, *One was Johnny*, *Alligators All Around*, and *The Sign on Rosie's Door*. The conceit of the television special is that the outgoing Rosie wants to make a movie about her life and friends.

Carole King, circa 1977. BY CAPITOL RECORDS / WIKIMEDIA COMMONS

This thirty-minute special, with music by King (who also voiced the character of Rosie) and lyrics and animations by Sendak proved so popular that Sendak expanded it for a stage production. *Really Rosie* eventually found its way to off-Broadway in 1980 at the Westside Theatre, where it was a success, running for 274 performances. Further, after the show received a cast album and was licensed, it became a favorite for children's theaters and school productions all over the country.

Sendak praised King's authenticity in writing for children to the *Kenosha News* and producer Sheldon Riss added, "When we received her music, it was so outstanding we had to lend even more importance to the music than we had originally planned for the show."[3]

The writer of songs like "Up on the Roof," "Natural Woman," and "Will You Still Love Me Tomorrow" also had a revue of her work produced at the Union Square Theatre off-Broadway in 1993. *Tapestry: The Music of Carole King* was short-lived, playing only nineteen performances after receiving negative reviews.

CHARLOTTE ANKER AND IRENE ROSENBERG
A Broadway Musical about the First Woman to Run for President

Victoria Woodhull was a groundbreaking political figure in the nineteenth century. She was the first female candidate for president of the United States; she fought for women's suffrage and equal rights; she founded a newspaper, a financial firm, and a spiritual practice; and she made her own fortune at a time when most women never worked outside the home.

Woodhull was a colorful character of the time. Her fights for justice included many actions that society felt were inappropriate, from publishing scandalous sex stories to expose hypocrisy in the upper class, to making speeches in favor of free love. In the 1870s, she told the public that women would not be equal anywhere until they were equal in the bedroom.

In 1980, a musical about Victoria Woodhull opened on Broadway. Titled *Onward Victoria*, the show has book and lyrics by Charlotte Anker and Irene Rosenberg and music by Keith Hermann. It was directed by Julianne Boyd, who told press while the show was in development that the title character would be played by "a woman, and not an ingenue."[4] The role would eventually be won by Jill Eikenberry.

Anker and Rosenberg first had the idea for the show when poking around in Woodhull's papers at the Library of Congress. The two writers from Washington managed to get their show a presentation in New York where its anachronistic writing—pop songs to flesh out the story of a nineteenth-century cutting-edge figure—was enjoyed and praised. Woodhull's story also seemed destined for dramatization.

---

3. "Carole King: Her Music Is Special." *Kenosha News*, 5 June 1976, p. 48.
4. Moody, Minnie Hite. "'One of Ours' on Broadway." *Newark Advocate*, 30 May 1979, p. 7.

Rosenberg told the press: "She fought against the notion that there were two kinds of women—the madonna and the whore. She believed that divorce should be easy to obtain. That people should be able to have intimate relationships without pledging they would last forever. That women had the right to sexual pleasure. In short, that women should have choices. She gave public lectures on sexuality, orgasm, and menstruation. And people found it very threatening."[5]

Onward Victoria tells Woodhull's story, but its characters also include many other real-life figures such as Susan B. Anthony, Elizabeth Cady Stanton, Cornelius Ward Beecher, and Henry Ward Beecher, with whom Woodhull had a controversial affair.

The show opened and closed on December 14, 1980. With poor advance sales, the show counted on positive reviews if it was going to stay open, and failing to obtain these, didn't continue past opening night.

Frank Rich's review in the *New York Times* was headlined: "'*Onward Victoria*: A Woman's Freedom Fight: Feminism, 1871 Style." He wrote, "[*Onward Victoria*] . . . looks like a dinner theater's home-grown answer to *Hello, Dolly!* . . . [The] musical aspires to be a feminist entertainment about the life and times of the provocative 19th-century suffragist Victoria Woodhull. . . . The script is full of hoary double-entendre jokes and sweaty liaisons that are apparently intended to dramatize Victoria's then-pioneering view of female sexuality. Such is the flat, smirky tone of the writing that the heroine comes off as a pioneering vulgarian instead."[6]

Critic Jacques LeSourd called the show "a setback for the feminist cause."[7]

Many critics blamed the show's scrappy production for its demise. The idea of doing a period piece as a low-budget small musical was criticized, but more than that, critics just didn't respond to the campiness and modern treatment of a nineteenth-century feminist figure. *Onward Victoria* received a cast recording, where listeners can judge for themselves songs like "Unescorted Women." where Woodhull is told she cannot eat at Delmonico's Restaurant without a man, and "Changes" where she proclaims all of the changes she'll make for women's rights.

5. Stephen, Beverly. "Victoria for a Song." *Daily News*, 14 December 1980, p. 602.

6. Rich, Frank. "Musical: *Onward Victoria*, a Woman's Freedom Fight: Feminism, 1871 Style." *New York Times*, 15 December 1980, p. C15, https://www.nytimes.com/1980/12/15/archives/musical-onward-victoria-a-womans-freedom-fight-feminism-1871-style.html.

7. LeSourd, Jacques. "*Onward Victoria* may be setback for feminist cause." *Journal News*, 15 December 1980, p. 24.

PAM GEMS
A British Take on Piaf and Dietrich

British writer Pam Gems authored three one-word Broadway shows: *Piaf* (1981), *Stanley* (1997), and *Marlene* (1999). They explore the lives of chanteuse Edith Piaf, painter Stanley Spencer, and actor Marlene Dietrich, respectively.

While both *Piaf* and *Marlene* include songs, *Piaf* was classified for Broadway purposes as a play with music while *Marlene* was labeled a musical. Such distinctions are largely important as they pertain to award qualifications. *Marlene* does feature a full score of songs that Marlene Dietrich had been known to sing, and so Gems was credited with the book of this Broadway musical, which played twenty-five performances at the Cort (now the James Earl Jones). The short run was due to largely negative reviews. The *Daily News'* headline read: "*Marlene* Impersonates Play" and explained, "It's hard, of course, for any writer to get under Dietrich's pale and ageless skin. She spent her life, after all, creating an alluring enigma."[8]

Gems had a long and fruitful career in her native England where she had over forty plays produced in her lifetime.

BARBARA SCHOTTENFELD
The Feminist Label

Barbara Schottenfeld wrote the book, music, and lyrics (and sometimes arrangements too) for three musicals that played off-Broadway: *I Can't Keep Running in Place* in 1981, *Sit Down and Eat Before Our Love Gets Cold* in 1985, and *Catch Me If I Fall* in 1990.

I Can't Keep Running in Place played the Westside Theatre upstairs for 208 performances. Schottenfeld also created the orchestrations, and the team was largely female. Susan Einhorn directed, Baayork Lee choreographed, Ursula Belden was the scenic designer, Christina Weppner was the costume designer, and Meryl Schaffer was the production stage manager.

The show had been Schottenfeld's undergraduate senior thesis project at Princeton. After staging the show there, Schottenfeld sent the script around and obtained an opportunity to bring *I Can't Keep Running in Place* to The Actors Playhouse Theater in New York. Using the money she had made from the production at the Princeton Inn, she brought the show intact to the city.

After this came several performances at La MaMa and then backer's auditions that allowed the show to be moved to off-Broadway. Schottenfeld knocked on producers' doors and introduced herself, cold, until she drummed up enough

---

8. O'Toole, Fintan. "*Marlene* Impersonates Play." *Daily News*, 12 April 1999, p. 262.

interest in seeing her show's readings that she eventually achieved a full New York run. At this point, its stars were well-known theatre professionals including Helen Gallagher, Marcia Rodd, Evalyn Baron, and Joy Franz.

I Can't Keep Running in Place is set at an assertiveness training session in modern-day Manhattan. Six very different women work through their issues, from self-esteem to codependency. Critic Mary Campbell for the *Associated Press* praised the music and lyrics, and wrote, "[*I Can't Keep Running in Place* gives] women's lib a good name....We heard the comment that this play would have been timely five years ago. Plays about what people really think and do, like this one, are also timely now."[9]

Schottenfeld was inspired to write about the topic of an assertiveness training session for women when she attended one such session herself, as a teenager. At the time, such sessions were only for women, which is why that is who comprises the show's character list. Leading up to the show's off-Broadway debut, several journalists were condescending about the content of the show, as well as its writer's age and gender. A song about the Freudian theory of penis envy was the butt of most jokes.

A *New York Times* feature on Schottenfeld during the show's run was written by Sandra Gardner. Gardner noted that *Running in Place* had a cast comprised of only women and concerned "women's issues" but that Schottenfeld "[refused] to call it 'a feminist play.'"

"If I had made a 'Feminist statement,' with a capital 'F,' it would have been a political doctrine, rather than a play," Schottenfeld told the *Times*. "Very few people have written political plays that are entertaining. That's why nobody wants to go see a 'feminist play.'"

The *Times* continued: "In personal politics, too, Miss Schottenfeld shrinks from what she calls the 'feminist label.' 'If you ask me, issue by issue, I'm for women's rights, the E.R.A., abortion,' she said. 'But people become so unreceptive when they hear the word feminism—it's like a disease.'"[10]

In *Off-Broadway Musicals Since 1919*, Thomas Hischak noted, "*I Can't Keep Running in Place* may seem dated and a bit simplistic today, but performed in the furor of the 1980s women's movement, it struck a chord in many audience members."[11] It was for this reason that the show played over five months of performances. It was recorded as an original cast album.

Schottenfeld's next shot was *Sit Down and Eat Before Our Love Gets Cold*, which she also starred in. The show opened off-Broadway in 1985 and the

---

9. Campbell, Mary. "*Can't Keep Running* Has Staying Power." *Associated Press*, 15 May 1981.

10. Gardner, Sandra. "Writer-Actress Running Hard." *New York Times*, 23 August 1981, p. NJ14.

11. Hischak, Thomas. *Off-Broadway Musicals Since 1919: From Greenwich Village Follies to The Toxic Avenger*. Lanham, MD: Scarecrow Press, 1911.

reception was not as friendly as it was for Schottenfeld's first show. The *New York Times* wrote, "The show began as a revue. The book grew out of the songs—but it did not grow far enough."[12] *Sit Down and Eat* found Schottenfeld playing a songwriter, who becomes romantically entangled with her best friend's ex-boyfriend. The love triangle was a chance to explore female friendship as well as dating mores of the 1980s.

Schottenfeld received an NEA grant for both *Sit Down and Eat* and for her next show, *Catch Me If I Fall*, for which she also won a Drama League Award. This show closed after only sixteen performances at the Promenade Theatre. *Catch Me If I Fall* is about a green card marriage and a man who is pursued by three different women. The *New York Times* noted that Schottenfeld's previous musicals "were collage-style shows dealing principally with questions of feminism. . . . But this time she has both a central story line and a male protagonist."[13] *The Times* review and most other write-ups were negative.

Leading up to *Catch Me If I Fall*'s debut, the *Boston Globe*'s Kevin Kelly wrote a piece centered on Schottenfeld. In the article, he noted that there were few women who wrote Broadway musicals, counting Elizabeth Swados, Gretchen Cryer and Nancy Ford, Carol Hall, and Mary Rodgers as the whole lot he could recall.

Kelly wrote: "Further (and sadly), none of these women seems to have creatively prospered after her initial early success. . . . If women have lapsed, there is still one of their intrepid number about to make a bid. Barbara Schottenfeld, in fact, has already made it. . . . *I Can't Keep Running in Place* [earned] her both popularity and critical favor." Kelly noted that after that show, Schottenfeld went on to write book, music, and lyrics for *Sit Down and Eat Before Our Love Gets Cold* and now was working on a new musical: *Catch Me If I Fall*.[14]

After *Catch Me If I Fall*'s negative reviews and quick closure, Schottenfeld continued to write, but has yet to have another Broadway or off-Broadway production. Her work continues to appear on Broadway performers' solo albums and in their cabaret acts, and she has her own cabaret act. Her latest work, *Hot and Sweet*, about an all-girl band in 1945 Chicago, is based on interviews she conducted; it was presented at the NAMT Festival.

---

12. Gussow, Mel. "Stage: *Sit Down and Eat*, a Musical." *New York Times*, 9 May 1985, p. C22.

13. Gussow, Mel. "Uncertain Hero Who Juggles Three Women, Musically." *New York Times*, 17 November 1990, p. 16.

14. Kelly, Kevin. "Composer of Off-Broadway's 'Catch Me If I Fall' makes music as few women do." *Boston Globe*, 7 September 1990, p. 39.

DEBRA MONK
A Broadway Star's Secret Writing Talents

Widely known as an actress and beloved in theatrical circles, Debra Monk has had a long and successful career. She is a Tony and Emmy Award-winning actor whose credits on Broadway include plays and musicals like *Redwood Curtain*, *Picnic*, *Steel Pier*, and *Curtains*. She has also worked to great acclaim in film and television.

Not many know of Monk's musical talents beyond singing, but in her earliest days in theatre, she cowrote, performed, and played instruments for both *Pump Boys and Dinettes* and *Oil City Symphony*.

Pump Boys and Dinettes was a rags-to-riches Broadway success story. The show originated as a concert act in a bar by Jim Wann and Mark Hardwick, and soon John Foley, John Schimmel, Debra Monk, and Cass Morgan joined to craft a loose narrative about a bunch of men who work at a gas station and two women who work at a diner—who sing of their lives, country-western style. The cast created the book and score together, with Monk and Morgan both responsible for cowriting several songs. *Pump Boys and Dinettes* started off-Broadway in 1981, transferred to Broadway in 1982, and was nominated for the Best Musical Tony Award. The show ran for 573 performances and has become a regional theatre favorite.

Oil City Symphony came along five years later and reunited Monk with Hardwick from the *Pump Boys* team. The two joined with new collaborators Mary Murfitt and Mike Craver for this wholly original show that played the Circle in the Square Downtown for 626 performances.

The concept of *Oil City Symphony* centers on a former high school musical group reuniting in their old gym to honor their music teacher with a concert program consisting of originals and standards. But in this case, the originals are outrageous autobiographical takes on the mundane lives of the characters, and the standards are hilariously re-envisioned. Circle in the Square Downtown was made to look like a high school gym and audience members even had to turn themselves around for "The Hokey Pokey." The show won the 1988 Outer Critics Circle Award for Outstanding Off-Broadway Musical.

In addition to cowriting and starring in *Oil City Symphony*, Monk also played drums. She stopped the show several times, impressing audiences with her ability to play heartfelt comedy and simultaneously dazzle, playing an instrument.

NAHMA SANDROW
Yiddish Theatre Expert

Nahma Sandrow is a theatre maker and historian whose focus on Yiddish theatre has made her one of the foremost experts in the field. In 1977, she wrote a book called *Vagabond Stars: A World History of Yiddish Theater*. The award-winning book, which Joe Papp gave a rave review to in a write-up for the *New York Times*, was later turned into a live show celebrating Yiddish theater, which played the Jewish Repertory Theatre.

In 1984, Sandrow was responsible for the significant off-Broadway success of the musical *Kuni-Leml*, a take on a classic Yiddish tale presented for modern audiences. *Kuni-Leml* took a nineteenth century Yiddish operetta about changing social mores and young Jewish love and adapted it. The show, with a book by Sandrow, won the 1985 Outer Critics Circle Awards for Outstanding Off-Broadway Musical, Best Book, Best Music, and Best Lyrics. It played 298 performances at the Audrey Wood Theatre.

Both *Vagabond Stars* and *Kuni-Leml* have been revived, and continue to be performed, especially by Jewish theatre groups.

Sandrow's work has mostly focused on Jewish theatre history and bringing Jewish theatre to light in the present, but she has also worked as a theatre historian separate from this, including penning pieces on the lasting impact of various musicals for publications including the *New York Times*.

ELLEN FITZHUGH
Four Decades of Musicals

Ellen Fitzhugh was a lyricist whose work included *Herringbone* (1982), *Diamonds* (1984), *Grind* (1985), *The Griffin and the Minor Canon* (1988), *Juno* (1992), *Paper Moon* (1993), *Luck, Pluck, and Virtue* (1995), *Saturn Returns* (1998), *Muscle* (2001), *Paradise Found* (2010), *Broadbend, Arkansas* (2019), and *Los Otros* (2022).

Herringbone, which premiered off-Broadway at Playwrights Horizons, is, as Frank Rich wrote in his *New York Times* review "a bizarre musical."[15] The tour-de-force central role was originated by David Round but was played in many subsequent productions by B. D. Wong, who recorded the show as well. *Herringbone*, with music by Skip Kennon and a book by Tom Cone, finds one man retelling the story of his upbringing and time in vaudeville while playing all of the characters. But the show is far more offbeat than that description implies, with its impressively original tone ranging from "absurdist family comedy" to "Gothic horror."

---

15. Rich, Frank. "David Rounds Plays 10 Roles in *Herringbone*." *New York Times*, 1 July 1982, https://www.nytimes.com/1982/07/01/theater/theater-david-rounds-plays-10-roles-in-herringbone.html.

Fitzhugh contributed four lyrics to the 1984 Hal Prince-helmed revue celebrating baseball called *Diamonds*. While most of the songwriters to lend their talents to *Diamonds* wrote only one song for the proceedings, Fitzhugh and her frequent collaborator, composer Larry Grossman, penned "Favorite Sons," "Song for a Pinch Hitter," "He Threw Out the Ball" and "The Boys of Summer," numbers that threaded together the theme of the evening. Part of the reason that Fitzhugh and Grossman became involved to that extent was that they were in the midst of simultaneously collaborating with Prince on their upcoming Broadway bow, *Grind*.

Grind is Fitzhugh's only Broadway credit. Her lyrics for this ambitious original musical about immigration and racial injustice as seen at a burlesque house at the height of the Great Depression earned her a Drama Desk nomination. *Grind* was nominated for Best Score at the Tony Awards that season as well. Fitzhugh's threading of both character and the accurate pastiche lyrics for the diegetic[16] numbers was skillful.

The Griffin and the Minor Canon was written by three women: Fitzhugh on lyrics, Mary Rodgers on music, and Wendy Kesselman on book. The show, based on the nineteenth-century story by Frank R. Stockton, as illustrated in 1963 by Maurice Sendak, tells the tale of the last living griffin who travels to a church to see a stone likeness of his species. As the townspeople descend on him in fear, his only friend is a minor church clergyman. A cautionary tale about how society treats outsiders, *The Griffin and the Minor Canon* premiered at Lenox Arts Center in Massachusetts and was intended for a run off-Broadway, which did not materialize. *The Berkshire Eagle* wrote, "Rodgers, Fitzhugh, and Kesselman have used Stockton's story as the pretext for a larger, more serious consideration of human values and how one discovers and then asserts one's sense of self-worth in a society whose concerns are far more venal and self-centered." The review went on to name the work's flaws and state that it needed much more work before a New York production. Judy Kuhn recorded one of the show's songs, "Am I?" on a 2015 solo album featuring the work of Richard Rodgers, Mary Rodgers, and Adam Guettel.

In 1992, Fitzhugh contributed additional lyrics for a new adaptation of the dark 1959 Broadway musical *Juno*, with a score by Marc Blitzstein and book by Joseph Stein, that played the Vineyard Theatre.

In 1993 Fitzhugh worked on *Paper Moon*, a musical with a much-heralded journey. *Paper Moon* was Broadway bound, with lyrics by Fitzhugh, music by Grossman, and a book by Martin Casella, based on the hit movie, when it played Paper Mill Playhouse in New Jersey. But its Broadway run was canceled even

---

16. A diegetic song in a musical is one that the characters can hear, whereas a non-diegetic song is one that they cannot hear although the audience can.

though the marquee for the show was already up at the Marquis Theatre. Other productions followed in the next decade at Walnut Street, Goodspeed, and Ford's Theatre, attempting to ready the show for a New York run, but it has yet to materialize. *Variety* likened the show to a new musical starring Harold Hill and Little Orphan Annie, and while the adventures of a con man and plucky girl seemed ripe for a Broadway bow, *Paper Moon* never showed up.[17]

In 1995, *Luck, Pluck, and Virtue* found several major players involved in an off-Broadway play with music. The Atlantic Theater presented this show with a script by James Lapine, and a few songs with lyrics by Fitzhugh, and music by Allen Shawn. Among its stars was Neil Patrick Harris. Harris played a man who learns through a lifetime of allegorical journeying that the credo implied in the show's title cannot give a man a good life, despite that philosophy being sold to us at birth. The show was presented as a vaudeville of sorts, necessitating its song breaks.

Fitzhugh contributed additional lyrics to Adam Guettel's 1998 Public Theater piece, *Saturn Returns*, which eventually evolved into the musical *Myths and Hymns*. In this, Fitzhugh had the distinction of working on musicals with both Mary Rodgers and her son, Guettel.

Muscle was the vision of James Lapine. He had found a book he thought ripe for musical adaptation, about competitive body building, and presented it to Stephen Sondheim in the early 1990s. Sondheim's *Muscle* was intended to be a companion piece to *Passion*, the two making up one entire evening. When *Passion* became a full-length musical, Lapine brought *Muscle* instead to Bill Finn. Finn wanted to compose only, so he brought Fitzhugh on as lyricist. Lapine, Finn, and Fitzhugh's *Muscle* had a production in 2001 in Chicago, but has yet to be seen in New York.

Another project of Fitzhugh's, again with a cast of high-profile players, that has yet to debut in New York was *Paradise Found*. One of the only Hal Prince musicals to not make it to New York, *Paradise Found* premiered at the Menier Chocolate Factory in London in 2010. The show was based on a novel called *The Tale of the 1002nd Night* by Joseph Roth, and has a book by Richard Nelson. Fitzhugh set her lyrics to music by Johann Strauss II for this show about Middle Eastern royalty and Austrian royalty who become romantically entangled.

Los Otros was a semiautobiographical musical that Fitzhugh wrote book and lyrics for, collaborating with Michael John LaChiusa, which premiered at the Center Theatre Group in 2012. Fitzhugh was inspired to write a show based on her experiences growing up in Southern California and relationships with many Mexican-American immigrants. The show received its off-Broadway premiere in

---

17. Daniels, Robert L. "*Paper Moon*." *Variety*, 27 September 1993, https://variety.com/1993/legit/reviews/paper-moon-2-1200433167/.

2022 as part of Premieres NYC. In 2014, Fitzhugh and LaChiusa collaborated again on *The Nine Fathers of Ariel*, a new musical which has been workshopped but has yet to receive its full stage premiere.

In 2019, Fitzhugh cowrote lyrics and book with Harrison David Rivers for the musical *Broadbend, Arkansas*, which depicts racial violence and inequality in America spanning two generations of the same family, during the 1960s civil rights movement and today. Music and additional lyrics were by Ted Shen for this show which played the Duke on 42nd Street.

Fitzhugh passed away in 2023.

JULIANNE BOYD, JOAN MICKLIN SILVER, AND *A … MY NAME IS ALICE*

Center of Evolution

A. … My Name Is Alice is worthy of unique contemplation in this collection of writers and musicals because it is at the crux of the evolution of feminist theatre in the twentieth century. A revue about modern women of all ages in all different situations, the revue features the work of numerous female writers and also numerous male writers. Its feminism was not reserved for only female voices, and in this manner of inclusion, it sent a message that feminism is for everyone.

The cast of the show did consist of all women, however, and they sang numbers like "All Girl Band," a delightful anthem to collective female power; "At My Age," about two women of different ages going on first dates; "Trash," about losing oneself in trashy romance novels; "Pretty Young Men," about women at a strip club; "Welcome to Kindergarten, Mrs. Johnson," about the expectations of motherhood; and "Friends," about long-term female friendship.

In the *Daily News*, Harry Haun noted that "the male of the species" could attend the show "without fear of catching any steel shrapnel in the eye,"[18] an opinion that several other critics echoed. According to the critical collective, the show was feminist but not angry-feminist. It was fighting for women but not scaring men. This was despite an impassioned scene with no punches pulled written by Anne Meara about women being heckled by men on the street, a hot-button topic in 1983 and a hot button-topic today.

In the *Central New Jersey Home News*, critic Ernest Albrecht's review had the headline "Feminine musical is more refreshing than militant." He went on to also note that, "In the cast of five, there are two black women, but they are not there to represent the black woman's point of view. They are there,

---

18. Haun, Harry. "*Alice* Rates an A for Agreeable." *Daily News*, 27 February 1984, p. 147.

obviously, because they are two dynamite talents and provide some variety of style."[19]

The Bechdel Test, popularized decades later, asks if women in a scene talk to each other about something other than men. *A . . . My Name Is Alice* does pass the Bechdel Test, as many of the sequences do revolve around the women's experiences and feelings about men, but just as many sequences revolve around other topics. The women at the helm of the show and the writing teams achieved a balance as far as content about the romantic and sexual lives of women and content about other elements of their lives.

In a way, the rejection of militant feminist expectations *was* feminist. As co-conceiver Joan Micklin Silver said to the press, "I personally don't relate to gynecologist jokes."[20] The pervading sentiment that all women should want to express themselves in the same way was anti-feminist by definition—and so this show, which to date still occupies a unique place in the canon, was revolutionary in doing its own thing, led by Boyd and Sliver.

Boyd and Silver initially met while working together on a benefit for the National Abortion Rights Action League. They solicited submissions for a revue about women and received many. The writers who contributed to the final version of the show included future *Friends* creator Marta Kauffman, the previously mentioned Meara, Lucy Simon, Winnie Holzman, Amanda McBroom, Carol Hall, Susan Birkenhead, June Siegel, and many more.

An article for the *Associated Press* reported, "Silver said she was looking for such ideas about women's common experiences that would let them be more relaxed, more self-confident and allow them to laugh at themselves. And she wanted to get past the defensive, sometimes bitter attitudes of the early days of women's liberation."[21]

A . . . My Name Is Alice was produced by the Women's Project at the Village Gate in 1983 and then transferred to the American Place Theatre for a more traditional off-Broadway presentation, which racked up 353 performances. A sequel, *A . . . My Name Is Still Alice*, premiered in 1992 and featured many of the same writers and several new ones, including Mary Bracken Phillips, Lynn Nottage, and Christine Lavin.

In 1995, *A . . . My Name Will Always Be Alice* combined the best parts of each revue together to create a highlights reel. This premiered at Barrington Stage Company and received a cast album.

---

19. Albrecht, Ernest. "Feminist Musical Is More Refreshing Than Militant." *Central New Jersey Home News*, 27 February 1984, p. 17.

20. Kuchwara, Michael. "A Musical by Women, for Women, about Women." *Associated Press*, 20 June 1984.

21. Ibid.

The show remains popular with schools and regional theaters, partially because of its all-female cast. Sadly, half of the songs from each show have never been commercially recorded since the existing recording only includes half of each edition's material.

The quality of the material in *A . . . My Name Is Alice*, and its sequels, does set it apart from other revues and other feminist musicals of its time. Boyd and Silver did a tremendous job assembling songs and scenes that are varied, compelling, moving, hilarious, and give a realistic portrait of where women were at in the 1980s and early 1990s.

MARTA KAUFFMAN
A Friends *Prequel*

One of the most successful television masterminds of all time, Marta Kauffman is the cocreator of *Friends*, alongside David Crane. Prior to *Friends*, Kauffman and Crane got their start writing off-Broadway musical material for the revues *Personals* and *A . . . My Name Is Alice*.

Together with Kauffman's then-husband Michael Skloff, who would also later work on *Friends* (including writing its theme song), Kauffman and Crane penned the title piece for *A . . . My Name Is Alice* as well as the songs "Trash" and "Welcome to Kindergarten, Mrs. Johnson," which appear on the show's original cast album compilation (consisting of highlights from the show and its sequel). In these pieces and their sketch "For Women Only Poems," one can experience the viewpoints and the style of humor that was later employed on *Friends*. "Trash" is a heightened tale of office drama as seen through the eyes of a woman obsessed with melodramatic romance novels. "Welcome to Kindergarten, Mrs. Johnson" is a twist on yuppie parenting woes of the 1980s as seen through the eyes of a parent-teacher conference. Each song is a self-contained story with fully painted modern characters.

Personals found Kauffman, as well as Crane and Skloff, sharing writing billing with career theatre writers like Alan Menken and Stephen Schwartz. This time, Crane and Kauffman wrote all lyrics with Seth Friedman, and other writers supplied the music. Thus, *Personals* feels more integrated than other revues, its songs and themes building on each other rather than complimenting each other from different perspectives. The overall concept is, as might be suspected, personal ads. Who are the people who place them, and why do they place them? In 1985, when *Personals* premiered at the Minetta Lane, personal ads were gaining new traction with twentysomethings and thirtysomethings, especially in urban centers. So the topic gave the future creators of *Friends* a chance to explore the love lives of characters much like the *Friends* characters, only in musical form, off-Broadway.

Personals ran for 265 performances, but sadly, its original off-Broadway cast of Jason Alexander, Laura Dean,[22] Dee Hoty, Jeff Keller, Nancy Opel, and Trey Wilson did not get to record an original cast album. A *Personals* album was recorded later with the original London cast and is a terrific listen—each song smart and tuneful, many tackling unexpected topics. "After School Special" slowly reveals a high schooler's devious plan to use double entendres in attracting "teachers" to give him lessons in love and other activities. "Moving in with Linda" is a musical sequence where the baggage brought when one moves in with a new partner is actualized in human and song form. "I Could Always Go to You" finds two female friends turning to each other romantically as an experiment. The songs have unexpected turns and are ultimately both funny and relatable.

Personals began at Brandeis University, when Kauffman was a student. All of its main creators knew each other in their early twenties, and set out to write a show about the singles scene as it currently stood.

Kauffman's other musical theatre writing credits from before she moved into the television realm include *Upstairs at O'Neal's*, a 1982 off-Broadway show where she also assisted creator Martin Charnin, and a children's musical of *Rapunzel*. Kauffman, Crane, and Skloff also wrote *Arthur: The Musical*, based on the film, which had its eye on Broadway during its 1992 premiere at Goodspeed Opera House, but fell short. The disappointment drove the writers to the West Coast.

WINNIE HOLZMAN
Writer of Wicked

The book writer of one of the most popular musicals of all time, Winnie Holzman, has but one Broadway credit to her name: *Wicked*. She has worked extensively in theatre and television.

Holzman started out as an actor and appeared in *Sister Mary Ignatius Explains It All for You* off-Broadway in 1982. She attended the NYU graduate musical theatre writing program where she met and began collaborating with David Evans. In 1983, the two collaborated with several other writers on a 1983 revue called *Serious Bizness* that was produced at the cabaret theatre O'Neal's. Then, Holzman and Evans wrote a musical called *Amateurs* that played Cincinnati Playhouse in the Park. Holzman also contributed to *A . . . My Name Is Alice* in 1984.

Birds of Paradise, Holzman and Evans's musical that played off-Broadway at the Promenade in 1987 began its life in the program at NYU. Holzman and Evans cowrote the book, with Holzman's lyrics and Evans's music. Arthur Laurents was their mentor and professor there; indeed, he introduced Holzman and

---

22. Dean later went on to play Rachel's coworker Sophie on *Friends*.

Evans to each other to begin their collaboration. Laurents directed *Birds of Paradise* and the illustrious cast included Mary Beth Peil, Crista Moore, Todd Graff, Donna Murphy, John Cunningham, J. K. Simmons, and Barbara Walsh.

Birds of Paradise is about an amateur theatre group filled with dreamers who are presenting a new show based on Chekhov's *The Seagull*. The backstage events mirror the plot of *The Seagull*, even as the play the characters are presenting is a departure from *The Seagull*. *Birds of Paradise* had its fans and has gained even more over the years thanks to a terrific and charming cast recording, but the show received damning reviews and closed after only twenty-four performances. Hischak wrote "With its triple-level plot, intricate songs, and complex characters, *Birds of Paradise* was invigorating theatergoing even though it didn't quite come off."[23]

Following *Birds of Paradise*, Holzman spent time in Los Angeles where she was a writer on the show *thirtysomething* until 1994 when she began work on *My So-Called Life* as cocreator, writer, and producer. As Holzman worked in television, she continued to make appearances as an actor in her projects and those of others.

In 2003, Holzman made her Broadway debut with *Wicked*, writing the book to Stephen Schwartz's score. In 1994, Holzman said to the *Associated Press* about *My So-Called Life*: "Everyone has been a teenager, no matter how much they don't want to admit it. It's like a country you have to pass through to get where you're going. That's what finally got me interested in the series: Teen-age is something that everybody shares." This quote relates to *Wicked* as well, as Holzman may as well have been speaking to the way she made the struggles of the young witches Elphaba and Galinda so relatable and universal.

Working with Gregory Maguire's original novel, Holzman crafted a book that has become one of the most beloved in musical theatre. She received a Tony Award nomination and won the Drama Desk Award for Best Book.

When asked in 2017 what had attracted her to *Wicked* originally, Holzman said, "It's the whole idea that . . . what you think you know you don't really know. People are never what they seem on the surface."

She shared that she had pursued the rights to the novel years before Stephen Schwartz was also inspired by it and brought her on board to cocreate a stage musical version. Holzman was immediately transported by the idea of "taking this extreme figure of iconic wickedness and making her the heroine." She commented, "I just love that she behaves in a human wicked way, and not in a wicked witch way."

While the story of Galinda and Elphaba's relationship is essential to Maguire's novel, Holzman and Schwartz elevated the friendship of the two women to

23. Hischak, Thomas. *Off-Broadway Musicals Since 1919: From Greenwich Village Follies to The Toxic Avenger*. Lanham, MD: Scarecrow Press, 1911.

become the central story of the stage musical *Wicked*.[24] The popular show is still running on Broadway today, more than 7,500 performances later, with a high profile film adaptation on the way.

AMANDA McBROOM
Writer of "The Rose"

Popular cabaret song stylist and writer Amanda McBroom is best known for her song "The Rose," which Bette Midler performed in the movie of the same name. She has also worked as an actress, mainly on television, appearing once on Broadway in the musical *Seesaw*.

McBroom's work is often performed by musical theatre actors in concerts and cabaret, as well as on recordings. She has written for several musicals as well.

In 1983, McBroom contributed to *A ... My Name Is Alice*. Her song "The Portrait," a lament sung by a daughter to a photo of her mother, is one of the most oft-performed pieces in the show. Her songs for the show's sequel, "Wheels" and "Baby" are equally emotional and moving.

In 1990, McBroom wrote *Heartbeats*, a musical with a plot that utilized many of her previously written songs as well as some new ones. The show started out a few years earlier as a revue of her work but morphed into a musical about characters and their romantic entanglements. McBroom appeared as an actor in the Los Angeles premiere of the work, which received a cast album. The reviews were unkind, feeling that hedging the existing songs into a plot created an evening of cliches. *Heartbeats* never moved to New York. In addition to the original cast album, songs from *Heartbeats* have been recorded and performed by notable artists such as Barry Manilow.

A Woman of Will was McBroom's 2005 musical which found her inspired by Shakespeare. A one-woman show, *A Woman of Will* utilizes McBroom's original songs to tell a story of a writer who draws upon Shakespeare's heroines to confront her own personal and professional demons. The show ran for one month at the Daryl Roth Theatre.

PATRICIA MICHAELS
Marilyn: An American Fable's *Librettist*

Librettist Patricia Michaels was credited with the book for *Marilyn: An American Fable*, a 1983 show about Marilyn Monroe that went through more changes

---

24. "Book Writer Winnie Holzman on Making a *Wicked* Heroine and Shunting Dorothy Aside." Broadway in Cincinnati, https://broadwayincincinnati.news/2017/08/08/interview-with-winnie -holzman-bookwriter-for-wicked/.

during Broadway previews than audiences could believe, with show doctors and new songwriters coming and going almost daily.

The show was Michaels's first time writing a libretto for a stage musical. She had largely worked in television production.

SYBILLE PEARSON
Baby *and* Giant

Sybille Pearson has been produced as a playwright at Manhattan Theatre Club, New York Theatre Workshop, the Vineyard Theatre, and on many other stages. Her two major works as a writer of musicals are *Baby* (1983) and *Giant* (2012).

Pearson wrote the book for *Baby*, an original musical about three couples of different ages and lifestyles on a college campus, who are all dealing with the change of life that a baby brings. Her collaborators were lyricist-director Richard Maltby Jr. and composer David Shire. Pearson was Tony-nominated for her work on *Baby*, which is her only Broadway show to date.

Pearson was born in Czechoslovakia, where her family had traveled while fleeing Hitler's Germany. This eventually brought them to New York, where Pearson worked as an actress until a lack of good roles and a need to be with her family sent her back to college to become a librarian. In school, she took a class with theatre writer Arthur Kopit that inspired her to try her hand at playwriting. Her first play, *Sally and Marsha*, was soon after produced at the O'Neill Center and then by Manhattan Theatre Club.

Maltby and Shire, who were familiar with her work, sought her out as book writer for their musical *Baby*, and at first, she balked. She had never written a musical. But she began collaborating with them eventually, and crafted a story that was notably realistic and filled with modern humanity, in great contrast with most Broadway musicals of the 1980s. From Lizzie and Danny, the unmarried pregnant young couple, to Pam and Nick who desperately want to get pregnant, to Arlene and Alan who think they are done having babies, Pearson gave each character in *Baby* layers of objective and personal history that made the show what it was.

In 2012, Pearson had another new musical premiere in New York. This was *Giant*, a collaboration with composer-lyricist Michael John LaChiusa, based on the Edna Ferber book. *Giant* received its world premiere at the Signature Theatre in Washington, D.C., in 2009 and three years later landed at the Public Theater, starring Brian D'Arcy James and Kate Baldwin. Pearson had her work cut out for her in adapting Ferber's dense, deeply written prose, the story of a family in Texas over many years. Her work on the sprawling and ambitious show earned her a Drama Desk nomination for Best Book of a Musical.

222

Pearson continued to collaborate with Michael John LaChiusa, and their musical adaptation of Somerset Maugham's *Rain* premiered at the Old Globe Theatre in 2016. Pearson was a longtime professor at the Graduate Musical Theatre Writing Program at NYU Tisch before her retirement.

PEGGY LEE
An Icon's Failed Musical Autobiography

Prolific songwriter, recording artist, actress, and icon Peggy Lee was one of the most well-known personalities in entertainment for much of the twentieth century. She recorded over eighty albums in her lifetime.

In 1983, Peggy Lee starred on Broadway at the Lunt-Fontanne in her own "musical autobiography." But this wasn't a specialty concert—it was a bona fide musical theatre piece. Lena Horne's hit Broadway retrospective the previous year presumably inspired Peggy Lee to create the same kind of show. But critical consensus wasn't as positive, and *Peg* closed after only five performances.

Frank Rich in the *New York Times* wrote that the show's selection of stories seemed awkward, much of the dialogue stilted, and the overall tone of the piece mislaid. In addition, he wrote, "Many of the anecdotes sound as if they were long ago homogenized by press agents for mass dissemination through talk shows. . . . Her manner can be blandly impersonal. Her speaking voice has few inflections, and her principal expression is a fixed, impassive smile."[25]

Lee wrote new songs to tell her life story as part of the proceedings. Many of her well-known hits were performed, interspersed with songs specifically crafted for this autobiographical stage piece. She was credited with writing the book of the show as well.

KAYE BALLARD
Writing for Herself

Musical theatre actor Kaye Ballard had a long career, stretching from the 1940s to the 2010s. She starred in revues, Broadway musicals, television shows, movies and was a favorite on the cabaret scene. Among her credits, she introduced "Fly Me to the Moon" and "Lazy Afternoon" to audiences.

While Ballard was a performer first, she also acted as writer for her one-woman show, *Hey, Ma . . . Kaye Ballard* off-Broadway at the Promenade in 1984. The show was a retrospective about Ballard's rise to success in show business and her adventures along the way. But it was more of a show than a cabaret act, and included original material by Ballard herself that was intended to craft the

25. Rich, Frank. "Stage: Peggy Lee Self-Portrait." *New York Times*, 15 December 1983, p. C17.

evening into a dramatization of events. Both her monologues and several of the songs in *Hey Ma*... were the work of Ballard herself. This predated a genre that would become more popular in the 1990s, as musical theatre actors and other entertainment personalities crafted semiautobiographical one-person musical acts around themselves for the legitimate stage.

BARBARA DAMASHEK AND MOLLY NEWMAN
The First All-Female Writing Team Nominated for a Best Musical Tony

Quilters was the third-ever Best Musical Tony Award nominee written solely by women. (The first was Micki Grant's *Don't Bother Me, I Can't Cope*, and second was Elizabeth Swados's *Runaways*.) Because *Quilters* had book by Molly Newman and Barbara Damashek, and music and lyrics by Damashek, and the other two shows were written by one author, *Quilters* was technically the first all-female writing *team* with a Best Musical nomination.[26]

Quilters originated at the Denver Center Theater Company in 1982. It was then presented in L.A., Pittsburgh, and Washington, D.C., as well as at the Edinburgh Festival, before heading to Broadway. *Quilters* played the Jack Lawrence on 48th Street, the same small now-demolished house off the beaten path that was home to *Don't Bother Me, I Can't Cope* and *Dear Oscar*.

The show is about pioneer women in the American west. The seven-woman cast plays a woman named Sarah and her six daughters, who experience many elements of pioneer life over the course of the show. *Quilters* presents the events of a lifetime chronologically, so the show begins with depictions of girlhood and ends in death—with everything from marriage to natural disasters in between. Each woman lends differing experiences to the universal framework for female pioneer life, through songs and stories. The show was based on the book *The Quilters: Women and Domestic Art* by Patricia Cooper and Norma Bradley Allen.

Frank Rich panned the show in the *New York Times*, which doomed its Broadway run. He wrote,

> Quilters, *the first Broadway production of the new season, is billed as a "musical," but it might better serve as a diorama at the Cooper-Hewitt Museum. This show means to celebrate those hearty pioneer women who turned a domestic craft into a spirited native form of autobiographical art. The women who created* Quilters, *Molly Newman and Barbara Damashek, clearly know a lot about quilting and the unsung heroines who practiced it. If the entertainment at the Jack Lawrence Theater is any indication, their*

---

26. As previously noted, Vinnette Carroll was the conceiver and director of *Cope*, but she counted herself as the director and not a "member of the writing team," in the case of that show.

knowledge of theater is somewhat less acute. Apparently proceeding from the misguided conviction that what works on cloth can work on stage, the authors have given their libretto a patchwork structure.

Quilters was the brain child of Newman. An actress, Newman auditioned for a play at Denver Center Theater with a monologue from a show she was writing herself. This play eventually became *Quilters*. Newman was encouraged to turn the show into a musical, and in doing so, began collaborating with Damashek. As Damashek added songs into the show, Newman traveled the American west, interviewing women and gathering regional history.

At the end of *Quilters*, a physical quilt displays patches from the women's lives which have come into play over the course of the show.

Since *Quilters*, Newman has mainly worked as a television writer and producer. Damashek, who also directed *Quilters*, mainly works as a theatre director.

ELLIE GREENWICH
The Queen of 1960s Pop

Ellie Greenwich, circa 1972. PHOTOFEST

Ellie Greenwich was the self-made queen of 1960s rock 'n' roll. While still in college, she became one of the Brill Building's most promising songwriters, a promise that was fulfilled when she wrote or cowrote songs like "Chapel of Love," "Leader of the Pack," "Be My Baby," "Do Wah Diddy Diddy," "(Today I Met) The Boy I'm Gonna Marry," "River Deep, Mountain High," "Christmas (Baby Please Come Home)," "Baby I Love You, "Da Doo Ron Ron," and many more. Greenwich was a huge part of the revolution in sound that happened in 1960s music.

In 1984, Greenwich began a road to Broadway in a very unique way. *Leader of the Pack* originated as a cabaret show at the downtown club the Bottom Line. The musical entertainment featured a first act that told the story of Greenwich's rise to fame as a songwriter. Iconic performers like Darlene Love who had originated Greenwich's songs performed numbers. In the last fourth of the show, Greenwich herself emerged to sing her own songs and finish the story.

Leader of the Pack was such a gigantic hit at the Bottom Line that it was sold out every night, with celebrities returning for repeat visits. While Greenwich was responsible for some of the most indelible hits of an era, she wasn't a public figure. She was at one time known as "The Demo Queen" for singing on more demos than anyone else—songs of her own and songs of others. And she did record her own work, especially toward the beginning of her career. But she never performed live, and she was known as a behind-the-scenes songwriter. The celebration of her songs brought out a nostalgia for the 1960s, and did so in a moving way that had never been seen before: incorporating bio-musical elements as well as a performance from the woman behind the music.

In *The Guardian*, Linda Blandford wrote that *Leader of the Pack* is "one of those joyous New York occasions that takes everyone by surprise."[27] She told readers how special it was to experience Greenwich singing her own songs, showing audiences that she was a triumphant survivor, whose work had deeply influenced the sound of American music. Blandford noted how ecstatic audiences were throughout every performance.

The story told in *Leader of the Pack* simplified Greenwich's life to a few key points so that focus could be on the songs in the show. Audiences saw her rise from a girl in Levittown writing songs on her accordion to a Brill Building songwriter, and got the Cliff's Notes version of her love story with Jeff Barry, which involved their marriage, career together as songwriters, and heartbreaking divorce—followed by Greenwich's rise back up to the top, by herself.

Greenwich spoke about her relationship with Barry, at home and at work, in an interview with *Spectropop*. She told the publication that when the two were clicking creatively, and also in love, there was nothing better—but that when they clashed at work, it was very hard to separate that from domestic life. She also said, "Jeff and I . . . were putting in the same hours. We'd finally get home from a long day's work at the office—writing the songs, rehearsing the groups, going in the studio—and be hungry. You tell me, who's gonna cook the meal? It wasn't like I was home all day, waiting for him: 'Here's your little dinner, dear.' There became some problems. It wasn't like, the man is the breadwinner, and this is what you do."[28]

Producers brought *Leader of the Pack* to the Ambassador Theatre on Broadway, where it opened in the spring of 1985 and was nominated for Best Musical in a particularly dry season that saw several categories eliminated from the Tony Awards. In fact, the show wasn't nominated in any other category.

Leader of the Pack was the first jukebox musical of its kind in the modern Broadway era. There had been shows before that used the songs of a popular musical artist of course, but these were largely revues. The way that *Leader of the Pack* used radio songs to tell a nostalgic story of American pop personalities in another era called forward to the success of shows like *Jersey Boys* and *Beautiful* decades later. In 1985, Broadway critics frowned upon the genre, and

---

27. Blandford, Linda. *"Leader of the Pack." Guardian.*

28. Greig, Charlotte. "Spectropop Presents Ellie Greenwich." Spectropop, http://spectropop.com/ EllieGreenwich2/index.htm.

found *Leader of the Pack* noisy and not-meant-for-Broadway. It closed after 120 performances.

Greenwich again appeared in *Leader of the Pack* on Broadway. The cast also included Dinah Manoff as young Ellie Greenwich, Darlene Love as herself, Annie Golden, Patrick Cassidy, Jasmine Guy, and Pattie Darcy. An original cast album was released.

Speaking about the show's Broadway life, Greenwich remarked that trying to create a hybrid of a Broadway musical and rock 'n' roll concert meant that *Leader of the Pack* had trouble pleasing fans of either genre. She thought *Leader of the Pack* had worked better in its original, smaller, downtown venue, and that leaning toward a revue format rather than a real book musical might've been a better strategy.[29]

In addition to *Leader of the Pack*, Greenwich's songs have appeared on Broadway in the shows *Bette Midler's Clams on the Half Shell Revue* (1975), *Rock 'N Roll! The First 5,000 Years* (1982), *Andrè DeShields' Haarlem Nocturne* (1984), *Uptown . . . It's Hot!* (1986), *The Cher Show* (2018), and *Tina* (2019). For *Leader of the Pack*, Greenwich also wrote several new songs to fill out the story.

Greenwich is widely regarded as one the most important pop-rock artists of the twentieth century.

ENID FUTTERMAN
A Musical about Anne Frank

A musical based on Anne Frank's diary, *Yours, Anne,* played off-Broadway at Playhouse 91 during the fall of 1985, and has since been a favorite of many theaters looking to present an educational show that musicalizes such an important work.

Yours, Anne used as its source material not just Anne Frank's diary itself, but also the 1955 play *The Diary of Anne Frank* by Frances Goodrich and Albert Hackett that had been a hit on Broadway. The book and lyrics were by Enid Futterman and music by Michael Cohen for this meaningful adaptation.

While *Yours, Anne* received largely respectful reviews, most agreed that the material didn't cry out for musicalization. Many felt the inclusion of songs was unnecessary for the piece, and further that it was awkward in many instances to have music interrupt the proceedings, whether it was the family singing in hiding or a musical interlude for Anne to sing about her Hollywood dreams. The show found an audience for a few months, many Jewish theatre groups among them, and was able to issue an original cast album and become licensed.

---

29. Ibid.

In 1987, Futterman wrote a musical called *Portrait of Jennie* based on the novel of the same name by Robert Nathan. She undertook the lyrics and cowrote the book for this show which premiered at the Berkshire Theatre Festival.

Futterman later wrote a book called *Bittersweet Journey: A Modestly Erotic Novel of Love, Longing, and Chocolate.*

POLLY PEN
Powerful Feminist Chamber Musicals

After appearing in several quick-closing Broadway shows including *The Utter Glory of Morrissey Hall* (1979) and *Canterbury Tales* (1980), Polly Pen made a name for herself off-Broadway as a writer. Thomas Hischak called Pen's breakthrough 1985 musical, *Goblin Market* "one of the most unusual and hypnotic musicals of the decade."[30]

Goblin Market started at the Vineyard Theatre, where Pen would return time and again throughout her career, before a run at Circle in the Square off-Broadway. The chamber musical has music by Pen and book and lyrics by Pen and Peggy Harmon,[31] based on the nineteenth-century book by Christina Rossetti. Rossetti's book had become seen as a powerful feminist work, for its tale of two sisters who are controlled and cursed by male goblins before regaining their power. According to Hischak, *Goblin Market*'s reviews called it the best musical of the season. The show's original performances by Ann Morrison and Terri Klausner were highly praised, and the show's dark and powerful ideas were put forth by its haunting score.

In 1994, Pen returned to the Vineyard with a show called *Christina Alberta's Father* for which she wrote book, music, and lyrics. The show, based on an H. G. Wells novel, received a Richard Rodgers Developmental Grant as well as a Drama Desk nomination for Pen's music. *Christina Alberta's Father* follows a man fixated on discovering Atlantis and his daughter who sets out to save him from his own folly. Those roles were originated by Henry Stram and Marla Schaffel.

Less than two years later, Pen returned to the Vineyard with *Bed and Sofa*, based on a controversial 1926 Russian film. *Bed and Sofa* is about a love triangle between two men and one woman in 1920s Moscow, where games and power struggles play out until eventually Ludmilla, the protagonist, becomes pregnant. While her two lovers wish for Ludmilla to have an abortion, she decides to keep the baby and leave both of them. *Bed and Sofa* received rapturous reviews from many of the papers with the *Village Voice* saying, "Wonderful! A must see! So

---

30. Hischak, Thomas. *Off-Broadway Musicals since 1919: From Greenwich Village Follies to The Toxic Avenger*. Lanham, MD: Scarecrow Press, 1911.

31. Harmon also largely worked as an actress, appearing in Broadway's *Big River*.

perfectly done it is almost unfair to the rackety hacks who infest our musical theater." Pen wrote music and lyrics (which were captured on an original cast album) and the book was by Laurence Klavan. This time, Pen won an Obie Award for her music. In 2003, Pen collaborated with Klavan again on a musical called *Embarrassments*, which played the Wilma in Philadelphia.

A 2000 feature article in *American Theatre* wrote: "Audiences and critics alike struggle to categorize Pen's take on musical theatre, describing her works as "vest-pocket musicals" or 'chamber operas,' on account of their miniature scale."

The piece was to mark the premiere of a new Pen show, called *The Night Governess*, based on an unknown Louisa May Alcott book called *Behind a Mask*. *The Night Governess* premiered at the McCarter (their first musical) and tells the story of a governess who secretly plots to marry a rich man. Like much of Pen's work, the show focuses on the Victorian era and the women who survived its patriarchal stranglehold in various ways.

In 2014, Pen wrote the music for *Arlington*, with book and lyrics by Victor Lodato, which premiered yet again at the Vineyard. The one-woman show originally starring Alexandra Silber is about a woman whose husband is off at war.

Pen's off-Broadway work, all with the Vineyard, was a function of a long creative relationship with that theater's artistic director, Douglas Aibel. Pen said, "If Doug hadn't persuaded me so persistently, I don't know whether I would have shown my work to anyone." She says. "It would have been a private pastime between acting assignments."[32]

JANE IREDALE
Casting Director, Writer, Producer, Makeup Line Entrepreneur

How many women that have been nominated for a Tony Award for writing also created their own successful all-natural makeup line?

The list is limited to one: Jane Iredale.

Iredale, originally from the United Kingdom, moved to New York in the 1970s and began working in casting and producing. During her time as a casting director and producer she came to feel that actors deserved better makeup—more natural choices that would not cause problems like acne later, even if they worked well for the task at hand at the moment. Iredale set out to start her own makeup line in the 1990s, and it is now a well-known brand.

In between, she made a pit stop working on a Broadway musical called *Wind in the Willows*. The 1985 musical version of the beloved classic by Kenneth Grahame played only four performances at the Nederlander Theatre, but was

---

32. Ahmad, Shazia. "The Perils of Polly Pen." *American Theatre*, 1 July 2000, https://www.american-theatre.org/2000/07/01/the-perils-of-polly-pen/.

nevertheless nominated for Best Book for Iredale, as well as Best Score (for William Perry and Roger McGough). Iredale's credit on the show was not "book by" but "dramatized by." Among the show's stars were Nathan Lane as Toad.

Wind in the Willows tried out at the Folger Theatre in Washington, D.C., before Broadway, where Iredale told the *Washington Post* that although she was first asked to cast the musical, she felt she was destined to write it instead. She also told the paper about her process adapting the original work for the stage. Iredale noted that as written, *Wind in the Willows* had no leading lady, so it was her idea to change the character of Mole into a woman, to expand the nature of the story.[33]

The paper noted that this gender change for a character inspired an extreme reaction when the show played London. The *Daily Mail* headline read "Storm Brews over Sex Change for Moley." Iredale told the press that because she found the character of Mole as originally written to have "feminine characteristics,"[34] she thought the creative choice was in the spirit of Kenneth Grahame's original book.

In the *New York Times* review that panned and closed the show, critic Mel Gussow concluded by asking that CARTOON (The Committee on Anthropomorphism and the Reckless Travesty of Our Nostalgia) stop creating any Broadway shows where actors played animals.[35] This was two years into *Cats'* record-breaking run and less than a decade before Disney would come to Broadway with shows starting with *Beauty and the Beast*.

A. M. (ANNAMARIE) COLLINS
Angry Housewives *Form a Rock Band*

In 1986, a musical called *Angry Housewives* opened at the Minetta Lane Theatre. The show had a book by A. M. Collins, and music and lyrics by Chad Henry.

The show had originated in Seattle in 1983, where it eventually became the longest-running musical in town, sticking around for six years.

In a sort of parallel to the plot of *The Full Monty*, *Angry Housewives* finds a group of women, down on their luck in different ways, financially, emotionally, in terms of self-esteem, and otherwise, who band together to win a contest. In this instance, they form a local punk-rock band. (It is, after all, the 1980s.) In creating songs together, and letting their rage and frustration out, the women come to

---

33. Brown, Joe. "Backstage." *Washington Post*, 1 August 1983, p. C7.

34. Ibid.

35. Gussow, Mel. "Stage: A Musical Tale, *Wind in the Willows.*" *New York Times*, 21 December 1985, p. 15.

terms with the problems they face. One of the angriest songs is called "Eat Your Fucking Cornflakes."

The show also puts on display the reaction to this new musical group by the men in the women's lives. In exploring the actions and reactions of so many characters to a heavy metal band formed by middle-aged women to express their anger, the show addresses a lot of different views on feminism in the 1980s.

Angry Housewives received lukewarm reviews but managed 137 performances in New York, and has continued to be a regional favorite, although less so than it might have managed had it received a cast album.

Seattle-based creators Collins and Henry continued to work in Seattle theatre, where Collins co-owned Pioneer Square Theatre, original home of *Angry Housewives*.

SUSAN ASTLEY, KIM SEARY, HILARY STRANG, AND CHRISTINE WILLES
Canadian Sex Tips

A Canadian hit musical called *Sex Tips for Modern Girls* made a splash off-Broadway at the Susan Bloch Theatre in 1986. The show was the product of several women who put their own stories on stage and developed a new musical from the material. With song titles like "Penis Envoy" and "Up to My Tits in Water," *Sex Tips* is nothing if not direct. The show played a fairly respectable 198 performances in New York, not becoming quite the success it was in Canada. As the *New York Times* wrote: "Blending smidgens of group therapy, sex education and musical comedy, the show gets lost in the wilderness between self-help and show business."[36]

MARY MURFITT
Actor, Musician, Writer, Director

In 1987, the off-Broadway Circle in the Square Downtown presented a new musical called *Oil City Symphony*. It became a smash hit, racking up 626 performances and winning the 1988 Outer Critics Circle Award for Outstanding Off-Broadway Musical.

Oil City Symphony joined two of *Pump Boys and Dinettes'* creators, Debra Monk and Mark Hardwick, with two new collaborators Mary Murfitt and Mike Craver. The concept of *Oil City Symphony* finds a former high school musical group reuniting in their old gym to honor their music teacher with a concert program consisting of originals and standards. But in this case, the originals are

---

36. Holden, Stephen. "Stage: *Sex Tips for Modern Girls.*" *New York Times*, 8 October 1986, p. C23.

outrageous, autobiographical takes on the mundane lives of the characters and the standards are hilariously re-envisioned. Circle in the Square Downtown was made to look like a high school gym and audience members even had to turn themselves around for "The Hokey Pokey."

The show began as an off-off-Broadway Christmas skit, and then was further developed by its creators. Sharon Scruggs initially played Murfitt's part in the first iteration but left the show. Monk, Hardwick, Murfitt, and Craver wrote, performed, and played all instruments for *Oil City Symphony*.

In *Time* magazine, Michael Walsh wrote, "*Oil City Symphony* lets the good times roll, and in the process skewers every high school music program in the country. . . . But fondly."[37]

In the *New York Times*, Mel Gussow wrote, "Ms. Murfitt, switching in midtune from violin to flute to saxophone, could have made a living with Phil Spitalny and his All Girl Orchestra."[38] Murfitt won a Theatre World Award for her performance.

Audiences who saw *Oil City Symphony* loved it, but, as historian Thomas Hischak points out, the title proved a significant detriment to the show's success. Many potential audience members misunderstood and thought they would be seeing a symphony instead of a musical, so they didn't buy tickets in the first place. The off-Broadway production eventually changed its title to just *Oil City*, to attempt to fix the issue, but the original title was used in licensing.[39]

Murfitt went on to perform the show in some of these productions, joined by three new cohorts on stage rather than the three other creators. She has also directed numerous productions of *Oil City Symphony*.

A decade later, Murfitt returned to off-Broadway, both writing and appearing on stage again. This time the show was *Cowgirls*, which played a 321-performance run at the Minetta Lane. Murfitt wrote music and lyrics to Betsy Howie's book for this show which celebrates the collision of classical and country music. *Cowgirls*, which Murfitt conceived, is about a Kansas saloon about to be closed, and the three women who love it and want to save it. Jo, whose father owns the saloon, invites a "Cowgirl trio" to come perform in an effort to save the place, but when the group shows up, it's the "Coghill trio," a classical music group. What

_____

37. Walsh, Michael. "In the Sweet, Funny by and by *Oil City Symphony*." *Time*, 24 June 2001, http://content.time.com/time/magazine/article/0,9171,145664,00.html.

38. Gussow, Mel. "Stage: *Oil City Symphony*, The Eternally Stagestruck." *New York Times*, 7 November 1987, p. 11, https://www.nytimes.com/1987/11/07/theater/stage-oil-city-symphony-the-eternally-stagestruck.html.

39. Hischak, Thomas. *Off-Broadway Musicals since 1919: From Greenwich Village Follies to The Toxic Avenger*. Lanham, MD: Scarecrow Press, 1911.

ensues is a marriage of two different kinds of music and six different women, each with their own problems to solve and lessons to learn.

Cowgirls was nominated for Outstanding Off-Broadway Musical by the Outer Critics Circle, and went on to be recorded and licensed. With a cast of six women, the show is a favorite for amateur theatre groups. The original production also had a female director, choreographer, musical director, arranger, and a majority female producing team.

In 2001, Murfitt wrote a site-specific musical to be performed in Jackson Hole, Wyoming, about the first all-female town government. In 1920, Jackson Hole's government was run by five women, even before women country-wide had been given the right to vote. *Petticoat Rules* has been performed in Jackson Hole constantly since its first production. Murfitt wrote book and lyrics, and Pam Drews Phillips wrote the music.

Murfitt's other musicals include *Eight Is Enough*, *Göttland*, and *Boomerangst!*

LYNN AHRENS
One of the Greatest Theatrical Lyricists of All Time

Lynn Ahrens and Stephen Flaherty have been one of the most beloved teams writing musicals for the last forty-plus years. Ahrens is the lyricist and sometimes-book-writer of the duo, and among their many credits are musicals including *Lucky Stiff* (1988), *Once on This Island* (1990), *My Favorite Year* (1992), *Ragtime* (1998), *Seussical* (2000), *A Man of No Importance* (2002), *Dessa Rose* (2005), *The Glorious Ones* (2007), *Rocky* (2014), and *Anastasia* (2017). In addition to their musicals, Ahrens has written for movies and television including *A Christmas Carol*, *Schoolhouse Rock*, and *Camp*.

Lynn Ahrens, circa 2009, by Steve Mack. STEVE MACK / ALAMY STOCK PHOTO

Like several other musical theatre writers featured, Ahrens got her start as a copywriter. While working in advertising, she managed to land a few opportunities to write songs for children's television programs such as *Captain Kangaroo*.

In 1982, Ahrens attended the BMI Musical Theatre Writing workshop. There, she met Stephen Flaherty who would become her long-term collaborator. The pair wrote two musicals that weren't produced before making their professional stage debut together with an adaptation of *The Emperor's New Clothes* for TheaterWorks USA in 1985.

The two followed this with *Lucky Stiff* which premiered in 1988 at Playwrights Horizons and put them on the map. On this show, they worked with Ira Weitzman, whom they would also collaborate with on many other musicals later at Lincoln Center. *Lucky Stiff* is a zany, small, musical comedy about mistaken identity based on a 1983 novel. The show has gained a cult following over the years and was even made into a film. Ahrens and Flaherty's song "Times Like This" is a favorite of many musical theatre performers and aficionados.

The next Ahrens and Flaherty show, *Once on This Island*, opened two years later at the same theatre and this is where the team really hit it big. *Once on This Island* received excellent reviews at Playwrights Horizons and transferred to Broadway, winning great acclaim, particularly for its score and lead performance by LaChanze. The show is a modern fable set in the Caribbean about a peasant girl's life—her village, her gods, and her doomed love story. The show has been much-revived, including on Broadway where it won a 2018 Tony Award for Best Musical Revival. Its style is wholly unlike that of *Lucky Stiff*, and Ahrens and Flaherty were continuously praised for their versatility from this time forward.

My Favorite Year marked the first Ahrens and Flaherty musical to premiere directly on Broadway and the team's first time of many working at Lincoln Center. The show is an adaptation of the film of the same name, and it opened at the Vivian Beaumont to largely negative reviews in 1992. The story of a bright-eyed young sketch writer (originally played by Evan Pappas) working on a 1950s television variety show who has to work with a former movie-idol turned alcoholic was ripe for musicalization. *My Favorite Year's* opening number, "Twenty Million People" is often hailed as one of the best opening numbers in musical theatre history, although the original production ran a disappointing thirty-six performances. *My Favorite Year* has a lot to offer with its colorful backstage atmosphere and personalities, who provide a foundation for the protagonist's coming-of-age story in entertainment.

Ahrens and Flaherty beat out several other writing teams for the opportunity to create *Ragtime*. In 1998, their perhaps most beloved show opened a new Broadway theater, the Ford Center for the Performing Arts. The adaptation of E. L. Doctorow's book about America at the turn of the twentieth century gave Ahrens and Flaherty the opportunity to incorporate varied musical styles and characters into one story addressing racism, immigration, violence, activism, industry, gender roles, poverty, and so much more. *Ragtime* boasts a story and score that have become a touch stone for a generation of theatre artists. The original cast featured Brian Stokes Mitchell, Audra McDonald, Marin Mazzie, and Peter Friedman, and included over fifty actors, a significant number for Broadway in 1998. Its songs such as "Wheels of a Dream" and "Make Them Hear You" have become popular anthems, and the entire score is often hailed as one of the greatest accomplishments of musical theatre in the 1990s. On *Ragtime*,

Ahrens and Flaherty collaborated with Terrence McNally as book writer, and all three took home 1998 Tony Awards—for Best Book and Score. The Best Musical prize went to *The Lion King*.

While *Ragtime* ran for 834 performances, the gigantic production failed to pay back its investment on Broadway. Ahrens and Flaherty's next Broadway show closed at an even higher loss. That was *Seussical*. A musical entertainment inspired by the writings of Dr. Seuss, the highly anticipated musical was one of the first to open in the new era of the internet marked by online Broadway gossip and message boards. During *Seussical's* out-of-town tryout in Boston, audience members took to the internet to criticize every step of the show's development, serving up a level of public scrutiny theretofore unseen. This torpedoed the show before it really had a chance to navigate the waters of development.

Seussical played six months on Broadway. This was followed by a high-profile tour; a 2007 off-Broadway revival that reworked the show to great acclaim; and numerous international, regional, and amateur productions. The show fully captures the spirit of Dr. Seuss's characters and zany style, incorporating the Cat in the Hat, Horton the Elephant, Gertrude McFuzz, and many other Seuss characters into one new story. The show also works in sociopolitical metaphors, true to the way this is done in Seuss's books.

Ahrens and Flaherty's next three major New York productions all opened at Lincoln Center's Mitzi Newhouse Theatre: *A Man of No Importance* in 2002, *Dessa Rose* in 2005, and *The Glorious Ones* in 2007.

A Man of No Importance starred Roger Rees as Alfie, a closeted homosexual man in 1960s Ireland who is determined to direct a production of *Salome*, with the local amateur theatre troupe. He befriends a young woman, Adele, who is unmarried but pregnant, and they form an unlikely alliance, with her agreeing to play the controversial title role. Alfie struggles with the idea of letting the townsfolk know about his sexuality and living openly. His long-suffering sister has been waiting to get married until he does, his fellow bus worker Robbie is the object of his unrequited affection, and the religious town overall does not seem like they would be open to Alfie revealing his secret. When finally it comes out, Alfie finds that some people do radically accept him and others do not, but that he has a new freedom.

Ahrens and Flaherty's score for this musical based on a film, with a book by Terrence McNally, has all of the flavor one has come to expect from their scores. "Princess" is a vulnerable, delicate "want song" disguised at first as an "I can't" song for Adele. "The Streets of Dublin" is an electrifying Irish celebration song for Robbie. The tenderness in Ahrens's lyrics for these characters is riveting.

Dessa Rose was based on a novel by Sherley Anne Williams about an enslaved woman named Dessa Rose on a plantation in the 1840s. When her lover Kaine is murdered by their owner, Dessa Rose attacks her and is sold to a new owner. When this owner tries to rape her, she kills him and Dessa is jailed. Eventually she escapes and comes to meet Ruth, a young white woman who becomes an unlikely ally—and the two escape the south together. Dessa and Ruth tell the entire story as elderly women and the story is about legacy and remembrance. Like all of Ahrens and Flaherty's scores, this one draws on the specific setting and time frame of the story as influence. The songs echo the style and sounds of the era, including the genres of music that were heard on plantations during the time of slavery.

The Glorious Ones boasts yet another completely different style from Ahrens and Flaherty. This time the team adapted a book by Francine Prose about the advent of Commedia dell'arte in seventeenth-century Venice. Their songs for this seven-person musical have a classical Italian style. "With buoyant music by Stephen Flaherty and a bawdy book and lyrics by Lynn Ahrens, the show mixes the lowdown pratfalls of Commedia dell'arte with the rosy sentimentality of classic American musical comedy.... The resulting musical is a sweet but strange hybrid, both joyfully naughty and totally innocuous," wrote Charles Isherwood in the *New York Times*.[40]

In 2014, Ahrens and Flaherty returned to Broadway with yet another project that displays their great range: *Rocky the Musical*. With a book by Thomas Meehan, this adaptation of the beloved film brought the unlikely boxer to the stage ... and to the audience at the Winter Garden Theatre, since director Alex Timbers staged a portion of the show in the orchestra section. While commercial mega-hit movies becoming stage musicals had been a significant trend during the time Ahrens and Flaherty had been writing, this was their first time working on a show of this sort. *Rocky* was a $20 million musical, with a twenty-member orchestra, and a production size that inspired awe in audience members. However the show was not appreciated by critics and was not nominated for Best Musical or Best Score at the Tonys. The prevailing sentiment was that the design elements and Andy Karl's central performance were the real stars of this show, and *Rocky* closed after 188 performances.

Anastasia, Ahrens and Flaherty's next big production, was a different story. Their stage adaptation of the popular animated film they'd contributed songs to in 1994 (earning two Academy Award nominations) ran for about two years on Broadway. The show about a young woman who may or may not be the grand duchess Anastasia in early twentieth-century Russia features songs like "Once upon a December" and "Journey to the Past."

In 2020, Ahrens and Flaherty's new musical *Knoxville*, based on a Pulitzer Prize–winning novel by James Agee, and with book by Frank Galati, was set to

---

40. Isherwood, Charles. "Those Smutty, Nutty Kids with Heart, Treading the Boards in Merry Olde Italy." *New York Times*, 6 November 2007, http://theater2.nytimes.com/2007/11/06/theater/reviews/06glorious.html.

premiere at Asolo Repertory Theatre. After a pandemic pause, the show finally opened in spring of 2022, starring Jason Danieley. An original cast recording was released.

In addition to her theatre work, Ahrens has also written for *Schoolhouse Rock*, and wrote the 2004 film *A Christmas Carol*, based on her 1994 stage version, written with Alan Menken, which played Madison Square Garden for ten years.

Ragtime's legacy has only expanded with the passage of time, and it is widely considered one of the great musicals of the twentieth century. The same is true of *Once on This Island*, which received an acclaimed revival on Broadway in 2017. Lynn Ahrens is one of the premiere lyricists of her generation, and the volume and variety of shows and scores she has written have earned her respect as one of the great theatre lyricists of all time.

MELINDA GILB
A Musical Soap Opera in a Laundromat

Melinda Gilb cocreated, cowrote the book for, and costarred in the 1988 off-Broadway musical *Suds*.

Suds had the distinction of opening the off-Broadway space, the Criterion Center Stage Left. From the late 1980s until the late 1990s, the complex on Broadway between 44th and 45th Streets contained two theatrical spaces: one off-Broadway venue (which had 436 seats) and one Broadway venue (which had 499).

The structure had once been Oscar Hammerstein's Olympia Theatre complex, built in 1895, which contained multiple venues as well. Then it was a movie house called the Criterion for much of the mid-to-late twentieth century. In 1988 and 1989, the two new legitimate theaters opened with *Suds* and *Starmites*, respectively. After its life as a legitimate theater space and home to Stage Left (off-Broadway) and Stage Right (on Broadway), it was transformed into a Toys R Us and then into a Gap and an Old Navy.

Suds' subtitle was "The Rocking 60's Musical Soap Opera." Like many other off-Broadway revues it capitalized on the popular songs of the 1960s to tell a story of "girl power." Ironically, *Suds* came about when a theatre group in San Diego couldn't afford the rights to the show *Beehive*, which fits that description. So, they created a new musical that utilized a similar song list. *Suds* is about a down-on-her-luck and brokenhearted young woman who gets a lot of advice in song form and a new lease on life in the setting of a 1960s laundromat.

In addition to cocreating and writing the show, Gilb played the role of Marge, one of two guardian angels (the other was originated by Susie Mosher) who help lovelorn Cindy (Christine Sevec) and with her, transform into a dream girl group who perform the songs of *Suds*.

Prior to *Suds*, Gilb appeared in the original 1985 Broadway cast of *Singin'* *in the Rain*.

TRACY FRIEDMAN
Musicalizing Harry Chapin and Randy Newman

Tracy Friedman's credits include two off-Broadway musicals featuring the work of popular music legends. In 1985, Friedman executed the musical staging for *Lies and Legends: The Musical Stories of Harry Chapin*. And in 1988, she was conceiver, book writer, choreographer, and director for *Middle of Nowhere*, a musical that utilized the songs of Randy Newman.

Middle of Nowhere was an outlier in 1988. The show is not a revue of Newman's work, or a jukebox musical with a framing device; it is a heavily planned concept musical set in Louisiana in 1969. Friedman placed four greatly differing white characters at a bus stop far from civilization with a Black station attendant, in the midst of the civil rights movement. In this context, the characters perform songs including "Short People," "I Think It's Going to Rain Today," "Louisiana," and "So Long, Dad."

On top of that, the musical is framed within the idea of a minstrel show. Friedman told the *Chicago Tribune* that she regards the genre of the minstrel show as "a blemish on the social consciousness of the American theatrical tradition." It is with this in mind that she made *Middle of Nowhere* utilize the format—heightened to be a nightmare minstrel show—to bring out Newman's commentary on stereotypes and racism.

Friedman also told the *Chicago Tribune*, "The whole bus station business relates to an experience I found myself having in 1969 in Louisiana. It was one of the most isolating, frightening, disorienting and nightmarish nights of my life. And I think Randy writes about the isolation, loneliness and bleakness of modern life, the feeling of five strangers who either have to deal with each other or be alone."[41]

While *Middle of Nowhere* received decent reviews, it closed after only a couple of weeks in New York.

Friedman's other credits include the choreography for the original Chicago production of *Do Black Patent Leather Shoes Really Reflect Up?* and as a writer, several children's books, television series like *Dr. Quinn, Medicine Woman* and *Murder, She Wrote*, and a musical called *The Black Tulip*, written with Brian Lasser, which premiered at the Center Theater in Chicago.

---

41. Smith, Sid. "'Middle of Nowhere, Middle of Night' Takes Scathing Look at Minstrel Shows." *Chicago Tribune*, 1 December 1985, https://www.chicagotribune.com/news/ct-xpm-1985-12-01 -8503230362-story.html.

Rena Berkowicz Borow, Miriam Hoffman, and Rosalie Gerut
All-Female Team Meets the Old Testament

In 1989, a musical written by three women opened at the Public Theater where it played 134 performances before transferring to a commercial run at the nearby Astor Place Theater. This was *Songs of Paradise*, a part-English, part-Yiddish stage interpretation of stories from the Old Testament, as interpreted by Itsik Manger in his poetry. Borow, Hoffman, and Gerut transferred this work to the stage, with Gerut composing, and Borow and Hoffman responsible for the libretto.

Songs of Paradise was ushered to New York by Joe Papp personally. He saw a presentation of the show at the YIVO Institute for Jewish Research and was inspired to produce an out-of-town tryout of the show in Riverdale, New York, before moving it to the Shiva Theatre at the Public. During the same season it premiered, the Public hosted another musical based on the Old Testament called *Genesis*, which was not as successful.

The stories told in *Songs of Paradise* focus on Adam and Eve and their descendants including Abraham, Jacob, and Joseph. The musical's five-person cast originally included Gerut, as well as its director Avi Hoffman and musical stager Eleanor Reissa.

The *Record* wrote about the show: "Mixing old and new is a grand tradition in folk plays, and Hoffman and Borow and composer Gerut go about it with glee. The music includes traditional Yiddish styles, jazz, rock, Broadway-style numbers, and whatever else seems to have come to hand. Most of the numbers are perky, and one or two are just beautiful."[42]

Linda Wallem
Comedy Beginnings Off-Broadway

Linda Wallem and Peter Tolan were a comedy team on the cabaret and comedy club circuit whose show *Laughing Matters* racked up eighty-five performances at the York Theatre off-Broadway in 1989. Wallem and Tolan wrote and starred in this topical two-person piece with a score by Tolan and sketches by both, which was shaped and directed by Martin Charnin.

One of *Laughing Matters'* most popular sequences found Wallem and Tolan postulating about if Stephen Sondheim musicalized *Dick and Jane*, Kander and Ebb musicalized *The Iliad*, and Irving Berlin musicalized *Metamorphoses*.

---

42. Wynne, Peter. "*Songs of Paradise*: Polished Gem of Yiddish Musical Theater." *Record*, 24 January 1989, p. 24.

Wallem went on to much acclaimed television work. She was part of the company of *SHE TV*, a 1994 sketch comedy series where women outnumbered men, that also starred Jennifer Coolidge. She guest-starred on shows, including *Seinfeld*, and wrote and acted on *Cybill* before writing and producing on *That 70s Show*. In 2008, she cocreated *Nurse Jackie*.

Wallem is the sister of actor Stephen Wallem and the spouse of singer-songwriter Melissa Etheridge.

MARY BRACKEN PHILLIPS
Metro *Adapter*

When *Metro*[43] was transferring to Broadway, its original Polish book and lyrics were adapted by Mary Bracken Phillips and the show's director, Janusz Józefowicz. *Metro* received a Tony nomination for Best Score, shared by all of its writers.

Phillips had previously worked on Broadway as an actor, appearing in the original productions of *Annie* and *1776*, among others. While *Metro* was her Broadway debut as a writer, she had already been represented as a writer on other stages.

In 1989, *Cradle Song*, about infant loss and contemporary parenting premiered at Musical Theatre Works off-Broadway. The show also received a production at Goodspeed. *Newsday* wrote that it was "a zesty, excellently performed little show—a tragicomic musical about love, death, ambition, and rebirth in Manhattan's dress for success trades."[44]

In 1994, Phillips's musical *Brimstone* premiered at Musical Theatre Works off-Broadway, and received an original cast recording. *Brimstone*, about the personal ramifications of one group of people affected by violence in Ireland in the 1990s, won the San Francisco Bay Area Critics' Awards for Best Musical.

Her other shows include *Sacagawea*, *Silver Dollar*, *Mountain Days*, *The Haunting of Winchester*, and *Crooked Lines*.

GLORIA NISSENSON
A Campy Musical Reaches Broadway from Florida

The Prince of Central Park opened at the Belasco Theatre in 1989 and closed after four performances. The show was first produced in Key West and then Miami, where it was presented by Jan McArt and starred Nanette Fabray. McArt and real estate magnate Abraham Hirschfeld decided to bring the show to Broadway and

---

43. See Agata and Maryna Miklaszewska section in chapter 11.

44. "Mary Bracken Phillips," http://www.marybrackenphillips.com/cradle-song.html.

Gloria DeHaven was cast as the lead. She was eventually fired and replaced by Jo Anne Worley, with Jan McArt as Worley's standby. The show was based on Evan H. Rhodes's best-selling 1974 novel about Jay Jay, a preteen boy who runs away from his abusive prostitute foster mother and finds shelter in a Central Park treehouse. There, he forms an unlikely friendship with Margie, an unhappy middle-aged woman whose husband has just left her for a younger woman.

Rhodes wrote the musical's book to Gloria Nissenson's lyrics and music by Broadway orchestrator Don Sebesky.

In 1970, Nissenson worked with composer Marcia Defren and book writer Ben Tarver on a musical version of *One of Our Millionaires Is Missing*, which also involves a young male runaway and a troubled adult becoming friends. The show was produced in Canada but never made it to New York. She had success in pop music and television writing before finally making it to Broadway with *The Prince of Central Park*. Among her credits were the pop songs "One Life to Live" and "After the Lovin'" and the country song "Heavenly Bodies" as well as the theme songs for the shows *Duffy* and *Brothers*.

The Prince of Central Park, featuring her lyrics, was skewered by critics, largely for how the outlandish adventures of the two protagonists were presented. In one part of the show, a rough and tumble street gang tries to get Jay Jay to join them and become a "druggie." As Ken Mandelbaum wrote in *Not Since Carrie*, "*The Prince of Central Park* was often camp heaven, mostly because of its wildly out of touch with reality portrayal of New York City. The musical's Central Park featured a friendly park ranger, a gang of not very threatening misunderstood teens, a quaint bag lady, and a couple of well-dressed men seen emerging from the park bushes. Specific camp highlights were a number set in Bloomingdales called "Red." . . . which culminated in a Dance of the Mannequins, and all the numbers for the gang, which defy description."[45]

With its older woman-younger boy friendship, the show intended to be another *Mame*, *Hello, Dolly!*, or even *Harold and Maude*. But the actual treatment and tone of the material was appalling to most people. Some were offended by how the show used an abused orphan to manipulate sympathies.

There were those who enjoyed the zany ridiculous nature of *The Prince of Central Park*. In *Backstage*, Roy Sander said, "It had a sweet sensibility that managed to shine through. . . and as Jay Jay, Richard Blake was terrific."[46] Indeed, the then 14-year-old Richard H. Blake, destined for a long Broadway career as an adult, received great reviews.

---

45. Mandelbaum, Ken. *Not Since Carrie*. New York: Griffin, 1992.
46. Sander, Roy. "The Prince of Central Park." *Backstage*.

The movie versions of the property were much more successful. And a note in the *Playbill* boasted that the novel currently had 100,000 copies circulating in the Soviet Union "as an example of what happens to an orphan in a decadent capitalist society."[47]

The Belasco had been dark for almost two years before *Prince of Central Park* came in, and it would be dark for over a year after it closed. Bookings were scarce at the time.

At the exact time that *The Prince of Central Park* was opening on Broadway, Nissenson also had a musical opening off-Broadway. This was *Frankie*, a modern version of *Frankenstein* at the York Theatre co-written with Joseph Turrin and the then 102-year-old George Abbott. While the show intended to be contemporary, it was accused of employing stereotypes in its characters and being generally out-of-touch.

Nissenson and Sebesky continued to collaborate and in 2007, their musical stage version of *The Velveteen Rabbit* was produced after many years of work.

---

47. Playbill for *The Prince of Central Park* at the Belasco Theatre, New York. *Playbill*, 1989.

11

1990s

Disney, Blues Music, and Autobiographical Work

QUEEN ESTHER MARROW
Mahalia Jackson's Champion

Queen Esther Marrow first made her Broadway debut as a performer, playing Aunt Em in *The Wiz* (1975), and appearing in *Comin' Uptown* (1979) and *It's So Nice to Be Civilized* (1980). Then, in 1990, she brought *Truly Blessed*, her musical celebration of Mahalia Jackson, for which she starred and wrote book, music, and lyrics, to Broadway.

Queen Esther Marrow, circa 1998. BY JOHN MATHEW SMITH, CC BY-SA 2.0 / WIKIMEDIA COMMONS

Truly Blessed premiered at Ford's Theatre in Washington, D.C., to great acclaim before opening at the Longacre Theatre on Broadway. The musical shares with audiences the life and music of Mahalia Jackson, one of the most important and influential singers of the twentieth century. Marrow sang numbers like "Happy Days Are Here Again" and "He's Got the Whole World in His Hands" in the style of Jackson. She headlined a cast of five. Morrow had never written a show before she wrote *Truly Blessed*.

Marrow founded The Harlem Gospel Singers.

CONNIE RAY
Christian Music in an Off-Broadway Hit

Actor and writer Connie Ray appeared on Broadway in recent years in *Hands on a Hardbody* (2013) and *Next Fall* (2010). Prior to that, she achieved success as the book writer of several musicals that became immensely popular in licensing.

In 1990, Ray made her off-Broadway debut as book writer of *Smoke on the Mountain*, an Outer Critics Circle Award-nominated musical. The show features a score of existing blues and gospel songs, used to tell the story of a family of performers in 1930s North Carolina. *Smoke on the Mountain* pokes light fun at Christian singers in America even as it celebrates them lovingly. Alan Bailey conceived the show, which Ray then wrote the book to, and the songs were arranged by *Pump Boys and Dinettes'* Mark Hardwick and Mike Craver. The show was a success at the Lamb's Theatre, running 452 performances,[1] and it received an off-Broadway revival in 1998 at the same house.

A local North Carolina paper during *Smoke on the Mountain*'s premiere in that town in 1991 wrote a feature about their "hometown girl" Ray. She is first referred to in the article as "the Chapel Hill dairy farmer's daughter."

---

1. This number includes performances when the show was technically on an off-off-Broadway contract as well as when it switched to an off-Broadway contract.

"And you know the old saying, she was only a farmer's daughter, but boy, could she milk a line.... Connie Ray's a young woman, but her church-going memories draw on a long tradition of fervent worship, the sound of Baptist stride pianos and singers caterwauling to beat the band, as if they were auditioning for the heavenly choir."[2]

Smoke on the Mountain became a cult favorite for licensing for professional, stock, and amateur productions, and Ray penned two sequels: *Sanders Family Christmas* in 1999 and *Smoke on the Mountain Homecoming* in 2006.

AGATA AND MARYNA MIKLASZEWSKA
Poland's First New Musical

Metro was considered Poland's first new musical. The show, with music by Janusz Stokłosa and original book and lyrics by Agata and Maryna Miklaszewska, premiered in Warsaw in 1991. *Metro* tells the story of a group of young people who decided to live in the subway tunnels and put on an underground show about their lives.

In Warsaw, the show was fresh and thrilling. The energy of this musical, created just after the fall of the Communist government, broke down barriers between people of all ages and moved audiences in unprecedented ways.

When the show planned a move to the Minskoff, the producer and director declared that they were going to show Broadway how it was done. They thought they had the next big mega-hit, and didn't listen to advice from anyone about how the show might need to be adjusted or developed for New York. Many thought that in their arrogance, they torpedoed the show. And yet, the young, talented Polish performers full of dreams still moved audiences nightly. The cast included blue-collar workers and a former miner that had been plucked from open auditions in Poland.[3]

SUSAN STROMAN
Integrally Involved

Five-time Tony Award-winning Broadway director/choreographer Susan Stroman is not known as a writer, but she has received "conceived by" credit on several of her musicals: *And the World Goes 'Round* (1991, Off-Broadway), *Steel Pier* (1997, Broadway), *Contact* (2000, Broadway), and *Thou Shalt Not* (2001, Broadway).

Stroman has often been integrally involved with the development of the musicals she has directed, and especially with the revues *And the World Goes*

---

2. Morrison, Bill. "*Smoke* Evokes Pure Pleasure." *News and Observer*, 11 June 1991, p. 27.

3. This section has been largely excerpted from Tepper, Jennifer Ashley, *The Untold Stories of Broadway Volume 4*.

'Round and *Contact*, has worked seamlessly with the writers involved to craft storytelling around the existing songs.

Separate from her conception credits, some of the musicals Stroman is best known for are *Crazy for You*, *The Music Man* (2000 revival), *The Producers*, *Young Frankenstein*, and *The Scottsboro Boys*.

PAULA LOCKHEART
Jazzaturg

Paula Lockheart was one of five writers who collaborated on book, music, and lyrics for the unconventional 1991 off-Broadway smash hit, *Song of Singapore*. The swing musical comedy set in a club played 459 performances.

Lockheart, along with fellow writers Erik Frandsen, Michael Garin, and Robert Hipkens, were composer-performers who, with Alan Katz, crafted the 1940s-set zany farce. The show won the Outer Critics Circle Award for Outstanding Off-Broadway musical, and the writers won the Drama Desk Award for Outstanding Music.

The three other writers were also in the cast; Lockheart was not, and was informally called the "jazzaturg."[4]

LYNDA BARRY
Creativity Master, Writer, and Cartoonist

Writer, cartoonist, and teacher Lynda Barry is well known for her work that focuses on encouraging the creativity of others. In addition to her acclaimed books, she teaches highly popular creativity workshops.

Barry made one foray into theatre. In 1991, her play with music *The Good Times Are Killing Me* ran for 242 performances off-Broadway. The show was adapted from her acclaimed 1988 illustrated novel of the same name. While not a musical, the use of music is integral to the show, which tells a coming-of-age story about the friendship of two girls, one white and one Black, in the 1960s.

The *Associated Press* wrote, "Barry . . . is a skillful writer. She has distilled the essence of being young—specifically, how children deal with fantasy and reality, good and evil, boredom and just plain fun—and put it into *The Good Times Are Killing Me*. The result is positively rejuvenating."[5]

---

4. Wright, Charles. "*Song of Singapore.*" Cast Album Reviews, https://castalbumreviews.com/song-of-singapore/.

5. Kuchwara, Michael. "Lynda Barry's *The Good Times Are Killing Me* Opens Off-Broadway." *Associated Press*, 9 August 1991, https://apnews.com/article/ecb110a9a90df7af8837df97feba141c.

Amy Powers
From Sunset Boulevard *to* Doctor Zhivago

Amy Powers was the original lyricist for *Sunset Boulevard*, chosen by Andrew Lloyd Webber to collaborate with him on the musical. After a workshop production of the show at the 1991 Sydmonton Festival, Lloyd Webber decided Powers was not a good fit for the project and replaced her with Don Black, whom he had worked with on *Song and Dance* and *Aspects of Love*. Powers receives an ongoing credit on *Sunset Boulevard* with the note: "The producer gratefully acknowledges the contributions in lyric development of Amy Powers." Four of the songs in the final version of the musical, "With One Look," "The Greatest Star of All," "As If We Never Said Goodbye," and the title song are acknowledged to contain her work.

The same year that the *Sunset Boulevard* development happened, Powers made her off-Broadway debut as a lyricist, writing a *Cinderella* adaptation, titled as such, with composer Dan Levy, who also cowrote lyrics, and book writer Norman Robbins. The show premiered at Playhouse 91. Peter Dinklage made his off-Broadway debut as an understudy.

Powers's *Lizzie Borden* musical, written with Christopher McGovern, has long been a cult hit among those who collect musicals that haven't played New York yet. The show's 1998 album and 2001 production at Goodspeed received positive attention. *Lizzie Borden* chronicles the true story of the woman of that name who purportedly murdered her father and stepmother in 1892 with a hatchet.

In 2003, Powers cowrote the lyrics and book (with David Topchik) for *The Game*, a musical adaptation of *Les liaisons dangereuses*, which premiered at Barrington Stage, with music by Megan Cavallari.

Powers's big Broadway moment came in 2015 when *Doctor Zhivago*, for which she'd cowritten lyrics with Michael Korie, premiered. The spectacular musical had only a quick run, and was a much bigger hit in its international productions, including in Korea and Australia. The show, based on the classic and beloved Russian novel, was a mammoth undertaking. The epic love story, taking place during World War I and the Russian Revolution, was brought to stirring dramatic life by Powers and Korie, as well as their collaborators composer Lucy Simon and book writer Michael Weller.

While Powers started her professional life as a lawyer, she has worked for decades now as a writer. In addition to her theatre projects, she is an Emmy-nominated writer for film and television. Powers was also a producer on *Heathers: The Musical*.

MARION ADLER
Collaborator with Alan Menken on a Howard Ashman Dream Project

Howard Ashman had always wanted to write a musical with Alan Menken based on the Damon Runyon short story, *Ballad of Little Pinks*. After Ashman passed away, Menken wanted to continue to pursue the project in his honor, so he began working on it with Marion Adler as lyricist.

Ballad of Little Pinks is a dark story about a 1920s Broadway chorus girl who is the victim of mobster violence and ends up in a wheelchair. She then teams up with a busboy named Little Pinks who is the only person who is loyal to her.

Adler and Menken worked on the show in the late 1990s and early 2000s, but it never fully came to fruition. A demo exists, featuring Frank Vlastnik, Lee Wilkof, and Sarah Jane Nelson, and the show has received several readings. The Nederlander Organization was involved in the show as producers and at one point it was announced that they'd be premiering the show on Broadway in 1999.[6]

In 1992, Adler contributed the moving song "Lifelines" to *A . . . My Name Is Still Alice*. The song, about women whose close friendship remains an anchor to each other throughout a lifetime, with music by Carolyn Sloan, can be heard on the show's cast recording.

In 1998, Adler wrote lyrics for a musical production of the Ferenc Molnár play *Enter the Guardsman*, to music by Craig Bohmler and a book by Scott Wentworth. The show premiered at London's Donmar Warehouse and then received a production at the New Jersey Shakespeare Festival.

Adler is also an actor, working frequently at the Stratford Festival. It was the Stratford Festival where *Ballad of Little Pinks* received its most recent showing in 2019.

FRANCESCA BLUMENTHAL
A "Hard Hat Woman"

Francesca Blumenthal contributed to two of the most iconic original off-Broadway revues of the decade: *A . . . My Name Is Still Alice* (1992) and *Secrets Every Smart Traveler Should Know* (1997). For the former, she collaborated with Doug Katsaros, writing lyrics to "Hard Hat Woman," a number about a group of female construction workers who assert that they want everything male construction workers want.

---

6. Brodesser, Claude. "Nederlander Gets Big Guns for *Little Pinks*." *Variety*, 23 September 1998, https://variety.com/1998/legit/news/nederlander-gets-big-guns-for-little-pinks-1117480697/.

JEANINE TESORI
Most Honored Female Composer in Broadway History

Jeanine Tesori, circa 2015. WENN RIGHTS LTD / ALAMY STOCK PHOTO

In the mid-1990s, a new generation of musical theatre writers was heralded as a group, as the next wave. This group included Jeanine Tesori, as well as Jason Robert Brown, Adam Guettel, Andrew Lippa, Michael John LaChiusa, and Ricky Ian Gordon. A 2001 *New York Times* article wondered when Broadway would take a chance on the exciting crop of new writers creating worthwhile original work, including Tesori, Brown, Guettel, and Lippa.[7]

At this point, Tesori had been working on Broadway for several years and had had a show she composed presented off-Broadway. The following year she would have a big break as a writer and soon she would become arguably the most celebrated and produced female composer in Broadway history.

Throughout the 1990s, Tesori worked on Broadway as a dance arranger, conductor, musician, and eventually composer. Her credits included *The Secret Garden* (dance arranger, associate conductor, keyboard), *The Who's Tommy* (associate conductor, keyboards), *How to Succeed in Business without Really Trying* (dance arrangements), *Dream* (dance arrangements), *The Sound of Music* (incidental music arrangements, dance arrangements), and *Swing!* (music arrangements). In 1998, a version of *Twelfth Night* for which she wrote an original score opened at the Vivian Beaumont Theatre on Broadway, and Tesori was nominated for Best Original Score at the Tony Awards, for her work.

Tesori worked consistently and successfully as an arranger, music director, and conductor, but she wasn't writing musicals—which she thought she was really meant to do. So, she moved to a lighthouse in upstate New York for almost a full year. It was there that she wrote the musical *Violet*.

In 1997, Tesori's first original musical presented in New York, *Violet*, opened at Playwrights Horizons off-Broadway. Written with Brian Crawley (book and lyrics) and based on an original story by Doris Betts, *Violet* tells the unconventional tale of a girl with a disfiguring scar on her face who tries to find her way in the South in the 1960s. For the show, Tesori wrote soaring ballads and rousing boot stompers infused with authenticity. Songs like "On My Way" immediately became popular among musical theatre performers.

---

7. Tommasini, Anthony. "They Do Write 'Em Like They Used To." *New York Times*, 20 May 2001, https://www.nytimes.com/2001/05/20/arts/they-do-write-em-like-they-used-to.html.

But the show closed quickly, after receiving a bad *Times* review. Tesori recalled in an interview, "I was pregnant and literally, I stayed in bed for three days. And finally, my then-husband said, 'You have got to get out of bed. That's all I'm asking you to do.' It was the kindest thing. . . . It was so hard of a lesson but thank God. If that had worked and been a success I would have never learned the real reason to write is to write and of course you have to write for coin and you have to do all of that stuff, but the real reason to write is to make something."[8]

In 1999, Tesori composed music for a play with music called *The First Picture Show*, a prequel to *The Last Picture Show* which played the Mark Taper Forum in Los Angeles. The *LA Weekly* critic wrote, "Director [David] Gordon's embarrassing use of slo-mo choreography seems less an homage to film technique than an expression of this show's lethargy, which Jeanine Tesori's faux-Sondheim, faux-ragtime score does nothing to conceal."[9] The show did not continue.

But Tesori said her only regret was that she spent a bulk of her early years in New York "talking about writing and not writing. You can talk yourself out of anything. I probably wasted seven or eight years of my 20s too afraid to be made a fool of. Now I just think that process of being so tortured when you're not even writing is kind of pathetic."[10]

In 2002, *Thoroughly Modern Millie* opened on Broadway. It heralded a new chapter for Tesori (new music) and Dick Scanlan (cowriter of the book and new lyrics), both of whom had worked in New York theatre for years before making a giant splash with this jazzy, lovable musical that would go on to win the big prize, Best Musical, at the Tonys. *Millie* used songs from the movie it was based on, and these were both updated and combined with new songs by Tesori and Scanlan, with such style and aplomb that those who didn't know couldn't tell the difference between old material and new.

The show made a star of Sutton Foster, and seemed to usher in a new era of theatre artists. Although it was a throwback to the 1920s, *Millie*'s exuberant celebration of New York City and finding your way as a young person there hit a nerve for a new generation. In the immediate post-9/11 atmosphere in the city, *Millie* was just what many audience members needed. The show ran for 903

---

8. Mishkin, Bud. "One on 1 Profile: Broadway Composer Jeanine Tesori Makes History with Tony Win after Life-Long Love of Theater." NY1, 8 June 2015, https://www.ny1.com/nyc/staten-island/one-on-1/2015/06/1/one-on-1-profile--broadway-composer-jeanine-tesori-hopes-for-tony-win-after-life-long-love-of-theater.

9. Mikulan, Steven. "They Lost It at the Movies" *LA Weekly*, 25 August 1999. https://www.laweekly.com/they-lost-it-at-the-movies/

10. Heyman, Marshall. "Shrek's Theater Queen." *W Magazine*, 1 December 2008, https://www.wmagazine.com/story/jeanine-tesori.

performances. Tesori and Scanlan were nominated for the Tony for their score but lost to the writers of *Urinetown*.

While *Millie* was still running on Broadway, Tesori was also downtown at the Public Theater developing *Caroline, or Change* with Tony Kushner and George C. Wolfe. One could not find two more different shows, in many regards, and yet Tesori composed both of them: the jazz-age, bright and brassy *Millie* and the 1960s-era, deep and complex *Caroline, or Change*.

Caroline, semi-based on Kushner's own childhood, is about a Black woman named Caroline (originated by Tonya Pinkins, in a galvanizing performance) in 1960s Louisiana who works for a white family comprised of a lonely eight-year old son named Noah, a recent widower father, and a Northerner stepmother adjusting to her new life. Caroline has two sons and a daughter whom she is trying to support on very little money, and when she is given permission to keep the money that Noah leaves in his pockets, a chain of small-but-large events is set off. The show employs anthropomorphism as the washer, dryer, bus, and more come to life and keep Caroline company as she cleans, cooks, waits, and endures. The score for *Caroline* is nearly sung-through and comprises many different styles, from Jewish klezmer music to Motown and blues, based on which character is singing.

Tesori was nominated, with Kushner, for a Best Score Tony Award, but lost to the writers of *Avenue Q*. While *Caroline* was highly exalted by a segment of the theatre community, the show closed prematurely on Broadway and faded into memory, as it was hard to produce in amateur and stock productions. That's not to say it wasn't treasured by fans, only that it was rarely performed live in the years following its 2004 Broadway closing. A Broadway revival was delayed by the COVID-19 pandemic shutdown, and eventually opened in 2021. The show has gained power in the years since, and is seen as an underappreciated masterpiece, written by some of the greatest dramatists of their generation.

Tesori followed *Caroline, or Change* with another Broadway musical that, again, was wildly different than her last. *Shrek the Musical* found her collaborating with David Lindsay-Abaire who wrote book and lyrics to the show based on the animated film. Tesori wanted to attempt to write something that could have a broader appeal, a show that was more commercial-minded than *Caroline, or Change*.

Shrek the Musical ran 441 performances at the Broadway Theatre. It received eight Tony nominations, winning for Costume Design for Tim Hatley during the 2009 season. Tesori and Lindsay-Abaire were nominated for Best Score and the show was nominated for Best Musical. *Shrek* has become a favorite in licensing, with hundreds of theatre makers presenting the musical each year, and a recent tour reimagining the show.

"I was taught to really lean backwards—to do my thing, be in the background, and not call attention to myself. I've had to really go against my training to really be present. I remember seeing Linda Twine conduct when I was nineteen. She is this beautiful African-American woman who was in complete command with all of the men on stage looking at her every move. So any woman who was claiming anything, it went right in and then I knew it was possible," Tesori told Victoria Myers for the *Interval*.[11]

In 2013, the musical that Tesori had been developing with Lisa Kron, *Fun Home*, had a workshop production at the Public Theater. Based on Alison Bechdel's graphic novel, *Fun Home* is about a woman who is a lesbian coming of age and her relationship with her father, who is a closeted gay man. *Fun Home* transferred in 2015 to Broadway's Circle in the Square where it won the Tony Awards for Best Musical, Best Book (Kron), Best Score (Tesori and Kron), Best Lead Actor in a Musical (Michael Cerveris) and Best Director (Sam Gold). In addition it was a finalist for the Pulitzer Prize for Drama, and the musical won the Obie Award, Outer Critics Circle Award, and Lucille Lortel Award. It was Tesori's fifth Tony nomination and first win.

When *Fun Home* won the Tony for Best Musical, it was the first time that a musical written entirely by women won the big award.

In 2010, Tesori composed the music for the Broadway play *A Free Man of Color* at Lincoln Center. In 2014, *Violet* was presented on Broadway for the first time by Roundabout Theatre Company, starring Sutton Foster in the title role. Tesori also wrote the music for the cherished *Gilmore Girls* in-episode musical in 2016, which featured performances from Sutton Foster and Christian Borle.

Tesori had a different writing collaborator for every one of her first six musicals that came to New York: Crawley on *Violet*, Scanlan on *Millie*, Kushner on *Caroline*, Lindsay-Abaire on *Shrek*, Kron on *Fun Home*, and next, David Henry Hwang on *Soft Power*.

Soft Power premiered in 2018 in Los Angeles and San Francisco, and opened at the Public Theater off-Broadway in 2019, where rumors of a Broadway transfer swirled until the COVID-19 pandemic shutdown put everything on pause. Like *Caroline*, *Soft Power* is a semiautobiographical story from Tesori's collaborator. In this case that was Hwang, who experienced a hate crime when he was stabbed in the neck by a criminal targeting him because of his Asian identity. *Soft Power* uses that event as an inciting incident to tell a story about racism, cultural appropriation, white supremacy, and politics. The show's framework surrounds a fantasy musical about Hillary Clinton and a Chinese businessman named Xuē Xíng, as created by Chinese artists making an American musical in the future.

---

11. Myers, Victoria. "An Interview with Jeanine Tesori." *Interval*, 18 March 2015, http://www.theintervalny.com/interviews/2015/03/an-interview-with-jeanine-tesori/.

This concept allows for an examination of how Western artists have created stories about Asian cultures, particularly *The King and I*. *Soft Power* was nominated for the Pulitzer Prize for Drama.

In 2021, the musical version of *Kimberly Akimbo* premiered off-Broadway at the Atlantic Theater. Tesori wrote music to the book and lyrics by previous collaborator David Lindsay-Abaire, who had written the play the musical was based on in 2001. The story, about a teenager who has a disease that causes her to age rapidly, came together into a poignant, funny, wacky, and ultimately acclaimed musical, that transferred to Broadway's Booth Theatre in 2022 after winning many accolades for its off-Broadway run, including the Drama Desk, Lucille Lortel, and Outer Critics Circle awards for Outstanding Musical. It was a hit on Broadway, winning five Tony Awards, including Best Musical and Best Score.

Tesori has the most Tony Award nominations of any female composer in history. She spent several years as the artistic director of Encores! Off Center. She has worked as the creative director of A BroaderWay, a program that brings the arts to underserved communities, and also produces shows.

In musing on how the theatre scene could be improved, Tesori told Myers, for a piece this time written for *Harper's Bazaar*: "We don't have a national theatre. If we had a national theatre you could make an initiative to fix a deficit and say, 'I've noticed that there are no women writing for theatre. Let's catch them at a time when they could be writing. Like at thirteen, fourteen, and fifteen, and let's start something at that level because they need music training—like the School of Rock but for musical theatre. I try to give as much time as possible, as people gave to me. You have to look backwards and give people a hand up.'"[12]

JULIA MCKENZIE
Longtime Sondheim Collaborator

English actress Julia McKenzie is well regarded for her award-winning performances. She is a six-time Olivier Award nominee and two-time winner; her London credits include *On the Twentieth Century*, *Guys and Dolls*, *Follies*, *Into the Woods*, and *Sweeney Todd*. Her sole Broadway credit as a performer came in 1977 when she transferred with the West End revue *Side by Side by Sondheim* and received a Tony nomination.

Throughout her long career, McKenzie has been associated with the work of Stephen Sondheim, and in 1992, she co-conceived the Sondheim revue *Putting It Together* with Sondheim himself. *Putting It Together* came about as a result of all of the requests for an updated version of *Side by Side by Sondheim*, which

---

12. Myers, Victoria. "Broadway's Leading Ladies: Composer Jeanine Tesori." *Harper's Bazaar*, 4 June 2014, https://www.harpersbazaar.com/culture/features/a2491/jeanine-tesori-interview-2014/.

would feature the material Sondheim had written since that revue came out in 1977.

Putting It Together premiered in Oxford, where McKenzie directed. She also directed the original off-Broadway production in 1993. In 1999, a Los Angeles production of the show directed by Eric D. Schaeffer transferred to Broadway.

McKenzie is credited in all versions of the show as having originally devised the show with Sondheim.

LUCY SIMON
Grammy-Winning Composer of The Secret Garden

Lucy Simon and her sister Carly wrote and released folk and rock albums as the Simon Sisters, starting when they were still teenagers. Carly went on to a career as a pop rock and folk singer-songwriter and Lucy went on to eventually focus on writing for theatre, after a recording career that won her a Grammy.

In 1984, Simon contributed to *A . . . My Name Is Alice*, writing music to Susan Birkenhead's lyrics for the show-stopping "Pretty Young Men," about women at a strip club.

In 1991, Simon made an auspicious Broadway debut, writing music for *The Secret Garden*. One of the rare musicals in Broadway history with an all-female writing team, the show has book and lyrics by Marsha Norman and was based on the novel by Frances Hodgson Burnett. In addition, the director and much of the design team were women; Susan H. Schulman directed, with scenic design by Heidi Ettinger (then Heidi Landesman), costume design by Theoni V. Aldredge, and lighting design by Tharon Musser.

The beloved novel *The Secret Garden* is about a young girl named Mary in 1906 who is orphaned and goes to live with her aloof uncle at his mysterious English estate. The musical starred Mandy Patinkin, Rebecca Luker, Alison Fraser, John Cameron Mitchell, Robert Westenberg, John Babcock, and, as Mary, Daisy Eagan, who became the second-youngest person to win a Tony Award.[13] Audra McDonald made her Broadway debut in the ensemble.

Simon's music for the show is lush, spirited, and emotional, featuring soaring tunes like "Lily's Eyes," "The Girl I Mean to Be," "Wick," "Hold On," and "How Can I Ever Know?" Simon had the initial idea to turn the novel into a musical, and then learned that book writer Marsha Norman was already working on this. So, she sought out Norman and they began writing together.

In *Newsweek*, Jack Kroll wrote: "There's immense talent among the four women chiefly responsible for *The Secret Garden*: Pulitzer Prize–winning playwright Marsha Norman, producer and Tony Award–winning set designer Heidi

---

13. Frankie Michaels was the youngest when he won for *Mame* in 1966.

Landesman, rising-star director Susan H. Schulman, [and] Grammy-winning composer Lucy Simon. In the man's world of Broadway such a collaboration is rare, especially [when] $6.2 million is on the line.... But you can't buy magic, and magic is what an adaptation of Frances Hodgson Burnett's classic novel must have."[14]

While many of the reviews were mixed or lukewarm, the show went on to have a 709-performance run at Broadway's St. James Theatre. Simon shared a Tony nomination for Best Score with Norman. During the busy and healthy 1991 Tony season including *Miss Saigon*, *Will Rogers Follies*, and *Once on This Island*, *Secret Garden* didn't receive as much attention as it might have otherwise, but it has gone on to a robust life around the world, following Broadway.

Simon's other big Broadway venture was *Doctor Zhivago* in 2015, for which she wrote the music. The spectacular musical had only a quick run, and was a much bigger hit in its international productions, including in Korea and Australia. The show, based on the classic and beloved Russian novel, was a mammoth undertaking. The epic love story, taking place during World War I and the Russian Revolution, was brought to stirring dramatic life by Simon as well as her collaborators, co-lyricists Amy Powers and Michael Korie, and book writer Michael Weller.

For a decade, Lucy Simon worked on a stage musical adaptation of *Little House on the Prairie*, but her version did not come to fruition.

About *The Secret Garden*, Lucy Simon told the *Philadelphia Inquirer*: "If I were to pinpoint anything that makes *The Secret Garden* different because four women created it ... it's the unfolding of the story. There is a patience that women have. We have a story to tell, and it can't be pushed—it will take its time in the way that when a flower is in bud, you can't force it open.... I don't know that men could have that patience."[15]

A potential revival of the show has been circling Broadway for many years. Simon spoke to *Playbill* about it in 2016, remarking, "I think *The Secret Garden* is always relevant. There's not a time in my life where there hasn't been a need to have that sense of rebirth and healing, whether it's the garden or whether it's the homeless or whether it's craziness in the world around. We have to heal. We have to come together as people, as human beings."[16]

Simon passed away in 2022.

14. "Broadway Hothouse." *Newsweek*, 5 May 1991, https://www.newsweek.com/broadway-hothouse -203852.

15. Klein, Julia M. "'Secret Garden' Composer Planning More Shows with 'Human Connections.'" *Philadelphia Inquirer*, 31 October 1993.

16. Fierberg, Ruthie. "The Hidden Lesson behind Marsha Norman and Lucy Simon's *Secret Garden*." *Playbill*, 27 February 2016, https://www.playbill.com/article/the-hidden-lesson-behind-marsha -norman-and-lucy-simons-secret-garden.

MARSHA NORMAN
Garden, Shoes, Purple, *and* Bridges

Marsha Norman is a prolific writer of plays, musicals, screenplays, and novels, who has largely built her career in the theatre. Her four major musicals have been *The Secret Garden*, *The Red Shoes*, *The Color Purple*, and *The Bridges of Madison County*.

In 1983, Norman received the Pulitzer Prize for her play, *'night, Mother*, about a mother and daughter in a tragic situation, dealing with suicide. While all of her other Broadway ventures have been musicals, Norman is perhaps still best known for *'night, Mother*, which was adapted into a film starring Sissy Spacek and Anne Bancroft.

Marsha Norman, circa 2011. BY UNKNOWN PHOTOGRAPHER/ WIKIMEDIA COMMONS

The idea for *The Secret Garden* musical started with scenic designer Heidi Ettinger (then known as Heidi Landesman). Ettinger brought the idea to Norman, who was immediately interested, as she had been wanting to write the book of a musical for years, but had been pigeonholed as a playwright.

Creating a show with a young girl as the central lead undertaking such a significant role was hardly conventional. Even though musicals like *Annie* existed, shaping a dramatic, serious musical theatre piece around such a young actor provided its own unique challenges.

Speaking about the musical in 2016 to Ben Coleman of *Breaking Character*, Norman, now a teacher of musical theatre, reflected upon her surprise that *The Secret Garden* had worked so well, since she knew far less what she was doing decades earlier, and was largely guided by instinct.[17]

In the same interview, Norman remarked that she did not think *The Secret Garden* was taken seriously as a contender for the Tony Award for Best Musical in 1991. She thought that *Will Rogers Follies* was "a creation of the old boy network," and when asked, said that she still thinks the theatre world is "controlled by men, for the most part. It's clear ... there are changes afoot. But *Waitress* is the first all-female creative team on a musical since *The Secret Garden*. Twenty-five years! *That's* what we are up against and that's why I founded The Lilly Awards with Julia Jordan. That's why we're on such a campaign now for gender parity in the theatre. We're training women, but that's not the issue—it's getting them heard."

---

17. Coleman, Ben. ""Come Spirit, Come Charm": An Interview with Marsha Norman and Lucy Simon on the 25th Anniversary of *The Secret Garden*." *Breaking Character*, https://www.breakingcharacter.com/home/2018/12/11/come-spirit-come-charm-an-interview-with-marsha-norman-and-lucy-simon-on-the-25th-anniversary-of-the-secret-garden.

Two years after Norman had a hit musical on Broadway with *The Secret Garden*, she had a musical called *The Red Shoes* become a legendary bomb on Broadway. The show is based on the classic 1948 movie, and Norman wrote the book as well as cowrote the lyrics with Bob Merrill (who wrote under the pseudonym Paul Stryker). The music is by Jule Styne. It was the last original Broadway production for both men, who had had long and successful careers in the theatre.

In fact, *The Red Shoes* was to be a reunion for Norman and her *Secret Garden* director Susan H. Schulman and scenic designer Heidi Ettinger. Schulman was eventually replaced by Stanley Donen, and Merrill was brought in to augment Norman's lyrics. They weren't the only two displaced; leading man Roger Rees was replaced by Steve Barton during a tumultuous preview period at the Gershwin Theatre.

The prevailing sentiment was that Norman and Schulman would be a good fit for the project since its main focus was a Russian Ballet company with a ballerina who is torn emotionally and navigating a choice between two men—and they had done such a terrific job with a heroine torn emotionally on their earlier musical. But Norman and Schulman wanted to update the story for the modern age, and their collaborators didn't. Despite some gorgeous extended ballet sequences choreographed by Lar Lubovitch, *The Red Shoes* flamed out after only five performances. It has not been seen since.

Norman's other two Broadway musicals were much more successful. A decade later, in 2005, Norman adapted another movie for the stage. This time she wrote only the book, not lyrics. *The Color Purple*, with music and lyrics by the pop songwriting team of Brenda Russell, Allee Willis, and Stephen Bray, ran for over two years at Broadway's large Broadway Theatre—one of the longest-running productions in that house. The story of Celie, a Black woman in the South in the early twentieth century and all of her struggles and triumphs, was brought to extraordinary life and was originally led on stage by LaChanze, who won a Tony Award for her performance. Norman was also nominated for her book, and the musical received eleven nominations overall, including for Best Musical. The show has received several high-profile productions since 2005 including a 2015 revival starring Cynthia Erivo. In 2023, the musical became a film.

In 2014, Norman returned to Broadway with another musical adapted from a beloved film. This time it was *The Bridges of Madison County*, written with Jason Robert Brown as composer-lyricist. The romantic movie depicting the brief and larger-than-life affair of a married woman with two teenage children and a traveling photographer who connect in an unprecedented way for both of them became a soaring and passionate musical starring Kelli O'Hara and Steven Pasquale.

Norman acknowledges that she got to work on musicals because of her success with *The Secret Garden.* "And making musicals is the best. . . . A lot of things can go wrong, but when they go right, it's ecstasy."[18]

LINDA WOOLVERTON
Disney's Go-To Book Writer

Beauty and the Beast, *The Lion King*, and *Aida* were Disney's first three shows on Broadway, and Linda Woolverton had credits on all three.

In 1991, Woolverton wrote the screenplay for the Disney animated film *Beauty and the Beast*. She was the first woman to write an animated Disney feature. When Frank Rich said that *Beauty and the Beast* contained "the best Broadway musical score of 1991,"[19] Disney became intent on actually bringing the work to Broadway. Woolverton adapted her screenplay for the stage in 1994, and the show ran for over thirteen years, with audiences delighting in her words as well as the songs by Alan Menken, Howard Ashman, and Tim Rice.

Woolverton cowrote the screenplay for *The Lion King*, and received "adapted from the screenplay by" credit when the show came to Broadway.

In 2000, Woolverton cowrote the book for Disney's *Aida* with Robert Falls and David Henry Hwang. Unlike the previous two works, *Aida* was not based on an animated movie. The show has music by Elton John, whom Woolverton would collaborate with on her only non-Disney Broadway musical: *Lestat.*

Lestat, the vampire musical based on *The Vampire Chronicles* by Anne Rice, with lyrics by Bernie Taupin, had a quick and troubled run in 2006.

Incidentally, all three Broadway shows Woolverton worked on played the Palace Theatre.

While Woolverton has certainly seen success on Broadway, most of her work has been in film. In 2010, she wrote the screenplay for *Alice in Wonderland*, making her the first woman to be screenwriter with sole writing credit on a billion-dollar movie.

About *Beauty and the Beast*'s protagonist Belle, Woolverton wrote, "[Belle] moved us forward a few inches. She was a reader. She didn't rely on her beauty to get herself through the world. She wasn't a victim waiting for her prince to come. She was a proactive character." *Medium* noted, "Though we're seeing far more female characters like that now, this wasn't something we'd ever seen before at Disney."[20]

---

18. Ibid.

19. Isenberg, Barbara. "Theater: The *Beauty* of Broadway : Disney eyes the future." *Los Angeles Times*, 10 April 1994, https://www.latimes.com/archives/la-xpm-1994-04-10-ca-44123-story.html.

20. Lee, Patrick. "6 Women Screenwriters You Need to Know." *Medium*, 7 March 2017, https://medium.com/outtake/our-experts-pick-6-women-screenwriters-you-should-know-c619018cafca.

CHAPTER II

DIEDRE MURRAY
From Jazz Opera to Adaptations

Diedre Murray, known as a jazz and classical cellist and composer, a record producer, and a theatre writer, has had an eclectic career in theatre and otherwise. In 1994, she wrote an a cappella musical with Marcus Gardley called *The Voices Within*, which was presented at the City College of New York. In 2010, the show received its official world premiere at Harlem Stage. In 1997, Murray composed *You Don't Miss the Water*, a musical adaptation of Cornelius Eady's twenty-one poems about his father's death and Black American family life, which premiered at the Vineyard Theatre.

In 1998, Murray collaborated with Diane Paulus and with Eady on the jazz opera *Running Man*. Paulus conceived and directed, Murray wrote music, and together Eady and Murray wrote book and lyrics, for this show about the disappearance of a young Black man. *Running Man* was a finalist for the Pulitzer Prize for Drama and won an Obie Award. (Murray also won an Obie for her music arrangements for the 2001 musical *Eli's Coming*.) About *Running Man*, the *New York Times* wrote, "Ms. Murray's arresting score for guitar, violin, accordion, cello and percussion gives anguish a discordant language; aching songlets and meandering melodies are passed back and forth among the performers like collection plates, in harmonies that are at times both beautiful and difficult to listen to."[21]

In 2012, Diedre Murray and Suzan-Lori Parks adapted the book of *Porgy and Bess* for its Broadway revival. The landmark musical with music by George Gershwin and lyrics by DuBose Heyward, Dorothy Heyward, and Ira Gershwin, returned to Broadway in a re-conceived production directed by Diane Paulus and starring Audra McDonald and Norm Lewis. During the development of the production, it was noted in press that Murray and Parks were brought on board specifically to address "the greatest obstacle for *Porgy and Bess* over the decades: the perception that this depiction of a black community in the American South, written in dialect by whites, is a racist work."[22]

Murray also composed *Songbird: The Life and Times of Ella Fitzgerald* and is currently working on a new musical about Richard and Mildred Loving.

---

21. Marks, Peter. "Theater Review; A Young Man of Promise Who Has Lost His Way." *New York Times*, 5 March 1999, https://www.nytimes.com/1999/03/05/movies/theater-review-a-young-man -of-promise-who-has-lost-his-way.html.

22. Collins-Hughes, Laura. "ART musical is Broadway-bound." *Boston Globe*, 7 August 2011, http:// archive.boston.com/ae/theater_arts/articles/2011/08/07/art_musical_porgy_and_bess_is_broadway _bound/.

YOKO ONO
A Musical About Life with John Lennon

Yoko Ono tried her hand at writing a musical officially one time, with the off-Broadway show *New York Rock* in 1994. The widow of John Lennon wrote book, music, and lyrics for *New York Rock*, which chronicled her life with Lennon in a thinly veiled manner. The show played the WPA Theatre, directed by Philip Oesterman and music directed by Jason Robert Brown.

In a way, *New York Rock* helped lead to *Songs for a New World*, since it was Brown's time music directing the show that contributed to his working relationship with the WPA's artistic director Kyle Renick. *Songs for a New World* premiered there in 1995. And Brown received some nice notices for *New York Rock*, with the *Times* writing, "Jason Robert Brown's sparkling arrangements, flecked with 1950s rock-and-roll, show off the songs to maximum advantage."[23]

New York Rock, with two female and eight male actors, has characters that are named Mother, Streetkid, Ignorance, Violence I, and Violence II. The show is comprised of songs Ono had previously recorded as well as some new compositions. *New York Rock* is an allegory more than an autobiography. It tells the story through song of a man and woman who fall in love after each experiencing trauma. The man is a rock musician who is eventually the victim of urban violence.

While most reviews leaned in a negative direction, the *New Yorker* did (after noting they had low expectations) write, "Endearing and enjoyable.... You'll leave buoyed up by the infectious tunefulness, gusto and life enhancing merriment. The tunes—and there are many of them—are lively and lilting, ear tickling and foot stomping."[24] This quote appears on the show's licensing page with Concord Theatricals.

The *Christian Science Monitor* noted what they considered wasted potential: "[*New York Rock* is a] word ... that has never been used to describe its controversial creator—bland. Overall, the show is mildly diverting, but considering that its author might have brought a provocative new voice to musical theater, its conformity is a bit of a letdown."[25]

Ono was also involved with the Broadway musical *Lennon* in 2005, although this time she was not officially a writer or member of the creative team. When

---

23. Holden, Stephen. "Another Chorus in the Ballad of John and Yoko." *New York Times*, 31 March 1994, https://www.nytimes.com/1994/03/31/theater/review-theater-another-chorus-in-the -ballad-of-john-and-yoko.html.

24. "New York Rock." Concord Theatricals, https://www.concordtheatricals.com/p/4276/new-york -rock.

25. Scheck, Frank. "A Bland Yoko Ono Mainstream Musical." *Christian Science Monitor*, 5 April 1994, https://www.csmonitor.com/1994/0405/05132.html.

New York Rock opened, Lennon had died only thirteen years earlier. The perspective of artists who hadn't known him and the additional time that had passed were one reason that *Lennon* was quite different than *New York Rock*.

Many noted that *New York Rock* was unabashedly optimistic, sentimental, and hopeful—trademarks of Ono's work—and that it was interesting to hear her songs sung by actors telling a story rather than in her typical personal style.

HELEN BUTLEROFF
That's Life! *and* Pets!

Helen Butleroff started her career in theatre as a dancer on Broadway in the 1970s. She became a director and choreographer, specializing in Jewish musicals and working both in New York and regionally.

Butleroff conceived and directed two off-Broadway revues: *That's Life!* and *Pets! That's Life!* is an exploration of Jewish identity and was nominated for the Outer Critics Circle Award for Outstanding Off-Broadway musical in 1994. The show played the Jewish Repertory Theatre. It tackles most of its topics comedically, from nose jobs to prejudice to Christmas.

Pets! opened in 1995 and is an homage to domestic animals and the love their people have for them. It was not as well received.

ANN DUQUESNAY
Bring in 'da Noise

As an actor, Ann Duquesnay appeared in the Broadway productions of *Blues in the Night*, *The Wiz* (1984 revival), *Jelly's Last Jam*, *Bring in 'da Noise*, *Bring in 'da Funk*, *It Ain't Nothin' but the Blues*, and *Hot Feet*. For *Bring in 'da Noise*, she was also a creator, writing the show's music (with Daryl Waters and Zane Mark), lyrics (with Reg E. Gaines and director George C. Wolfe), and vocal arrangements.

Duquesnay was mentored by Wolfe, who brought her on board for *Bring in 'da Noise* Off-Broadway at the Public in 1995, before it transferred to Broadway. They had previously worked together on *Jelly's Last Jam* and *Spunk*. *Bring in 'da Noise*, a nominee for Best Musical, told a story of Black history, from slavery to the present, through original songs, and choreography including tap from Savion Glover (who also starred). Duquesnay won the Tony for Best Featured Actress in a Musical and shared a nomination for Best Score. She and fellow original cast member Jeffrey Wright provided a vocal through line, as the majority of the show's performers told the story through dance.

Newsday wrote, "Duquesnay's name actually appears on the title page three times—the most of anyone. She is the show's singing actress and its vocal arranger, and was part of the trio credited with the music. . . . Two Tony nominations in the show's nine have her name on them."[26]

DEEDEE THOMAS
A Brief History of White Music

DeeDee Thomas was one half of the team, with David Tweedy, responsible for creating the provocatively titled *A Brief History of White Music*. The musical had a successful 308 performance run at the Village Gate in 1996 and has been seen in regional productions since.

Throughout the twentieth century, musical genres that were first created and developed by Black singers and musicians were taken over by the white establishment. Rhythm and blues was adapted for white artists as it was thought by some that songs would hit bigger if Elvis Presley or Buddy Holly sang them. *A Brief History of White Music* aimed to turn this on its head by having three Black performers sing music of the 1940s through the 1970s that was originated by white artists. Songs including "Who Put the Bomp," "I Got You Babe," and "Leader of the Pack" were reimagined.

As *Variety* wrote: "The show presents its point of view—that "white" music lacks soul—without getting heavy-handed or heavy-hearted."[27]

TINA LANDAU
From Floyd Collins *to* SpongeBob SquarePants

Known for her expansive, spectacular, and immersive work, as well as her intellectual focus as a Steppenwolf member and otherwise, Tina Landau is an acclaimed director and writer. While the majority of her career has been focused on directing, Landau has also collaborated as a writer on two off-Broadway musicals and conceived one Broadway musical as well.

Floyd Collins in 1996 helped put Landau on the map as an inventive director of unconventional work. Based on the true story about a man stuck in a cave, the show has music and lyrics by Adam Guettel, and a book by Landau, who also originally directed. *Floyd Collins*, presented at Playwrights Horizons, won the Lucille Lortel Award for Best Musical and became a cult favorite after its quick run. With its stunning score and surprising topic treated seriously and with powerful storytelling, *Floyd Collins* became a benchmark musical for a new generation of writers that was emerging in the mid-to-late 1990s. A

---

26. Green, Blake. "Getting Their Acts Together." *Newsday*, 30 May 1996.

27. Waxman, Howard. "*A Brief History of White Music*." *Variety*, 4 January 1997, https://variety.com/1997/legit/reviews/a-brief-history-of-white-music-1117436786/.

much-anticipated revival directed by Landau has been in the works for several years.

In 1999, Landau partnered with another writer in that new group, Ricky Ian Gordon, to create *Dream True: My Life with Vernon Dixon* at the Vineyard Theatre. Landau wrote book and lyrics, and Gordon wrote music and additional lyrics. The *New York Times* review stated: "*Dream True*, which opened last night at the Vineyard Theater, is a truly perplexing experience. The story it tells is on the self-important side, yet the way it spins it is wholly original: the first musical, perhaps, to make a conscious appeal to the subconscious. Like the dream world itself, *Dream True* orbits in an alternate universe where rationality takes a back seat to sensation."[28]

In 2017, Landau was at the helm of *SpongeBob SquarePants*, which she conceived and also directed for Broadway.[29] The show, based on the Nickelodeon animated television series of the same name, was a creative take-off on the original property featuring avant-garde staging, thoughtful and relevant themes, and an adult musical sensibility. The story about SpongeBob and his fellow undersea creatures trying to save their world from extinction, crafted by book writer Kyle Jarrow, was scored by a large variety of popular music artists. Unlike any other recent Broadway musical, each song was written by a different prominent pop music writer.[30] Contributors to *SpongeBob SquarePants* included Cyndi Lauper, Yolanda Adams, Sara Bareilles, and Lady A (formerly known as Lady Antebellum).

The show's spectacular Palace Theatre engagement on Broadway was nominated for both Best Musical and Best Score at the Tony Awards, and a 2019 television special version of the musical featured members of its original Broadway cast.

JULIE TAYMOR
Acclaimed Director—and Writer Too

A highly acclaimed and provocative director of stage and screen work, Julie Taymor is not known as a writer. But she has had a hand in writing several of her projects, including all three of her Broadway musicals: *Juan Darien* (1996), *The Lion King* (1997), and *Spider-Man: Turn Off The Dark* (2011).

---

28. Marks, Peter. "Theater Review; Oh, to Be Back Home in Wyoming." *New York Times*, 19 April 1999, https://www.nytimes.com/1999/04/19/arts/theater-review-oh-to-be-back-home-in-wyoming.html.

29. See *SpongeBob SquarePants* section in chapter 13.

30. This hearkened back to the decades depicted earlier in this book, when Broadway shows would boast scores by a list of different writers, each one contributing one or two numbers.

Juan Darien, subtitled "A Carnival Mass," is an avant-garde musical utilizing puppets that first premiered off-Broadway in 1988. Taymor collaborated with her partner Elliot Goldenthal on the script, and she directed while he composed. She also designed the show's masks and puppets and co-designed scenery and costumes. The piece was based on the fable of the same name by Horacio Quiroga, about a baby jaguar who becomes a human and has to contend with the violence of human society. The show received a nomination for Best Musical at the Tony Awards, and Taymor received nominations for Best Director of a Musical and Best Scenic Design of a Musical (with G. W. Mercier).

In 1997, Taymor made a gigantic splash on Broadway with her adaptation of *The Lion King* for the stage. She kicked off a new era where Disney would explore unconventional takes on their stage musicals. Bringing her expertise in puppetry to the table was one part of it, not to mention her expertise in directing. Taymor wrote additional music and lyrics for the show, as her level of authorship with the material extended into many departments as usual. This time she won Tony Awards for Best Direction and Best Costume Design and *The Lion King* took home the Tony for Best Musical as well.

The much-maligned *Spider-Man: Turn Off the Dark* famously had the longest preview period in Broadway history without actually opening. For more than six months, starting in 2010, *Spider-Man* played 182 previews as the show went through several iterations and writers, even dropping entire characters from the show during the process. Taymor was eventually credited with original direction and as having designed the show's masks and cowritten the book with Glen Berger and Roberto Aguirre-Sacasa. Having worn nine different hats on Broadway shows, sometimes six at the same time, Taymor is one of the top multihyphenates of her generation.

Tsidii Le Loka
Rafiki's Chants

Tsidii Le Loka originated the role of Rafiki in *The Lion King* and also wrote the character's chants, which are part of the score of the 1997 musical. Originally from South Africa, Le Loka came to America to attend college as a teenager with aspirations of becoming a singer and musical artist. Her knowledge in South African music became essential to the fabric of *The Lion King*.

About Le Loka's presence in the show, Michael Kuchwara in the *Associated Press* wrote, "Among the astonishments that occur during the opening moments of *The Lion King* . . . one in particular delights the eye and the ear. It is the appearance of a painted comic creature, a wild yet wise woman whose powerful, almost primeval voice soars through "Circle of Life," the anthem that trumpets the hit musical's message about the interconnection of all things. . . . To play [Rafiki], director Julie Taymor chose a South African performer-songwriter named Tsidii Le Loka who was studying music and economics at the University of Massachusetts in Amherst."[31]

Before auditioning, Le Loka had never seen the movie. In the movie, Rafiki is a male character, but Taymor wanted to switch the character's gender for the stage show so there would be an adult female character anchoring the show. Le Loka was recommended to Taymor by Lebo M, a South African writer who contributed musical material to *The Lion King* as well. He became familiar with Le Loka and was impressed with her work with traditional African music. Le Loka received a call to audition for *The Lion King* in July of 1996, and three days later, landed the job.

In 2005, Le Loka premiered a show about her inspiration, Miriam Makeba, called *Song on the Mountain*. The concert piece tells about the life of Makeba, a South African singer known as Mama Africa and the Empress of African Song. She was a cultural force in America in the mid-twentieth century, working and performing with everyone from Harry Belafonte to Paul Simon. Le Loka looked up to her activism and politics as much as her artistry, and crafted the piece to educate people about who she was.[32]

IRENE MECCHI
Lion King *Scribe*

Irene Mecchi cowrote the screenplay for the animated film, *The Lion King*. When the show was brought to the Broadway stage by Disney, Mecchi adapted her screenplay, cowriting the book with Roger Allers. For this she received a Tony Award nomination. While Mecchi is mostly a writer for film and television, also penning the screenplays for *The Hunchback of Notre Dame* and *Hercules*, she does have roots in the theatre as well, having written a play based on the columns of journalist Herb Caen.

NAN KNIGHTON
Minskoff Queen

Best known for her book and lyrics for the well-loved musical *The Scarlet Pimpernel*, Nan Knighton has largely collaborated with composer Frank Wildhorn throughout her career.

---

31. Kuchwara, Michael. "Woman at Spiritual Center of *The Lion King*." *Associated Press*, 12 January 1998.

32. Yellin Outwater, Myra. "Mamas of Africa." *Morning Call*, 10 July 2005.

In 1997, Knighton made her Broadway debut with *Pimpernel,* which played 772 performances on Broadway in a rare situation where a show was shut down, revised, and reopened, at great expense. Knighton received a Tony nomination for Best Book of a Musical, and her songs with Wildhorn became popular favorites. "Into the Fire," "When I Look at You," "She Was There," "Storybook" and "You Are My Home" are among the songs that have often been sung at concerts and on recordings since *The Scarlet Pimpernel* burst onto the scene. Originally, Knighton was only writing the lyrics, but after the show went through several book writers, she wound up writing the book as well.

Knighton's work on the show about a hero during the French Revolution is spirited, filled with humor and style. Reviewers largely skewered the show, with the *New York Times* calling Wildhorn's music "pulpy" and Knighton's words "wooden."[33] But audiences ate the show up, resulting in its more-than-two-year run.

While *Pimpernel* was still running, Knighton opened *Saturday Night Fever* on Broadway. *Pimpernel* had actually opened at the Minskoff and moved to the Neil Simon so that *Saturday Night Fever* could have the Minskoff. Knighton adapted the popular 1970s movie about the intersection of disco culture and working-class life for the stage. It premiered first in London.

Knighton was already a big fan of the movie, which made her excited to adapt it for the stage. She remarked to the press that she felt the film was underrated. "It takes incredible skill to capture the rhythms of street language, ennui, and kids who have nothing to do with their time. But every single scene of these kids bumming around the streets was just so full of energy and so real and so raw."[34]

Much like *The Scarlet Pimpernel, Saturday Night Fever* had a decent run (501 performances) although it didn't make back its investment, and it received negative reviews (but found adulatory audiences). In 1999 when the show opened, Broadway audiences had not yet seen the coming wave of popular semi-recent movies being made into musicals. *Saturday Night Fever* was one of the first. Like *Footloose* shortly before, it utilized songs from its movie version with a few new additions to help with storytelling. This kind of adaptation was looked down upon by critics and the industry at large.

Again with Wildhorn, Knighton wrote the musical *Camille Claudel,* about the French sculptor who did not achieve fame in her lifetime but became widely praised after she died. The show premiered at Goodspeed in 2003. One element

---

33. Brantley, Ben. "Two Faces, and Both in Trouble." *New York Times,* 10 November 1997, https://timesmachine.nytimes.com/timesmachine/1997/11/10/049913.html?pageNumber=67.

34. Trussell, Robert. "*Saturday Night Fever* boogies from screen to stage." *Kansas City Star,* 1 November 2002.

covered in the musical is the romantic relationship Claudel had with fellow sculptor Auguste Rodin. She eventually left him so that she could be seen as an artist independent from him. Knighton said, "I insisted from the beginning that this be an uplifting musical. I have injected a lot of natural humor in it. As far as I'm concerned, it's not a tragedy if a woman got to do what she wanted with her life."[35] A song from *Camille Claudel* was performed at the 2002 Winter Olympics.

Pimpernel continues to be performed all around the world with great regularity. Knighton's other musicals include *Rudolf* and *Snapshots*.

ANN HAMPTON CALLAWAY
Swing!

Ann Hampton Callaway is a beloved multihyphenate of the concert, cabaret, and theatre world. Her biography describes her as "a singer, pianist, composer, lyricist, arranger, actress, educator, TV host and producer." Among her credits, Callaway contributed music and lyrics to the Broadway musical, *Swing!* which she also starred in.

Swing! is a 1999 Broadway dance revue celebration of the big band era that ran for 461 performances and received a nomination for the Best Musical Tony Award. Callaway also received a nomination for Best Featured Actress in a Musical, for her performance delivering numbers like "Blues in the Night" to the rafters of the St. James Theatre.

Callaway's writing contribution was heard in the numbers "Two and Four" (music), "I Won't Dance" (updating Dorothy Fields's lyrics), and "Stompin' at the Savoy" (updating Andy Razaf's lyrics).

A MasterWorks summary of the show noted that its creators imagined "an Ann Hampton Callaway type" in the show before they even pursued her. "Her contribution of the song 'Two and Four' is a perfect introduction for costar Laura Benanti, and her additional lyrics to 'Stompin' at the Savoy' aid in giving the show its historical context."[36]

LITA GAITHERS
Book Writer About The Blues

In 1999, *It Ain't Nothin' but the Blues* opened off-Broadway at the New Victory Theatre for a limited run by the Crossroads Theatre Company. It was such a

---

35. Ibid.

36. "SWING! – ORIGINAL BROADWAY CAST RECORDING 1999." *Masterworks Broadway*, https://masterworksbroadway.com/music/swing-original-broadway-cast-recording-1999/.

success that it moved to a nonprofit run on Broadway at Lincoln Center's Vivian Beaumont—and was such a success there that it transferred to a commercial run at the Ambassador.

The show received a Best Musical Tony nomination as well as three other nominations. One of these was Best Book, for writers Charles Bevel, Lita Gaithers, Randal Myler, Ron Taylor, and Dan Wheetman. This honor made Gaithers one of four Black women ever nominated in the category. Gaithers was also credited as the vocal director.

The revue about the history of blues music had humble beginnings as a show that the Denver Center in Colorado toured to schools in 1994. It then had a production at Arena Stage before making its way to New York.

It Ain't Nothin' but the Blues is stuffed with over fifty songs. In their review of the show at the New Victory, the *New York Times* wrote, "*It Ain't Nothin' but the Blues*... is a potent blend of visual eloquence and historical sweep that engages the eye and touches the heart while its songs soothe the ear, occasionally work mischief on the funny bone and always raise the spirits."[37]

The show covers the history of blues, as it intersects with events that fight for social justice and racial equality. Some songs tell stories of slavery and violence; other songs tell stories of celebrations and success in show business.

Gaithers works as an actor, writer, and director. While she was not in *It Ain't Nothin' but the Blues* on Broadway, she did appear in previous incarnations, at the same time as she was working as vocal director and one of the book writers. About the New Jersey production that she appeared in in 1998 at Crossroads, she told the *Central New Jersey Home News*,

This is a fusion of all the creative media. You have a little bit of a play, a little bit of musical theatre . . . and you have a little bit of gospel, a little bit of blues, a touch of rock 'n' roll. I think that's what is exciting. . . . When it comes to American music as we know it today, it has gone through a bunch of changes, and it started with the Africans coming to America. There were building blocks that led up to the music we know today, and those building blocks are spirituals, field hollers, gospel, and country music. We are trying to take the audience on a journey through those building blocks.[38]

Gaithers performed "Strange Fruit," the song originally popularized by Billie Holiday, about the lynching of a Black man, in the production. She shared

37. Van Gelder, Lawrence. "Theater Review; In Every Color, Finding the Blues." *New York Times*, 1 April 1999, https://www.nytimes.com/1999/04/01/theater/theater-review-in-every-color-finding-the-blues.html.

38. Granieri, Laurie. "Made in America." *Central New Jersey Home News*. 20 November 1998.

that it was hard to perform "Strange Fruit" without crying, and that sometimes she did cry. Gaithers noted that many of the actors were going through real emotions while performing the songs that meant so much to them, and she thought that was why audiences were so responsive to the show.

JACKIE DEMPSEY AND JANA LOSEY
Bigsmörgåsbørdwünderwerk

Squonk was a unique Broadway venture, a commercial entry from a group with the goal of bringing opera to the people, in a modern, accessible form. Squonk Opera was founded in 1992 and comprises a group of artists who create shows that combine music, dance, multimedia elements, pop culture–related concepts, and experimental elements of performance.

Jackie Dempsey, one of Squonk Opera's two artistic directors, directed the group's Broadway debut at the Helen Hayes Theatre in 2000, a transfer of their summer 1999 off-Broadway production, originally titled *Bigsmörgåsbørdwünder-werk*. The show's lyrics are by Jana Losey, and both women were also part of the five-member cast.

On Broadway, *Squonk* closed in a month, shot down by Ben Brantley's *New York Times* review. He had been charmed by the scrappiness of the off-Broadway production, but found the transfer to be unwise. "Visiting a little show called *Squonk* during its brief run in the East Village last summer was like walking into a neighbor's garage and discovering a homemade fun house. [But on Broadway,] *Squonk* has shrunk, almost to the point of invisibility. Placing this small, eccentric charmer in a Broadway house is a brutally misguided transplant."[39]

Despite its short Broadway run, *Squonk* has continued to tour the world with different productions. Its legacy in New York included a billboard on the southwest corner of 42nd Street and Ninth Avenue, which remained visible, disintegrating slowly, for the better part of fifteen years following the show's month on Broadway.

MARCY HEISLER AND ZINA GOLDRICH
An All-Female Team for a New Generation

Marcy and Zina heralded a new era for cabaret and theatre singer-songwriters. The two began collaborating in 1993 and in 1999 burst onto the scene in a major way with "Taylor the Latte Boy." Kristin Chenoweth performed the now-iconic

---

39. Brantley, Ben. "Theater Review; A Downtown Head Trip Plants Its Feet Uptown." *New York Times*, 1 March 2000, https://www.nytimes.com/2000/03/01/theater/theater-review-a-downtown -head-trip-plants-its-feet-uptown.html.

cabaret standalone song on *The Rosie O'Donnell Show* and musical theatre enthusiasts everywhere took note of the team.

"Taylor the Latte Boy" is emblematic of the cabaret song style of Marcy and Zina (as the two advertised themselves): colloquial, modern, personal, original, and very much wrapped around the experience of being a woman in New York City, and specifically in the theatre scene, in the modern day. Their two cabaret sampler CDs, which were sold at their myriad concerts included songs like "Alto's Lament," a comedic showstopper about a performer who is saddled with the alto lines and roles in theatre, "I Want Them . . ." about a woman who loves bald men, "Let Me Grow Old," an ode to the simple joys of life one wishes for, and "Now That I Know" about the struggle to get over a love affair.

The deliberate feminine perspective of Marcy (lyrics) and Zina (music)'s work was refreshing, as they burst onto the scene. The two tackled both earnest ballads and comedy songs with equal skill, and in both, explored situations and feelings one might have seen in female-helmed books or television, but rarely in cabaret-musical theatre at the time. "Make Your Own Party," the opener of their first cabaret sampler is a triumphant declaration of unbreakable women living in New York making their own party—and Marcy and Zina did. "Fifteen Pounds" opens with Marcy telling Zina she won't believe all of the outrageous things men have said to her—and goes on to tell the story of a guy who told her she was "fifteen pounds away from my love." If *I Love You, You're Perfect, Now Change* was the male perspective on dating in the 1990s in musical theatre form, Marcy and Zina took the cake on the female flip side. Many of the songs on Marcy and Zina's cabaret sampler CDs were commercially released on a 2009 album.

Marcy and Zina became the first all-female team to win the Fred Ebb Award, and they count MAC Awards, Drama Desk nominations, a Lortel nomination, and the Kleban Award among their accolades together or separately as well.

Performing their own work, Marcy and Zina are reminiscent of singer-songwriters who wrote musical theatre and preceded them, from Carol Hall to Nancy Ford and Gretchen Cryer. While they have never performed in their own stage musicals, Marcy and Zina record and perform their own songs in concert with expert style.

In 2000, Marcy and Zina's musical *Adventures in Love* premiered in St. Paul, and contained several of their better-known cabaret songs—but it did not transfer to New York. In 2004, the team's *Junie B. Jones* premiered at the Lortel as part of TheaterWorks USA. Successfully received, *Junie B. Jones* went on to have two off-Broadway revivals and receive positive reviews and award nominations. In 2008, their musical *Dear Edwina*, also based on a popular children's book series, premiered off-Broadway. The show was actually written more than a decade earlier in the BMI Workshop.

In 2012, Marcy and Zina collaborated with Julie Andrews on a musical adaptation of the book she'd written with her daughter Emma Walton Hamilton, *The Great American Mousical*. The show, with book by Hunter Bell, premiered at Goodspeed and was directed by Andrews. A love letter to show business, *Mousical* is told through the lens of a theatrical troupe of mice.

Their closest brush with a Broadway debut to date has been *Ever After*, the adaptation of the popular film version of the Cinderella story. In 2015, *Ever After* received an out-of-town tryout at Paper Mill and in 2019 continued with another run at the Alliance Theatre. *Ever After*'s defiantly feminist perspective on the classic tale has been embraced by Marcy and Zina and seems a perfect match for their well-established style and voice.

During the COVID-19 pandemic, Marcy and Zina contributed to a project called *Breathe: Portraits from a Pandemic*, with book by Jodi Picoult and Tim McDonald.

WENDY WASSERSTEIN
Groundbreaking Playwright with One Posthumous Musical

Wendy Wasserstein,
circa 1990. PHOTOFEST

Wendy Wasserstein was one of the great playwrights of her generation, a trailblazing writer who won both a Tony Award and a Pulitzer Prize. Her plays include *Uncommon Women and Others*, *Isn't It Romantic*, *The Heidi Chronicles*, *The Sisters Rosensweig*, *An American Daughter*, and *Third*. She also worked in film and wrote short stories and novels.

The one musical that Wasserstein penned is, like so much of her work, significantly personal. *Pamela's First Musical* started out as a book that Wasserstein created in honor of her young niece Pamela. In 1996, Wasserstein wrote a book that was meant to inspire a young generation of theatergoers and New York City dreamers. *Pamela's First Musical* is a colorful depiction of a young girl who is taken on an adventure to experience Broadway with her eccentric aunt.

Wasserstein wrote the book, Cy Coleman the music, and David Zippel the lyrics for a stage musical adaptation of the show. *Pamela's First Musical* was set to premiere at Goodspeed in 2005, but this was canceled when Coleman died in 2004. Wasserstein passed away in 2006. *Pamela's First Musical* finally received its first performance at Town Hall in 2008, and then its premiere full production at Two River Theater in 2018. Christopher Durang, who had been a close friend of Wasserstein, came on board to work on the book since Wasserstein was gone.

Wasserstein also contributed sketches to the 1988 off-Broadway musical *Urban Blight*, a Manhattan Theatre Club revue about city living. The show featured songs by Richard Maltby Jr. and David Shire as well as Ed Kleban, and sketches by Wasserstein as well as Terrence McNally, A. R. Gurney, Christopher Durang, George C. Wolfe, Shel Silverstein, and more.

12

2000s

Tongue-in-Cheek Comedy, Jukebox Phenomena, and New Media

DOLORES PRIDA
Latinx Trailblazer

Dolores Prida's claim to fame was being "the Latina Dear Abby." From the 1970s until she died in 2013, Prida was a journalist who wrote largely for the Latinx community. She was a cofounder of *Latina Magazine* where her column was called *"Dolores Dice"* (Dolores Says).

In 2000, Prida, with David Coffman, conceived a musical celebrating Latinx songs and culture called *4 Guys Named Jose . . . and Una Mujer Named Maria*. The title and plot are a take-off on the 1992 revue *Five Guys Named Moe*.

The conceit of *4 Guys Named Jose . . . and Una Mujer Named Maria* finds four men—Puerto Rican, Cuban, Mexican, and Dominican—meeting by chance and discovering that they share a name and an interest in the same woman. The evening's events follow, with the men using this premise to string together a series of performances of beloved Latinx numbers from "La Bamba" to "Bailamos"— originated by the show's producer, Enrique Iglesias.

Prida wrote the book for the show that delighted audiences at the Blue Angel off-Broadway for six months. It was originally produced by Amas Musical Theatre (founded by Rosetta LeNoire).

Off-Broadway of the 2000s was filled with musicals that were an offshoot of the jukebox musical—shows that didn't capitalize on the work of one artist, or tell the story of a specific musical group, but used previously written popular songs, performed in revue style, connected by a loose story.

KIRSTEN CHILDS
Young, Female, and Black Characters

Kirsten Childs started her theatrical career as a performer. She was the first Black woman to play Velma Kelly (and did so opposite future director-choreographer Susan Stroman as Roxie Hart) on the *Chicago* tour, as directed and choreographed by Bob Fosse himself. Childs performed in the 1970s through the 1990s before she decided to write her own work.

The autobiographical *The Bubbly Black Girl Sheds Her Chameleon Skin* premiered off-Broadway at Playwrights Horizons in 2000 and won an Obie Award. The musical tells the story of a young Black woman coming of age in Los Angeles who dreams of moving to New York and becoming a dancer. She also dreams

Kirsten Childs, circa 2010. WENN RIGHTS LTD / ALAMY STOCK PHOTO of escaping racism in the world around her. She has a white doll and fantasizes about a white prince and wants to avoid the kids on the playground who tell her she looks just like one of the young female victims of a hate crime bombing at a church in Alabama. Bubbly just wants a chance to be, well, bubbly, without all of the trappings that come from being inside her own skin. Childs' own *Chicago* experience is even touched upon in a song called "Director Bob," where a seductive stand-in for Fosse encouraged the lead not to 'go white on him' during a monologue.

The complicated issues in *Bubbly* are explored with depth, honesty, and humor, in this show that introduced Childs as a voice to watch. *Bubbly* was revived in New York City Center's Encores! Off-Center series in 2017,[1] and the word-of-mouth was overwhelmingly positive for this show that powerfully addresses many current issues at the forefront of society, which have persisted since 2000.

In 2005, Childs' musical *Miracle Brothers* premiered at the Vineyard Theatre. This is a story about two brothers: one Black and enslaved and one white and free, and how they escape from plantation life in 17th century Brazil. Like *Bubbly*, *Miracle Brothers* has all three elements written by Childs. Her score is filled with Brazilian-inspired melodies.

Miracle Brothers was produced thanks to a Kitty Carlisle Hart commission that Childs received. She has also been the recipient of a Jonathan Larson Grant, an NEA Grant, a Weston New Musical Award, a Kleban Award, and many other prizes.

In 2007, Kirsten Childs' *Funked Up Fairy Tales*, a reimagined re-telling of stories like Rumpelstiltskin, opened at Barrington Stage Company. *Variety* wrote: "It gives multi-hyphenate Childs, the Obie-winning composer of *The Bubbly Black Girl...*, the chance to show off her musical range and lyrical dexterity. Childs taps into the vibes of country rap, gospel and R&B, not following any genre's expectation but bringing her own bright, natural and offbeat sensibility to the music."[2] The show has yet to play New York in a full production.

Fly, a new interpretation of the Peter Pan story, opened at Dallas Theater Center in 2013 with book by Rajiv Joseph, music by Bill Sherman, and lyrics by Joseph and Childs. *Fly* centers on Wendy. The show also received a 2020 production at La Jolla Playhouse.

In 2016, Childs' *Bella: An American Tall Tale* burst onto the scene at Playwrights Horizons and inspired positive word of mouth, its boldness and originality striking a spark. Set in the 1870s, *Bella* tells a story about the American

---

1. Childs had previously worked at Encores! adapting Truman Capote's original book for the musical *House of Flowers*.

2. Rizzo, Frank. "Funked Up Fairy Tales." *Variety*, 10 August 2007, https://web.archive.org/web/20180128214224if_/http://variety.com/2007/legit/reviews/funked-up-fairy-tales-1200557245/.

frontier from the not oft-explored perspective of a young Black woman, who counts among her claims to fame her gigantic booty. *Bella* shares a story about the Wild West that is filled with actual history about Black Americans at the time, and celebrates Black Americans of today through anachronistic choices as well.

Childs shared in an interview while working on *Bella*:

> *Because Bella's a wanted criminal, she has to change her name. There's a history of black people in this country [having] to forget their name . . . forget their culture. . . . [The] grandmother [wants] to make sure that even though Bella has forgotten her name, she doesn't forget where she's come from. She's a griot, an African historian from an oral tradition. . . . Where do I get a link to my people's history in Africa and America, when my history is ignored by the dominant white society and the cultural memory delivered to me by my own people is fading from generation to generation?*[3]

LINDA KLINE
What She Did for Love

Three years after *A Chorus Line* opened on Broadway and took it by storm, its lyricist, Ed Kleban, met Linda Kline.

"I met Ed on Memorial Day in 1978, at a party Peter Stone threw in East Hampton," Kline told me during a 2015 interview for the *Dramatist*. "Ed and Peter had written a musical together called *Subject to Change*. I went up to Ed when he was making hamburgers on the grill and I said: "I want to know: is Mr. Karp in the song "Nothing" really Larry Oldman? He was my homeroom teacher at Performing Arts. Ed replied, "How'd you know?" "That's how we met.""[4]

Kline was Kleban's girlfriend for much of the last decade of his life before he died in 1987 at the age of forty-eight. She is also the co-librettist, with Lonny Price, of *A Class Act*, the 2001 Broadway musical that tells the story of Kleban's life through his songs.

Both Kleban and Kline spent time in Lehman Engel's BMI Workshop during its pivotal early years. Kline wrote the librettos for the musicals *The Secret Garden* (TheaterWorks USA), *My Heart Is in the East* (Jewish Rep), and *Cut the Ribbons*. She was head writer for the television show *FYI: For Your Information* and a staff writer on *Captain Kangaroo*.

---

3. "Artist Interview: Kirsten Childs." *Playwrights Horizons*, 12 June 2017, https://www.playwrights-horizons.org/shows/trailers/artist-interview-kirsten-childs/.

4. Tepper, Jennifer Ashley. "How the 'Real People' of *A Chorus Line* Changed Broadway." *Dramatist*, March/April 2015.

In 1987, Ed Kleban's memorial at the Public Theater was a powerful tribute to a musical theatre writer who made a significant mark and yet left the world without ever achieving his dream: to find success as a composer as well as a lyricist. Kleban was a force as a human being, a neurotic, brilliant, mass of contradictions, and as the community paid tribute to him, Kline realized that perhaps this could be crafted into a theatrical evening that would celebrate all of his work.

All but two of the songs heard in Kleban's memorial wound up being used in *A Class Act*, the musical that tells the story of his life and career through his own songs. In 2000, the musical premiered off-Broadway at MTC and in 2001, it transferred to Broadway's Ambassador Theatre, where it was nominated for Best Musical. Kleban received his dream posthumously, through the work of Kline and Price.

NELL BENJAMIN
Strong Young Female Protagonists

Musical theatre writer Nell Benjamin is best known for cowriting the music and lyrics for *Legally Blonde* (with her husband Laurence O'Keefe) and writing the lyrics for *Mean Girls*.

Benjamin and O'Keefe's first major work for the stage was *The Mice*, a musical that became part of the three-parter titled *3hree*, which was helmed by Hal Prince and premiered in Philadelphia in 2000 before receiving a cast album. With O'Keefe, Benjamin also wrote *Sarah, Plain and Tall* for TheaterWorks USA.

In 2007, Benjamin made waves with her and O'Keefe's score for *Legally Blonde*, which became one of the most beloved musicals and scores of the decade on Broadway. With its sharp attention to character detail, unforgettable hooks, energetic spirit, and authentically funny takes on the story at hand, *Legally Blonde*'s score manages to find endless comedy without sacrificing the characters' humanity.

Reviews were largely negative, with the majority male critic base showing more misogyny than usual in putting down not just the musical but the character of Elle, the pink color that pervaded the proceedings, and the entire feminist slant behind the enterprise. But *Legally Blonde* prevailed. While it did not recoup on Broadway, the show has become a financially successful property; its life in stock and amateur is extensive and showing no signs of slowing down. The show ran for over two years in the West End and won three Olivier Awards, including Best Musical.

On *Mean Girls*, Benjamin collaborated with composer Jeff Richmond and book writer Tina Fey to adapt another beloved film centered around young women for the stage. This time critics were slightly kinder, and the show received a Tony nomination for Best Musical. Benjamin received her second nomination for Best Score.

Two of Benjamin's musicals have been in development in recent years with sights set on Broadway. *Dave*, another film-to-stage adaptation, was produced at Arena Stage in 2018. Benjamin wrote the lyrics and cowrote the book with the late Thomas Meehan to this show about a man hired to impersonate the president of the United States. On *Because of Winn Dixie*, which premiered at Goodspeed in 2019 following several other out-of-town tryouts, Benjamin wrote book and lyrics. Duncan Sheik wrote the music for this show about a dog named Winn Dixie.

A playwright as well, Benjamin's *The Explorers Club*, about a woman who tries to gain entry to an all-male group of explorers in the 1800s, premiered off-Broadway in 2013.

"I don't think this is purely a 'woman thing,'" Benjamin told broadway.com in an interview about the play. "There are unfortunate times in life when you have to suck it up and be polite to people you think are being . . . stupid. That . . . translates across the board. . . . It's kind of fun to make bigots and bullies into big, cheerful idiots so that we can laugh at them. I didn't get the opportunity to laugh at them when it was happening to me, but now I do and I'm enjoying it thoroughly."[5]

AMANDA GREEN
Musical Theatre Writing Royalty Carves Her Own Niche

A descendant of musical theatre royalty, Amanda Green is the daughter of Adolph Green—half of the legendary writing team of Comden and Green—and musical theatre great Phyllis Newman. Thus, Amanda grew up not only experiencing her parents' Broadway careers from a front-row seat, but also surrounded by the top talent in musical theatre writing, from Leonard Bernstein to Stephen Sondheim to Cy Coleman.

Green decided to train as a performer, but this soon gave way to writing and performing her own material in nightclubs, much as her father had done early in his career, with his partner Betty Comden.

Amanda Green, circa 2023. UPI / ALAMY STOCK PHOTO

Amanda Green's work was raunchy and country-tinged, and this inclination eventually led her to move to Nashville to pursue writing country music.

5. Benjamin, Nell. "Nell Benjamin on Laughing at Bullies and the Sentimental Inspiration behind Her Play *The Explorers Club*." Broadway.com, 11 June 2013, https://www.broadway.com/buzz/170035/nell-benjamin-on-laughing-at-bullies-the-sentimental-inspiration-behind-her-play-the-explorers-club/.

But by the early 2000s she was back in New York, collaborating with Tom Kitt, whom she met in the BMI Workshop, on a stage musical version of the book and movie *High Fidelity*, about the romantic entanglements of a man who works at a record store. The musical, which starred Will Chase and Jenn Colella, had a disappointingly short run on Broadway in 2006, despite many who praised its score. Green wrote lyrics and Kitt wrote music for the pop-rock score, which gave voice to the story's modern characters. The show's witty and biting song titles include "Desert Island Top 5 Break Ups," where protagonist Rob goes into his dating history and tells his recent ex-girlfriend Laura that she "wouldn't even make the list" and "Ready to Settle," a diegetic number about giving up on true love.

High Fidelity is true to its roots, deep in music culture. "Goodbye and Good Luck" finds Bruce Springsteen's influence providing guidance through a galvanizing rock number, and "I Slept with Someone" calls upon Green's country influences even as it finds its roots in musical comedy lyrics like those of Comden and Green. (The other half of the phrase in the song's title is "Who Slept with Lyle Lovett" or "Who Handled Kurt Cobain's Intervention.")

The show had a small cast and is an intimate story about modern love—an idiosyncratic fit for Broadway's Imperial Theatre. Without marquee stars or rave reviews, it folded after only fourteen performances.

In 2012, Amanda Green contributed lyrics to the Broadway musical *Bring It On*, also based on a movie. Again she collaborated with Kitt, and this time they were joined in writing the score by Lin-Manuel Miranda. *Bring It On* was nominated for Best Musical and featured a thrilling cast of young artists, almost all making their Broadway debuts and executing highly impressive cheerleading stunts at the St. James, where Green had spent time watching her father's musical *On the Twentieth Century* in the 1970s.

By this point, Green was a staple at cabaret venues like Birdland and Feinstein's, known for putting a wry, sexy spin on her own songs and for assembling raucous evenings where actors interpreted her work in a cabaret setting as well. Her album *Put a Little Love in Your Mouth!*, recorded live during a concert performance, displayed this to acclaim in 2003.

In 2013, Green returned to Broadway with *Hands on a Hardbody*. She wrote the lyrics and cowrote the music for this musical based on the documentary about a contest to win a truck, with music also by Trey Anastasio and book by Doug Wright. *Hands on a Hardbody* is an ensemble musical about ordinary, down-on-their-luck Texans who each try to keep their hands on a truck the longest, in order to walk away with the prize. The show tried out at La Jolla Playhouse before moving to the Brooks Atkinson, where it displayed Green's aptitude for country-infused musical theatre. The show has an extraordinary score, outstandingly deployed to tell its story of ordinary people, but it wasn't shiny enough for critics and audiences, and closed after only twenty-eight performances. A cast album displays just how special the musical is.

Green's next two Broadway projects were revivals. In 2015 she participated in furthering her father's legacy by rewriting some additional lyrics for an *On the Twentieth Century* revival. She had previously done the same for a regional production of his *Hallelujah, Baby!* In 2019, Green provided additional material for a *Kiss Me, Kate* revival, updating the libretto for a modern audience without sacrificing its integrity.

Green told Sarah Rebell at the *Interval* about one change she made to Cole Porter's original lyric for "I've Come to Wive It Wealthily in Padua." In that song, the character Fred Graham/Petruchio had previously sung a line that Green noted wasn't working for her. According to Green: "[I changed] *'If she fight like a raging boar, I've oft stuck a pig before.'* [to] *'I've oft bed a bore before.'* . . . You can't fight what the song is about and what the characters are. . . . But you don't have to say *'I've oft stuck a pig before,'* because it's just unnecessarily icky. I did not want to be anachronistic and make it something it's not. It's not a play about 2019. You won't hear about a woman's choice and I didn't want to bring in. There is so much that is delightful about this musical, and that's what you're seeing up there."[6]

In 2022, Green wrote the lyrics for *Mr. Saturday Night*, a Broadway musical that starred Billy Crystal, with music by Jason Robert Brown. In addition to starring, Crystal cowrote the book (with Lowell Ganz and Babaloo Mandel) based on his 1992 movie. Green's lyrics on that show, while updating the characters and plot of the film with her own personal touch, earned her a second Tony Award nomination for Best Original Score.

Green's unique voice comprises a juxtaposition of classic musical comedy, country radio hits, modern singer-songwriter, and her own completely original style. She has carved a niche in the industry.

One of her upcoming projects, *Female Troubles*, about an unwed pregnant woman in the nineteenth century, has received a developmental concert at Bucks County Playhouse, and is aimed at Broadway. It will receive a 2024 out-of-town tryout at the Goodman Theatre.

In 2021, Green became the first woman to hold the position of president of the Dramatists Guild.

---

6. Rebell, Sarah. "Amanda Green on Kiss Me, Kate and More." *Interval*, 7 May 2019, https://www.theintervalny.com/interviews/2019/05/amanda-green-on-kiss-me-kate-and-more/.

CATHERINE JOHNSON
Creator of Mamma Mia!

Catherine Johnson is a British playwright whose work on a musical made her one of the top-earning female musical theatre writers of all time. The musical is *Mamma Mia!* In 1997, producer Judy Craymer commissioned Johnson to write the book for the ABBA jukebox musical based on the strength of her plays, and in 1999 it premiered in the West End. A Broadway bow in 2001 followed.

Discussion of *Mamma Mia!*'s Broadway success is often accompanied by a dissection of the fact that the escapist, joyful musical with its comforting nostalgic hit songs opened the month after September 11, and hit a sweet spot of exactly what theatergoers wanted to see at that time. *Mamma Mia!* became the ninth-longest-running Broadway musical of all time and its most successful jukebox musical. The show is a mega-hit, with productions all over the world, a film adaptation, and a film sequel.

For all of *Mamma Mia!*'s success, Catherine Johnson's name is not a well-known one to Broadway crowds. Although they have more than enjoyed her clever storytelling and dialogue that shape the now-iconic musical, her name has been eclipsed by the success of the show title itself and the visible driving force of ABBA.

JEANIE LINDERS
Over Nine Million People Have Seen Her Musical

A worldwide phenomenon, *Menopause: The Musical* began its life in Orlando, Florida. Jeanie Linders wrote the book and new lyrics for this show that capitalizes on nostalgia for classic mid-twentieth-century pop and rock songs and the relatable theme of menopause. Linders took songs from "I've Got You Babe" to "I Heard It through the Grapevine" and set them with new lyrics, filled with puns, to musicalize what women go through when the "change of life" occurs.

The show was a huge girls-night-out hit with women of a certain age, and soon productions hit major cities all over the globe including Theater Four off-Broadway in New York, where it eventually played 1,724 performances from 2002 to 2006. *Menopause* paved the way for the modern girls-night-out musical genre off-Broadway. The main theatrical ticket-buying audience for years has been women around the age of the characters in the show, and this musical and the ones that came after strove to show characters and stories on stage that were directly relatable to this demographic.

Menopause: The Musical has been seen by more than nine million people worldwide.

ERICA SCHMIDT
Adapting a Porn Flick into a Musical

Director Erica Schmidt has worked steadily off-Broadway and regionally for the last two decades. Her notable musical credit as both director and writer is the 2002 musical *Debbie Does Dallas*. The show parodying a pornographic movie played at the Jane Street Theatre, and starred Sherie Rene Scott in the title role. It was conceived by Susan L. Schwartz, adapted and directed by Schmidt, and had music by Andrew Sherman with additional music and lyrics by Tom Kitt and Jonathan Callicutt.

Debbie Does Dallas started out at the Fringe Festival. The story about a high school cheerleader and her squad who discover they can make it to the big time by engaging in paid sexual escapades was deliberately but lightly musicalized, with the score only consisting of about half a dozen full songs. The enjoyable original cast recording consists of much underscored dialogue as well, in its forty-seven tracks.

While the original off-Broadway production did not contain nudity, *Debbie Does Dallas* has inspired nudity and increasingly sexually explicit interpretations in its licensed productions.

DEBRA BARSHA
Music Woman

A prolific writer in multiple media, Debra Barsha has worked in musical theatre as a composer, lyricist, librettist, orchestrator, vocal arranger, dance arranger, conductor, performer, musical director, and musician.

In 2003, Barsha was composer and co-lyricist for the cult hit musical *Radiant Baby*, about artist Keith Haring, which played at the Public Theater. The musical, which chronicles the 1980s club and pop art worlds, has gained a following, and its eclectic score is often praised by aficionados who believe *Radiant Baby* to be one of the best scores of its decade that was never commercially recorded.

Barsha also contributed to *Songs from an Unmade Bed*, which played New York Theatre Workshop in 2005. In 2016, Barsha collaborated with Hollye Levin, with both women sharing credit for book, music, and lyrics, on *A Taste of Things to Come*, a new musical about a Betty Crocker cooking contest in the 1950s and the lives of the women who enter it. The York Theatre–originated musical featured an all-female cast and band. Several of Barsha's musicals written for family audiences have been licensed for schools.

On Broadway, Barsha associate-conducted and played both *Summer* and *Jersey Boys* and was musical director for *Oh, Calcutta!*

A recipient of multiple ASCAP Awards and Jonathan Larson Foundation Awards, Barsha has forged a long career in theatre writing.

RUTH WALLIS
Queen of the Party Songs

Ruth Wallis entered the arena of musical theatre in 2003 when *Boobs! The Musical* opened at the Triad Theatre off-Broadway. Wallis was a jazz and cabaret singer, at the peak of her career in the 1940s through the 1960s, who was known for pushing the envelope with songs about risqué topics. Wallis wrote her songs herself, and they had titles like "Queer Things Are Happening" and "Ugly Man with Money."

Wallis was called "Queen of the Party Songs," and her albums were often hidden behind music dealers' counters, since they were so controversial that they couldn't appear on public shelves. *Boobs!* brought her work to a new generation, and the show has been licensed and performed regionally.

JOANNE BOGART
Five Parodies in One

Joanne Bogart is the Drama Desk-nominated book cowriter and lyricist of *The Musical of Musicals—The Musical!* with Eric Rockwell. The satiric show premiered off-Broadway at the York Theatre in 2003, before moving to New World Stages for much of 2005. It received an original cast album, featuring both of the show's writers as well as Craig Fols and Lovette George.

Each of the five acts of *The Musical of Musicals—The Musical!* tells the same story, but through the lens of a different musical theatre writer or team. The leading lady can't pay her rent, the landlord is after her, the leading man loves her, and the matron (originated by Bogart) wants to help. The acts include *Corn!* in the style of Richard Rodgers and Oscar Hammerstein II, *A Little Complex* in the style of Stephen Sondheim, *Dear Abby* in the style of Jerry Herman, *Aspects of Juanita* in the style of Andrew Lloyd Webber, and *Speakeasy* in the style of John Kander and Fred Ebb. Bogart and Rockwell made fun of tropes with dexterity and each act is equally attuned to its individual style.

The Musical of Musicals—The Musical! followed in the footsteps of *Forbidden Broadway*. The off-Broadway genre of the clever small musical poking fun at Broadway was an offshoot of the Broadway revue of the first half of the twentieth century, which once did the same, but on a large scale. The wit and jokes of the show are sharp, specific, and enjoyed by critics and audiences alike.

KAIT KERRIGAN AND BREE LOWDERMILK
Changing New Musical Theatre

Kait Kerrigan and Bree Lowdermilk spearheaded a new generation of "new musical theatre writers"—even going so far as to brand the very phrase.

When they broke onto the scene with their popular songs "Run Away with Me" and "Say the Word," written for a musical called *The Unauthorized Autobiography of Samantha Brown*, Kerrigan and Lowdermilk found a following in a brand new way: on the internet. In the early 2000s, as the internet was becoming fertile ground for new musical theatre to gain popularity, reaching humans at their computers everywhere via audio tracks, chat boards, reviews, videos, and so on, Kerrigan and Lowdermilk were just starting out. They led the way in embracing new technology as a means of dispersing new material—and as time went on, they led the way in embracing new technology within theatre itself as well.

Lowdermilk is the composing half of the team, and Kerrigan writes lyrics and sometimes book. Together and separately, they are the recipients of a Jonathan Larson Grant, Richard Rodgers Award, Dramatists Guild Fellowship, and Ed Kleban Award. Their earliest work together includes *The Woman Upstairs*, which premiered in the first-ever New York Musical Theatre Festival in 2004 and *Henry and Mudge*, a 2006 TheaterWorks USA musical that subsequently toured the United States for a decade. The team first met as high schoolers and began writing together in college.

In 2014, Kerrigan and Lowdermilk received their first major production with *The Unauthorized Autobiography of Samantha Brown*, which premiered at Goodspeed. The musical about a high school student on the verge of graduation who loses her best friend in a car accident and tries to navigate life without her and her adventurous spirit, boasts the team's heart-wrenching ballads and irresistible melodies. The five-character musical centered around young people appealed greatly to the young audiences who had become rabid fans of Kerrigan and Lowdermilk's work.

The Unauthorized Autobiography of Samantha Brown was further developed following its Goodspeed run, and with a different title, one fewer character, and many other changes, opened off-Broadway in 2017 under the title *The Mad Ones*. An original cast album was released.

Tales from the Bad Years is Kerrigan and Lowdermilk's song cycle revolving around people in their twenties. This conceit became very popular among their generation of musical theatre writers, with everyone's ' "twenties song cycle" becoming their calling card to write more commercial book musicals. In Kerrigan and Lowdermilk's case, *Tales from the Bad Years* began its life as a conventionally staged song cycle including songs like "Twenty-Something," "Party Worth Crashing" and "Vegas," and evolved into an immersive house party musical, rebranded as *The Bad Years*. The musical was produced in New York in a warehouse setting, where audience members could wander around and experience different scenes in different sequences. While immersive theatre of this sort gained in popularity throughout the 2010s, it was not a popular format for a new musical; *The Bad Years* was one of the first.

Kerrigan and Lowdermilk cofounded newmusicaltheatre.com, an outlet for the new generation of writers to sell their own sheet music online. The website started with a small group of writers and over a decade expanded to sell the work of dozens, introducing a legal and accessible way for people to perform new songs from musicals by younger writers.

In terms of sharing their work on YouTube, making one of the first kickstarted new musical theatre albums, premiering new musicals in new formats, and more, Kerrigan and Lowdermilk have always explored the cutting edge of media when it comes to new musical theatre.

Lowdermilk, who is a queer, transgender woman who uses she/they pronouns, has released original song content in unique formats, from living room concerts to music videos. Some have been improvisational, in collaboration with folks commenting on the internet, often in real time.

Justice: A New Musical, with book by Lauren Gunderson, music by Lowdermilk, and lyrics by Kerrigan, premiered at Arizona Theatre Company in 2022 and then played the Marin Theatre in 2023. The show is about the first women to be Supreme Court Justices, Sandra Day O'Connor, Ruth Bader Ginsberg, and Sonia Sotomayor. "It feels vital to engage with the women whose seat on the bench forced our justice system to reckon with gender, inclusivity, race, and equality," Kerrigan told the press.[7]

In April of 2023, Kerrigan and Lowdermilk had their work performed on the White House lawn for Easter, when their TheaterWorks USA musical, *Rosie Revere, Engineer*, written with Gunderson, was chosen to be part of the celebration. Kerrigan also wrote additional lyrics for *The Time Traveller's Wife*, with book by Gunderson, which premiered in the West End in fall 2023. Also in fall 2023, the new musical version of *The Great Gatsby*, with book by Kerrigan, opened at Paper Mill Playhouse. It transferred to Broadway in 2024, marking Kerrigan's Broadway debut. Kerrigan and Lowdermilk's current projects in development also include *ERNXST*, a gender-expansive new version of *The Importance of Being Earnest* in collaboration with Justin Elizabeth Sayre.

As Kerrigan noted, "We've tapped into an audience that's pretty young because our musical sensibility and because the kinds of moments we're interested

---

7. Gans, Andrew. "Marin Theatre Premiere of Bree Lowdermilk and Kait Kerrigan's *Justice: A New Musical* Begins February 16." *Playbill*, 16 February 2023, https://playbill.com/article/marin-theatre -premiere-of-bree-lowdermilk-and-kait-kerrigans-justice-a-new-musical-begins-february-16.

in writing really appeal to teenagers and young 20-somethings. And that audience is very tech savvy—they know how to find things online. Most writers don't get to connect with that audience, and if they do, it's after they've had a couple successes. Through our use of technology, we sort of jettisoned that step and have remained very connected with the younger audiences."[8]

BARRI MCPHERSON
Adapting a Real Homeless Existence into a Broadway Musical

Brooklyn the Musical, oft spelled as *BKLYN*, has one of the more unique origin stories of any Broadway musical. Barri McPherson was a New York City cabaret singer in 1982, when Mark Schoenfeld heard her sing and invited her to record some of his work. Shortly after, McPherson left the business. In 1991, while visiting the city, McPherson saw a homeless man singing on a corner and realized it was Schoenfeld. She invited him to live with her family while he got back on his feet.

During this convalescence, McPherson and Schoenfeld became collaborators, eventually writing a musical about homeless street singers and cabaret performers. They both wrote book, music and lyrics. *Brooklyn* is a street fairy tale of sorts, a fable about a girl named Brooklyn whose troubled parents (dad deserts mom and becomes drug-addicted, mom hangs herself) leave her as an orphan, who seeks to make a name for herself with her voice, in a competition against a wicked foe named Paradice, all narrated by a homeless storyteller.

In 2004, when the show opened at the Plymouth (which was incidentally renamed the Schoenfeld during the run),[9] it was the peak era of Broadway sampler CDs, and so *Brooklyn* CDs were aplenty anywhere that Broadway fandom was present. The world was watching *American Idol*, and so singing and performance had begun to modulate accordingly in many places, to an *American Idol*-style. Many write-ups of *Brooklyn* noted its embrace of this belted, money-note approach.

Brooklyn starred Eden Espinosa (Brooklyn), Kevin Anderson (Taylor Collins, her father), Karen Olivo (Faith, her mother), Ramona Keller (Paradice), and Cleavant Derricks (the narrator, called Street Singer). It managed to run 284 performances on less-than-stellar reviews, mainly because word of mouth on the singing in the theater was so positive. Those who knew how the show had come

---

8. "Interview with Book Writer/Lyricist Kait Kerrigan." *ContemporaryMusicalTheatre.com*, https:// contemporarymusicaltheatre.wordpress.com/2012/03/06/interview-with-book-writerlyricist-kait -kerrigan/.

9. This was done in honor of Gerald Schoenfeld of the Shubert Organization, no relation to *Brooklyn* writer Mark Schoenfeld.

to be tended to have more respect for it, and several of the moments in McPherson and Schoenfeld's lives were paralleled in *Brooklyn*. But *Brooklyn* was perhaps most noted for its costumes. Tobin Ost crafted each character's look out of what essentially amounted to street garbage, the most notable being given to Ramona Keller, whose costumes and head pieces were comprised of garbage bags, duct tape, caution tape, and bags of chips.

In a rare move, the cast recording of *Brooklyn* was recorded live.

MEERA SYAL
Bringing South Asian Culture to Broadway

A multihyphenate to an extreme degree, Meera Syal is an actor and a novelist, a singer and a journalist, a comedian and a playwright. She has written and performed in many different media, mostly in England where she is from. Syal grew up as the only South Asian girl in a British town, and her parents are from Punjab. Some of her material is autobiographical and involves this experience.

In 2002, Syal was the cowriter of the book with Thomas Meehan for *Bombay Dreams*, the spectacular musical about Bollywood with music by A. R. Rahman and lyrics by Don Black that was produced Andrew Lloyd Webber. *Bombay Dreams* first premiered in the West End where it had a celebrated two-year run before a Broadway run that was not quite as well received but still made a splash at the Broadway Theatre in 2004.

Syal made a guest appearance in the West End run of the show, performing as Kitty for one week only during the run. The show, about a poor man from a slum in Bombay who dreams of being a Bollywood star and saving his town, is filled with show-stopping numbers in the Bollywood style. *Bombay Dreams* was revised significantly between the West End and Broadway, with the creators seeking to share the Bollywood culture successfully with Americans who would be familiar with it in a different way than British audiences were. Meehan was brought on to Americanize the book Syal had written.

"The problem with doing lots of things is that you are looked on as a Jill of all trades and a mistress of none," Syal told the *Evening Standard* during a 2004 interview about *Bombay Dreams*. "I've only just got over the feeling that I'm the girl who tries so hard at school she gets an A for effort."[10]

---

10. "Meera's *Bombay Dreams*." *Evening Standard*, 12 April 2010, https://www.standard.co.uk/culture/theatre/meera-s-bombay-dreams-7287519.html.

MINDI DICKSTEIN
"Christopher Columbus!"

Mindi Dickstein is a lyricist-librettist-playwright whose most well-known work is the Broadway musical *Little Women*. In 2005, *Little Women* opened at the Virginia Theatre (now the August Wilson), and Broadway favorite Sutton Foster belted out Dickstein and collaborator Jason Howland's show-stopping number "Astonishing" eight times a week. "Astonishing" became not only a trademark number of Foster's career but a favorite solo for a generation of musical theatre singers.

Little Women spent four months on Broadway and then became a popular property in licensing, with many theaters eager to present the musical version of the beloved classic.

Dickstein's other musicals include *Benny and Joon*, which received its premiere at the Old Globe Theatre in 2017, and *If You Give a Mouse a Cookie*, a TheaterWorks USA production she contributed to off-Broadway in 2006.

RACHEL SHEINKIN
Spelling Bee's *Tony Award–Winning Book Writer*

Only six women have ever won the Tony Award for Best Book of a Musical: Bella Spewack (for *Kiss Me, Kate* in 1949 with Samuel Spewack), Betty Comden (for *On the Twentieth Century* in 1978, with Adolph Green), Marsha Norman (for *The Secret Garden* in 1991), Rachel Sheinkin (for *The 25th Annual Putnam County Spelling Bee* in 2005), Lisa Kron (for *Fun Home* in 2015), and Diablo Cody (for *Jagged Little Pill* in 2020).

Sheinkin was the fourth woman to ever win, and the second to ever win as sole book writer of a musical.

The book for *The 25th Annual Putnam County Spelling Bee* is a feat of creative theatrical engineering. The show started out as an improvisational play by Rebecca Feldman, off-off-Broadway. Sarah Saltzberg was one of the actors in the play and at the time, she was writer Wendy Wasserstein's nanny. Because of this, Wasserstein saw the play and recommended that her close friend William Finn see it—and Finn was inspired to turn it into a musical.

Finn, writer of musicals including the *Falsettos* trilogy, invited his former student at the NYU graduate musical theatre writing program, Rachel Sheinkin, to write the book to his music and lyrics. The musical version of the show premiered at Barrington Stage Company in 2004, opened off-Broadway at Second Stage in 2005, and moved to Broadway later that year, at Circle in the Square. All along the way it was developed by its creative team as well as its cast of actors, with the actor who originated the role of Vice Principal Panch, Jay Reiss, eventually being credited with "additional material by."

Spelling Bee was a runaway hit, becoming the longest-running production ever at Circle in the Square. The original Broadway production lasted 1,136 performances, quite an accomplishment for a musical on Broadway based on no existing source material, with no brand name, and no stars with mainstream name recognition. Sheinkin's book for the musical was heaped with praise; its special qualities were essential to making the musical take off. The book of *Spelling Bee* treats its young characters like individuals, and the humor is character-based, original, and grounded in real emotions that can turn from hilarious to heartbreaking in seconds.

In a 2005 interview with *Backstage*, Sheinkin said: "This is a story about growing up, figuring out what winning means. Different characters find different answers. Often it's not what they expected when they walked in. The show also zeroes in on the absurdity of language. The way in which we build meaning and use words is often absurd. I think the play ultimately suggests we find meaning in each other."[11]

Sheinkin's other musicals include *Striking 12*, which played off-Broadway in 2006, *Sleeping Beauty Wakes*, and *The Royal Family of Broadway*, also written with Finn. *Spelling Bee* is one of the most popular twenty-first-century musicals in stock and amateur licensing.

CHERI STEINKELLNER
Sister/Spousal Act

Cheri Steinkellner is one half of a husband-wife writing team, with her spouse, Bill, who have been responsible for work on popular television shows including *The Jeffersons*, *The Facts of Life*, *Cheers*, and *Who's the Boss*. In particular, the Steinkellners' work on *Cheers* as writers and producers was crucial to the franchise, and they won multiple Emmy Awards for this over the years.

The Steinkellners branched out into musical theatre with their book for the 2011 musical *Sister Act*, an adaptation of the treasured movie. They collaborated with Alan Menken (music), Glenn Slater (lyrics), and Douglas Carter Beane (additional book) to adapt the story of singer Deloris Van Cartier who escapes a criminal situation and finds herself hiding in a lively convent full of nuns. Steinkellner received a Tony nomination for Best Book for *Sister Act*.

In addition to *Sister Act*, Steinkellner has also worked on the musicals *Princesses*, an adaptation of *The Little Princess* that premiered at the 5th Avenue Theatre in 2005, *Mosaic*, *Jailbirds on Broadway*, and *Our Place*, as well as *Instaplay*, which is the longest-running improvised musical comedy in Los Angeles. She

---

11. Horwitz, Simi. "Rachel Sheinkin: Weaving a Spell." *Backstage*, 2 March 2005, https://www.backstage.com/magazine/article/rachel-sheinkin-weaving-spell-40017/.

conceived and wrote the book and new lyrics for *Hello! My Baby*, a chronicle of popular music in New York City at the turn of the twentieth century, written for use in schools, which she collaborated on with Georgia Stitt.

In 2023, the stage musical version of the classic film *Summer Stock*, with book and additional lyrics by Steinkellner, premiered at Goodspeed and received positive reviews.

"Looking at 1950s characters through a contemporary lens meant making crucial changes, not only in motivation—but in the people we want to see onstage," Steinkellner wrote in a program note for *Summer Stock*. "One challenge was crafting a story to support a diverse cast of characters with intention, authenticity, and care."[12]

BETSY KELSO
The Great American Trailer Park Musical

During the first year of the New York Musical Theatre Festival's existence, 2004, *[title of show]*, *In Transit*, *Altar Boyz*, *The Great American Trailer Park Musical*, *Captain Louie*, *Shout! The Mod Musical*, *Yank!*, and *The Blue Flower* all premiered. While NYMF turned out many shows over the years that made it to off-Broadway and Broadway, no festival was quite as successful as its first. New York and its theatre industry were ripe and ready for a festival of NYMF's kind.

The Great American Trailer Park Musical was directed by Betsy Kelso, who also wrote the book, with David Nehls composing music and lyrics. The show is set in a trailer park in North Florida, and follows its inhabitants' romantic entanglements, all within a comedic framework celebrating trailer park culture.

The cast for *Trailer Park* boasted an impressive lineup: Shuler Hensley, Kaitlyn Hopkins, Orfeh, Wayne Wilcox, Leslie Rodriguez Kritzer, Marya Grandy, and Linda Hart. With songs like "Flushed Down the Pipes" and "Road Kill," the original musical gave its setting authentic flavor. This was also reflected in Kelso's book, which is ripe with ribald jokes and outrageous twists for the characters. The plot is kicked off by an affair between a newcomer to the park, a stripper played by Orfeh, and a married toll-collector, played by Hensley, who is wed to an agoraphobic woman who doesn't leave her trailer.

Reviewers largely enjoyed the show, or at least some elements of it, like the anthem to "make like a nail and press on"—but many thought the show was too flimsy to live off-Broadway and belonged on the scrappier festival circuit, despite the Broadway-caliber cast.

The Great American Trailer Park Musical received a cast recording and is licensed.

---

12. Steinkellner, Cheri. "Writer's Notes." Program for *Summer Stock* at the Goodspeed Opera House, Connecticut, pp. 18–19.

BRENDA RUSSELL AND ALLEE WILLIS
Chart Topping Pop Writers Learn How to Write The Color Purple

The 2005 hit Broadway musical *The Color Purple*, based on the iconic book and movie, has a book by Marsha Norman and a score by Brenda Russell, Allee Willis, and Stephen Bray. Russell, Willis, and Bray were all making their Broadway debuts although they were well established in other areas. When they landed the job, the three writers spent a year listening to and studying cast albums in preparation.

Producer Scott Sanders attained the rights to create a stage musical version of *The Color Purple* in 1998 and was auditioning writers to create it when his friend Willis asked for a shot at the job. She was collaborating with Russell and Bray on a television project at the time and so they wrote on spec for *The Color Purple* together, and got the gig.

Willis, who passed away in 2019, was a hit pop songwriter whose credits included everything from "September" recorded by Earth, Wind & Fire, to the *Friends* theme song "I'll Be There for You." Willis was also a multimedia artist and director. She was inducted into the Songwriters Hall of Fame and her songs sold over sixty million records.

Russell is a singer, writer, and producer, whose prolific career began in the 1960s and has included everything from singing backup for Elton John to chart-topping solo albums to producing for Diana Ross.

The Color Purple was nominated for Best Musical and ran for over two years, its rousing, contemporary score playing a huge part in the show's success. An acclaimed and stripped-down revival of the musical came to Broadway in 2015. A film adaptation of the stage musical came to screens in 2023.

In a 2006 interview, Russell said, "It was an extraordinary experience to write for Broadway. . . . I was able to channel my music into this broader vision; these songs didn't have to conform to a radio format. We wrote blues, big band, gospel and other genres of music. It's expanded me tremendously as a writer." Russell went on to thank the show's producer Scott Sanders, mentioning that he took a risk by hiring three pop songwriters to create *The Color Purple*, who had no previous Broadway experience.

"I also wanted to thank Alice Walker," Russell told *Songwriter Universe*. "She's . . . wise. She said that the characters [would] come to us, to help us write the songs. I would open up creatively when I was at the piano, and just let the music come through me. I could relax and let things flow."[13]

---

13. Kawashima, Dale. "Brenda Russell Co-Writes the Songs for Hit Musical *The Color Purple*; Receives Tony Award Nomination." *Songwriter Universe*, 8 February 2006, https://www.songwriter-universe.com/russellpurple-123.htm.

LISA LAMBERT
A Wedding Gift Turned Broadway Hit

In 1997, three friends put together a musical entertainment for a private party celebrating their other two friends getting married. Nine years later, it was on Broadway.

The Drowsy Chaperone was created by Don McKellar, Lisa Lambert, and Greg Morrison as a wedding gift of sorts for Robert "Bob" Martin and Janet Van De Graaff. The Canadian friends were largely performers involved in improvisational comedy. Lambert, McKellar, and Martin had been friends since high school, and the musical was meant to honor Martin's obsession with Marx Brothers revues and Lambert's obsession with 1920s musicals. *The Drowsy Chaperone* was plotted around the wedding of Robert Martin and Janet Van De Graaff, and nothing was planned beyond its performance in honor of their actual wedding.

But *The Drowsy Chaperone* took on a life of its own. The group brought it to the Toronto Fringe Festival in 1999, where producer Roy Miller saw it and eventually had it presented at the National Alliance for Musical Theatre Festival in New York in 2004. From there, it was catapulted to a Broadway bow at the Marquis Theatre in 2006.

Lambert, who mainly worked as an actor otherwise,[14] was the co-composer and co-lyricist with Morrison, as Martin and McKellar became the cowriters of the book. There were several other friends who contributed to the initial presentation who were financially compensated for their work but did not continue with the show.

Along the way, the character of Man in Chair was added to *The Drowsy Chaperone* and was played by Bob Martin himself. More than a narrator, Man in Chair has the whole show shaped around him, a lonely musical theatre fan alone in his apartment, bringing his favorite album, *The Drowsy Chaperone*, to life. Robert Martin was played by Troy Britton Johnson and Janet Van De Graaff by Sutton Foster, with the cast rounded out by Beth Leavel in the title role, Danny Burstein, Georgia Engel, Edward Hibbert, Eddie Korbich, Lenny Wolpe, Jennifer Smith, Kecia Lewis, Garth Kravits, and Jason Kravits. *The Drowsy Chaperone* sends up musical theatre conventions on stage but also behind-the-scenes as Man in Chair tells outlandish tales about each of the personalities who originated roles in the show. The result is an entirely original-feeling show business musical.

The Drowsy Chaperone was a success on Broadway, nominated for thirteen Tony Awards. It won five—including Best Book for Martin and McKellar and Best Score for Lambert and Morrison. It ran 674 performances on Broadway.

---

14. Lambert played the title character in the original presentation.

The Drowsy Chaperone was a failure on London's West End—the show's style of comedy just did not catch on with British audiences. *The Drowsy Chaperone* has definitely caught on as a favorite in schools and regional theaters in America.

MELISSA MORRIS
Evil Dead: The Musical

Evil Dead: The Musical ran for half a year at New World Stages in 2006 and 2007, winning over audiences with its full-throttle comedic adaptation of the cult favorite horror film franchise. The score for the show was the work of four individuals: Melissa Morris, George Reinblatt (who also wrote book and lyrics), Christopher K. Bond (who also codirected), and Frank Cipolla. The show garnered an Outer Critics Circle Award nomination for Outstanding Off-Broadway Musical.

Evil Dead's five-person cast energetically brought to life the story of five college kids who spend a weekend in the woods, their cabin haunted by an evil force that threatens to kill them one by one. The show's tuneful score, captured on a cast album, has inspired hundreds of amateur and professional productions of the show since 2007. Its tongue-in-cheek treatment of the horror elements of the movie and rock score make it feel part of the generational line created by shows like *The Rocky Horror Show* and *Little Shop of Horrors*, side by side with off-Broadway musicals like *Zombie Prom* and *Bat Boy*. *Evil Dead*'s characters are grounded less in realistic emotion and developed relationships than many sci-fi horror musicals, but the style of the show fits into this musical family.

Morris is a writer of plays and musicals who also works as a musical director, including eight seasons as musical director/composer with the St. Lawrence Shakespeare Festival.

The first decade of the twenty-first century found a venue-based genre taking root: the New World Stages (formerly Dodger Stages) musical. While the musicals that opened in New World Stages' five theaters during the decade varied greatly, there was a lean toward pop-rock scores, satiric comedy, and a fringy camp element. All of these were trends off-Broadway in general during the decade, but they thrived in an even more extreme sense in this place that contains five theaters under one roof.

The complex opened as a place for live theater, following its life as a movie theater, in 2004. In its first six years, musical productions included *Evil Dead*, *The Great American Trailer Park Musical*, *Rooms—A Rock Romance*, *Rock of Ages* (prior to its Broadway transfer), *Avenue Q* (after its Broadway run), *The Toxic Avenger*, *The Musical of Musicals—The Musical!*, *How To Save the World and Find True Love in 90 Minutes*, *Celia*, *Mimi LeDuck*, the long-running *Altar Boyz*, *Naked Boys Singing!*, *Sidd: A New Musical*, *Make Me A Song: The Music of William Finn*, *Pinkalicious*, and *What's That Smell: The Music of Jacob Sterling*.

Variety wrote about *Evil Dead*: "[the show] should be a disaster. . . . It has self-aware jokes, ironically earnest songs and a tacit assertion that the creators think their entire project is a goof. And yet it works. The show's wit, gore and stage magic make it a ridiculous amount of fun."[15]

VALERIE VIGODA
Musical Theatre Writer and Electric Violinist

GrooveLily is a musical group comprised of Valerie Vigoda, Brendan Milburn, and Gene Lewin, who, since the early 1990s, have crafted a notably eclectic style. The press response from the beginning has been that the group's rejection of being made to fit a mold has confused record labels.

Vigoda said in response: "There is a strong element of theater in many of our songs, and it's common knowledge in the music industry that musical theater is NOT cool. . . . But after years of chasing the industry . . . our career is happening just fine without its help."[16]

Vigoda is on lead vocals as well as electric violin, with Milburn on keyboard and Lewin on percussion instruments, for most of GrooveLily's club and cabaret appearances. Around 2002, GrooveLily began performing in more theatrical venues, with their piece *Striking 12*.

Striking 12 is a New Year's Eve–themed musical piece about a man alone on the holiday, intertwined with the classic Hans Christian Andersen tale "The Little Match Girl." The show was originally performed by the trio, who both played instruments and brought the story to life theatrically through dialogue, written by Vigoda and Milburn, along with Rachel Sheinkin. *Striking 12* premiered off-Broadway at the Daryl Roth Theatre in 2006 and was nominated for a Lucille Lortel Award for Outstanding Musical. That same year, Vigoda won The Jonathan Larson Award.

GrooveLily's second major theatrical piece was *Wheelhouse*, an autobiographical take on life as a touring band. *Wheelhouse* premiered at TheatreWorks Silicon Valley in 2012 but has yet to play New York.

In 2017, *Ernest Shackleton Loves Me*, a new musical by the group, played Second Stage off-Broadway. Vigoda and Milburn, who had been married, were divorced by then. As Vigoda said about the *Ernest* process: "We did our readings, and our workshops and the show was getting some buzz. We were going to take it on the road. Right in the middle of all of that, one morning my husband came

---

15. Blankenship, Mark. "*Evil Dead: The Musical.*" *Variety*, 1 November 2006, https://variety.com/2006/legit/markets-festivals/evil-dead-the-musical-1200512248/.

16. Keating, Douglas J. "GrooveLily's *Striking 12* is part theater, part concert." *Philadelphia Inquirer*, 21 December 2012.

to me and told me, 'I've fallen in love with one of our best friends, I don't want to be married to you anymore.' I did not see this coming. I was devastated for months. Eventually, we got divorced, and we dissolved our writing partnership. But this *Shackleton* show was still moving forward."[17]

Ernest Shackleton Loves Me is a surrealistic two-person musical that starred Vigoda along with Wade McCollum, as a single mother and video game composer who discovers a famous explorer named Ernest Shackleton, who died almost one hundred years ago, on a dating website. In the show, the two take an adventure together, and the central character, Kat, learns from Shackleton's quest to explore Antarctica.

A 1982 *Washington Post* feature on Vigoda profiled the then-fifteen-year-old, hailed as a genius, heading off to Princeton. The article noted Vigoda's overwhelming talents in music, as well as in math, science, and literature. According to the *Post*, Vigoda scored a 212 on the Stanford-Binet IQ test at age seven. As the article stated, "100 is average, over 132 is considered gifted, over 180 extremely gifted."[18] Thirty-seven years later, the same publication reviewed *Striking 12*, calling it "an engaging concert-style entertainment."[19]

MASI ASARE
Racial History and Themes in Musical Theatre

Composer, lyricist, playwright, and educator Masi Asare is a leader in the conversation about racial history and musical theatre. Her book, *Voicing the Possible: Technique, Vocal Sound, and Black Women on the Musical Stage* explores the history and future of Black women interpreting musical theatre.

In 2022, Asare made her Broadway debut, cowriting the lyrics (with Nathan Tysen) for *Paradise Square*, a new musical about Irish Americans and Black Americans living in New York City during the American Civil War and the ensuing draft riots. The show received nine Tony Award nominations, including one for Best Score.

Asare is also the composer-lyricist of the musical *Sympathy Jones* (music and lyrics, book by Brooke Pierce), a show about an unconventional secret agent in the 1960s that was presented as part of the New York Musical Theatre Festival in 2007. For *The Family Resemblance*, Asare penned book, music, and lyrics. The show about a mixed-race family during Christmas was commissioned by Theatre

17. Matthews, Mitch. "Creating a Life of Peak Experiences, with Val Vigoda." *Mitch Matthews*, https://mitchmatthews.com/creating-a-life-of-peak-experiences-with-valerie-vigoda/.

18. Rimer, Sara. "Brainchild: Not Your Normal Everyday 15-Year-Old, Though at Times Valerie Vigoda Would Certainly Like to Be." *Washington Post*, 10 October 1982, p. SM12.

19. "Chart Topping Hits." Groovelily, https://www.groovelily.com/chart-topping-hits/.

Royal Stratford East. Asare is the sole writer of *Rishvor*, a show about racial passing.

She is the cowriter of lyrics for a Broadway-bound adaptation of the hit movie *Monsoon Wedding*, about the unlikely wedding of an Indian bride and an American groom. The show premiered at St. Ann's Warehouse in mid-2023, with a book by Arpita Mukherjee and Sabrina Dhawan, music by Vishal Bhardwaj, and lyrics by Asare and Susan Birkenhead, conceived and directed by Mira Nair. Asare's plays include *Mirror of Most Value*, a licensed play for young audiences about Marvel teen super hero Kamala Khan.

About her experience working as both sole writer of a musical and collaborating on musicals, Asare told the *Clyde Fitch Report* that she fell into book writing accidentally. She had stories she wanted to tell, and couldn't find collaborators that felt correct, so she took on entire projects by herself. One of the potential pitfalls of this, as pointed out by Asare, was that she might not hear necessary alternative perspectives on the piece during the early steps of the process. A higher level of confidence was required in order to write alone, since only the sole writer could determine which feedback from outside sources should be considered and which ignored.[20]

Quiara Alegría Hudes
Pulitzer Prize–Winning Writer of In the Heights

Quiara Alegría Hudes is best known for her book to the hit musical *In the Heights*, written in collaboration with Lin-Manuel Miranda. She is also a Pulitzer Prize–winning playwright and essayist.

Quiara Alegría Hudes, circa 2021. BY GBH FORUM NETWORK/ WIKIMEDIA COMMONS

In 2007, *In the Heights* opened off-Broadway at 37 Arts. The book was by Hudes, and music and lyrics were by Lin-Manuel Miranda. The show transferred to Broadway and received rave reviews as well as the Tony Award for Best Musical. Hudes's book gave voice to the Latinx community in Washington Heights through the show's individual characters. One goal that the creators of *In the Heights* had was to present Latinx characters on Broadway who were not gang members, like in *West Side Story* or *The Capeman*. Hudes, who is both Puerto Rican and Jewish, painted a portrait of real modern-day Latinx people and their everyday struggles.

---

20. Rothstein, Robin. "Masi Asare and Her Radical, Creative Musical Theater." *Clyde Fitch Report*, 27 June 2018, https://www.clydefitchreport.com/2018/06/musical-theater-masi-asare/.

Hudes was brought onto *In the Heights* by Miranda as well as director Tommy Kail. They attended a reading of a play she wrote and invited her to join the *Heights* team and further develop the show they had already been workshopping. Much of Hudes's earlier work had been plays, and after *In the Heights*, she would go on to write both plays and musicals. She also collaborated with Miranda on the animated film *Vivo*, for which she wrote the screenplay in 2021.

Hudes was a Pulitzer Prize finalist for her play *Elliot, a Soldier's Fugue* in 2007 and for *In the Heights* in 2009. She received the Pulitzer for her play *Water by the Spoonful* in 2012. These two plays are the first two parts in a trilogy that also includes *The Happiest Song Plays Last*.

Hudes's children's musical *Barrio Grrrl!* played the Kennedy Center in 2009 and is licensed, giving youth theatre groups an opportunity to play young Latinx characters. The show is about a protagonist named Ana who considers herself a superhero in her neighborhood but also has to contend with issues within her family, including her mom serving overseas in Iraq.

As Hudes told the *Interval*, "I think we need to actively, committedly be trying to produce the most diverse pool of plays possible. I'm not just talking about ethnicities, race, and gender. I'm talking about aesthetics and everything that goes into theatre. I don't see that happening without a very committed pressure put on ourselves as artists and theatres. If I feel that pressure from anything, it's from myself. It's not from the outside world, but it's me going, challenge your assumptions, [and ask], who is not being spoken about that needs to be spoken about. It's very important to my practice."[21]

In 2016, Hudes had a new musical premiere at La Jolla Playhouse. This was *Miss You Like Hell*, which the *LA Times* called "an immigration musical for the new Trump era."[22] *Miss You Like Hell* centers on a mother-daughter story, a rarity in musical theatre.

In *Miss You Like Hell*, teenage Olivia reconnects with her estranged mother Beatriz. Beatriz is an undocumented Mexican immigrant and while she hasn't been in Olivia's life in years, she wants her to testify at her hearing to stay in America. The show takes the form of a road trip odyssey where mother and daughter come to terms with each other as they try to take on the issue of immigration. In the end, Beatriz is deported from America and sent back to Mexico.

Miss You Like Hell's book is by Hudes and the score is by Erin McKeown. In addition to the show's two Latinx female leads, the characters that the show

21. Myers, Victoria. "An Interview with Quiara Alegría Hudes." *Interval*, 17 May 2016, https://www.theintervalny.com/interviews/2016/05/an-interview-with-quiara-alegria-hudes/.

22. "Review: *Miss You Like Hell*, an immigration musical for the new Trump era." *Los Angeles Times*, 14 November 2016, https://www.latimes.com/entertainment/arts/la-et-cm-miss-you-like-hell-review-20161114-story.html.

was populated with are diverse in all respects, trading off roles of those who the women encounter on their journey. The show played the Public Theater in 2018 and received a cast album. It has been further produced regionally.

In the same 2016 interview with Victoria Myers of the *Interval*, Hudes said, "I get asked a lot of questions that I'd be willing to wager a lot of money that Edward Albee never gets asked. He never gets asked, 'What does being a white male playwright mean?' He never gets asked that kind of stuff. But actually I think he'd have a lot to say about it that would be interesting. I don't find it a bad question, I just wish it were a question that was asked to those quote-unquote outside the mainstream, but we need to have critical eyes on ourselves inside the mainstream too. So definitely, the work gets engaged in a very different way. I have Albee envy because when he sits down and talks to interviewers, they get right to the meat of the play, which is something I don't often get to do in interviews. Usually the interview is about my identity, and then the interview is over and it doesn't even get to the work. That gets really boring really quickly."[23]

HEATHER HACH
The Real Elle Woods

Heather Hach is a writer for theatre and film who is known in the Broadway community for her book to the musical *Legally Blonde*. In 2007, Hach penned the libretto for the beloved musical based on the beloved movie.

She gained additional fame for appearing on the reality television program to select the second Elle Woods on Broadway, called *Legally Blonde: The Search for the Next Elle Woods*. Viewers noted that Hach herself seemed to contain the spirit of Elle Woods with her blonde hair and strong spirit.

As broadway.com shared in an interview with Hach at the time, "Hach used her storytelling skills to triumph in high school speech and debate. "I used to show up for debates as this little sophomore against senior boys," she recalls. "They'd think I was this cream puff, and then I'd beat them!""

"A traumatic divorce threatened to upend Hach's seemingly idyllic life in the late '90s. But much like Elle Woods, she was determined to bounce back. "It was a great opportunity to ask myself, 'What do I want to do?'" she reflects. "If I couldn't have a good personal life, I'd have a great professional life—or at least try!" Relocating to L.A., Hach pounded the pavement as a budding screenwriter."

Her film credits include the screenplays for *Freaky Friday* (2003) and *What to Expect When You're Expecting* (2012).

Hach was Tony-nominated for her book for *Legally Blonde*.

---

23. Myers, Victoria. "An Interview with Quiara Alegría Hudes." *Interval*, 17 May 2016, https://www.theintervalny.com/interviews/2016/05/an-interview-with-quiara-alegria-hudes/.

HEIDI RODEWALD
A Girl in a Rock Band

There are a lot of committed couples writing musicals in these pages, but it's much rarer to see a Broadway musical by a *former* couple. Heidi Rodewald and Stew were romantically linked for a decade while they toured with the band The Negro Problem.

Passing Strange was inspired by Stew's interest in writing an autobiographical rock musical about discovering his art and identity as a young, middle-class, American Black artist on travels through Europe. It premiered at Berkeley Repertory Theatre in 2006 and played off-Broadway at the Public Theater in 2007 before moving to the Belasco Theatre on Broadway in 2008.

The original musical's book and lyrics are by Stew, and music is by Stew and Rodewald. They also shared orchestrator and music supervisor duties on the show, and Rodewald was on bass and vocals in the band, as she was on tour.

Passing Strange opened on Broadway in a year when a significant number of the new musicals that opened had their writers originating roles, often semiautobiographical. This included Stew in *Passing Strange*, who narrated the proceedings and commented on them, as well as Lin-Manuel Miranda in *In the Heights*, Hunter Bell and Jeff Bowen in *[title of show]*, and Harvey Fierstein in *A Catered Affair*.

Despite being part of this Broadway trend, Stew and Rodewald felt ill at ease with the logistics of the theatre world. "The Tonys mean too much," Rodewald told a *New York Times* reporter directly after the awards were given out. *Passing Strange* was nominated for seven, and Rodewald was included in two of these: Best Score and Best Orchestrations. But the show only took home the Tony Award for Best Book, and thus its chances of surviving on Broadway as an original musical were greatly diminished. Rodewald said, "I admit I was getting my hopes up that we'd win for best musical. Not because Stew and I care anything about Tony Awards—we're a rock 'n' roll band—but because in this crazy place called Broadway, winning is what tells people to come see the show."[24]

Rodewald's musical work on *Passing Strange* was integral to the show's success as many praised the sound in bringing the Afro-baroque style of The Negro Problem to Broadway.

"I'm a girl in a rock band and I'm on Broadway," Rodewald commented. "Stew will be mad at me, but I really don't feel we compromised. We're in this money world that has nothing to do with the stuff Stew and I have ever done."

Rodewald and Stew's romantic relationship ended during the Berkeley Rep run, and the two were asked about this during nearly every interview about

---

24. Finn, Robin. "When Brush with Broadway Ends, She'll Play On." *New York Times*, 20 June 2008, p. B4.

Passing Strange. It seemed the typical tensions of putting a musical together had broken up this relationship but not their professional one.

Spike Lee filmed the Broadway production of *Passing Strange* for film release. The show has also lived on in further productions, but the narrator character, as originated by Stew, has been edited out of these.

Rodewald and Stew have continued to collaborate with the Negro Problem as a band as well as on theatrical projects. Their next show, *Making It*, played off-Broadway at St. Ann's Warehouse in 2010. This was also an autobiographical project, this time about their relationship, which Stew had to convince Rodewald to do. As Stew told NPR, "At first we thought there was no way [our professional relationship] was going to be able to continue. But you . . . realize there's a different kind of love. . . . There's nobody like her who was born in the same part of the United States, [consumed] the exact same radio, TV shows, [and] punk bands as me. You can't break up with that. Romance can end, but I don't think art really ends, as romantic as that might sound."[25]

The album of *Making It* came out shortly after. More an album by their band than a cast album, *Making It* is emblematic of the unconventional way that Rodewald and Stew intersect with the theatre world. Their musicals are still extensions of the work they do with their band, and they can be divorced from their theatrical presentation. Rodewald and Stew's other theatrical collaborations include *Notes of a Native Song*, inspired by the work of James Baldwin, which premiered at Harlem Stage in 2015, and *The Total Bent*, about a young artist's relationship with his preacher father, which premiered at the Public Theater in 2016.

The Public Theater commissioned *Passing Strange*, committing to Stew and the Negro Problem, since they believed their work had the ability to bridge a gap between theatre and rock music in a unique way. They also wanted to give Stew an opportunity to reach a larger audience, toiling as he had been, and struggling to make a living despite being an incredibly well-regarded artist.

Stew told the *New York Times:* "We know that fame just isn't the judge of quality, except in America. Only in America do they go: 'You've made six records? You're making a play? But I've never heard of you.'" "There has been this constant drumbeat here of reinventing how musicals are done, especially in order to talk about social subject matter," said Oskar Eustis, artistic director of the Public Theater. "Stew's whole story is about crossing cultural and aesthetic boundaries, mixing genres and identities in a way that is really complicated and contemporary."[26]

---

25. "Stew: *Making It* After a Tough Breakup." NPR, 30 January 2012, https://www.npr.org/2012/01/30/144318767/stew-making-it-after-a-tough-breakup.

26. "A Musical Star Plucked from the Underground." *New York Times*, 21 May 2007, https://www.nytimes.com/2007/05/21/theater/21stew.html.

CATHERINE CAPELLARO
Musicalizing Walmart Culture

Like *Debbie Does Dallas, Walmartopia* originated at the New York Fringe Festival. This tongue-in-cheek musical takedown of corporate America and its chain stores has a book by Catherine Capellaro and a score by Andrew Rohn, a husband-wife team. The performers of its 2007 run at the Minetta Lane included Bradley Dean, Stephen DeRosa, Cheryl Freeman, Nikki M. James, John Jellison, Pearl Sun, Heléne Yorke, and Charl Brown. The fifteen-person cast was a large one for off-Broadway, considering mid-2000s economics, but the musical managed a four-month run. The musical, about the exploitation of the American workforce, received an original cast album.

Capellaro and Rohn, who hail from Wisconsin where *Walmartopia* was a local hit, also wrote musicals called *Temp Slave* and *Blasphemy*. A write-up in the Wisconsin paper the *Capital Times* when *Walmartopia* originated proclaimed its headline: "Everyday High Energy: Catherine Capellaro edits a magazine, raises twins, and skewers Wal-Mart in her spare time."[27]

CARMEN RIVERA
Writer of the Longest-Running Spanish-Language Play in NYC History

Carmen Rivera is an oft-produced playwright whose Obie Award-winning play *La Gringa* is the longest-running Spanish-language play in New York history. The play has been running in repertory at Repertorio Español for over twenty-eight years.

While largely a playwright, Rivera's show about Celia Cruz featured Cruz's music, and therefore drifts into musical territory. Rivera and her coauthor, her husband Candido Tirado, crafted *Celia: The Life and Music of Celia Cruz* about the Cuban musical artist rising to the top. The show uses her popular songs, such as "La vida es un carnaval," "Que le den candela" and "Quimbara" to tell the story of the "Queen of Salsa." The show features a large amount of Spanish lyrics and dialogue.

Celia: The Life and Music of Celia Cruz ran for nine months at New World Stages.

JILL WINTERS
She Ran Away with the Circus

In 2008, *Cirque Dreams Jungle Fantasy* played a special engagement at the Broadway Theatre. Its main composer-lyricist was Jill Winters, who was

---

27. Troller, Susan. "Everyday High Energy." *Capital Times*, 29 July 2006.

Cirque Dreams' regular music director and had started out as a vocalist with the group.

The Cirque Dreams franchise, similar to the Cirque du Soleil franchise, is a modern take on the circus for contemporary audiences. Since 1993, different editions of the show have toured, been seen on cruises, and played residencies at amusement parks like Busch Gardens and Six Flags.

JILL SANTORIELLO
The Tradition of Adapting Dickens

The 2008 Broadway musical adaptation of *A Tale of Two Cities* by Charles Dickens had book, music, and lyrics by Jill Santoriello. Santoriello saw her musical premiere in Florida before it transferred to the Al Hirschfeld Theatre, where it starred James Barbour and was nominated for three Drama Desk Awards.

As the sole author of the musical, Santoriello didn't have a single professional theatre credit to her name prior to her Broadway bow. Her brother Alex Santoriello, who had appeared in Broadway shows including *Les Misérables* and eventually became one of the *Cities* producers, encouraged her to push the show forward since in 2008, *Les Misérables* was no longer running and there might be a vacant space for a musical with similar tone and themes. Like *Les Misérables, Cities* involves the French Revolution, a tragic former-prisoner protagonist, and the suffering of people longing for a different world. Santoriello had actually begun writing *Cities* in the 1980s.

There has been a plethora of Broadway musicals based on the work of Charles Dickens. They date back to 1867 when a musical called *Little Nell and the Marchioness,* based on Dickens's *The Old Curiosity Shop,* opened. This was followed by *Dolly Varden,* based on *Barnaby Rudge* in 1902; *Mr. Pickwick* in 1903 and *Pickwick* in 1965, both based on *The Pickwick Papers; Oliver!* based on *Oliver Twist* in 1965; *Comin' Uptown* in 1979 based on *A Christmas Carol;*[28] *Copperfield* in 1981, based on *David Copperfield;* and *The Mystery of Edwin Drood* in 1985, based on an unfinished Dickens novel.

A Tale of Two Cities is the most recent new Dickens musical adaptation for Broadway. Its reviews were uniformly negative, with *TheaterMania* summarizing thus: "[It] never rises above the level of mediocrity."[29] The show closed after sixty performances. After opening, it played to an average capacity of about 56 percent throughout the early fall of 2008. The show was filmed for PBS in London in

---

28. There is also a popular musical stage version of *A Christmas Carol,* thus titled, that has never played Broadway.

29. Finkle, David. "*A Tale of Two Cities.*" *TheaterMania,* 18 September 2008, https://www.theatermania.com/new-york-city-theater/reviews/a-tale-of-two-cities_15288.html.

2009 and received an international cast recording. It has gone on to receive several international productions and is licensed for stock and amateur.

Santoriello also wrote *It Happened in Key West*, which premiered in London in 2018.

DOLLY PARTON
Working 9 to 5

Popular culture icon Dolly Parton made a foray into the Broadway sphere in 2009 when she wrote music and lyrics for the stage musical adaptation of *9 to 5*, the iconic film celebrating powerful women in the workplace. The 1980 movie starred Parton in the role of Doralee, a secretary who teams up with two other women to seek revenge on their misogynist, harassing boss. For the musical, Megan Hilty took on this role, singing Parton's jubilant score alongside Stephanie J. Block, Allison Janney, and Marc Kudisch. The musical's book was by Patricia Resnick, who also cowrote the original screenplay.

The 2009 musical opened at the Marquis Theatre and despite receiving fifteen Drama Desk nominations and four Tony Award nominations including one for Best Score for Parton, it only lasted for 148 performances. The musical was overshadowed in its season by four bigger hits: *Billy Elliot*, *Next to Normal*, *Rock of Ages*, and *Shrek*, all of which received a Best Musical Tony nomination while *9 to 5* did not. Although *9 to 5* had its fans, it could not sustain a run at the large Marquis Theatre for longer than a few months, with its largely negative reviews. The show has found great success in licensing and also internationally, with a 2019 West End production receiving significant acclaim.

About Parton's *9 to 5* score, Elisabeth Vincentelli wrote in the *New York Post*: "It shouldn't surprise anybody she's taken so well to the stage: She's always been a storyteller first and foremost. Her countrified pop . . . fits perfectly on Broadway. Of all the mainstream artists who've tried their hand at show music in the past few years, she may be the most convincing."[30]

Parton infused her trademark personal style into the musical in a way that is both authentic and charming. In fact, the same year as the musical opened she released a solo album, titled *Backwoods Barbie*—also the title of a song that is used to speak to the heart of the character Doralee in the show.

In the 2000s and 2010s, as an increasing number of pop artists came to Broadway with musicals, many chose to present jukebox musicals consisting of existing songs, but Parton was one of the first, followed by Cyndi Lauper and Sara Bareilles, to craft original scores for new musicals on Broadway.

---

30. Vincentelli, Elisabeth. "Parton's Musical Works." *New York Post*, 1 May 2009, https://nypost.com/2009/05/01/partons-musical-works/.

SHERIE RENE SCOTT
You May Now Worship Me

Broadway star Sherie Rene Scott also began writing her own work over a decade into her career. In 2008, the star of *Aida, Rent, Dirty Rotten Scoundrels,* and *The Little Mermaid* created a piece called *You May Now Worship Me,* a semiautobiographical show crafted around music from her youth. The show premiered as a BC/EFA benefit presented on Broadway, and Scott, who conceived the show with Dick Scanlan, performed the one-woman piece to great acclaim.

Sherie Rene Scott. BY SHERIE RENE SCOTT, CC BY 4.0 / WIKIMEDIA COMMONS

You May Now Worship Me was further developed and eventually became *Everyday Rapture,* the musical which premiered in full theatrical form at Second Stage Theater off-Broadway in 2009, also featuring performances by Eamon Foley, Lindsay Mendez, and Betsy Wolfe. *Everyday Rapture* is a deeply personal, utterly original regaling of stories from Scott's Kansas childhood to early years navigating New York City to her time becoming a "semi-star" on Broadway.

The show transferred to Broadway as part of Roundabout Theatre Company's season and earned Scott two Tony nominations: one for Best Actress in a Musical and one for Best Book of a Musical, shared with Dick Scanlan.

Everyday Rapture received rave reviews, including from Ben Brantley in the *New York Times,* who wrote: "Just as the Broadway theater season is drawing to its close, a smashing little show has arrived to remind us of why so many of us keep going back to Broadway, even though it's broken our heart so many times. . . .In telling the story of Sherie, Ms. Scott embellishes, overstates, understates, bends and weaves the complexities and inconsistencies of one life into the whole-making harmonies of a musical fable. . . . She has created a beautiful, funny fiction that is both utterly removed from and utterly true to real life. Which is what I, at least, always hope a musical will do."[31]

Scott has continued to write in addition to performing, including the play *Whorl Inside a Loop* and several original shows in concert.

---

31. Brantley, Ben. "A Semi-Star Torn between Two Superstars." *New York Times,* 29 April 2010, https://www.nytimes.com/2010/04/30/theater/reviews/30everyday.html.

13

2010s

Celebrities, Playwrights, and Crossover Artists

GEORGIA STITT
Composer and Maestra Founder

Georgia Stitt is a composer of musicals, founder and president of Maestra, a music director/conductor, vocal coach, music supervisor, arranger, and producer.

With Cheri Steinkellner, she wrote *Hello! My Baby*, about kids in the early days of Tin Pan Alley, and *Mosaic*, a one-woman piece that premiered as part of the Inner Voices series at 59E59. Both were produced in 2010. *Samantha Spade—Ace Detective* premiered at TADA Youth Theatre in 2014, a collaboration with writer Lisa Diana Shapiro. Stitt's musical *Snow Child* received its world premiere at Arena Stage in 2018. Stitt is the composer of *Big Red Sun*, about a family of musicians contending with the parents' past as swing musicians in World War II, which premiered in Philadelphia in 2018, after over a decade of development. Her other produced musicals include *The Water* (winner of the 2008 ANMT Search for New Voices in American Musical Theatre award) and *The Danger Year*, a musical revue that premiered in 2021 at College Light Opera Company, directed by Hunter Foster, a frequent Stitt collaborator.

Georgia Stitt, circa 2014. EVERETT COLLECTION INC / ALAMY STOCK PHOTO

Stitt has released three albums of her work: *This Ordinary Thursday: The Songs of Georgia Stitt* (2007), *My Lifelong Love* (2011), and *A Quiet Revolution* (2020). All feature an array of well-known theatre performers interpreting Stitt's work. She has also worked as a composer, producer, and/or arranger on solo albums by Susan Egan, Lauren Kennedy, and Kate Baldwin.

On screen, Stitt has acted as music director, music supervisor, on-screen vocal coach and more on projects including movies *The Last Five Years* and *13: The Musical* (written by her husband Jason Robert Brown), and television programs *America's Got Talent*, *Grease: You're The One That I Want*, *Clash of the Choirs*, *Once Upon a Mattress*, and *The Sound of Music Live!*

In addition to her theatre work, Stitt has also composed choral and symphony pieces.

Maestra is an organization for women and nonbinary individuals who are musicians and music professionals. Stitt founded the group, which has grown steadily in size and reach, contributing to important connections and jobs for members. She is also on the board of directors for The Lillys, an organization that fights for parity in theatre and since 2010, has distributed awards to women accomplishing outstanding work in theatre.

SUZAN-LORI PARKS
The First Black Woman to Win the Pulitzer Prize for Drama

Writer Suzan-Lori Parks is best known for her plays, including the 2001 Pulitzer Prize for Drama-winner, *Topdog/Underdog*. Parks was the first Black woman to win this award. She has had many of her plays produced at the Public Theater, including the Obie Award-winning *Venus* and *In the Blood*, which was a Pulitzer finalist. In addition to her theatre work, Parks has also worked notably in film. In 2023, Parks was named one of the 100 most influential people in the world by *Time* magazine.[1]

In 2010, a jukebox musical about the life and work of Ray Charles, was announced for Broadway. Titled *Unchain My Heart*, the show has a book by Parks and had previously been presented at Pasadena Playhouse in 2007. *Unchain My Heart* is set during the legend's final recording session and features songs like "Hit the Road, Jack" and "Georgia on My Mind," knit together by Parks's book about Charles's artistry and rise to fame. The Broadway production never materialized.

As previously noted, Parks also adapted the 2012 Broadway revival of *Porgy and Bess*, alongside Diedre Murray.

In 2023, Parks's stage adaptation of the iconic 1972 Jamaican film *The Harder They Come* premiered at the Public Theater. The show includes songs by Jimmy Cliff written for the original film as well as new songs by Parks. *The Harder They Come* tells the story of an aspiring music artist in Jamaica whose climb to the top is beset by issues of systemic poverty, violence, and lack of opportunity. The film was known for bringing reggae music to a wider audience. About her work on the musical, as well as several other new shows simultaneously, Parks told Michael Paulson of the *New York Times*. "If you can hear the world singing, it's your job to write it down."[2]

IRIS RAINER DART
Female Bonding amid Tragedy

Novelist and writer for stage and screen Iris Rainer Dart is best known for *Beaches*, the story of two lifelong best friends who navigate joy and tragedy together. The emotional tale of Cee Cee Bloom and Bertie White in the book was made into a 1988 film starring Bette Midler and Barbara Hershey, and featuring the beloved song "Wind Beneath My Wings." When *Beaches* was adapted

---

1. *"Time* 100: Most Influential People 2023." *Time,* https://time.com/collection/100-most -influential-people-2023/.

2. Paulson, Michael. "Suzan-Lori Parks Is on Broadway, Off Broadway, and Everywhere Else." *New York Times,* 5 October 2022, https://www.nytimes.com/2022/10/05/theater/suzan-lori-parks.html.

into a stage musical, Dart wrote lyrics and collaborated on the book with Thom Thomas, and David Austin composed the music. The show has received several productions, but has yet to reach New York.

Dart has written eight other best-selling novels, and was also the first female writer on *The Sonny and Cher Show*.

In 2011, Dart wrote the book and lyrics for *The People in the Picture*, which was supposed to premiere at Pasadena Playhouse, but had to forego its out-of-town tryout. The original musical, about three generations of Jewish women in 1970s New York, has music by pop icon Mike Stoller and Artie Butler. The show opened cold on Broadway in 2011 in a Roundabout Theatre production starring Donna Murphy. While Murphy received massive praise for her role as the eldest matriarch, the show suffered from not having proper development opportunities before its New York premiere.

The People in the Picture finds Raisel Rabinowitz (Murphy) telling her grand-daughter Jennie about her time as an actress in the Yiddish theatre during the time of the Warsaw Ghetto Uprising. Raisel also seeks to repair her relationship with her daughter, Red, before she passes away. Tales of Poland on the brink of the Holocaust alternate with current-day scenes where the three women learn from each other.

The Hollywood Reporter wrote, "*The People in the Picture* is an odd duck. While it's ultimately touching and contains some charming melodies, the show's earnestly old-fashioned blend of multi-generational melodrama, Holocaust tragedy and Borscht Belt humor makes for a lumpy stew."[3]

But the show proved a tearjerker for audiences, and found devoted fans during its Broadway run. Dart and her collaborators continued to refine the piece after its Broadway run, cutting several peripheral characters and focusing the show on the three main women.

JILL ABRAMOVITZ
Comedic Chops

An actor and writer, Jill Abramovitz brings her comedic chops to both arenas. On Broadway she has appeared in shows like *Beetlejuice* and *Cinderella*, and was a contributing lyricist to *It Shoulda Been You*. As a writer, Abramovitz wrote the lyrics and cowrote the book (with Leah Napolin) for *The Dogs of Pripyat* (music by Aron Accurso); wrote the lyrics for *Martha Speaks* (book by Kevin Del Aguila and music by Brad Alexander); and book and lyrics for *Bread and Roses* (music by Brad Alexander).

---

3. Rooney, David. "*The People in the Picture*: Theater Review." *Variety*, 28 April 2011, https://www.hollywoodreporter.com/review/people-picture-theater-review-183295.

The Dogs of Pripyat received development at Goodspeed, NAMT and Weston Playhouse, and tells the story of the dogs left behind during the Chernobyl disaster. *Martha Speaks* is a 2012 TheaterWorks USA show for young audiences about a talking dog. *Bread and Roses* has been developed at Amas and at NYMF, and is an adaptation of the movie of the same name about janitors who attempt to unionize to overcome unfair working conditions.

Abramovitz has also contributed to the web series *Submissions Only*. Her song "Happy" with music by Joy Son is a cabaret favorite.

MARKÉTA IRGLOVÁ
"Falling Slowly"

Czech writer, actor, and musician Markéta Irglová cowrote the music and lyrics for the 2012 Best Musical Tony Award winner *Once* with Glen Hansard. The show, which began as a 2007 film, is a semiautobiographical tale. Irglová and Hansard played fictional versions of themselves named Guy and Girl, and penned numbers like "Falling Slowly" (which won the Academy Award for Best Song) for their struggling musician characters, who were later brought to life on stage by Cristin Milioti and Steve Kazee.

Only nineteen years old when the film came out, Irglová was just twenty-four when the musical opened on Broadway, making her one of the youngest women to ever write music and lyrics for a Broadway show.

While many hypothesized that what made *Once* spark was the presence of Irglová and Hansard performing their own songs, the musical took off at New York Theatre Workshop off-Broadway and was soon aimed at a Broadway run. It received a positive-to-mixed *New York Times* review, but Ben Brantley wrote "The songs (written by Mr. Hansard and Ms. Irglova) soar with rough-edged, sweet-and-sad ambivalence that is seldom visited in contemporary American musicals." The show transferred and received even more positive notices on Broadway, where it won the Tony Award for Best Musical and ran for 1,168 performances.

KATHIE LEE GIFFORD
A Scandalous *Religious Musical*

Popular talk show host, author, and performer Kathie Lee Gifford has worked on Broadway on two occasions. The first was as a performer in the 1999 Sondheim revue *Putting It Together*, and the second was as book writer, lyricist, and additional music composer for the short-lived musical *Scandalous*, about the life of Aimee Semple McPherson.

Aimee Semple McPherson was an evangelist preacher who became a celebrity in the early days of the megachurch in the 1920s and 1930s. McPherson used radio to get her messaging out to a wider audience and led a controversial and scandalous life, including several marriages and supposed affairs, and at one point was accused of staging her own kidnapping. But at her core, she was known to be a brilliant visionary with innovative ideas about how to use new media to bring faith and religion to more people.

In 2012, Gifford told *Playbill* that she had been interested in McPherson's story since she was a teenager. "I couldn't believe that anybody could've lived that much of a life.... I was fascinated with her as ... a woman who accomplished what she did in that time period. She was a fearless, fierce force of nature in feminine form, and we haven't seen anyone like her before or since."[4]

In 2000, *Time* magazine called McPherson one of the most influential people of the twentieth century. Gifford had already started writing *Scandalous* at the time, and the article further motivated her to deliver McPherson's story to a wider audience.

"How did she fall through the cracks of history? It's not right. [She fell through the cracks because] she was a woman, [and] because she was a woman of faith.... Also, because of her tabloid problems, many people wrote her off as a phony."[5]

McPherson was portrayed by Carolee Carmello in this show with music by David Pomeranz and David Friedman, directed by David Armstrong, which sought to theatricalize the already theatrical preaching and lifestyle of McPherson. Two of the show's lead producers were Betsy and Dick DeVos, conservative Republicans who gained attention in the community for being unconventional producers for a Broadway musical.

Scandalous received negative reviews and closed after only twenty-nine performances on Broadway.

JULIA JORDAN
A Steamy Murder Ballad *and The Lillys*

A murder ballad is a traditional form of song where a murder is described. Playwright Julia Jordan was inspired to create a whole musical based around the idea of a murder ballad, and she enlisted Juliana Nash, a singer-songwriter with a rock band, to collaborate with her on it.

---

4. Voss, Brandon. "Kathie Lee Gifford, the Saintly and *Scandalous* Scribe, Talks about Her Passion for Musicals and More." *Playbill*, 6 October 2012, https://www.playbill.com/article/kathie-lee-gifford -the-saintly-and-scandalous-scribe-talks-about-her-passion-for-musicals-and-more-com-198353.
5. Ibid.

Thus was born *Murder Ballad*, the 2012 off-Broadway musical that oozes sex and danger and featured John Ellison Conlee, Rebecca Naomi Jones, Karen Olivo, and Will Swenson. The show tells the story of Sara, who has a wild romance with a bartender and musician named Tom until she settles down with an academic named Michael. Sara and Michael have a baby and a calm, loving life together until Sara and Tom begin having an affair.

The sung-through pop opera is filled with memorable songs and with a modern rock kind of recitative. Nash and Jordan collaborated on the lyrics, with Nash writing music and Jordan conceiving and writing the book.

A *Playbill* article revealed the origin story of the musical. "[Jordan] came to me in December '09 with this idea of rewriting some old songs of mine," Nash remembered. "We were inspired by our own experiences. We were young and worked in bars and were wild. Then we stopped to be mothers and eventually began to miss our earlier lives. She missed writing plays. I missed playing bars. *Murder Ballad* was our way to connect with our past."

The show began at Manhattan Theatre Club's off-Broadway space and then transferred to the Union Square Theatre, where Karen Olivo was replaced by Caissie Levy. In both places, *Murder Ballad* sought to create an immersive environment, part of the ongoing trend that at that moment included *Here Lies Love* and *Natasha, Pierre, and The Great Comet of 1812*.

Jordan originally planned *Murder Ballad* to be part of a trio of musicals about "the one who came before." Her other credits include the book for *Sarah, Plain and Tall* which won her several awards.

Jordan is also a founder and executive director of the Lillys, an organization (named after Lillian Hellman) that honors female writers and women working in all areas of theatrical production, and has provided important research about parity.

LISA KRON
A "Ring of Keys" Moment

Lisa Kron had a long and prolific career as a playwright, specializing in autobiographical work that she often performed in herself, before she made her musical theatre debut with *Fun Home*. *Fun Home* was not only Kron's first musical but her first time adapting the work of another writer, in this case graphic novelist and memoirist Alison Bechdel.

Kron wrote the book and lyrics for *Fun Home*, collaborating with composer Jeanine Tesori. "One of the great experiences of my artistic life has been collaborating with composer Jeanine Tesori. Whereas I knew nothing about musicals except as a person who loves them and has been in them, Jeanine is a master of the form. Combining our different backgrounds and strengths was really glorious," Kron said in an interview.[6]

While *Fun Home* was not directly autobiographical for Kron, she related deeply to the material. The story about a girl coming of age in the 1960s and 1970s and navigating coming out as gay to her parents was something that Kron experienced as well. *Fun Home* is one of the first Broadway musicals to have a lesbian protagonist. The song "Ring of Keys," where the young protagonist, Alison, discovers her sexuality through an encounter with a woman that she sees from afar, became iconic, with the term "Ring of Keys moment" entering the lexicon.

The show chronicles Alison's story by having three actresses play her at different ages, and also looks at the lives of her parents. Alison's father, Bruce, is a closeted man who runs a funeral home and who has affairs with young men. The show has a nine-person cast, and is an intimate story about family and identity.

The show was developed at the Public where it opened off-Broadway in 2013. It then transferred in 2015 to Broadway's Circle in the Square, where it won the Tony Awards for Best Musical, Best Book (Kron), Best Score (Tesori and Kron), Best Lead Actor in a Musical (Michael Cerveris) and Best Director (Sam Gold). In addition it was a finalist for the Pulitzer Prize for Drama, and the musical won the Obie Award, Outer Critics Circle Award, and Lucille Lortel Award.

Alison Bechdel, who wrote the original material, is the namesake of "the Bechdel test." This is a test where a book, show, or other dramatic media is looked at to determine if two women speak to each other about something other than a man. If they do, then the work passes the Bechdel test. Bechdel has long been an advocate for more expansive storytelling about women.

When *Fun Home* won the Tony for Best Musical, it was the first time that a musical written entirely by women won the big award. In an interview with the *Interval*, Kron commented on the moment.

> *First of all, let me just start by saying that it's absurd that we don't just fix the parity issue. There's no reason to not just fix it. At some point in our world of interviews here, I felt like every single interview that Jeanine and I had was about being a woman in the theatre and why there weren't more women on Broadway. I wrote an email to our press department—they were great about it and I didn't have that many of those interviews after that—and I was like,*

---

6. Chessler, Suzanne. "There's No Place Like Home—Interview with *Fun Home* writer Lisa Kron." *Broadway in Detroit*, 17 November 2016, https://www.broadwayindetroit.com/news/interviews/theres-no-place-like-home-interview-with-fun-home-writer-lisa-kron.

"This question has been asked and answered so many times. Stop asking us." Why don't you ask some men? Why don't you ask some producers? Why don't you ask some artistic directors? In a way there's this echo chamber of being stuck in this moment. There are so many reasons that plays are chosen—cast size, budget, shaping the season—why not make that kind of diversity part of it?

We now know, thanks to the work Julia Jordan has done, that all the myths we were taught to believe are not true: plays by women make as much money, they win as many awards, they are about the same diversity of topic. Women are writing enormous plays. The only reason for it is unconscious bias on the part of men and women in positions to make those decisions. So let's just stop it. So I start with that.

There is another thing that I've been thinking about this discussion and that is this idea that this has never happened before. There are particulars about Fun Home *that have never happened before and I feel very excited about those things. The idea of a song from* Fun Home *being on* The Tonys *on national television feels really moving and exciting to me. But I also think there's a thing that happens, which is that over and over again we're always here. It's always, "Here's this person who has done amazing work and now things will be different," and then it's not different. Part of the reason it's not different is that we forget those productions, we forget those women.*[7]

AMANDA YESNOWITZ
Crackerjack Lyricist

Lyricist Amanda Yesnowitz is known for her quick wit and talent for word play. In 2013, Yesnowitz wrote the lyrics to Doug Katsaros's music for the stage musical adaptation of the romantic time-traveling movie *Somewhere in Time*. The old-fashioned story about a young playwright visiting a hotel, who falls in love with an actress who stayed there decades earlier, had its premiere at Portland Center Stage.

Yesnowitz is known for her standalone songs as well, which have been sung by everyone from Stephanie J. Block to Lea Michele. She has also written lyrics for the revue *In the Name of Love, By the Numbers, The History of War, The Caucasian Chalk Circle,* and *Building a Wing*. She was the first individual lyricist to win the Jonathan Larson Award and is a nationally ranked crossword puzzle solver.

---

7. Myers, Victoria. "An Interview with Lisa Kron." *Interval*, 13 May 2015, https://www.theintervalny.com/interviews/2015/05/an-interview-with-lisa-kron/.

CYNDI LAUPER
Girls Just Wanna Have Tony Awards

Pop icon Cyndi Lauper, known for hits like "Girls Just Wanna Have Fun" and "True Colors" has been a record-breaking, chart-topping music star since the 1980s, selling over eighty million records. She is also a notable activist, advocating for LGBTQ+ rights since early in her career.

Lauper became involved in *Kinky Boots* because of her friend, Harvey Fierstein, who had been brought on board to write the musical's book. *Kinky Boots* is based on a 2005 film about a young British man with a struggling shoe store who decides to produce footwear for drag queens to try to save his family business. Producer Daryl Roth had the initial idea to turn the property into a musical, and pursued the rights and began to assemble a team in 2006.

When Fierstein approached Lauper to see if she'd want to collaborate and write her first musical, she thought the show was a great fit.

"The story has real heart," Lauper wrote in her memoir. "And it's been freeing for me as a writer, because I can write in the style that's right for the character. To get inspiration I listen to songs from Rodgers and Hammerstein, which I sang to when I was five. . . . I guess Harvey must have known all along that I'd love it."[8]

The show was initially an underdog, overshadowed during its Broadway season by *Matilda*, but *Kinky Boots* came out on top, winning the Tony Award for Best Musical. The show was a *New York Times* critic's pick, and Ben Brantley opened his review talking about Lauper, whose presence on Broadway was a big moment as far as crossover music artists making writing debuts.

"Cyndi Lauper knows how to work a crowd. Making her Broadway debut as a composer with *Kinky Boots*, the new musical that opened on Thursday night at the Al Hirschfeld Theater, this storied singer has created a love- and heat-seeking score that performs like a pop star on Ecstasy. Try to resist if you must. But for at least the first act of this tale of lost souls in the shoe business, you might as well just give it up to the audience-hugging charisma of her songs."[9]

At the 2013 Tony Awards, Lauper became the first woman to ever win the Best Score award as a sole writer without a collaborator.[10]

8. Dunn, Jancee, and Lauper, Cyndi. *Cyndi Lauper: A Memoir*. New York: Atria Books, 2017.

9. Brantley, Ben. "High Spirits, Higher Heels." *New York Times*, 4 April 2013, https://www.nytimes.com/2013/04/05/theater/reviews/kinky-boots-the-harvey-fierstein-cyndi-lauper-musical.html.

10. Betty Comden (three times), Lynn Ahrens, and Lisa Lambert were the only previous female winners. Since 2013, Jeanine Tesori, Lisa Kron, and Anaïs Mitchell have won.

The show had a long Broadway run, and continued on to have a successful West End run as well. *Kinky Boots* catapulted stalwart Broadway actor Billy Porter to stardom, after he stole the show playing the character of Lola. The title of the show was initially thought to make *Kinky Boots* unsellable to tourist groups, families, and those from the more conservative states, but its hit status meant that it became a must-see. This meant that unlikely audiences were taking in the story about drag queens and gender identity, and being won over. It was very on-brand for Lauper to use her star power to change minds and hearts with regard to queer culture, allying with queer artists to do so.

SARA WORDSWORTH
Broadway's First A Cappella Musical

The aptly named Sara Wordsworth was one of the four writer-creators of *In Transit*, the off-Broadway show about interconnected New Yorkers performed entirely a cappella that transferred to Broadway in 2016. Prior to *In Transit's* Broadway bow, Wordsworth largely wrote musicals for families, including adapting *Frozen*, *Beauty and the Beast*, and *Aladdin* for their Disney Cruise Line productions.

Her original shows on stage include *Dear Albert Einstein*, for which she wrote lyrics and collaborated on the book with Russ Kaplan, who composed the music. The show, about a girl coming of age in the 1950s who is followed around by an imaginary Albert Einstein, had an off-Broadway run in 2014. Wordsworth also collaborated with Kaplan on *The Elf on the Shelf: A Christmas Musical*, which regularly tours during the Christmas season.

Wordsworth also did the adaptation of *Frozen* into both *Frozen Jr.* and *Frozen KIDS* for licensing.

KIM ROSENSTOCK
Hit TV Writer's Off-Broadway Origins

Best known as producer and writer for the hit television show *New Girl* starring Zooey Deschanel and the cult favorite *Glow*, Kim Rosenstock is also a playwright and musical theatre writer. In 2014, the musical *Fly by Night*, which she conceived, received a run off-Broadway at Playwrights Horizons.

Rosenstock wrote book, music, and lyrics, in collaboration with Will Connolly and Michael Mitnick, for this original musical that takes place during the 1965 blackout in New York City. *Fly by Night* revolves around two sisters who fall in love with the same man, an aspiring musician who is mourning the death of his mother. The romantic and whimsical small musical, infused with the style and charm of 1960s NYC, is a dark fable that was said by *TheaterMania* to have a "beautifully melodic score and ... absolutely heartwarming story."[11] *Fly by Night* received a cast recording and is licensed by Concord Theatricals.

About the show's 2011 premiere in San Francisco, Rosenstock told the *San Francisco Examiner* she was enjoying collaborating fully on all three elements of the show's writing, with Connolly and Mitnick. Like many other writers who work on both sole writing projects and collaborative ones, she noted that she enjoyed having company in the creative process.

About the show, she said: "[*Fly by Night*] is a bittersweet story.... I believe there's nothing like laughing with a group of people at the same thing. But there's also nothing quite as satisfying as creating characters you can really invest in. Hopefully we'll have that mix."[12]

LYNN NOTTAGE
Two-Time Pulitzer Prize Winner

Lynn Nottage, circa 2017. BY THE TONY AWARDS - YOUTUBE, CC BY 3.0 / WIKIMEDIA COMMONS

Playwright Lynn Nottage is the only woman to have won the Pulitzer Prize for Drama twice—for *Ruined* (2009) and *Sweat* (2017). Her other plays include *Intimate Apparel*, *By the Way*, *Meet Vera Stark*, and *Mlima's Tale*. Nottage's plays feature Black female protagonists and chronicle different moments of real history through their lenses.

When asked by the *Guardian* about her opinion that she has to speak for her gender, class, and race in a way that white men are never required to do, Nottage said, "We feel this need to assert ourselves because we are absent in mainstream spaces, but at the same time feel the frustration that there is even a need to assert our voices. So that's the paradox."[13]

Nottage's first time contributing to a produced musical was with the show *In Your Arms*, a dance piece consisting of individual vignettes, which premiered at the Old Globe in 2015. Christopher Gattelli directed and choreographed this

---

11. "Reviews: *Fly by Night*." *TheaterMania*, 11 June 2014, https://www.theatermania.com/new-york -city-theater/reviews/fly-by-night_68849.html.

12. Rowe, Georgia. "NY Playwright Hits the City with Gusto." *San Francisco Examiner*, 23 June 2011, https://www.sfexaminer.com/culture/new-york-playwright-kim-rosenstock-hits-san-francisco-with -gusto/article_df3e4430-1332-598d-a4d8-095e4312c009.html.

13. Crompton, Sarah. "Playwright Lynn Nottage: 'We are a country that has lost our narrative.'" *Guardian*, 2 December 2018, https://www.theguardian.com/stage/2018/dec/02/lynn-nottage -interview-play-sweat-america.

show about romantic love that utilizes a diverse set of stories and musical styles. Nottage was one of the ten vignette writers.

In 2019, Nottage wrote the book for the stage musical adaptation of *The Secret Life of Bees*, which premiered off-Broadway at the Atlantic Theater Company. The music is by Duncan Sheik and lyrics by Susan Birkenhead, for the show based on Sue Monk Kidd's best-selling novel. *The Secret Life of Bees* is about a teenage white girl, Lily, and her Black caregiver, Rosaleen, in the 1960s, who run away when Rosaleen is punished for trying to vote. They move in with three sisters who are beekeepers.

In *The Hollywood Reporter*, David Rooney wrote that the show had "some of the most gorgeous female-forward musical storytelling seen on a New York stage. The first-rate ensemble, dominated by women of color, sings the score with transporting spirit."[14]

In 2022, *MJ: The Musical*, a Michael Jackson jukebox musical with book by Nottage, opened on Broadway. This made her one of the only writers in Broadway history to open a new musical, *MJ*, and a new play, *Clyde's*, in the same season. Her opera, *Intimate Apparel*, based on her play, also received its premiere production in the same season at the Mitzi Newhouse Theatre off-Broadway. *MJ* has been playing to sold out houses, with high grosses at the Neil Simon Theatre since early 2022.

BARBARA ANSELMI
It Shoulda Been You

Barbara Anselmi is a composer and music director best known for *It Shoulda Been You*, the heartwarming and hilarious 2015 Broadway musical that featured a veritable Mary Poppins bag of star actors including Sierra Boggess, Tyne Daly, Harriet Harris, Lisa Howard, David Burtka, Montego Glover, Josh Grisetti, Adam Heller, Edward Hibbert, Michael X. Martin, Anne L. Nathan, Nick Spangler, and Chip Zien.

Anselmi is the conceiver and composer of *It Shoulda Been You*, which has book and lyrics by Brian Hargrove and was directed by David Hyde Pierce. The show tells the story of a man and woman on their wedding weekend—who are both secretly gay and in love with other people. Meanwhile, the bride's exboyfriend who tries to break up the wedding is actually in love with the bride's sister, both the bride's and the groom's parents have their own agenda, and between the massive secrets and the farcical guests and wedding planner, everything is upside down.

---

14. *"The Secret Life of Bees*: Theater Review." *The Hollywood Reporter*, 13 June 2019, https://www.hollywoodreporter.com/review/secret-life-of-bees-theater-1218075.

The show is reminiscent of a 1990s romantic comedy film on stage and each character is given a great opportunity to shine, particularly Jenny, the underdog sister and maid of honor. While the show was not a hit on Broadway, it has gone on to productions everywhere from Australia to Scotland and is gaining traction as a popular choice for community theaters.

Anselmi is also the composer of *The Orphan Train* (book and lyrics by Susan and Sasha Nanus).

NATALIE TENENBAUM
Multihyphenate of a New Generation

A celebrated multihyphenate, Natalie Tenenbaum is known as a music director, pianist, arranger, producer, singer-songwriter, and composer of many different genres.

Her work as a composer for the theatre includes music for *More Stars Than There Are in Heaven*, a play by John Guare that premiered in Provincetown in 2015, the stage musical version of *Benjamin Button*, for which Tenenbaum wrote music to Brett Boles's book and lyrics, *Juliet and Juliet*, a modern day high school *Romeo and Juliet*, and *Little Black Dress*, which toured in the United States and Canada from 2018 to 2020.

Both *Benjamin Button* and *Juliet and Juliet* have received development at the York Theatre, off-Broadway.

On Broadway, Tenenbaum created vocal arrangements for *Mean Girls*.

CLAUDIA SHEAR
Tuck Everlasting

Writer and actor Claudia Shear rose to prominence for her autobiographical one-woman show *Blown Sideways through Life*, chronicling her more than sixty job experiences. The show was the first of several acclaimed plays, many semiautobiographical, which Shear wrote starting in the early 1990s.

Shear closely collaborated with several artists known for their musicals, on plays. In 2000, she and director James Lapine premiered *Dirty Blonde*, their play about Mae West's life, on Broadway. But Shear did not work on a musical herself until 2015 when she cowrote the book, with Tim Federle, to the Broadway musical *Tuck Everlasting*. The musical, based on the beloved children's book, has music by Chris Miller and lyrics by Nathan Tysen.

The emotional and whimsical tale about mortality found audience members wiping away tears every night, but closed after only a quick five weeks on

Broadway. As Shear told *TheaterMania* in an interview prior to opening, "This show is so gentle and it's a loud season.[15] I hope people can hear us."[16]

LAUREN PRITCHARD
Southern Roots

Singer-songwriter, actor, and writer Lauren Pritchard began her theatre career auspiciously, originating the role of Ilse in the landmark 2006 Broadway musical *Spring Awakening*. After *Spring Awakening*, Pritchard focused on her music career, releasing the albums *Wasted in Jackson* (2010), *In Loving Memory of When I Gave a Shit* (2016), *X* (2021), and *lauren* (2022), fusions of pop, rock, soul, R&B, and Southern music influences. In 2013, Pritchard began going by the name LOLO professionally in her pop music career.

In 2015, Pritchard's swing at writing a musical landed off-Broadway at 59E59 where it was very well received. *Songbird*, with music and lyrics by Pritchard and book by Michael Kimmel, is a modern update of Anton Chekhov's *The Seagull*, set in a small Tennessee town. Pritchard fused her Southern roots and the musical style she developed during her pop career into a score to dramatize the desperate yet joyful lives and struggles of a group of people who frequent the same bar.

Charles Isherwood made the show a critic's pick in the *New York Times*, writing, "Powered by a terrific country score by Lauren Pritchard, with a strong assist from Michael Kimmel's smart contemporary version of the text, the show succeeds in snugly reframing the story in the world of country music, with the actress Arkadina becoming the country music star Tammy Trip, played with her usual lush magnetism by Kate Baldwin, who drapes her beautiful voice in a smooth Southern accent."[17]

Songbird was next seen at Two River Theater in a production that continued to develop the material.

Speaking to the *Interval* about her experience with *Songbird* and with parity in theatre, Pritchard said, "There are times where you're not being seen, you're not being heard. And that's really frustrating. My *Songbird* environment is like

---

15. *Tuck Everlasting* was part of the 2016 Tony season, which also included new musicals *Allegiance*, *Amazing Grace*, *American Psycho*, *Bright Star*, *Disaster!*, *Hamilton*, *On Your Feet!*, *School of Rock*, *Shuffle Along, or the Making of the Musical Sensation of 1921 and All That Followed*, and *Waitress*.

16. Gordon, David. "Partners in Crime: Claudia Shear and Tim Federle on Adapting *Tuck Everlasting*." *TheaterMania*, 13 March 2016, https://www.theatermania.com/broadway/news/claudia -shear-tim-federle-interview-tuck-everlasting_76296.html.

17. Isherwood, Charles. "Review: *Songbird*, a Honky-Tonk Take on Chekhov." *New York Times*, 28 October 2015, https://www.nytimes.com/2015/10/29/theater/review-songbird-a-honky-tonk-take -on-chekhov.html.

an alternative universe because it is the most considerate, kind space I've ever had the opportunity to work in. It's been an amazing and emotionally helpful place.

"There have also been times in my life where I've been in collaborative situations where all of a sudden, my stance as a female collaborator or creative gets jeopardized because all of a sudden the person thinks because I laugh at their jokes that I'm fucking hitting on them or falling in love with them or something, which is really annoying. It doesn't happen that often. I get to be a bit more choosy these days about some of the things I want to do or some of the people I want to work with. But that shit still happens all the time and it's really weird when it does because you're like, I just want to be here and to create. I have no interest in pursuing you whatsoever."

"It still feels like we have to remind people that they need to hire us, which is confusing to me. I don't know why that is, but sometimes it feels like we still have to have these conversations like, don't forget to call the girls first before you make any decisions. That's very strange to me. Sometimes I'll be in workrooms and it will be mostly women, and I feel so encouraged and I go, yes, nobody had to remind these people to call the ladies. They just did. They did it on their own. They knew to do that. Good for them. And then sometimes and I'm in a room and it feels the exact opposite. So I'm not really sure how we fix that."[18]

EDIE BRICKELL
Bright Star, *a Bluegrass Fable*

A rock and bluegrass concert and recording artist, Edie Brickell has been a successful singer-songwriter since the 1980s. In 2013, she wrote and performed an album with Steve Martin, where she wrote the lyrics and he composed the music. Two of the songs on this album, titled *Love Has Come for You*, later wound up in Brickell and Martin's musical *Bright Star*.

Bright Star was inspired by a folkloric tale of a baby who was thrown off a train and abandoned in 1902 Missouri. After writing their album together, Brickell and Martin were inspired to create an original musical using their bluegrass style and expanding on this story. *Bright Star* had pre-Broadway tryouts at the Old Globe and the Kennedy Center before premiering at the Cort (now the James Earl Jones) in 2016, starring Carmen Cusack and Paul Alexander Nolan.

In *Bright Star*, Alice Murphy is a successful 1940s editor, who shares through flashbacks to the 1920s the story of how the baby she had with her young love Jimmy Ray was taken against her will and put up for adoption. A secondary plot

---

18. Myers, Victoria. "Lauren Pritchard on *Songbird*." *Interval*, 12 June 2018, https://www.theintervalny.com/interviews/2018/06/lauren-pritchard-on-songbird/.

line involves aspiring writer Billy Cane who has just returned home from serving in World War II.

Both Brickell and Martin were credited with the story for the show. Martin wrote the book, Brickell wrote the lyrics, and both collaborated on the music. They won the Outer Critics Circle Award for Outstanding New Score and Outstanding Broadway Musical, and the Drama Desk Award for Outstanding Music. The show was nominated for five Tony Awards including Best Musical and Best Score, but did not win any, during the 2016 season which was dominated by *Hamilton*.

In a *New York Times* feature anticipating the show's opening on Broadway, Dave Itzkoff wrote, "While working on their albums, whose songs combine Ms. Brickell's elliptical lyrics and airy vocals with Mr. Martin's bluegrass compositions, the collaborators began to feel that some of their tunes were telling a story—one Ms. Brickell said was infused with 'the spirit of a young girl who's forthcoming and self-possessed.'"

Originally, more than two of the songs from Martin and Brickell's album were part of the draft of *Bright Star*. But as the musical developed, its characters were honed and hefty revisions were done to focus the stories of Alice Murphy, Jimmy Ray, Billy Cane, and the people in their lives in the 1920s and 1940s. The tone of the show hearkened back to a different time on Broadway; the storytelling was sincere, without self-referential humor or modern music, in great contrast with the other shows that season like *School of Rock* and *Waitress*. In addition, while country music had certainly been heard on Broadway before, the kind of bluegrass heard in *Bright Star* was unorthodox.

Bright Star closed after 109 performances but gained legions of dedicated fans and continues to be a favorite as it is produced regionally.

JENNY STAFFORD
Original Musicals and Circus Work

Prolific musical theatre writer Jenny Stafford has had several musicals receive significant development regionally, and contributed additional lyrics to Cirque du Soleil's *Paramour*, which played Broadway in 2016.

Stafford penned the book, with Sam Salmond writing music and lyrics, for *The Homefront*, an original musical about women who are forced out of the workforce when men return home at the end of World War II. *The Homefront* was presented in the Village Festival of New Musicals, and won a NAMT grant.

With Scotty Arnold, Stafford cowrote the lyrics and wrote the book for *Extended Stay*, about a hotel guest afraid to leave his room. With Willem Oosthuysen, Stafford wrote *Prodigy*, about a cellist contending with her father's legacy. With J. Oconer Navarro (music) and Joel B. New (lyrics) Stafford wrote the book for a musical adaptation of Kate Chopin's *Awakening*. The rock musical *The Artist and the Scientist*, featuring Stafford's book and lyrics, received a run at CAP 21 in 2015.

In 2016, Stafford wrote additional lyrics for *Paramour*, the Cirque du Soleil show that had a Broadway run at the Lyric. *Paramour* is a plot-driven Cirque show about a love triangle during the Golden Age of Hollywood, accompanied by all of the spectacular contemporary circus elements the company is known for.

SARA BAREILLES
Sugar, Butter, Broadway

Singer-songwriter Sara Bareilles was long a favorite of musical theatre artists for concerts and recordings at the time it was announced that she was writing a musical of her own: *Waitress*. A collaboration with Jessie Nelson (book) based on the film by Adrienne Shelly, *Waitress* received its Broadway premiere in 2016. The show is an intimate, contemporary one, powered by Bareilles's score, and became a Broadway hit, running for almost four years.

The story of a waitress named Jenna who gets pregnant by accident while in an abusive relationship and dreams of opening her own pie shop, *Waitress* was a revered indie movie. With Nelson, Bareilles translated the complex human elements of the film to the stage. From the larger ensemble numbers to Jenna's tour de force "She Used to Be Mine," the score is filled with Bareilles's trademark style. Bareilles received a Tony nomination for Best Score.

Sara Bareilles, circa 2015. BY JUSTIN HIGUCHI FROM LOS ANGELES, CA, USA; CC BY 2.0 / WIKIMEDIA COMMONS

Alongside the cast recording for *Waitress*, Bareilles released an album titled *What's Inside: Songs from Waitress*, featuring her own interpretations of the songs from the musical, often with slightly different lyrics than what wound up in the final version of the show. Bareilles stepped into the role of Jenna several times during the musical's run, after the part was originated by Jessie Mueller. Bareilles also played Jenna during the show's West End production.

As Bareilles told *Elle*, "The greatest difference between writing for a Sara Bareilles record and this show is the liberation in terms of stylistically what I'm trying to achieve. I get to sort of play in a way that I don't always feel is available to me on my own records. I'm somebody who grew up listening to a lot of musical theater, so getting to finally write musical theater songs and songs that sound that way—the emphasis being on the storytelling, but the arrangements and the orchestrations can be really varied—I found that to be, actually, a really joyful discovery."[19]

Bareilles also contributed a song to the musical *Spongebob SquarePants* in 2017. She starred as Mary Magdalene in the 2018 live television musical *Jesus Christ Superstar* and as the Baker's Wife in Broadway's 2022 *Into the Woods* revival. She currently appears in the musical theatre-adjacent series *Girls5eva*. Her credits also include cohosting the 2018 Tony Awards. Bareilles is reportedly at work on a Broadway-bound musical adaptation of Meg Wolitzer's book, *The Interestings*.

JESSIE NELSON
Strong Women on Stage and Screen

Renowned film writer, director, and producer Jessie Nelson counts among her credits *Corrina, Corrina*, *Stepmom*, *The Story of Us*, and *I Am Sam*.

In 2016, Nelson made her Broadway musical debut writing the book of the musical *Waitress*, and collaborating with Sara Bareilles to bring the film to life as a stage musical. In doing so, she sought to pay tribute to the film's creator Adrienne Shelly, who died tragically after the movie was made.

Nelson said, "Adrienne Shelly was the original architect and I came in to do the renovation. . . . You are taking all these beautiful puzzle pieces you have been given and playing with them. . . . It is really that you are kind of collaborating with the original writer in your mind. But you don't want to be so beholden to it that you can't turn it into a musical which is a very different beast. You have to be inspired but have to let scenes lead to song."[20]

Nelson was a waitress herself early in her career, while trying to build a career in show business. This helped her to craft the musical in a realistic way. She had also seen the film dozens of times before seeking to adapt it, since her daughter was obsessed with watching it at sleepovers. With Bareilles and director Diane Paulus, Nelson achieved an exploration of the lives of working-class people at a diner without any form of condescension or class snobbery.

In 2019, Nelson worked on a very different kind of musical: *Alice by Heart*, for which she cowrote the book (with Steven Sater) and directed. Sater penned lyrics and Duncan Sheik the music for this new retelling of *Alice in Wonderland* set during the London Blitz of World War II. Teenage Alice is in hiding in a

---

19. Rodulfo, Kristina. "Sara Bareilles Doesn't Want You to See *Waitress* Only for the Woman Thing." *Elle*, 9 March 2016, https://www.elle.com/culture/celebrities/news/a34732/sara-bareilles-waitress -the-musical-interview/.

20. Robb, Peter. "*Waitress* Writer Jessie Nelson Honed Her Writing Skills Serving in Restaurants." *artsfile*, 23 December 2019, https://artsfile.ca/waitress-writer-jessie-nelson-honed-her-writing-skills -serving-in-restaurants/.

London tube station, with her best friend Alfred who is very sick from tuberculosis. In order to escape their dark reality, Alice encourages Alfred to imagine their favorite book, *Alice in Wonderland* together, and reality blends with the story. The show received its off-Broadway premiere at MCC Theater.

Although *Waitress* and *Alice by Heart* are very different in terms of their stories, settings, and styles, they do both have strong female protagonists. Nelson commented to *Women and Hollywood*, "It's important for me to work on honest, deep, hopeful material. If the story comes as it did in a male voice as it did with "*I Am Sam*," I'm open to exploring it. I love both male and female stories with heart in them. At this moment in time, it's particularly meaningful to get to work on these stories about women finding their authentic voices and coming into their selves."[21]

KRISTEN ANDERSON-LOPEZ
"Let It Go"

Known for her work on stage and screen, Kristen Anderson-Lopez is a book writer, composer, and lyricist who regularly collaborates with her husband Bobby Lopez.

Anderson-Lopez began her theatre career as an actor but was inspired to start writing lyrics after attending the BMI Workshop, where she also first met Lopez. In 2006, the two wrote songs for the stage

Kristen Anderson-Lopez with Robert Lopez, circa 2018. BY THE TONY AWARDS - YOUTUBE, CC BY 3.0 / WIKIMEDIA COMMONS

version of *Finding Nemo* for Walt Disney World. This was toward the beginning of a long relationship with Disney, which had already included some songs for animated television programs, and would in 2011 include songs for the film *Winnie the Pooh*.

In 2013, Anderson-Lopez and Lopez wrote the songs for Disney's smash hit animated film *Frozen*. *Frozen* became the highest-grossing animated movie of all time, winning praise from critics. The movie tells the tale of two princesses, Elsa and Anna, in a kingdom called Arendelle. Elsa has magical powers that allow her to control snow and ice, but she does not know how to handle them, and inadvertently hurts Anna when she uses them. The sisters have to become heroes in their own right in order to save their kingdom.

---

21. Rosen Fink, Holly. "Jessie Nelson on Her New Off-Broadway Show *Alice by Heart* and Advice from Nora Ephron." *Women and Hollywood*, 22 March 2019, https://womenandhollywood.com/jessie -nelson-on-her-new-off-broadway-show-alice-by-heart-and-advice-from-nora-ephron/.

The songs written for *Frozen* were instantly popular, with "Let It Go" becoming a worldwide phenomenon. "Let It Go" was performed in the film by Idina Menzel, voicing Elsa, and also covered by Demi Lovato over the movie's credits. The Anderson-Lopez and Lopez song won an Academy Award for Best Original Song, and many other awards as well.

In 2018, *Frozen* became a Broadway musical when it opened at the St. James. Anderson-Lopez had made her Broadway debut one season earlier, with *In Transit* (2016), the a cappella musical for which she was one of the four creators, sharing book, music, and lyrics credit. *Frozen* earned her her first Tony Award nomination for Best Score. On Broadway, "Let It Go" was performed by Caissie Levy.

About writing the song, Anderson-Lopez told NPR: "We got very emo. We decided we didn't want this song to be a traditional Disney princess song, so we were listening to singer-songwriters like Aimee Mann and Tori Amos and Sara Bareilles, and we just wanted to approach this song in a different way. . . . I did [most] of the feminist [lines]."[22]

Frozen has inspired endless spin-off properties, from *Frozen Jr.*, which can be performed in licensing by schools, to the feature-length film *Frozen II*. "Let It Go" entered the zeitgeist, becoming a ubiquitous phenomenon of a song.

Anderson-Lopez's other stage musical work includes several family musicals for TheaterWorks USA: *The Tell Tale Heart*, *Fancy Nancy*, and *Diary of a Worm*. It also includes the original musical *Up Here*, a show with Broadway-bound aims that stalled after a 2015 La Jolla Playhouse production.

Up Here, on which Anderson-Lopez and Lopez share all three writing credits, for book, music, and lyrics, is about a modern relationship between a schlubby, insecure computer nerd and a beautiful T-shirt designer who needs her computer fixed. The show largely takes place in the mind of the male half of the romance, exploring his doubts and fears. After a largely negative *New York Times* review from Charles Isherwood, *Up Here* did not come to New York.

Up Here had been gestating for almost two decades at the time of its premiere. Lopez began working on it in the early 2000s, even before starting work on *Avenue Q* (on which he was co-composer and co-lyricist). A few years later, Anderson-Lopez joined him in developing the show, which they approached as a challenge: to dramatize the life of an introverted character, unorthodox for a musical comedy.

In 2023, *Up Here* premiered as a television series on Hulu. Anderson-Lopez and Lopez adapted their stage show, collaborating with Steven Levenson and Danielle Sanchez-Witzel to bring it to the screen.

---

22. "Songwriters Behind *Frozen* Let Go of the Princess Mythology." NPR, 10 April 2014, https://www.npr.org/2014/04/10/301420227/songwriters-behind-frozen-let-go-of-the-princess-mythology.

Anderson-Lopez also cowrote songs for the beloved animated movie musical *Coco* as well as the Marvel television series *WandaVision*. For *Coco*, a 2017 film about ancestry and music, Anderson-Lopez and Lopez penned "Remember Me," the central anthem. For *WandaVision*, their contributions include a different theme song for each episode as well as integral, non-diegetic numbers for the characters, which have become iconic among Marvel fans.

SHAINA TAUB
Singer-Songwriter-Suffragist

Shaina Taub is a musical theatre writer, singer-songwriter, actor, and activist. Two of her long-gestating stage musical projects both received their world premieres in 2022: *Suffs*, with book, music, and lyrics by Taub, a musical about the history of the women's suffrage movement in the United States, premiered at the Public Theater, and *The Devil Wears Prada*, an adaptation of the popular film, with Taub penning lyrics to Elton John's music, and Kate Wetherhead's book, premiered at the Nederlander Theatre in Chicago.

Suffs had a sold out run at the Public's Newman Theater, eliciting comparisons to *Hamilton*, which played the same theater and was also sold out, created by a sole writer, about a historic era in America, utilizing musical vernacular, and counted among its stars Phillipa Soo. *Suffs* was directed by Leigh Silverman, with music direction and supervision by Andrea Grody, and choreography by Raja Feather Kelly. The show's cast featured Ally Bonino, Jenn Colella, Nadia Dandashi, Aisha de Haas, Nikki M. James, Grace McLean, Phillipa Soo, and Taub herself.

The musical followed multiple trailblazing women on their quest to achieve the right to vote for women in the United States. According to press materials: "A thrilling story of brilliant, flawed women working against and across generational, racial, and class divides, *Suffs* boldly explores the victories and failures of a fight for equality that is still far from over." Real-life historic figures depicted in the show included Carrie Chapman Catt, Doris Stevens, Alva Belmont, Mary Church Terrell, Ida B. Wells, Inez Milholland, and Alice Paul.

Suffs received mixed reviews, with many critics sharing the view that the musical had enormous potential but needed further development. The show continued to receive private developmental steps, and is set for an April 2024 opening on Broadway.

The Devil Wears Prada, based on the book by Lauren Weisberg and the subsequent movie, ran in Chicago during the summer of 2022. Produced by Kevin McCollum, with direction by Anna D. Shapiro, the show had its eyes on Broadway, but middling-to-negative reviews seemingly scuttled these plans, at least temporarily. The story, iconic to a generation, about a relatable, downtrodden assistant in the fashion world with a tyrannical diva of a boss, was adapted with Taylor Iman Jones and Beth Leavel in the central roles.

About working on *The Devil Wears Prada*, Taub told *Deadline*, "it's thrilling. Usually I write music and lyrics, but to focus on creating lyrics that will work with his melodies, I'm learning so much. I feel like I'm going to grow a lot as an artist, and feel doubly lucky that it's a story and characters that I love, and that I think really belong onstage, a story where two women are at the center of it, and the main plot has to do with their ambition and their business and power. That's a story I haven't seen a lot in musicals onstage."[23]

In October 2024, *The Devil Wears Prada* will open on the West End, starring Vanessa Williams.

Taub has previously written a slew of shows that have premiered with the Public Theater off-Broadway, and also spends time at the Public with a concert residency at Joe's Pub. During this residency, she has included songs from *Suffs* before its full stage premiere, and songs from other projects in the works.

Taub wrote music, lyrics, and orchestrations for a Public Works production of *Twelfth Night* at Shakespeare in the Park in 2016. The production, where Taub also music directed and played the role of Feste, was revived in 2018. In the summer between, she adapted *As You Like It*, also for the Delacorte Stage as part of the Public Works program. This time she played Jaques. Taub's talent for writing rousing collective choral numbers came to use during these large productions, which were highly touted.

In 2016, Taub collaborated with David Shiner and Bill Irwin on *Old Hats*. The show is a clowning piece by the two which premiered in 2013. For the 2016 off-Broadway production at the Signature Theater, Taub joined to perform original songs as part of the proceedings.

Taub often performs in her own work, and also performs in the work of others. She appeared in the off-Broadway productions of *Natasha, Pierre, and the Great Comet of 1812* and of *Hadestown*, and played Emma Goldman in *Ragtime* on Ellis Island.

Taub's three albums, *Visitors*, *Die Happy*, and *Songs of the Great Hill* feature her performing her soulful original songs, many of which have also been heard during her frequent concerts at Joe's Pub.

23. Evans, Greg. "From Shakespeare to Elton John: Composer Shaina Taub Gets Ready to Wear *Prada*—on Theater." *Deadline*, 15 August 2018, https://deadline.com/2018/08/shaina-taub-elton -john-devil-wears-prada-shakespeare-in-the-park-1202445084/.

ANAÏS MITCHELL
Way Down in Hadestown

Singer-songwriter Anaïs Mitchell came to Broadway in a roundabout fashion. In 2006 she began working on a stage musical adaptation of the Greek myth of Orpheus and Eurydice. Mitchell decided to turn the show into a concept album, which was released in 2010. Unlike her other albums, *Hadestown* featured a cast of singers, with Mitchell herself singing the role of Eurydice in the story.

The myth of *Hadestown* is a love story between Orpheus and Eurydice, who seek to overcome their need for money and material things in a world full of temptation. The two attempt to navigate the underworld, dominated by Hades, in order to be together. The album was well received, and Mitchell continued developing the work into a stage musical.

In 2016, *Hadestown* received its off-Broadway premiere at New York Theatre Workshop. Its road to Broadway continued to be an unconventional one, with subsequent productions in Alberta, Canada, and in London, before its Broadway premiere. *Hadestown* received significant development during these steps, with the show evolving during each production. In 2019, when *Hadestown* premiered on Broadway, it won Tony Awards including Best Musical and Best Score for Mitchell.

In a *Town and Country* article with the headline "Why It Took 13 Years for *Hadestown* to Become Broadway's Hottest Show," Mitchell said, "I started working on [*Hadestown*] when I was in my twenties and living in Vermont. The first version of the show was a do-it-yourself community theater project.... The company was made up of friends from different bands from all around Vermont. We toured in this bus that was painted silver and played town halls and music venues, and it was a much more abstract version of the show. We did that for two years, and then I made a studio recording [of the songs]. I always wanted to see it on stage again, and it took a while to figure that out."[24]

Hadestown's themes of extreme wealth and extreme poverty within the same community have resonated with audiences in the 2010s and 2020s. The song "Why We Build the Wall" has been particularly resonant, being performed at a time when immigrants in need are being kept out of the country.

Director Rachel Chavkin was instrumental in the development of *Hadestown* as a stage piece. Fifteen new songs were written as the show was being developed further, after the initial album release.

In January of 2023, *Hadestown* became the longest-running production in the history of Broadway's Walter Kerr Theatre, with its 918th performance.

---

24. Rathe, Adam. "Why It Took 13 Years for Hadestown to Become Broadway's Hottest Show." *Town and Country Mag*, 24 April 2019, https://www.townandcountrymag.com/leisure/arts-and -culture/a27258853/hadestown-broadway-anais-mitchell-interview/.

IRENE SANKOFF
The Unexpected Mega-Hit About 9/11

Half of the writing team responsible for one of Broadway's biggest hits of the 2010s, *Come from Away*, Irene Sankoff is a Canadian book writer, lyricist, and composer. She and her husband, David Hein, collaborated on both *Come from Away* and an earlier work, *My Mother's Lesbian Jewish Wiccan Wedding*.

In 2009, *My Mother's Lesbian Jewish Wiccan Wedding*, based on Hein's own experience with his mother and her later-in-life marriage to a woman, was a runaway hit at the Toronto Fringe Festival. For this show, Hein wrote the songs and both Sankoff and Hein wrote the book. The show transferred to a long run at a larger theater and received a production at the New York Musical Theatre Festival in 2010, which *Backstage* described as "unique and thoroughly enjoyable."[25]

Producer Michael Rubinoff saw *My Mother's Lesbian Jewish Wiccan Wedding* and was inspired to ask Sankoff and Hein if they'd like to work with him to create an original musical based on the events in Gander, Newfoundland, on September 11, 2001. In 2011, the writers visited Gander on the tenth anniversary of the attacks, and interviewed residents about their experience of that day and the days that followed.[26] These interviews became the earliest basis for a forty-five-minute stage version of *Come from Away*, which was workshopped at Sheridan College in Canada.

Continuing its unique trajectory, *Come from Away* had productions at La Jolla Playhouse (2015), Seattle Repertory Theatre (2015), Ford's Theatre (2016), Steele Community Centre in Gander (2016, a special one-night concert), and the Royal Alexandra Theatre (2016) before opening at the Schoenfeld Theatre on Broadway in 2017. While the show was on Broadway, prior to the launch of a United States national tour, it premiered a Canadian national tour.

Because of the September 11th attacks, thirty-eight commercial planes were rerouted to Gander, Newfoundland. The remote town doubled its population when the planes landed, and the influx of visitors on such a tragic and historic day, amid terror and fear, made for a connection of unlike people that was unique unto itself. The show finds actors playing both residents of Gander and unexpected visitors. The twelve-person cast portrays real people as well as conglomerations. One stand-out moment in the show is the song "Me and the Sky," a solo for pilot Beverley Bass, originated by Jenn Colella, who was a pioneer as a female pilot and who flew one of the planes to Gander. Bass was one of many

---

25. Penketh, Tom. "*My Mother's Lesbian Jewish Wiccan Wedding*." *Backstage*, 16 October 2010, https://www.backstage.com/magazine/article/mothers-lesbian-jewish-wiccan-wedding-56786/.

26. Sankoff and Hein, while Canadian, were in New York City studying theatre during the time of the 9/11 attacks.

real-life participants in Sankoff and Hein's interviews who were a presence at the Schoenfeld.

Come from Away was a somewhat unexpected hit on Broadway, receiving unanimous rave reviews. There was initial doubt that a story about 9/11 would gain favor on Broadway, with New Yorkers who had experienced that day first hand in the city. But *Come from Away* was not the musical one might expect about 9/11, and its original approach to telling a story about that day, far away from the place where the attacks happened, felt authentic and meaningful across the board.

Ben Brantley, who named the show a critic's pick in the *New York Times*, wrote: "Try, if you must, to resist the gale of good will that blows out of *Come from Away*, the big bearhug of a musical that opened on Sunday night at the Gerald Schoenfeld Theater. But even the most stalwart cynics may have trouble staying dry-eyed during this portrait of heroic hospitality under extraordinary pressure.... As it proceeds, the show—based on interviews with the people who inspired it—covers a vast expanse of sensitive material with a respect for its complexity."[27]

At the 2017 Tony Awards, *Come from Away* competed against *Dear Evan Hansen* and while it was nominated for seven awards including Best Musical and Best Score for Sankoff and Hein, it only won one: Best Director for Christopher Ashley. The show did win the Drama Desk for Outstanding Musical and for Best Book and the Outer Critics Circle Award for Outstanding Broadway Musical and Outstanding Book of a Musical.

Originally a film adaptation of the musical was planned, but due to the COVID-19 pandemic, these plans evolved into a filmed version of the Broadway production, which was released in September 2021, to commemorate the 20th anniversary of the September 11 attacks.

At the time of its closing in September 2022, *Come from Away* was the longest-running show in the history of the Schoenfeld Theatre.

JULIANNE WICK DAVIS
LGBTQ+ Stories

Composer-lyricist Julianne Wick Davis is best known for her musicals *Trevor* and *Southern Comfort*, two acclaimed shows that explore LGBTQ+ stories.

Trevor, based on the film about a bullied gay teen, had its world premiere in Chicago in 2017, winning the Jeff Award for Best New Musical.[28] The show was

---

27. Brantley, Ben. "Review: *Come from Away*, a Canadian Embrace on a Grim Day." *New York Times*, 12 March 2017, https://www.nytimes.com/2017/03/12/theater/come-from-away-review.html.

28. The Jeff Awards are theatre awards for Chicago-area produced work.

set for a New York run in 2020, which was halted by the COVID-19 pandemic. For *Trevor*, Davis wrote music to the book and lyrics by her frequent collaborator Dan Collins.

Southern Comfort was also written with Dan Collins and also based on a film—this time a 2001 documentary. The show is about a group of transgender friends who form their own commune of sorts in rural Georgia. *Southern Comfort* had a 2016 off-Broadway production at the Public Theater, where it was a *New York Times* critics pick.

Deadline wrote: "The book and lyrics by Dan Collins and music by Julianne Wick Davis are of a piece with the story and include several gems. The songs are played by a bluegrass band whose members also take on roles. . . . It's a beautiful show; bring the family."[29]

Davis's other musicals include *The Pen*, *When We Met*, and *Lautrec at the St. James*.

HELEN PARK
KPOP

Rising musical theatre writer star Helen Park cowrote music and lyrics (with Max Vernon) for the original musical *KPOP*, which had a sold-out off-Broadway run at Ars Nova in 2017. The show, which won Best Musical at the Lucille Lortel Awards, has a book by Jason Kim and chronicles the Korean pop music genre phenomenon by zeroing in on fictional groups.

About the score, the *New York Times* wrote, "Ms. Park's and Mr. Vernon's pastiche fusion musical numbers, choreographed with slashing wit by Jennifer Weber, are as synthetically sweet and perversely addictive as the real thing. (Think of them as ear Skittles.)"[30]

Park also received Drama Desk nominations for Outstanding Music and Outstanding Lyrics for her and Vernon's score. In addition, she created the show's orchestrations. Park is originally from Korea, and has always been interested in the musical genre of K-pop. She was approached by Ars Nova to work on the show in 2014 after director Teddy Bergman and book writer Jason Kim started developing the show there and needed a composer-lyricist. At that point, the show was an immersive musical about the music genre K-pop without a set script. The three collaborators spent several years working out exactly what they

---

29. Gerard, Jeremy. "Alex Timbers' *Robber Bridegroom* Revival Takes Flight; *Southern Comfort* Is the Public Theater's Latest Musical Triumph—Review." *Deadline*, 13 March 2016, https://deadline.com/2016/03/the-robber-bridegroom-and-southern-comfort-review-1201719729/.

30. Brantley, Ben. "Review: *KPOP Sings* and Dances Its Way through a Divided Culture." *New York Times*, 22 September 2017, https://www.nytimes.com/2017/09/22/theater/kpop-musical-review.html.

wanted their show to be, and researching K-pop as a genre and Korean culture in general so the show would be accurate and authentic.

About this work, Park said, "It's very easy to work off of a brief impression of a genre, and that's when things can get skewed or misinterpreted. . . . I wanted to make sure that none of the songs sound like a bad parody or mockery of the Korean pop phenomenon that is already widely popular around the globe. That meant really studying pop hit songs, breaking them apart and analyzing them. Also, as the music producer for this show on top of the composing component, I had to work on bettering my electronic music producing skills as well. It's been a continuous learning experience."[31]

In 2022, *KPOP* opened in a new Broadway production at Circle in the Square. The five-year stretch between the show's Off-Broadway and Broadway productions was partially because of the COVID-19 shutdown. A planned pre-Broadway tryout in Virginia at the Signature Theatre was canceled. The show was revised significantly from its 2017 off-Broadway run, and the new version premiered to the public on Broadway in 2022.

KPOP's preview period at Circle in the Square in fall of 2022 was beset by COVID-19 infections among the company that caused several performances to be canceled and others to be presented featuring many understudies. While this was the norm for Broadway productions throughout 2021 and 2022, it was particularly burdensome for a new original musical trying to work out fresh material, dependent on sales and word of mouth spreading rapidly during previews in order to catch on. Without traditional stars or a known brand, and with five years since its hot off-Broadway run, *KPOP* fought an uphill battle during its transfer. The show closed after only forty-four previews and seventeen regular performances.

After reviews came out, there was an uproar from *KPOP*'s producers, other members of the *KPOP* team, and the public about the "casual racism" in Jesse Green's *New York Times* review. Park further commented, in a guest essay for *Playbill*, on the disappointing early closure as well as how she addressed the cultural phenomenon of K-pop while contending with the white gaze throughout the development process of the show. She explained the conversations that took place around the theme of the show. How would the genre have to be presented in order to be compelling to the predominantly white Broadway audience? How could the show remain authentic and true to the individuality of K-pop while trying to be understood by all? "Despite the pressure from all sides, I made it my mission to stay authentic to this complicated, unique experience of mine, of being in between two languages, two cultures, two worlds," Park wrote, citing her

---

31. Struck, Chris. "BroadwayWorld Interview: Helen Park." *BroadwayWorld*, 2 March 2020, https:// helenparkmusic.com/news/2020/3/2/broadway-world-interview-helen-park.

experience as a Korean-American writing the show. "In transferring the show to Broadway, we were determined to fearlessly embrace our voice. We were not interested in tweaking our story simply to satisfy the stereotype-drenched expectations from the white gaze. The Koreans on the creative team tirelessly advocated for authenticity, from making a slick logo design and casting K-pop stars, to making sure the makeup and hair styles felt true to the genre."[32]

What Park and the entire team at Circle in the Square did with *KPOP* was lauded by many in the industry as breaking new ground, and the show certainly had its fans. Many were devastated by its early closure.

Park's other credits include music for *Baked Goods*, a ten-minute musical that won the Samuel French Short Playwriting Contest in 2015, and songs for *Over the Moon*, an acclaimed original animated film for Netflix that came out in 2020. A *BroadwayWorld* review of Park's 2020 concert at 54 Below called her "the calmest, coolest, chicest, young prodigy in town."[33]

ABIGAIL BENGSON
Autobiography and Trauma

Abigail Bengson burst onto the scene with her husband and creative partner, Shaun Bengson, in 2017. The duo's *Hundred Days* made a splash at New York Theatre Workshop, and the following year they were back on the boards with *The Lucky Ones* at Ars Nova.

Both shows are personal memoir musicals, with *Hundred Days* looking at the Bengsons' beginnings as a couple, including getting married three weeks after their first date, and *The Lucky Ones* examining a traumatic event from Abigail's childhood and its ripple effects. The shows deal with issues of mental health and major tragedy, all the while celebrating the joys of living and of family. Both musicals have books cowritten by Sarah Gancher and were directed by Anne Kauffman.

"The task, I think, of storytelling," Abigail told the *New York Times*, "is the reintegration of the dark and the light—going back and saying, 'Yes, this darkness is here and it's true.' And, 'There was light on us once, and there will be again.'"[34]

---

32. Park, Helen. "KPOP Songwriter Helen Park Reflects on a Broadway Run Cut Short" *Playbill*, 8 December 2022, https://playbill.com/article/kpop-songwriter-helen-park-reflects-on-a-broadway -run-cut-short.

33. Mosher, Stephen. "BWW Review: Audience Cheers New Writers at 54! Helen Park in Concert at 54 Below." *BroadwayWorld*, 1 February 2020, https://www.broadwayworld.com/cabaret/ article/BWW-Review-Audience-Cheers-new-writers-at-54-helen-park-in-concert-at-54-Below -20200201.

34. Collins-Hughes, Laura. "A Childhood Eden Seared by Violence. Set to Music?" *New York Times*, 6 April 2018, https://www.nytimes.com/2018/04/06/theater/bengsons-the-lucky-ones-ars-nova .html.

The Bengsons, with their earthy and personal style, had been working in theatre for many years prior. Their previous shows include *Sundown, Yellow Moon, Anything That Gives Off Light, Hurricane Diane, You'll Still Call Me by Name, The Place We Built*, and *Iphigenia in Aulis*. They perform their own work on concert and cabaret stages as well.

The exuberant folk-rock style of the Bengsons has gained them legions of fans both in person and digitally. Their work also includes self-taped original songs, such as "The Keep Going Song" that went viral on the internet during the COVID-19 pandemic.

In 2022, the Bengsons performed their own songs in the new play with music *Where the Mountain Meets the Sea*, by Jeff Augustin, at Manhattan Theatre Club's Stage I space, off-Broadway.

Jennifer Lee
Frozen *Queen*

Jennifer Lee is known as the chief creative officer of Disney Animation Studios. She cowrote and codirected (with Chris Buck) the animated films *Frozen* and *Frozen II*. When *Frozen* came to Broadway in 2018, Lee adapted her book for the stage. She received a nomination for Best Book of a Musical at the Tony Awards and the show also received a nomination for Best Musical.

Frozen tells the tale of princesses Anna and Elsa, who are sisters. Elsa acquires powers that she doesn't know how to control, and ends up freezing their kingdom, Arendelle, and putting Anna in danger. Both sisters need to figure out how to come together and save Arendelle.

In an interview with *Elle*, Lee addressed several questions about the story of *Frozen*. Asked where she found inspiration for the new material in the stage musical, Lee told the magazine that the writers visited Norway, Finland, and Iceland. "Iceland . . . has its own interpretations of the stories and sagas. I got lost in them." The interviewer also asked why the character of Elsa doesn't get a love story and Lee said, "That's not everyone's journey, and romantic love is not the only goal."[35]

Erin McKeown
A Musical about Undocumented Immigrants

A concert and recording artist with eclectic style and dynamic presence, Erin McKeown has made one foray so far into musical theatre. It was a high-profile

---

35. Kovan, Brianna. "How Writer-Director Jennifer Lee Made *Frozen* Broadway a Reality." *Elle*, 6 April 2018, https://www.elle.com/culture/movies-tv/a19691866/jennifer-lee-broadway-frozen-disney/.

one: *Miss You Like Hell*, which played the Public Theater off-Broadway in 2018, with book and a portion of the lyrics by Quiara Alegría Hudes.

McKeown composed the music and cowrote lyrics for *Miss You Like Hell*, which tells the devastatingly relevant story of a mother and daughter who are separated due to the immigration laws of modern-day America. Olivia doesn't want to give her mother, Beatriz, another chance when she shows up and suggests a road trip; Beatriz has been an absent mother for too long. But once they are on the road, the two begin to deal with many issues from their individual and collective pasts—all leading to Beatriz's deportation hearing since she is an undocumented immigrant. The New York premiere production was directed by Lear deBessonet and starred Daphne Rubin-Vega and Gizel Jiménez.

Variety wrote, "McKeown makes an impressive stage debut with music that is eclectic and appealing, though the lyrics she co-wrote with Hudes are too often an odd mix of fleeting grace and awkwardness. . . It's hard not to be moved by the newly earned parent-child bond [and] by walls that stand in the way of loving families."[36]

Miss You Like Hell was developed at La Jolla Playhouse, where it premiered in 2016.

TINA FEY
So Fetch

Comedy icon Tina Fey is best known for her time on *Saturday Night Live*, her show *30 Rock*, and her big-screen performances. Much of her work in film and television is bolstered by music, so it made sense for her to write the book of the stage musical adaptation of *Mean Girls* on Broadway in 2018.

Fey wrote the screenplay for and played Ms. Norbury in the 2004 smash hit film *Mean Girls*, which gave birth to more colloquial catchphrases for a young generation than almost any other film of its time. When the beloved movie became a musical, it had music by Fey's husband, Jeff Richmond (who had also penned music for *30 Rock* in collaboration with her), and lyrics by Nell Benjamin. The screenplay of *Mean Girls* was originally based on Rosalind Wiseman's book *Queen Bees and Wannabes*, and Fey has reported that she also based a good amount of the story on her own experience.

An article about the movie's impact stated: "Now, more than a decade after the film's release, its legacy—and cult following—continues to transcend the tests of time." The reason, according to Fey, is *Mean Girls'* universal relatability. "It has this little net that catches girls as they pass through preteen and high school

---

36. Rizzo, Frank. "Off Broadway Review: 'Miss You Like Hell'." *Variety*, 10 April 2018, https://variety.com/2018/legit/reviews/miss-you-like-hell-review-musical-1202749363/.

age," Fey has said. "Girls will come up to me and say it helped them get through a terrible year."[37]

The musical received twelve Tony nominations but won zero in a season that was dominated by the musicals *The Band's Visit* and *Once on This Island*. Notably, the Tony Awards broadcast the award for the category of Best Book of a Musical, which has in recent years not always been on the broadcast, because they wanted to get Tina Fey on television if she won. She didn't win, but Itamar Moses of *The Band's Visit* did accept the award on screen.

Mean Girls was shuttered on Broadway prematurely due to the COVID-19 pandemic. The stage musical of *Mean Girls* was adapted into a film that was released in 2024.

DOMINIQUE MORISSEAU
Ain't Too Proud

When Dominique Morisseau discovered the lack of roles for her as a young Black female actor in college, she began to write plays. Her three-play cycle called *The Detroit Projects* includes *Detroit '67*, *Paradise Blue*, and *Skeleton Crew*, which won her significant acclaim and awards citations. In 2018, she received a MacArthur Genius Grant.

In 2019, Morisseau made a high-profile entry into musical theatre, writing the book for the Broadway musical *Ain't Too Proud: The Life and Times of The Temptations*. The big budget jukebox musical explores the ups and downs of the iconic music group and Morisseau's book guides the story, from the members' childhood traumas to trouble with drugs to scandalous affairs to the effects of racism and financial power struggles on their careers. The Temptations' chart-topping hits were shaped into a story by Morisseau and director Des McAnuff.

When speaking with NPR about the relevance of *Ain't Too Proud* at the time it opened, Morisseau remarked, "We are all writing about the themes of love and power and power struggle and economics. Everything about 1963, '64, '65 could be mirrored right now—which is scary, but it's also profound that art gets to do that, to catch up to the time and give us a way of looking at something differently and getting dialogue about it."[38]

---

37. Witter, Brad. "Tina Fey Used Her Real Life as Inspiration for the Unforgettable Characters in *Mean Girls*." *Biography*, 12 May 2019, https://www.biography.com/news/tina-fey-mean-girls-characters.

38. Bowman, Emma. "*Ain't Too Proud* Playwright Dominique Morisseau Tackles the Temptations Origin Story." NPR, 1 July 2018, https://www.npr.org/2018/07/01/624790393/playwright-dominique-morisseau-on-ain-t-too-proud.

Morisseau also noted that her interest in this story was about exploring the Black identity of the Temptations as artists who made their way in the world and achieved stardom during a time of great civil unrest.

GRACE MCLEAN
Eleventh-Century Religious Leaders

Actor-writer-musician-orchestrator Grace McLean has a singular style in all that she does. Her New York musical theatre writing debut, *In the Green* (2019), is about the unlikely topic of Hildegard von Bingen, a saint and mystic from the eleventh century, and her religious mentor Jutta von Sponheim. The two women were locked in a cell for thirty years and *In the Green* tells their story through song, where characters are portrayed both literally and more experimentally. Three actors portray Eye, Hand, and Mouth, parts of Hildegard that express themselves.

In the *New York Times*, Ben Brantley wrote about the show, "This strained presentation of Hildegard as a singing sufferer of post-traumatic stress disorder is one of several wildly inventive musicals to have arrived in New York recently. . . . But for audacity and opacity it's hard to top "*In the Green.*"[39] Brantley credited the show with experimenting boldly but thought that many audience members would probably not understand what was happening on stage.

In The Green was nominated for six Lucille Lortel Awards and won one, Outstanding Lead Actress in a Musical for McLean, who portrayed Jutta. It is now released for licensing, and has become popular among students.

In the Green was part of McLean's work as an artist-in-residence at Lincoln Center. For Lincoln Center, she has also presented several American Songbook concerts with her band, Grace McLean and Them Apples. In her concert work, she is known for creating loops, layers of sound using recorded music on top of live singing and playing.

McLean's roles on stage in shows not written by herself include *Natasha, Pierre, and the Great Comet of 1812, Alice by Heart, Suffs, Brooklynite*, and *Bad Cinderella*.

KATORI HALL
Tina Turner's Story

Katori Hall made her Broadway debut with the play *The Mountaintop*, a fictionalized account of Martin Luther King Jr.'s last night before his assassination,

---

39. Brantley, Ben. "Review: A Singing Nun Struggles with PTSD in *In the Green.*" *New York Times*, 27 June 2019, https://www.nytimes.com/2019/06/27/theater/in-the-green-review.html.

which starred Samuel L. Jackson and Angela Bassett. The show was a huge hit in London before it came to Broadway, winning the Olivier Award for Best Play. Hall was the first Black female playwright to hold this honor.

Hall's other plays include the acclaimed *Our Lady of Kibeho*, about young women in Rwanda, which premiered off-Broadway at the Signature in 2014. Hall was a resident playwright at the theater, and her *Hot Wing King* (2020) and *Hurt Village*, which won the 2011 Susan Smith Blackburn Award also premiered there.

In 2019, Hall made her musical theatre writing debut with *Tina*, the Tina Turner jukebox musical which tells the story of Turner's life using her songs. Hall collaborated on the book with Frank Ketelaar and Kees Prins. She was brought onto the project by *The Mountaintop* and *Tina* producer Tali Pelman, who felt she would be a good fit for the show because of her skill in dramatizing the stories of real people.

Hall spoke to the press about the show's treatment of Tina Turner's ex-husband, Ike Turner. "It's . . . easy to have a villain in the story. And of course, [Ike] is [a villain], in that there was a lot of domestic abuse. However, I wanted to provide a psychological and social context. . . . It really allowed a kind of re-humanization of Ike that I don't think happened in previous tellings of her story, to the point where Tina has said to us that she wished that Ike and her mother were alive to see this show. Yes they did horrible things, monstrous things, but we were able to show their complexity and humanity, and give some social context."[40]

Tina was building great momentum on Broadway prior to the COVID-19 pandemic shutdown and received twelve Tony Award nominations including for Best Book and Best Musical. The show also had major buzz around its star, Adrienne Warren, giving one of the most talked-about performances of the season as Tina.

Hall interviewed Turner several times over the course of years in order to write *Tina*. In order to tell her story truthfully and really pull back the curtain on things that had been told incorrectly in the past, she dramatized the story with great attention to detail. About the themes of the show, Hall said, "This is the darkness that she had to overcome, and there are a lot of people who sit in an audience [and] are dealing with the same darkness. And whether you have dealt with that kind of trauma or not, to see somebody fall into an extremely deep abyss and pull themselves out of it is just one of the most inspiring things."

Tina's successful North American tour began in 2022.

---

40. Vadnal, Julie, "Why Tina Turner Trusted Playwright Katori Hall to Tell Her Story." *Shondaland*, 7 November 2019, https://www.shondaland.com/live/a29703428/katori-hall-tina-turner-musical -interview/.

DIABLO CODY
A Story for Alanis Morissette's Songs

Diablo Cody made an auspicious entrance into the musical theatre world, writing the book for the Broadway musical *Jagged Little Pill* in 2019.

Cody previously rose to prominence for writing and directing for film and television, including her Academy Award–winning screenplay for the 2007 movie *Juno*. Some of the publicity surrounding her Hollywood success was framed in a sexist way based on Cody's previous time as a stripper, which she had written about on a popular blog. The *New York Times*' headline for a 2007 article about *Juno* was "Climbing the Stripper Pole to Hollywood Stardom."[41]

Alanis Morissette knew that she didn't want the Broadway jukebox musical featuring her songs to be about her life. Cody came on board to craft an original story with Morissette and director Diane Paulus that would use the existing numbers from the album. Cody had never written a musical or a play before, and she studied many existing jukebox musicals in order to understand the form.

"I know there are some people who feel that there might be too many issues in this show, and that's fine with me," Cody told *Vulture*. "That makes me want to pile on more, because the reality is there are too many issues in the world. I wish we were living in a simpler narrative where we only had one or two things keeping us awake at night. But I have like seven, and they are all represented in this show. The opioid epidemic has affected my family personally in a major way, and for me to write about that has been cathartic."[42]

The story of *Jagged Little Pill* is about a family who might seem to the outside eye like a picture-perfect, cookie-cutter American household, but who are very much not. The mother, Mary Jane, is addicted to painkillers, the father, Steve, is addicted to pornography, the daughter, Frankie, is experimenting with her sexuality, and the son, Nick, is witness to a rape. Other main characters include Bella, who is raped at a party the teenagers attend, and Jo, Frankie's best friend who is trying to make their mom understand their sexuality and gender identity. The show, initially developed at ART, includes Morissette songs like "Ironic," "Hand in My Pocket," and "Thank U" to tell its story.

Jagged Little Pill received fifteen Tony Award nominations during the 2020 season, which had its award ceremony postponed due to the COVID-19 pandemic. Cody received a nomination for her book and the show also received a nomination for Best Musical.

---

41. Carr, David. "Diablo Cody: Climbing the Stripper Pole to Hollywood Stardom." *New York Times*, 3 December 2007, https://www.nytimes.com/2007/12/03/arts/03iht-juno.1.8567521.html.

42. "Diablo Cody on Writing the Jagged Little Pill Musical." *Vulture*, 19 November 2019, https://www.vulture.com/2019/11/diablo-cody-jagged-little-pill-musical.html.

Cody spoke about the nature of her collaboration with Morissette, as she was crafting her songs into the show: "She gives you the best notes ever, then she backs off. So I've had a ton of creative freedom. I have found myself sitting in my garage, rewriting Alanis Morissette lyrics. At the same time, she will let us know if something in a performance isn't working for her. We hear from her at least once a week."[43]

43. Ibid.

Acknowledgments

I wish to give a special thank-you to the following individuals who made this book possible in various ways: Lynn Ahrens, Mana Allen and her Contemporary Musical Theatre class at Barnard, David Berlin, Brisa Carleton, Ted Chapin, Kristin Chenoweth, Kirsten Childs, Tim Federle, Sierra Fox, Jill Fritzo, Amanda Green, Joe Iconis, Julie James, my sweet sister Jessica Kent Esq., Bree Lowdermilk, Shannon Mackay, Lin-Manuel Miranda, Victoria Myers, Roberta Pereira, Lance Rubin, Seth Rudetsky, Stephanie Wessels, Nick Wyman, and Eric Zohn. Thank you also to all my colleagues at 54 Below.

Immense gratitude is due to Katherine Odom-Tomchin and Claudia Cross for believing in this book and working hard to continually champion it. *Women Writing Musicals* could not have happened without you.

Thank you to Emily Burr, John Cerullo, Chris Chappell, Barbara Claire, Ashleigh Cooke, Carol Flannery, Emily Jeffers, Gary J. Hamel—and everyone else at Rowman & Littlefield/Globe Pequot, for giving your energy, expertise, time, and support to *Women Writing Musicals*.

I am immeasurably indebted to the musical theatre writers featured in this book that I've gotten to speak with, work with, and interview directly over the years. Your perspectives were essential. Thank you also to the writers and others involved in the hundreds of sources I used in order to write *Women Writing Musicals*. And thank you to everyone at Photofest and ALAMY for your collaboration regarding the photos utilized here. Much gratitude is due the photographers of the images included herein as well.

Thank you to my parents, Larry and Janis Tepper, who have always made me believe I can do anything.

Index of Musicals

Chronologically by Opening Date

Below is a chronological list of musicals by opening date that are featured in this book. When a musical played New York, the opening date determining the order of listing is the date of the first New York opening. (For example, if a musical played off-Broadway and then transferred to Broadway, both dates are listed, and the musical is ordered according to its off-Broadway opening.) When a musical did not play New York, the opening date given is the date of the first significant out-of-town opening. Only original productions are included, not revivals. (An exception is made for revivals, where a female writer was introduced to the process for the revisal.) Where plays with music were chosen for inclusion in the volume, they are also included in this list. Shows that include a large amount of songs by different contributors not explicitly written for the musical are not included. In rare cases, musicals with source material by a female writer are included. Shows that played New York prior to 1900 are labeled only by opening date. Work that premiered after 2020 is included where relevant, although the book stops at that year, as far as new writers making debuts.

PRE-1900S

Needs Must, or The Ballad Singers (December 26, 1793)
Tammany; or, The Indian Chief (March 3, 1794)
Norman Leslie (January 11, 1836)
Last Days of Pompeii (1858)
In and Out of Bondage (1876)
Slaves' Escape, or, The Underground Railroad (also called Peculiar Sam) (1879)
By the Sad Sea Waves (February 28, 1899)

1900s

Mam'selle 'Awkins (February 26, 1900, Broadway)
The Belle of Bridgeport (October 29, 1900, Broadway)
Madge Smith, Attorney (December 10, 1900, Broadway)
The King's Carnival (May 13, 1901, Broadway)
The Liberty Belles (September 30, 1901, Broadway)
The Supper Club (December 23, 1901, Broadway)
The Hall of Fame (February 5, 1902, Broadway)
The Show Girl (May 5, 1902, Broadway)
The Girl from Kay's (November 2, 1903, Broadway)
An English Daisy (January 18, 1904, Broadway)
Sergeant Brue (April 24, 1905, Broadway)
The Rollicking Girl (May 1, 1905, Broadway)
When We Were Forty-One (June 12, 1905, Broadway)
The Catch of the Season (August 28, 1905, Broadway)
The Duke of the Duluth (September 11, 1905, Broadway)
Fritz in Tammany Hall (October 16, 1905, Broadway)
Mexicana (January 29, 1906, Broadway)
The Social Whirl (April 9, 1906, Broadway)
The Man from Now (September 3, 1906, Broadway)
Mizpah (September 24, 1906, Broadway)
The Top o' th' World (October 19, 1907, Broadway)
The Lancers (December 5, 1907, Broadway)
A Knight for a Day (December 16, 1907, Broadway)
Miss Innocence (November 30, 1908, Broadway)
Peggy Machree (December 21, 1908, Broadway)
Ziegfeld Follies of 1909 (June 14, 1909, Broadway)

1910s

Ragged Robin (January 24, 1910, Broadway)
The Jolly Bachelors (January 6, 1910, Broadway)
Naughty Marietta (November 7, 1910, Broadway)
Little Miss Fix-It (April 3, 1911, Broadway)
A Certain Party (April 24, 1911, Broadway)
The Enchantress (October 19, 1911, Broadway)
The Wedding Trip (December 25, 1911, Broadway)

Glorianna (October 28, 1918, Broadway)
The Canary (November 4, 1918, Broadway)
Little Simplicity (November 4, 1918, Broadway)
Hooray for the Girls (December 16, 1918, Special Benefit)
The Voice of McConnell (December 25, 1918, Broadway)
Come Along (April 8, 1919, Broadway)
She's a Good Fellow (May 5, 1919, Broadway)
The Lady in Red (May 12, 1919, Broadway)
Shubert Gaieties of 1919 (July 17, 1919, Broadway)
Elsie Janis and Her Gang [1919] (December 1, 1919, Broadway)

1920s

The Night Boat (February 2, 1920, Broadway)
Lassie (April 6, 1920, Broadway)
The Sweetheart Shop (August 31, 1920, Broadway)
Tip Top (October 5, 1920, Broadway)
Hitchy-Koo [1920] (October 19, 1920, Broadway)
Lady Billy (December 14, 1920, Broadway)
The Midnight Rounders of 1921 (February 7, 1921, Broadway)
The Choir Rehearsal (February 28, 1921, Broadway)
Chinese Love (February 28, 1921, Broadway)
Snapshots of 1921 (June 2, 1921, Broadway)
Ziegfeld Follies of 1921 (June 21, 1921, Broadway)
Tangerine (August 9, 1921, Broadway)
The Greenwich Village Follies [1921] (August 31, 1921, Broadway)
Music Box Revue [1921] (September 22, 1921, Broadway)
Blossom Time (September 29, 1921, Broadway)
Good Morning Dearie (November 1, 1921, Broadway)
Elsie Janis and Her Gang [1922] (January 16, 1922, Broadway)
Marjolaine (January 24, 1922, Broadway)
Just Because (March 22, 1922, Broadway)
Michio Itow's Pin Wheel (June 15, 1922, Broadway)
Orange Blossoms (September 19, 1922, Broadway)
Queen O'Hearts (October 10, 1922, Broadway)
The '49ers (November 6, 1922, Broadway)
The Bunch and Judy (November 28, 1922, Broadway)
The Clinging Vine (December 25, 1922, Broadway)

Tales of Rigo (May 30, 1927, Broadway)
A la Carte (August 17, 1927, Broadway)
My Maryland (September 12, 1927, Broadway)
Enchanted Isle (September 19, 1927, Broadway)
My Princess (October 6, 1927, Broadway)
Take the Air (November 22, 1927, Broadway)
Keep Shufflin' (February 27, 1928, Broadway)
Blackbirds of 1928 (May 9, 1928, Broadway)
Grand Street Follies [1928] (May 28, 1928, Broadway)
Say When (June 26, 1928, Broadway)
Earl Carroll's Vanities [1928] (August 6, 1928, Broadway)
Three Cheers (October 15, 1928, Broadway)
Hello, Daddy (December 26, 1928, Broadway)
Fioretta (February 5, 1929, Broadway)
Pleasure Bound (February 18, 1929, Broadway)
Ziegfeld Midnight Frolic [1929] (April 1929, Broadway)
The Little Show (April 30, 1929, Broadway)
Grand Street Follies [1929] (May 1, 1929, Broadway)

1930s

The International Review (February 25, 1930, Broadway)
And So On (April 25, 1930, Out of Town)
Jonica (April 7, 1930, Broadway)
Three Little Girls (April 14, 1930, Broadway)
The Tavern (May 19, 1930, Broadway)
Garrick Gaieties (June 4, 1930, Broadway)
Mystery Moon (June 23, 1930, Broadway)
Earl Carroll's Vanities [1930] (July 1, 1930, Broadway)
Fine and Dandy (September 23, 1930, Broadway)
The Vanderbilt Revue (November 5, 1930, Broadway)
Sweet and Low (November 17, 1930, Broadway)
Ziegfeld Follies of 1931 (July 1, 1931, Broadway)
Shoot the Works (July 21, 1931, Broadway)
Fast and Furious (September 15, 1931, Broadway)
Singin' the Blues (September 16, 1931, Broadway)
The Great Day (January 10, 1932, Broadway)
A Little Racketeer (January 18, 1932, Broadway)

Hey Nonny Nonny! (June 6, 1932, Broadway)
Chamberlain Brown's Scrap Book (August 1, 1932, Broadway)
Belmont Varieties (September 28, 1932, Broadway)
Manhattan Varieties (October 21, 1932, Broadway)
The Threepenny Opera (April 13, 1933, Broadway)
Candide (May 15, 1933, Broadway)
Shady Lady (July 5, 1933, Broadway)
Blackbirds of 1933 (December 2, 1933, Broadway)
Ziegfeld Follies of 1934 (January 4, 1934, Broadway)
Four Saints in Three Acts (February 20, 1934, Broadway)
New Faces of 1934 (March 15, 1934, Broadway)
Gypsy Blonde (June 25, 1934, Broadway)
Singing Steel (November 23, 1934, Out of Town)
Fools Rush In (December 25, 1934, Broadway)
Alma Mater (March 1, 1935, Broadway)
Porgy and Bess (October 10, 1935, Broadway)
Provincetown Follies (November 3, 1935, Broadway)
The Illustrators' Show (January 22, 1936)
New Faces of 1936 (May 19, 1936, Broadway)
Ziegfeld Follies of 1936 (September 14, 1936, Broadway)
How Long Brethren? (May 6, 1937, Broadway)
A Hero is Born (October 1, 1937, Broadway)
Three Waltzes (December 25, 1937, Broadway)
Right This Way (January 5, 1938, Broadway)
Who's Who (March 1, 1938, Broadway)
The Two Bouquets (May 31, 1938, Broadway)
You Never Know (September 21, 1938, Broadway)
Leave It to Me! (November 9, 1938, Broadway)
The Race of Life (January 30, 1939, Broadway)
With Red Fires (January 30, 1939, Broadway)
To the Dance (January 30, 1939, Broadway)
One for the Money (February 4, 1939, Broadway)
Stars in Your Eyes (February 9, 1939, Broadway)
Adelante (April 4, 1939, Broadway)
Sing for Your Supper (April 24, 1939, Broadway)
The Straw Hat Revue (September 29, 1939, Broadway)
Swingin' the Dream (November 29, 1939, Broadway)
Two for Tonight (December 29, 1939, Off-Broadway)

1940s

Earl Carroll's Vanities [1940] (January 13, 1940, Broadway)
Two for the Show (February 8, 1940, Broadway)
Reunion in New York (February 21, 1940, Broadway)
A Case of Youth (March 23, 1940, Broadway)
All in Fun (December 27, 1940, Broadway)
Crazy with the Heat (January 14, 1941, Broadway)
Viva O'Brien (October 9, 1941, Broadway)
Let's Face It! (October 29, 1941, Broadway)
La Vie Parisienne (November 5, 1941, Broadway)
Priorities of 1942 (March 12, 1942, Broadway)
Count Me In (October 8, 1942, Broadway)
Oy Is Dus a Leben! (October 12, 1942, Broadway)
New Faces of 1943 (December 22, 1942, Broadway)
Something for the Boys (January 7, 1943, Broadway)
Mexican Hayride (January 28, 1944, Broadway)
Martha (February 22, 1944, Broadway)
The Maid as Mistress/The Secret of Suzanne (May 14, 1944, Broadway)
On the Town (December 28, 1944, Broadway)
Up in Central Park (January 27, 1945, Broadway)
The Girl from Nantucket (November 8, 1945, Broadway)
Billion Dollar Baby (December 21, 1945, Broadway)
The Duchess Misbehaves (February 13, 1946, Broadway)
Three to Make Ready (March 7, 1946, Broadway)
Annie Get Your Gun (May 16, 1946, Broadway)
If the Shoe Fits (December 5, 1946, Broadway)
Barefoot Boy with Cheek (April 3, 1947, Broadway)
Louisiana Lady (June 2, 1947, Broadway)
Sleepy Hollow (June 3, 1948, Broadway)
Kiss Me, Kate (December 30, 1948, Broadway)
Lo and Behold (1949, Out of Town)
Touch and Go (October 13, 1949, Broadway)
Regina (October 31, 1949, Broadway)
Gentlemen Prefer Blondes (December 8, 1949, Broadway)

1950s

Alive and Kicking (January 17, 1950, Broadway)
Arms and the Girl (February 2, 1950, Broadway)
Katherine Dunham and Her Company (April 19, 1950, Broadway)
Tickets, Please! (April 27, 1950, Broadway)
A Tree Grows in Brooklyn (April 19, 1951, Broadway)
Two on the Aisle (July 19, 1951, Broadway)
Bagels and Yox (September 12, 1951, Broadway)
Lo and Behold! (December 12, 1951, Broadway)
Curtain Going Up (February 15, 1952, Out of Town)
Paris '90 (March 4, 1952, Broadway)
Shuffle Along [1952] (May 8, 1952, Broadway)
Leonard Sillman's New Faces of 1952 (May 16, 1952, Broadway)
Wonderful Town (February 25, 1953, Broadway)
Anna Russell's Little Show (September 7, 1953, Broadway)
John Murray Anderson's Almanac (December 10, 1953, Broadway)
By the Beautiful Sea (April 8, 1954, Broadway)
Peter Pan (October 20, 1954, Broadway)
Hit the Trail (December 2, 1954, Broadway)
Seventh Heaven (May 26, 1955, Broadway)
Almost Crazy (June 20, 1955, Broadway)
Joyce Grenfell Requests the Pleasure ... (October 10, 1955, Broadway)
The Littlest Revue (May 22, 1956, Off-Broadway)
New Faces of 1956 (June 14, 1956, Broadway)
Autobiography (October 2, 1956, Broadway)
Bells Are Ringing (November 29, 1956, Broadway)
Candide (December 1, 1956, Broadway)
Ziegfeld Follies of 1957 (March 1, 1957, Broadway)
Kaleidoscope (June 13, 1957, Off-Broadway)
Mask and Gown (September 10, 1957, Broadway)
Joyce Grenfell: Monologues and Songs (April 7, 1958, Broadway)
Goldilocks (October 11, 1958, Broadway)
Demi-Dozen (October 11, 1958, Off-Broadway)
Salad Days (November 10, 1958, Off-Broadway)
A Party with Betty Comden and Adolph Green (December 23, 1958, Broadway, February 10, 1977, Broadway)
Redhead (February 5, 1959, Broadway)

This Was Burlesque (March 16, 1965, Broadway)
Wet Paint (April 12, 1965, Off-Broadway)
Hotel Passionato (October 22, 1965, Off-Broadway
The Mad Show (January 5, 1966, Off-Broadway)
Sweet Charity (January 29, 1966, Broadway)
Let's Sing Yiddish (November 9, 1966, Broadway)
Viet Rock (November 10, 1966, Off-Broadway)
Walking Happy (November 26, 1966, Broadway)
Hallelujah, Baby! (April 26, 1967, Broadway)
Now Is the Time for All Good Men (September 26, 1967, Off-Broadway)
In Circles (November 5, 1967, Off-Broadway)
Curley McDimple (November 22, 1967, Off-Broadway)
How Now, Dow Jones (December 7, 1967, Broadway)
George M! (April 10, 1968, Broadway)
I'm Solomon (April 23, 1968, Broadway)
Leonard Sillman's New Faces of 1968 (May 2, 1968, Broadway)
The Believers (May 9, 1968, Off-Broadway)
Walk Down Mah Street! (June 12, 1968, Off-Broadway)
Promenade (June 4, 1969, Off-Broadway)
Jimmy (October 23, 1969, Broadway)
Gertrude Stein's First Reader (December 15, 1969, Off-Broadway)

1970s

The Last Sweet Days of Isaac (January 26, 1970, Off-Broadway)
Georgy (February 26, 1970, Broadway)
Applause (March 30, 1970, Broadway)
Cry for Us All (April 8, 1970, Broadway)
Mod Donna (April 24, 1970, Off-Broadway)
Colette (May 6, 1970, Off-Broadway)
Light, Lively and Yiddish (October 27, 1970, Broadway)
Touch (November 8, 1970, Off-Broadway)
Blood (March 7, 1971, Off-Broadway)
To Live Another Summer, To Pass Another Winter (October 21, 1971,
    Broadway)
Inner City (December 19, 1971, Broadway)
Don't Bother Me, I Can't Cope (April 19, 1972, Broadway)
Mother Earth (October 19, 1972, Broadway)

But Never Jam Today (July 31, 1979, Broadway)
King of Schnorrers (November 28, 1979, Broadway)

1980s

The Housewives' Cantata (February 18, 1980, Off-Broadway)
Changes (February 19, 1980, Off-Broadway)
The Haggadah, a Passover Cantata (March 31, 1980, Off-Broadway)
Tintypes (April 14, 1980, Off-Broadway, October 23, 1980, Broadway)
It's So Nice to Be Civilized (June 3, 1980, Broadway)
FOB (June 8, 1980, Off-Broadway)
Really Rosie (October 14, 1980, Off-Broadway)
Onward Victoria (December 14, 1980, Broadway)
Alice in Concert (December 29, 1980, Off-Broadway)
Piaf (February 5, 1981, Broadway)
I Can't Keep Running in Place (May 14, 1981, Off-Broadway)
The Dance and the Railroad (July 16, 1981, Off-Broadway)
Family Devotions (October 18, 1981, Off-Broadway)
Pump Boys and Dinettes (October 1, 1981, Off-Broadway, February 4,
    1982, Broadway)
Lullabye and Goodnight (February 9, 1982, Off-Broadway)
Herringbone (June 30, 1982, Off-Broadway)
A Doll's Life (September 23, 1982, Broadway)
Upstairs at O'Neal's (October 29, 1982, Off-Broadway)
Portrait of Jennie (December 19, 1982, Off-Broadway)
Mama, I Want To Sing! (March 23, 1983, Off-Broadway)
Serious Bizness (September 30, 1983, Off-Broadway)
A ... My Name Is Alice (November 2, 1983, Off-Broadway)
Sound and Beauty (November 6, 1983, Off-Broadway)
Marilyn: An American Fable (November 20, 1983, Broadway)
Doonesbury (November 21, 1983, Broadway)
Baby (December 4, 1983, Broadway)
Peg (December 14, 1983, Broadway)
Hey, Ma ... Kaye Ballard (February 27, 1984, Off-Broadway)
What about Luv? (April 15, 1984, Off-Broadway)
Quilters (September 25, 1984, Broadway)
Rap Master Ronnie (October 3, 1984, Off-Broadway)
Kuni-Leml (October 9, 1984, Off-Broadway)

2010s

2020s

The Danger Year (August 18, 2021, Out of Town)
Six (October 3, 2021, Broadway)
Trevor (November 10, 2021, Off-Broadway)
Kimberly Akimbo (December 8, 2021, Off-Broadway, November 10, 2022, Broadway)
MJ: The Musical (February 1, 2022, Broadway)
Paradise Square (April 3, 2022, Broadway)
Suffs (April 6, 2022, Off-Broadway, April 18, 2024, Broadway)
Justice: A New Musical (April 15, 2022, Out of Town)
Knoxville (April 23, 2022, Out of Town)
Mr. Saturday Night (April 27, 2022, Broadway)
The Devil Wears Prada (August 7, 2022, Out of Town)
Los Otros (August 31, 2022, Off-Broadway)
KPOP (November 27, 2022, Broadway)
The Harder They Come (March 15, 2023, Off-Broadway)
Monsoon Wedding (May 22, 2023, Off-Broadway)
Summer Stock (July 26, 2023, Out of Town)
The Great Gatsby (April 25, 2024, Broadway)

Index

South Pacific, 109, 119, 132
Southern Comfort, 336–337
Spewack, Bella, 90–92, 292
Spewack, Samuel, 90–92, 292
Spider-Man: Turn Off the Dark,
    264–265
SpongeBob SquarePants,
    263–264, 329
St. Ann's Warehouse, 300, 304
St. James Theatre, 62–63, 112, 133,
    256, 268, 283, 331
Stafford, Jenny, 327–328
Stage Door Canteen, 27, 190
Stein, Gertrude, xii, 85–86, 164
Stein, Joseph, 119, 185, 214
Steinkellner, Cheri, 293–294, 312
Stew, 303–304
Stewart, Michael, 76, 161
Stitt, Georgia, 294, 312
Stoner, Joyce, 185–186
Stowe, Harriet Beecher, 14, 52
Strand Theatre, 18–19
Strand, Chuck, 186–187
Streep, Meryl, 61, 194
Street Dreams. See Inner City
Streisand, Barbra, 130, 150,
    170, 196
Striking 12, 293, 298
Stroman, Susan, xii, 246–247
Student Prince, The, 40, 42
Styne, Jule, 103–105, 113, 125, 258
Subways Are for Sleeping, 105, 202
Successful Calamity, A, 14, 16
Suds, 237–238
Suesse, Dana, 76–78

Suffs, 332–333, 343
Sullivan, Dan, 146, 154n17
Sunset Boulevard, 178, 248
Swados, Elizabeth, 192–196,
    211, 224
Sweeney Todd, 152, 197, 254
Sweet Charity, 60, 125
Sweet and Low, 67, 77
Sweethearts, 34–35
Swift, Kay, x, xiv, 62–65, 77–79
Swing!, 250, 268

Tangerine, 44–45
Tanguay, Eva, 36–37
Taub, Shaina, 196, 332–333
Taymor, Julie, 194, 264–265
Temple, Shirley, 156–157
Temptations, The, 342–343
Tennille, Toni, x, 122, 176–179
Terkel, Studs, 134, 198
Terry, Megan, 154–155
Tesori, Jeanine, xi, 250–254,
    317–318, 320n10
Theater Four, 205, 285
Theater de Lys. See Lucille Lortel
    Theatre
Theatre Guild, 37–38, 74–75
Theatre World Award, 107,
    178, 232
TheaterWorks USA, 160, 233,
    271, 280–281, 288–289, 292,
    315, 331
TheatreWorks Silicon Valley,
    198, 298